Theories of International Relations

Theories of International Relations ✺

Transition vs. Persistence

Michael P. Sullivan

palgrave

First published 2001 by
PALGRAVE™
175 Fifth Avenue, New York, NY 10010 and
Houndmills, Basingstoke, Hampshire, England RG21 6XS.
Companies and representatives throughout the world.

Palgrave is the new global publishing imprint of St Martin's Press LLC Scholarly and Reference Division and Palgrave Publishers Ltd (formerly Macmillan Press Ltd).

ISBN 0–312–23074–5 hardback

Library of Congress Cataloging-in-Publication Data
Sullivan, Michael P., 1942-
Theories of international relations : transition vs. persistence / Michael Sullivan.
   p. cm.
  Includes bibliographical references and index.
  ISBN 0–312–23074–5
  1. International relations—Philosophy—History.   I. Title.
JZ1242.S85   2001
327.1'01—dc21

                                    00–068844

Design by Letra Libre, Inc

First Edition: May 2001
10 9 8 7 6 5 4 3 2 1

Printed in the United States of America.

For Gail,
Who gave it the title it should *have had,*
Stalking Chameleons
and provided encouragement, help,
and support all along the way.

Contents

Acknowledgments

S everal individuals have read portions of this manuscript and have provided helpful, sometimes extensive, comments. Given the nature of the vetting process, they remain anonymous, but they know who they are, and I truly appreciate all of them, even the most acerbic.

I would especially like to thank Ole Holsti for having carefully perused the entire manuscript and for his encouragement and valuable suggestions.

I am of course solely responsible for any errors, omissions and lacunae.

Chapter One ❀

The Territoriality of Theory

The Minefield

On the day the United States Navy—in a driving rain—pulled out of Subic Bay, the Philippines, in October 1992, history did not especially note it. The American departure seemed to "make sense," which is why it received short-term coverage in most world media. It would not have made sense 40 years earlier, in 1952 certainly, nor in 1962 or 1972, and would have been out of place during the presidency of Ronald Reagan. It may, however, go down ultimately as one of many signals of the end of an era, or perhaps even the end of an empire, but certainly as part of the end of the Cold War. Oddly enough, it is an event not often included in that latter phenomenon, and yet in the context of much American activity of the previous century and a half, it should have been quite inconceivable. Nonetheless, it "made sense."

Three years earlier, in late 1989, the Berlin Wall's demise occasioned much greater attention, surprise, ideological cheering, and ultimately theoretical consternation for practitioners of international relations theory and their critics. It rather quickly seemed to fit into the stream or flow of events—fading from great public attention much faster than the original building of the Wall in 1961, an event surrounded with much hoopla, fanfare, and continuous Cold War rhetoric. Both the withdrawal from Subic Bay and the Fall of the Wall were in their own rights extraordinary events, although the latter has secured greater attention—in today's jargon, it has been "privileged"—and the former treated as an insignificant by-product of contemporary historical change. Explaining them singly or in conjunction with other events brings us into what has become even more of a minefield than it was a generation ago: the contending theories of international relations. The past half century has produced a very contemporary consciousness about theory not existent as the last great war—World War II—drew to an end. Some years ago an attempt was made going beyond the recitation of anecdotes to bring together the burgeoning corpus of theoretical formulations with the then-flourishing domain of empirical findings. In essence, it was to attempt a coherent analysis of the developing body of empirical evidence and its relationship to consciously developed theoretical propositions (Sullivan, 1976).

Much has happened, both in the world and in theory development, and to reenter the fray requires placing the latter within a context of historical development, reflecting how approaches have evolved over the past several decades. Some changes are rather clear. "National security" studies, for one, have faded as a dominating component of the discipline, although proposals materialized in the early 1990s for a resurgence (Walt,

1991). "National interest," despite its centrality and popularity for many years, also faded from the scene, primarily because "the concept is useless for guiding us in the choice of policies in the future or as a yardstick for evaluating those that were followed in the past" (Singer, 1995: 247), but it remains central to realism, and attempts have been made recently to stage a comeback (Kimura and Welch, 1998).

What has become known as the "democratic peace" literature, however, truly represents the phoenix rising from the ashes: early empirical studies had found, with some exceptions, a moderating relationship between type of political system and conflict, but findings were slim, and given the overly charged Vietnam-era anti-war feelings of the 1970s, the consensus mitigated against that research agenda. Scholars moved on. A decade later, beginning in 1983, the same research agenda reemerged, and findings from this large and growing body of empirically based research have become enshrined by some as one of the true "laws" in international politics. Likewise, cyclical theories have had—we might say—their ups and downs. In the 1960s, with the exception of a relative few focusing on the heavily disputed relationship between cycles and war, cycles were considered on the theoretical fringe. Twenty years later they emerged as a major theme and came to be accepted as almost an established fact of international politics, despite continuing and heated debates concerning specifics, definitions, and measurement.

More intriguing have been the shifts in the view of the nation-state itself, a core concept that had given way in some peoples' minds to a broader focus on larger international structures. After a time, the cry went forth to "Bring the State Back In!" Strongly related to these shifts has been the growing controversy over "realism" and "power": both concepts have suffered periodic bouts of attacks and renewals, falling by the wayside in the early 1970s only to be reasserted in the 1980s both by real-world events and with a resurgence in interest in anarchy. By the mid-1990s a major symposium[1] devoted itself to what might be called "the death of realism—again," accompanied by the emergence of a new concept, neoidealism.

It is said that these are turbulent times (Rosenau, 1990), a prosaic refrain to be heard at all times,[2] and extending this observation to the world of theories of international relations may appear as stereotyped as well. It is not trite, however, to contend that it is a complex world (witness the recent popularity of "complexity" and "chaos" theories), a reality that seems so often scorned in the desire to impose one model or explanation. International relations consists of such a broad range of behavior, encompassing multiple levels, that no one image, explanation, or model, in any composite sense, could be expected to explain *all* of international behavior.[3] If a minefield mentality exists, it results partly from unwillingness to recognize clear differences in what is conventionally called the dependent variable: the recognition that distinct theories may operate at different levels of analysis and are probably better at explaining certain types, ranges, or domains of behavior than other explanations.[4] Dissension has always been present and is healthy, although things can become treacherous and unpleasant—some even call it "fratricide" (Brecher, 1999: 234), perhaps reflecting the substantive area under study. Certainly, "territorial" is not too strong a word to describe some of the divisions.

Hits and Misses

Not too many have missed the apparent significance of the fall of the Berlin Wall. As for the American departure from Subic Bay, it may turn out to be one of the big "misses" in terms of scholarly predictions, especially if viewed at some future date as the beginning of the end of the "American empire" in the Pacific, which began with Perry and his ships in Edo (Tokyo) Bay in 1853. But at least for the moment it was the "Wall" and the "Fall"—the *Soviet* Empire's demise two years after the Wall's—that riveted the attention of theorists. Keeping score, assessing "hits and misses," choosing winners and losers is a common pastime, and, defining the dependent variable in a certain way, it has become popular to argue that the fall of Communism and the end of the Cold War were significant "misses" for a certain genre of theorists of International Relations. But missing the end of the Cold War implies a great deal: what "missing" means, what the Cold War was and what would constitute its "end," as well as the function of theory.

For one thing, that "miss" was not limited to one small group of academic theorists nor even to academics as a whole. Scholars generally had been lulled into a false sense of complacency concerning their understanding of international phenomena, especially major *change* in the international system and the possibility of major, revolutionary transformations in relations among state systems. Communism ended at a time most observers had, even if only by default, arrived at the position of silently taking it for granted. One critic relates a telling story about a foreign policy conference in 1985 to investigate United States' policy toward the Soviet Union through the end of the decade. After watching fellow participants discuss many issues but rarely looking beyond that decade, he wondered out loud whether they should not be discussing the possibility that the Cold War might end, how they might like it to do so, and what would replace it. The embarrassing silence that followed was met by the comment, from a highly respected senior diplomat, "'Oh, it hadn't occurred to any of us that it ever would end'"(Gaddis, 1992: vii).

"Missing" the end of the Cold War was widespread, but critiques were more narrowly aimed, mostly at quantitatively oriented theorists for their having been unable to predict or forecast that event (Gaddis, 1992/93).[5] The argument, however, requires seeing an abrupt end to the very complex phenomenon of the Cold War. It characterizes the Persian Gulf War as "unanticipated"; and views the Soviet Union as having suffered "sudden disintegration," all of which "astonished almost everyone" (Gaddis, 1992/93: 5). No criteria exist for establishing, however, *when* the Cold War ended (the Wall in 1989 and the final disintegration of the Soviet Union in 1991 were perhaps only specific incidents in a much longer-term *process* that began as early as the early 1970s), nor setting out even *what* the Cold War *was*.[6] In the "hits and misses" game, few individuals' averages would likely be very good. Even historians do not fare well. Paul Kennedy's well-received *Rise and Fall of the Great Powers*—a work not known for heavy theory, or empirical and quantitative terminology—touted the decline of the United States as the most recent "Great Power" at the very time the exact opposite was happening: the Soviet Union was in fact teetering on the brink of impending disaster.

Thus, no one has a monopoly on "misses." The Cold War "miss" applies to a variety of observers. Another less noticed "miss" would be of those observers who had expunged consideration of "nationalism" as a fundamental process in international politics. As World War II receded, the dominating impact of communist ideology, as well as the overpowering effect of growing—and, it was thought, inevitable—strides toward international interdependence and "globalism" were proving the nation-state-generated phenomenon of nationalism, like the dinosaur, extinct. Events since 1989 would appear to contradict those evaluations, but they were perceptions not confined to one circumscribed group.

The integration of Europe might be considered an unrecognized "near-miss." After a spurt of early research in the 1950s and 1960s, scholarly analysis in the next two decades shifted to interdependence, transnationalism, and regimes, all the while the actual reality of growing European integration proceeded apace. While nods of journalistic attention were given to events in Europe, little systematic research was focused on the growing EC and its potential implications for internal European relations as well as for broader, world structural changes. By the early 1990s, the actual events had quietly overtaken academic foci, and research began to emerge once again.

While misses have occurred, by the same token rather dramatic "hits" have been scored in the scholarly ballpark. For years a central focus was on the differential effects of varying international structures on international behavior, as well as the expected behavior when those structures began to change. Debates were perhaps too limited to the effects of bipolar or multipolar systems, but the larger question of structural effects and change was long a concern—long before, in fact, the venerable "agent-structure" debate. From this general perspective developed the focus on what was later to be called, among other things, "globalism" or transnationalism, starting with a somewhat naive idealist-oriented concentration, followed by a more realist one. Nonetheless both perspectives focused attention on the phenomenon of change in international structure.

From that more general concern emerged the focus on international political economy. Even analysts in the business community were missing the boat on which some academics had already traveled quite far. A top management guru of the 1980s admitted in a review of his own book ten years after its publication, "We missed or glossed over . . . things, such as the onrush of globalism."[7] Such issues had played no sustained part in United States' political campaigns prior to 1992, even though the scholarly community had been busy at work since at least the mid-1970s, not only describing such an emerging world but also the potential global implications of such transformations.

The turn toward "international political economy" took many forms; much focused on in-depth case studies, including the first serious discussions about a possible American "decline," how it might fit into perennial "long cycles" of the rise and decline of nations, and how these cycles themselves relate to war and conflict. Long-term changes in these three phenomena—America's decline, its possible relationship to longer-term cycles, and the patterns of cycles and war—had been carefully profiled at least on the theoretical dimension, with empirical elaboration following in slow and halting moves. Shifts in world politics, which began to unfold at the systemic level in only the barest fashion in the 1970s and continued into the 1980s, were easily imbedded within certain consistent theoretical formulations that had been developing as early as the late 1950s.

The sports analogy of "hits and misses" can be humbling, but also misleading. What exactly would a "hit" have been in the context of forecasting or predicting the end of the Cold War?[8] No agreement exists on what the Cold War was, and its ending should be even more troubling and perplexing, despite the immediate euphoria. No doubt in the near future systematic attempts will be made to assess whether anything and what it was that "ended" sometime in the late 1980s and early 1990s, a noteworthy and more complex task than implied by the simple "endings" nomenclature. The scorecard criterion implies a "game" with agreed-upon rules, established and played by all. None of these parameters are present in the assessment of theories of international behavior. Thirty years ago it was written:

If students of world politics could come to accept the idea that each is playing a game that can be assessed only in terms of its own rules, progress in the field would surely occur more rapidly . . . instead of assessing a colleague's performance in terms of the game he is playing, international-relations scholars will often criticize him for not playing another game and dismiss his findings on the grounds that he would have come to different conclusions if he had played the game he ought to have played (Rosenau, 1967: 297–298).

The Dependent Variable as Chameleon

Charles Hermann once told the story of how former Secretary of State Dean Acheson discovered with amazement that in Hermann's early research on the Korean crisis of 1950 he, Acheson, had been an "independent variable." Acheson's response has gone unrecorded, but certainly he must have viewed his role much differently. No doubt he would have been even further amazed to find that for other purposes he may have served as a *dependent* variable, which, not surprisingly, is the subject of this section. The dependent variable as an object of inquiry in and of itself has been one of the great understudied phenomena in international relations, and yet it is that phenomenon that should *drive* the entire research endeavor. Like the chameleon, the dependent variable *does* mutate and, again like the chameleon, it confuses the predator, in this case the scholar. The result might be confusion about what exactly is being explained in any specific instance, a general dissatisfaction with what appears to be lack of coherent progress toward an end-goal, or a failure to realize that some things perhaps *cannot* be explained. Shifts and changes in the dependent variable can run the gamut from simply flighty fads of the moment all the way to significant shifts in orientation that reflect serious reformulations in the field.

In recent years it has become fashionable to assert that the dependent variable for the realist is narrowly confined to war and conflict, whereas for others, idealists, liberals, or those investigating "cooperation under anarchy," the focus is cooperation and international integration. To some degree this is true, but to some extent also misleads. More important is that even during the early heyday of realism after World War II, when the innovating research on integration by Karl Deutsch and others turned the focus toward the potential integrating tendencies of European states, a future lacking the disintegrative or conflictual tendencies thought inherent in the realist school, both—regardless of the specific substantive form—were united in focusing on the dependent variable at the macro or systemic level. Interest in the specificity of the dependent variable was mostly lost in the macro world of the larger international system, realists dealing with war and conflict, and integrationists dealing with cooperative outcomes. Early decision-making frameworks, however, brought with them a conceptual apparatus informed implicitly by the complexity of foreign policy decision-making hidden or subsumed within the "realist" model. Remembered rightly for their implication about the necessity for more complex models to understand decision-making, the mostly ignored implication of these models was the transformation of the dependent variable. War and conflict in the macro sense faded into the background in favor of a directed focus on *decisions*. While a specific decisional outcome might be war or conflict, it could also be cooperation or have integrative tendencies. The key point was that the *decision* and *decision process* became the focus of analysis.

To confuse things even more, others began to view decision-makers' *perceptions,* not the processes within which they operated, as the operative *independent* variables, and concomitantly focused on even more micro decisional *outputs* at times limited to specific *daily* changes in aggregated events, a long cry from both the large, macro dependent variables of the systems analyst, or the larger decisions of the decision-making theorists. Both perspectives—decisions and perceptions—were the first to seriously and effectively question the large, macro, realist, rational-actor approach to international politics, not as a broadside critique, but out of a recognition of the breadth and complexity of phenomena to be explained and the apparent inability of the standard "realist" approach to account for elements of that behavior. It would take another 30 years for the volatile broadside to surface.

In the 1960s, the nation-state emerged as a unit of analysis for the first time in an explicit, painstakingly empirical sense, reasserting, in a way, assumptions about black-boxing the individuals that had been present in realism but had momentarily vanished, and the definition and essence of the dependent variable was once again transformed. Now the comparative behavior of *nations,* called "Comparative Foreign Policy," became the focus: how did nations differ from one another and how did this affect their behavior as specified, recognized, empirically distinct, and yet categorizable units? Omitted were the large exogenous factors of the international system, the complex internal decision-making processes, and the multiple, diverse and idiosyncratic perceptions of the individual decision-makers. Now the focus was on how *nations* differed in terms of their makeup *as nations* and, concomitantly, how the dependent variable changed to the external output of *nations.*

With the readvent of post–World War I idealism in the guise of "transnationalism" in the 1970s, an even more momentous shift occurred, characterized by two ingredients. The first, substantively, was the turn from the traditional focus on war and national security concerns toward economic issues, as a result the dependent variables now focused not on the military-security but rather on the economic relations among nations. The second ingredient of this shift was a reemergence of case study methodology, in which the chameleon-like character of the dependent variable becomes even more apparent because of the methodology's reluctance to isolate it explicitly—both a drawback and a major attraction. Case studies produce data in the form of specifics— at times endless, mind-numbing, innumerable specifics—resulting in such a yield of data that a mushy dependent variable too often produces a pulpy independent-dependent variable *linkage.*[9]

With the development of transnational studies into the full-fledged field of international political economy, along with the later emergence of liberal institutionalism's focus on the impact of organizations and institutions on economic as well as political behavior, a major threshold was crossed. What becomes clear, however, is that the history of contemporary theories of international relations, viewed by some as continual revolutionary shifts in theoretical orientation—and by others as merely "fads"—may be characterized as a reconsideration, redefinition, or more accurately, respecification of the dependent variable. Once that fact is understood, then the promise of "new theoretical orientations" takes on a much different hue.[10]

Criteria for the importance of specific dependent variables are at times rather apparent: if a new *phenomenon* emerges in international politics in need of explanation, the criterion is immediacy or relevancy. "Terrorism," for instance, was widely advertised some years ago as a—perhaps *the*—new "non-nation-state" behavior that would revolutionize thinking about theories of international politics. But several items are of note. First, non-state behavior had always been present, and, second, in many instances apparent non-state behavior had in fact the backing—very often direct—of nation-states. Switching the specifics of the dependent variable in this case—from nation-state war or conflict to terrorism—did not change a more important point: while the existence of subnational, terrorist activity itself was certainly interesting, an equally important question hinged on why that behavior was exhibited at certain times rather than at others, in certain locales rather than others, and which nations might in fact be the operatives in such behavior (Thomson and Krasner, 1989: 208–214; Sullivan, 1990: 25–32).

A more recent illustration of whether to decorate the chameleon one color rather than another was the debate over "Big Wars vs. Little Wars." The "big wars" proponents viewed these as major system-transforming events to see who will emerge as the "hegemon." The opposing position was that *all* wars are important: "If . . . big wars are not begun with the expectation of satisfying an *ex post* view of bigness, then there are critical problems inherent in focusing attention on large conflicts to the exclusion of others" (Bueno de Mesquita, 1990: 167). There is even disagreement on what events fit into the "big war" category (Bueno de Mesquita, 1990: 168).

Such debates are not just petty quarrels over academic jargon or a trivial measurement question—rearranging the deck chairs on the *Titanic*. They involve fundamental procedures of theory-building. The distinction between types of wars relates to key theoretical explanations. A structural war may be a function of long-term variables—inequalities, alliance formations and memories, and changes in the balance of power, that dependent variable is not less important than other wars, but simply caused by different phenomena. A "mobilization" war, on the other hand, might need a "mobilizing leader," which suggests a relationship between the two types of wars:

> The period between a structural and mobilization war witnesses a power interregnum as the result of the material exhaustion of the principals during the earlier structural war, which in turn, "invites" the aggressive entry of the mobilizing leader into the international arena (Midlarsky, 1990: 177).

Thus the *theoretical reasons* dictate establishing the dependent variable in one distinctive way rather than another. While some may feel this produces an unpleasant problem called "nonintegration" of empirical findings (Dessler, 1991: 341–342), at the same time it produces the very definite theoretical benefit of recognizing that, indeed, the world is complex, and therefore different theories may explain different dependent variables. This need not detract from complex understanding of that dependent variable.[11]

Thus, dependent variables are not unchanging nor is that change unfortunate, but that does not mean unpleasant ones *must* change. The process of clearly establishing distinctions between dependent variables is a far cry from endeavors to eliminate altogether certain dependent variables—war—because they are nasty, costly, and, so the argument goes, inconceivable in the contemporary era: "A war between the great powers simply would be impossible to wage today" (Goldgeier and McFaul, 1992: 482). Such claims come along from time to time; the most recent spate of which occurred in North America near the end of America's involvement in the Vietnam War, but have historically and consistently proved, unfortunately, to be wishful thinking.

Nonetheless, a subtle restyling in perceptions could be afoot. It has been proposed that the twentieth century's chief warmongers have changed their tune; leaders still managed to get into wars, of course. But no longer was it possible simply and honestly to proclaim like Julius Caesar, "I came, I saw, I conquered." Gradually this has changed to "I came, I saw, he attacked me while I was standing there looking, I won." (Mueller, 1989: 18).

While "this might be seen as progress" (Mueller, 1989: 18), it is also true that when war *was* considered "normal," moral justification was the name of the game, and a relatively easy one at that: a few Jesuits, a little posturing, one or two references to God's will, and that was that. As those moral justifications became a bit more difficult to carry off (one subtitle says it all: "War Becomes Rather Embarrassing" (Mueller, 1989: 18)), they have withered, and in the process at least the perception of war as a viable behavior and therefore as a relevant dependent variable declined.

A positivist perspective on the possible end of war (Ray, 1989) compares the abolition of slavery to the same potential fate for war. Arguments against slavery had been both economic and moral, and to the extent that slavery was still economically feasible the moral component entered into play. When it came to the question of war, World War II depleted the ranks of the idealists, "leaving a relatively hardy few to combat the realistic tide in the 1950s" (Ray, 1989: 416). But idealism resurfaced in the 1970s and with it a very changed perspective about war. Keohane and Nye's classic *Power and Interdependence* is "explicitly antirealist in some important respects, de-emphasizing the role of states and downplaying the significance of military force" (Ray, 1989: 416–417). Regime analysis emphasizes "at least by fairly clear implications the impact of ethical constraints and moral values . . . There is, in short, enough idealism in interdependence/regime analysis to make it a tempting target for moral skeptics from various points on the ideological spectrum" (Ray, 1989: 417).

But altruism *does* exist, and that idealistic view could hypothetically cause repercussions for the dependent variable of war. In electoral politics, for instance, one person's vote rarely "counts," yet many people vote. Outpourings of sympathy for victims of natural disasters are common, and,

> the disappearance of slavery and recent trends in international warfare suggest that ethical constraints and moral progress have had an important impact on international politics (Ray, 1989: 421).

The observation that Caesar's "Veni, Vidi, Vici" became "I came, I was attacked while I was standing there watching, I won" displays growing moral constraints against war-like behavior, and the specific effect on war should be in the area of leaders *initiating* war. If this moral "progress" were to continue, fewer leaders might be led to develop "deceptive strategies and rationalizations in defense of war initiation, as well as a decline in the number of those who will be inclined to accept those rationalizations" (Ray, 1989: 422). At that point, suspicions that one is about to be attacked might lose their "logical base, and accusations regarding imminent attacks will lose their credibility" (Ray, 1989: 422).[12]

What has become of our chameleon? This quick, somewhat circuitous historical survey suggests one story of how the chameleon-like dependent variable has changed over the years, from straightforward assumptions about what was important, all the way to a suggestive and positivist reevaluation of a specific dependent variable, namely war, which in the context of the 1990s appears to many to be an anachronistic behavioral phenomenon and therefore perhaps of little relevance for the contemporary scholar.

Many have argued this, and recent elaborations on this time-worn theme seem particularly attractive. It is, unfortunately, not likely to disappear.

More relevant, however, is the fact that war is only one of a multitude of potential dependent variables that may ebb and flow in importance in the world of international politics as well as in the focus of scholarly research. This lengthy interest in the chameleon-like character of the dependent variable flows from the fact that much of the talking past one another and the debates that persist among different schools[13] are not so much invariably over competing theoretical approaches as much as, at the root, a failure to recognize that the foci of different studies is in fact on very different dependent variables. The debates take place ostensibly over what are the best explanations when in fact the differing explanations are often being applied to very different—perhaps even mutually exclusive—behaviors. Without carefully specifying the latter, the focus turns to the former—but it becomes misplaced. It might even be hypothesized that frustration about truly understanding the traditionally most important dependent variable, war, shifted attention to a picture of the world that thrusts other dependent variables into the spotlight. It became fashionable at one point to ask how cooperation, the obverse of conflict, could possibly exist in the "anarchical" world supposedly coexistent with the realist model of incessant conflict between nations. But the more fundamental question is perhaps even more interesting and relates at least indirectly to the chameleon factor: admitting cooperation to the hierarchy of interesting dependent variables raises the question of whether the "anarchical" description of world politics was ever accurate.

The Myth of Anarchy

The dependent variable may not be the only chameleon; the very "definitional cores" that guide the discipline also exhibit a chameleon-like existence.

> Why do states cooperate at all in a world marked by international anarchy? This question has received enough renewed scholarly attention in the past few years to qualify as the definitional core of a distinctive theoretical literature (Dixon, 1990: 109).

Others echo these sentiments: "anarchy and the security dilemma make cooperation among sovereign states difficult . . . when international politics is viewed from this perspective, the central question is not, 'Why do wars occur?' but 'Why do wars not occur more often?'" (Jervis, 1986: 58). Some take it a step further: "Achieving cooperation is difficult in world politics. There is no common government to enforce rules, and by the standards of domestic society, international institutions are weak. Cheating and deception are endemic" (Axelrod and Keohane, 1986: 226). If, however, anarchy appears as a basic backdrop, perhaps even as a constant (Axelrod and Keohane, 1986: 226), then the "renewed scholarly attention" is something of a misnomer, and produces a misguided sense of "newness" not coincident with the real world.

The comparison of international relations with the relative tranquility of "home, the family . . . the nation" (Goldstein and Freeman, 1990: 10–11) has been the time-worn stock comparison, an image in which international relations is a prisoner's dilemma, derived from "realist themes of international anarchy and national self-interest in the great power system" (Goldstein and Freeman, 1990: 10), at the heart of which is the concept of anarchy:

International relations is not like the safe, domestic world of the home, the family, and by extension, the nation; rather it is a dangerous world of all against all—the jungle out there (Goldstein and Freeman, 1990: 10–11).

To counter this widespread view, a "new school of international relations theory" emerged, variously labeled "cooperation under anarchy," a "theory of cooperation," or "cooperation after hegemony."

Accepting most realist assumptions, this school attempts to show that it is possible to achieve cooperation even under conditions of anarchy. This school synthesizes two traditions in international relations theory, bringing together "neorealism" and studies of "international interdependence" (Goldstein and Freeman, 1990: 11).

Political philosophers have historically, however, imbedded their writings on international affairs in the concept of "anarchy." Machiavelli, Bertrand Russell, Reinhold Niebuhr, Hans Morgenthau, and others traditionally used the concept as a backdrop, sometimes even as a central core. It has been called the "defining characteristic of the field" (Ferguson and Mansbach, 1988: 186), although one still sketched so broadly that it can range from simple lack of central government to complete lawlessness and political disorder. Most, however, would probably agree that an anarchical system is not "chaotic or riven by disorder," but simply one with no central authority (Mearsheimer, 1999: 3). Still, ambiguity persists and allows much straddling of the definitional and operational fences, yielding on the one hand that "we cannot dismiss the 'anarchy' concept lightly," but recording, nonetheless, its "limited analytic value." It cannot be dismissed "because, as a metaphor, it has exercised and continues to exercise a powerful hold on the *imagination* of observers and participants" (Ferguson and Mansbach, 1988: 187; emphasis added), and the absence of authority becomes "'a permissive or underlying cause of war' in the sense that 'wars occur because there is nothing to prevent them'" (Ferguson and Mansbach, 1988: 187; citing Waltz, 1959: 232).

But imagination and metaphors, like analogies, are as often misleading as they are helpful. Analogies with domestic societies clearly break down (Bull, 1977: 50–51), but the parallel has had profound effects nonetheless. But why now in international relations? Certainly one ingredient facilitating the success of a recently popular concept, "regime," might help us understand this transformation: "regimes" have been viewed "as an important tool for explaining states' patterned behavior in an anarchic world" (Cheon, et al., 1990: 117), a conceptual apparatus for handling or analyzing what was thought to be that unordered, anarchical system. Subscribing to the anarchy picture allows the observer to gaze with awe and marvel at the cooperation that does transpire in international relations, and "regime" is one way to handle the alleged contradiction imbedded in "cooperation under anarchy." How else to explain something that should not be there—or, like war, of which there should be more—if the "metaphor" is correct?

But the relationship between rules and anarchy decomposes a bit from one perspective, namely, where the existence of "rules" would seem to imply that anarchy doesn't exist. However,

Scientific realism insists that *all* social action depends on the preexistence of rules, implying that even under anarchy, rules are an essential prerequisite for action. It asserts the impossibility and inconceivability of social behavior without rules; the issue of whether a centralizing authority exists or not is beside the point (Dessler, 1989: 458–459).

Extensive recent elaboration of rules has taken place within the constructivist paradigm (Onuf, 1997), but has been present in various forms for almost a generation (Bull, 1977: 67–71). Thus, one could have anarchy within a world of rules, although it is not quite clear what becomes of anarchy. Should one *not* concede "anarchy" at all, however, then cooperation is not all that astonishing, and anarchy becomes nothing more than a colorful metaphor that sparks the imagination, with not much lost by dropping it except perhaps lengthy debates about how to figure out whether nations *can* cooperate under anarchy, when in fact we can observe as an empirical fact that nations *do* cooperate, and extensively.

One reformulation of "power transition" theory (first put forward in its classic formulation many years earlier (Organski, 1968: chapter 14)) bluntly questions the utility and veracity of anarchy:

> Power transition sees the international order not as anarchical at all, but as hierarchically organized in a manner similar to the domestic political system. Actors accept their position in the international order and recognize influence based on differences in the power distribution among nations. This fundamentally different assumption separates power transition from preceding realist models (Organski and Kugler, 1989: 172).

In acting, in other words, nations follow strategies that produce a "path of compromises and concessions leading to the actor's preferred outcome."

> We might conclude from the chaos theorems that we live in a turbulent world. Yet most of the time this seems not to be so. More often than not, nations appear to abide by precepts of international law and custom and are expected to honor the agreements they make. Indeed, reactions such as shock are far more commonly associated with breaches of international accords than they are with the honoring of such arrangements (Bueno de Mesquita, 1990: 318–319).

In more specific terms,

> The periodically recurring "summits," the establishment and dissolution of international alliances, and the convening of ad hoc conferences to address specific problems such as ecology (Rio 1992) or to negotiate a comprehensive regime for the oceans (UNCLOS III) all suggest that the web of interactions among government and subnational groups is much richer than the imagery of an international anarchy, in which states face each other in a "state of nature" (Kratochwil, 1994: ix).

The solution to all of this is therefore deceptively simple: aggregate behavior in the international system is not as disordered and disruptive as the metaphor of "anarchy" implies.[14] Ironically, even the "father" of modern realism was clear on this point:

> It is also worth mentioning, in view of a widespread misconception in this respect, that during the four hundred years of its existence international law has in most instances been scrupulously observed . . . to deny that international law exists at all as a system of binding legal rules flies in the face of all the evidence (Morgenthau, 1965: 277).

Cooperation *does* occur, and often, and it always has. Moreover, the comparisons or analogies with domestic systems seem more and more to be overdrawn: disorder in domestic societies can realize the level of international disruption, ranging from rampant crime to domestic unrest and violence, riots, and at times the disappearance of government itself. Less developed societies seem more prone to such activity and more so—interestingly— subsequent to the transformation in the international system usually referred to as the "end of the Cold War," a structural phenomenon paradoxically labeled as a "new world order." And such disruptions are true not only of less developed countries; developed countries also go through periods of major disruptions, which many who lived through the Vietnam era seem to have forgotten.

Returning to the original question, to ask "why does cooperation occur" assumes implications from imposing the anarchy metaphor; a more fruitful direction is to ask what accounts for changing levels in the mix of cooperation and conflict. One might lament the lack of institutions and the fact that cheating and deception seem to be "endemic," but one also finds that " . . . cooperation is sometimes attained. World politics is not a homogeneous state of war: cooperation varies among issues and over time" (Axelrod and Keohane, 1986: 226). Much behavior *is* ordered and patterned, and the task is to find out what explains those varying patterns of order as well as disorder, cooperation as well as conflict. To use as a definitional core, therefore, "cooperation under anarchy" is to impose a colorful but misleading metaphor. To focus on "cooperation after hegemony" fails to see that hegemony varies and its variation has potential as an explanatory factor in international behavior.

The argument so far is based largely on empirical observation: the bulk of international behavior is in fact cooperative, the opposite position of that implied by "cooperation under anarchy." We have noted already: rules exist (Bull, 1977). Recently, the argument has been pressed by constructivists:

> There is no "logic" of anarchy apart from the practices that create and instantiate one structure of identities and interests rather than another; structure has no existence or causal powers apart from the process. Self-help and power politics are institutions, not essential features of anarchy (Wendt, 1992: 394–395).

In other words, in a somewhat ambiguous but now famous phrase: "Anarchy is what states make of it" (Wendt, 1992: 395). By extension, states can make either cooperation or conflict. "This may all seem very *arcane*" (Wendt, 1992: 402), and in a sense it is, except that it raises doubts about anarchy beyond the empirical ones noted already. Concerning the domestic analogy, for instance, buying into the anarchy argument focuses on the worst-case scenario, and even domestic society would be impossible

> if people made decisions purely on the basis of worst-case possibilities. Instead, most decisions are and should be made on the basis of probabilities, and these are produced by interaction, by what actors *do* (Wendt, 1992: 404).

It is "only through a process of signalling and interpreting that the costs and probabilities of being wrong can be determined. *Social threats are constructed, not natural.* The process of signalling, interpreting, and responding completes a 'social act' and begins the process of creating intersubjective meanings" (Wendt, 1992: 405; emphasis added). "It is through reciprocal interaction, in other words, that we create and instantiate the relatively enduring social structures in terms of which we define our identities and interests" (Wendt, 1992: 406). In other words, to complete the circle the admonition should be: watch what nations *do*, not what people *say* nations do,[15] or—worse yet—what other people say nations should be doing according to some externally imposed and colorful metaphor that in fact describes only a small portion of what nations do.

Two studies published within two years of each other exemplify the problematic status of combining the anarchy metaphor with the chameleon dilemma. Both focused on the chameleon-like "dependent variable" from two very different ends of history concerning the nation-state: prior to its beginning and, according to some, in its waning years. Focusing on feudal Europe between 800 and 1300 might seem completely irrelevant, but provides an enticing way of analyzing certain attacks on realism, and argues

> the structure of anarchy constrains states to control natural and human resources in order to procure military forces sufficient to deter potential aggressors. It constrains states to arm and to form alliances in accordance with the distribution of capabilities with the aim of balancing each other's war-making potential (Fischer, 1992: 429).

The feudal period "strengthens the principal belief of political realists that lawless conflict and arbitrary violence constitute the natural condition of individuals deprived of the blessings of central authority" (Fischer, 1992: 463).[16] Such a conclusion stands in stark contrast to an alternative, much more optimistic deduction concerning how the "condition" of nuclear deterrence produced a structural change in the international political system, a change that

> has created a new organizing principle that follows from joint custodianship, a function which was acquired by the United States and the Soviet Union and which fundamentally differentiates them from other states. If the international system permits functional differentiation of this sort, then it will no longer operate precisely as an anarchy (Weber, 1990: 77).

Hence, "we should expect to see behavior and international outcomes inconsistent with or unpredicted by theories that take anarchy as a starting point." Few doubt now that by the late 1980s, evidence suggested that the role of nuclear weapons in international politics had been transformed—INF and START would be examples, as would be the clear desire of the "international hierarchy" to come down very hard on maverick states wishing to break into the nuclear club—but the disutility of anarchy had really nothing to do with it.

What then befalls this "definitional core" called anarchy? It becomes little more than a metaphor or analogy that—as with most analogies—has little predictive capacity and trivial immediate relevance to the real world. Moreover, mutating or embellishing on the analogies to convince ourselves we are moving away from anarchy adds only more confusing terminology:

> all but the most hard-core neorealists would probably say that the international system is characterized by "particles" of governance and that as such it is not a pure anarchy. With the deepening and proliferation of international institutions, these particles are rapidly becoming "sediment" (Wendt, 1994a: 392).

Distinguishing "pure" anarchy from the emergence of "particles," and then validating the next step to "sediments" is intriguing, but demands operational clarification and empirical testing.

Anarchy serves as a colorful metaphor, conveys a distinctive picture of the international system, but, like beauty, has no objective referent. It is cumbersome, produces varied and vague implications, but intrigues nonetheless. Nations cooperate; cooperation is not a *deviant status* for international politics or its actors. Cooperation, like conflict, is not a constant or a given. But just as national systems do not always possess effective national authority, so also international systems fluctuate between order and discord, cooperation and conflict. The particles and sediments were there all along—Morgenthau saw them in the distinct workings of international law operating more than half a century ago. We end up working very hard trying to generate conceptual approaches thought to be able to explain the decline of something that probably doesn't exist.

> To say that world politics is anarchic does not imply that it entirely lacks organization. Relationships among actors may be carefully structured in some issue-areas, even though they remain loose in others . . . Anarchy, defined as lack of common government, remains a constant; but the degree to which interactions are structured, and the means by which they are structured, vary (Axelrod and Keohane, 1986: 226).

Therefore why do states cooperate? States have always cooperated, and *that* has been a definitional core of international relations from the beginning, not something discovered during the most recent "turn toward cooperation."

Dialectics

Anarchy represents only one of the cyclical debates in what was once described as "games international relations scholars play" (Rosenau, 1967), a ballpark viewed as revolving around the endless, continuing "debates" about appropriate models, paradigms, and methods. Reflecting on this phenomenon more recently, one keen observer concluded:

> What has not changed . . . is the enduring divisiveness in our field of study which, it seems to me, reflects a persistent immaturity. Sometimes the conflict between "schools" is wrapped in the superficially civil discourse of a "debate," sometimes not. What seems to me beyond question, however, is the intolerance attending these debates, often accompanied by rancor, that takes the form of denigrating alternative approaches, methods, models, and theories (Brecher, 1995: 5).

In addition to anarchy, any review of the ongoing debates would merely mean rounding up the usual suspects: the first and continuing idealist-realist debate, followed by the methodological dual of "behavioralists" vs. "traditionalists," followed in turn by a replay of the first debate, only now called the realist-globalist debate, and finally, the most recent variation of this particular debate encompassing first the emergence of "neorealism," to some a more nasty variant of realism because of its insistence on "structure" as an operative cause as opposed to individual "agency," which then meshed in the 1990s with the so-called "end of the Cold War" and the new "neo-idealist" movement involving "neo-liberalism" and institutionalism, and representing yet one more challenge to that broad category called realism. The most recent innovation in the debate mode appears in the "post-positivist" or "post-modern" reaction, issuing in many ways in a rehash of both the realist/idealist as well as the traditional/behavioral debates.

While some fear that "our discipline is at risk of self-destruction" (Brecher, 1995: 8), the admonitions noted 30 years ago about "playing games" also counseled that such debates "should not be denigrated" (Rosenau, 1967: 293). While much in recent polemics resurrect components of controversies more than a generation ago—perhaps either still unresolved or unimportant—a more fruitful focus on important theoretical elements has also emerged. One illustration concerns the contentious nature and role of the nation-state. While representing only one theoretical focus, it shares with others the nucleus of concern about "realism," which continues to be the source of growing intellectual tension. Allegedly "new" theoretical approaches are claimed all the time, and while they take multiple specific, operational forms and are given many labels,[17] a central focus is on the continuing debate pitting realists and neo-realists against neo-liberals and institutionalists, which has seemingly hijacked the discipline. The debate can at times appear futile, but insofar as it concentrates on the central unit of analysis for traditional realism, the nation-state, interesting progress can be made. While for many years the nation-state suffered nothing more than a benign, resigned acceptance, these more recent avenues have enlivened its stature. Some cast it as one more of the male-created and male-dominated hierarchical structures at the central core of the major problems in international politics (Peterson, 1992; Sylvester, 1994), and others view it as having served as a positive step forward in the efficient organization of human beings into large groupings (Spruyt, 1994) despite its alternating and contested status with respect to changed perceptions of its essential element, sovereignty (Barkin and Cronin, 1994).

Nonetheless, the "hits" taken by realism and the nation-state have been numerous, sometimes specified through the vehicle of particular contentious areas. Major "issues" in international politics based on the preeminence of the nation-state have been called outmoded, with power and realism failing to comprehend contemporary international politics because the underlying premise was wrong: the "issues" of import had shifted from the old ones of power, military might, and national security, to the newer ones of depletion of natural resources, international pollution and population, terrorism, multinational corporations and—more recently—reborn nationalism (Mansbach and Vasquez, 1981; Sullivan, 1990: 21–72). These were the "modern" problems; war, power, and international conflict of the traditional variety were outmoded—or too intractable—and so scholars moved on (Sullivan, 1990: 57–71, 98–102).

Concerning the broader nation-state *system*, the dirge is reminiscent of those heard in the 1920s: the nation-state is dead, internationalism is the new "reality" in the world, and peace will reign. Later, in the 1950s, the panacea was "integration," especially in Europe. Later still, beginning in the 1970s, the demise of the nation-state was heralded as concomitant with the onslaught of growing interdependence and "globalism" (Sullivan, 1978; 1982). More recently, the process has manifested itself in multiple distinctive constructs, some imbedded in the generalized notions of neo-idealism and others in more specific manifestations. One illustration carrying many ramifications as well as policy and theoretical implications is "epistemic" communities, defined as "networks of knowledge-based experts" who ideally share a set of normative and "principled" beliefs, "which provide a value-based rationale for the social action of community members," "shared causal beliefs," and a

common policy enterprise—that is, a set of common practices associated with a set of problems to which their professional competence is directed, presumably out of the conviction that human welfare will be enhanced as a consequence (P. Haas, 1992a: 2–3).

These communities relate not to national but to *international* policy coordination. Their members "become strong actors at the national and transnational level."

> To the extent to which an epistemic community consolidates bureaucratic power within national administrations and international secretariats, it stands *to institutionalize its influence and insinuate its views into broader international politics* (P. Haas, 1992a: 4; emphasis added).

The position and role of the nation-state take a back seat, for the epistemic communities' "approach" assumes a "nonsystemic origin for state interests" and identifies a dynamic for consistent cooperation "*independent of the distribution of international power*" (P. Haas, 1992a: 4; emphasis added). Epistemic communities provide a conceptual underpinning for transcending the nation-state, wherein its traditional and central role fades into the background, and processes associated with its traditional essence—"realism"—should accordingly, over time, fade from the scene.

Should that come to pass, then the chameleon-like character of international behavior should in fact change. Some insist that it already has: "as recently as two decades ago, economists and political scientists in the United States and similar nations barely talked to each other about their overlapping interests" (Cohen, 1990: 263). For many the locus of the behavior of interest has changed to economic as opposed to purely political behavior, resulting in outcome variables at times only tangentially related to nation-state structure, even though the role of realism may remain.

Whether ongoing contentious dialectics reflect "divisiveness," "rancor," and "a persistent immaturity" that puts the discipline "at risk of self destruction" (Brecher, 1995: 5–6, 8) or produce a "greater self-consciousness" (Rosenau, 1967: 293) probably depends on which side of the divide one sits. Debates are not necessarily indicative of fatalistic characteristics; they can symbolize and forecast changing interests and boundaries of research, spawn provocative conceptual realignments and developments, and as such can be healthy. However, persistence of essentially repetitive debates, perhaps cast in different specific forms over the years, or the continuation of metatheoretical disputes so far removed from the reality of politics as to become caricatures, suggests not so much immaturity as lack of directed focus wherein central research questions serve as markers to facilitate progress.

Conclusion

Theory and the "real world" constantly badger and hound each other, the former straining to corral the latter, and the latter racing away, producing a necessary tension in an "interactive" mode because both dimensions—the theoretical and the world it tries to represent—are dynamic.[18] That tension can produce a tendency to see the development of theory *responding* to events in the world, with seemingly new phenomena requiring fresh theories, the most recent manifestation involving the end of the Cold War, the demise of bipolarity, and—at least up through the mid-1990s— questions about the status of American hegemony, all of which, unproven as yet in terms of veracity or at least not very well specified, have resulted in yet *new* calls for *new* ways of dealing with this *new* world. Such constitutes a normal process when observed facts appear no longer to fit the previous theoretical structure, but in a sense the process witnessed in international relations unfortunately masks a subtle form of intellectual laziness: that is, implicitly accepting the existence of communism, an acceptance confining research to an agenda *assuming* communist systems ad infinitum, as well as accepting the continued existence of the "Cold War system," and, for some, American hegemony. It is remarkable how little attention was focused—by almost *anyone* other than the most casual journalists—on forecasting changes potentially bringing about these multiple transformations. Of all these processes, only the "fall" of American hegemony received sustained attention, and it remains a very much debated empirical phenomenon.

These failures, while associated with the academic community, were more widely prevalent. One White House national security advisor upon leaving his position and returning to the army in 1989 found, after traveling to numerous military bases around the United States, the "same old policies," with high-level military planners operating under the same old models: "you would think the Soviet threat had not been altered one iota" (Woodward, 1991: 76–77). The affliction so effectively outlined as having plagued a small group of quantitative scholars (Gaddis, 1992–93) had obviously disseminated to high-ranking policy-makers also.

An equally tenacious affliction of post–Cold War theoretical dogma may already be forming: just as the Cold War, bipolarity, and the continued existence of communism and communist systems had become accepted as normal, now the dawning, newly accepted wisdom seems to be the assumed linear and uninterrupted beneficial effects of the movement away from communist systems and *toward* market-based democratic processes, as well as the spread of "globalization." While empirical evidence suggests that the "democratic domino theory"—as opposed to the popular "communist domino theory" of the 1950s and 1960s—has validity (Starr, 1991a), nonetheless it would be just as foolhardy now to forecast a linear trend in these dimensions as it was, with hindsight, to forecast such a linear continuance of alternative processes in Eastern Europe, Russia, and the world political system in an earlier era.

Assessing major long-term changes over the short term is thus hazardous. When events occur that appear to contradict timeworn—and especially unpopular—paradigms, a natural tendency is to reject the unpopular in favor of "new" paradigms and theories. It has happened before and will again, and such calls would seem especially treacherous when the transformations said to necessitate new approaches have had perhaps a decade to produce their effect. A decade is a short time, and while it is too facile to contend that what results is merely old wine in new bottles, still we do tend to find similarities between new and old. No one suggests hitching an entire discipline to outmoded paradigms but certainly some recognition should be given to the short time frame within which we have had to assess these major transformations, and also, quite bluntly, the possibility that unfortunately some things do not change. Venerable theories survive, although perhaps with new labels; some have sprouted new viewpoints. Certain paradigms—constructivism, agent-structure, critical theory—all have antecedents, some close, some more distant.

A structure such as the one to follow, which unabashedly uses Waltz's classic three-image organization of international relations, is still a construction, and one that itself has become heartily contested (Caporaso, 1997: 563–566). Whatever faults it may have had, however, it does attempt, if—unlike Waltz—one gives credence to all three levels of analysis, to reflect the complex reality of multiple behaviors combined with multiple explanations. Because the following chapters are structured loosely around the traditional three-level scheme of individual, state, and system, it is open to many of the same attacks that have occurred over the years, but it is a scheme that survives and has even been utilized, in rough format, in at least one recent symposium (Lebow and Risse-Kappen, 1995). We do not follow this slavishly, but its outlines can be detected.

Characterizing international relations theory as analogous to a minefield might convey an overly pessimistic message, but when truisms such as "national interest" and "power politics" are deemed no longer relevant or part of the serious component of the discipline, such a judgment seems pertinent. References to "hits and misses," "chameleons," and "myths" also might seem cavalier. But possibly a bit of whimsy—or humility—might help.[19] The Vietnam War produced multiple effects, with theory-building constituting one affected area.[20] That war, for many contemporaries of the time, however, "Had Such Promise!"[21] The new promises of the current era must now be assessed, and the following chapters hope to mesh the best of the old and the new.

Chapter Two ✿

Individuals, Agency, and Ideas

Introduction

The revolutionary transformations between 1989 and 1991 so frequently hailed as marking the latest "modern" era—post–Cold War—occurred on the "watch" of two specific individuals: Mikhail Gorbachev and Ronald Reagan. Present at potentially a momentous juncture in recent history, one would expect an understandable focus on those two leaders, following a research agenda first tangibly proposed before World War II and continued in earnest during at least the first two decades after the end of that major war. While such a focus on them has not emerged, systematic analyses of the role of individuals, which had flowered in the 1950s and 1960s in an early anti-realist movement, continued but gave way in some quarters toward extra-individual explanations of larger, aggregated phenomena. Many reasons account for that metamorphosis, one being the chameleon factor: the change by the 1970s in the definition of the most relevant-appearing dependent variables.

Almost perversely, as research gravitated away from what some viewed as "reductionist" reliance on individual-level variables, two public figures emerged who caught the imagination of the populace in the two largest powers, and the world witnessed the "Gorby phenomenon" and the two-term presidency of a Hollywood actor. From the respective depths of the Soviet bureaucracy and Hollywood studios emerged two *individuals,* who, in a few short years, seemed to have unleashed monumental transformations in international politics: the fall of the Berlin Wall, the end of communism and Soviet—or "evil"—empire, the end of the Cold War, and the pronouncement—authorship here is somewhat up for grabs—of the "New World Order." It would be doubly ironic to ignore these individuals since it was Gorbachev himself who delivered, in the spring of 1992, a major speech in Fulton, Missouri—home of Churchill's "Iron Curtain" speech—contending that the major *cause* of the Cold War in the first place had been the misperception of the Soviet Union by American leaders in the immediate post–World War II period.

In the glow of post–Cold War hubris, the "individual" reemerged for some as a newly found revelation of a post-realist, post-structuralist intellectual ferment. In fact, systematic analysis of the individual's role in world politics first emerged in the immediate post–World War II era, spawned by an intellectual reaction to Morgenthau's "realpolitik" model, by the view that World War II had been a function of *one* individual, namely, Hitler, the sense that through the mid-1960s individual characteristics of the leaders of the time—Stalin in the East and Dulles in the West—were crucial in understanding the unfolding instability, and finally the succession of acute international crises also viewed as a function of "leader characteristics"—Stalin, Mao, and Castro if you were in the West, and Dulles, Eisenhower, and Kennedy if you were in the East.

The individual view—Waltz's "first image"—endures through many attacks, and transcends academic boundaries. The specifics of the general approach vary, of course. Anthropological and psychological studies have been "overlaid" onto international phenomena and the "fit" was often seen as quite good.[1] Freudian terminology has on and off had its day in imputing to individual leaders psychological predispositions plausibly associated with their international behavior. The biological reasons behind war, which always retains an interest, seem almost to have dropped by the 1970s (Sullivan, 1976: 23–26), though they have been revived periodically since then. Even though a group of scientists "rejects the contention that 'biological factors' play any meaningful role in the causation of war," nonetheless ethologists and biologists "have almost unanimously agreed that human aggression has a substantial biological component," demonstrating the incendiary possibilities of the entire genre:

> once we grant a role to biological factors, it may be impossible to draw the line at aggression and war. If aggression is the product . . . of our evolutionary past, so too are dominance and subordination, behaviors which are just as consistently manifested by all social primates (Somit, 1990: 581).

In the context of critical theory and postmodern approaches, such discussions manifest a relevance much beyond the narrowly defined issue of aggression and war, but the conclusion drawn long ago—that the puzzles posed by behavior that varies across time and space could in no way be solved by relatively stable, perhaps constant factors, such as human nature—still remains (Sullivan, 1976: 23–26). Nonetheless, a broad range of behavior susceptible to individual-level causality also lingers, viewed today in terms of "agency," which could be reduced to one slice of the traditional debate pitting free will versus determinism.

But that debate resides at the metatheoretical level; at the real-world level, personal characteristics have always represented the messiest part of "agency," and the following section addresses this perspective. Following that, we begin addressing the variety of ways in which "rational" and "psychological" models differ: rational choice, motivated bias, and cognitive bias paradigms each contain their "own basic logic of how decision makers use information to evaluate alternative courses of action" (Kaufmann, 1994: 559). The core of rational choice, elaborated on in the next chapter, is that "people maximize their interests subject to constraints." Motivation-based models assume a basic dynamic called "ego defense," and these processes operate "only when individuals are confronted with consequential choices, which involve risks to important values as well as tradeoffs between conflicting values" (Kaufmann, 1994: 559). For "unmotivated" models, the central idea is "cognitive economy," wherein complexity and an incoherent world produces cognitive "short cuts," which "reduce mental strain and . . . impose a tolerable degree of simplicity, consistency, and stability in our perceptions and beliefs," which can engender certain "systematic errors and biases" (Kaufmann, 1994: 559). These in turn can lead to a variety of methods of assessing such cognitive processes, much of which we will analyze: operational codes, image theory, and conceptual complexity (Young and Shafer, 1998).

Despite differences, the two latter approaches predict "broadly similar divergences from rational standards: insufficient information search before forming a judgment, biased evaluation, and excessive resistance to re-evaluation" (Kaufmann, 1994: 559), all implying a contrast with the "rational," a sense that things that may look on the surface as if they were the result of someone's great "plan," in reality result from multiple, non-"rational" factors.

Personal Characteristics:
The Ultimate Draw or Reductionism?

"Agency" has become attractive but remains inordinately generalized, and the core component would seem to revolve around "agents" themselves. "Overlaying" personality factors onto international behavior, however attractive, often creates more difficulties than it resolves. First, personality contains within it such diversity that the research agenda as well as any "design" other than the most simple ends up becoming overly detailed and nuanced. Theories of personality constitute a panoply of potential explanations, but the diversity and disagreement within that field concerning basic underlying dynamics suggests that

> The transfer of knowledge from one discipline to another would be fairly unproblematic if there were an established body of theory and research that had been experimentally verified and widely accepted within the parent discipline. Unfortunately, this is not the case in cognitive psychology (Shimko, 1991: 27).

Basic determinants of personality are still not precise, and application, for instance, of Freud's notions to international actors has not advanced very far (Winter, 1992: 80–83, 96), which should certainly raise warning flags about overlaying such theories onto complex, multilayered international behavior. In fact, trends that have occurred reflect this realization, from fairly simple "transference" methodologies of mid-century to the recognition that individual-level variables, at least for large portions of international behavior, constitute perhaps residual explanations, in the scheme of things accounting for fairly small amounts of international behavior. For instance, in "complex and highly threatening" negotiating situations, the "negotiators are locked into rigidly defined roles and share a subculture with their opposite numbers. Under these conditions, the effects of personality characteristics have been shown to be minimized" (Druckman, 1973: 71).

Nonetheless, personality possesses a "draw," and plausible linkages between leaders' individual traits and subsequent international behavior can be made. Illustrations abound, and the references to Ronald Reagan and Mikhail Gorbachev above were not presented casually. The "Gorby phenomenon" was not limited to public reactions to him; despite his swift political demise he has received much attention by scholars as well, but the focus, interestingly enough, has not been directed at innate personal characteristics. In the heyday of the "transference" school, an authoritative study on Woodrow Wilson noted that for Wilson, "the basic hypothesis concerning [his] political behavior is that power was for him a compensatory value, a means of restoring the self-esteem damaged in childhood" (George and George, 1964: 320). Plagued by "bottled up" aggressive impulses, Wilson needed to purify his exercise of power by taking on tasks only on a moral plane. On American entry into World War I, Wilson's wish was:

to transform the war into a great crusade for an ideal peace; his tendency to overrate the efficacy of moral appeals; his inclination to substitute vaguely worded aspirations and general principles for concrete proposals (George and George, 1964: 172).

The then standard "relationship with his father" (Post, 1983) categorized Wilson's personality and thus plausibly linked his characteristics to his behavior.

> When Wilson had a small degree of personal involvement in a task and did not link success with his need for self-esteem, he could be extremely skillful in handling the situation. He could be very flexible, select political goals that were ripe for development, and be both shrewd and inventive in his leadership. It was only when the situation related to his unconscious problems that he became inflexible . . . (deRivera, 1968: 199).

However, explaining a president's behavior from such "character" attributes is very enigmatic, for while "it is not difficult to find evidence that a subject's character-rooted needs or motives . . . are *expressed* in his behavior," such evidence is nonetheless "a necessary *but insufficient* condition for establishing the *critical causal importance* of those personality factors in the explanation of that behavior" (George, 1974: 253, emphasis in original).

Such cautions have not stopped the enterprise, and Wilson continues to be a popular subject, all the way from psychoanalytical to medical accounts (Winter, 1992: 80–86). The psychoanalytical accounts can certainly plausibly explain what has been called "Wilson's puzzling behavior" (Walker, 1995: 698), with the Versailles Treaty debate viewed as an opportunity for expressing "deep personality needs" whereas the decisions to occupy the Mexican port of Vera Cruz and to enter World War I occasioned different responses; ultimately, however, especially with the treaty decision, "ego-defensive processes emanating from the depths of Wilson's personality produced a flawed decision-making process and a suboptimal outcome" (Walker, 1995: 715).

Three key events spanning a decade and a half of America's involvement in the Vietnam conflict have also been "linked" with the absence or presence of a specific type of narcissistic character in Presidents Eisenhower, Johnson, and Nixon. Dismissing the press of domestic constraints or the influence of respective advisory systems (Steinberg, 1996: 292–293), the three presidents are depicted as possessing differential personality characteristics that led to one avenue of decision for Eisenhower over Dien Bien Phu in 1954 and to another for Johnson in early 1965 and Nixon over Cambodia in 1970:

> leaders with a narcissistic personality structure manifesting itself in a strong sensitivity to issues of shame and humiliation may be influenced in the making of foreign-policy decisions by unconscious efforts to avoid shame-inducing experiences and alleviate painful feelings of low self-worth (Steinberg, 1996: 307).

In terms of such specific decisions—and the three under consideration are specific, although key, decisions—the constructs of personality certainly emerge from the painstaking and enumerated details of the three presidents' lives as potentially determinant explanations of their behaviors in the three instances.

Nonetheless, at bottom we are faced with three specific decisions—in a very long line of many other specific decisions. Imposing personality characteristics is thus plausible but tenuous, especially when they convey subtle invidious connotations. The continuing drawback in investigating individual characteristics of leaders is the inability to "touch" them, not unlike the astronomers who cannot "touch the heavens." Such a drawback, however, has not prevented innovative ways of attempting to bridge that gap, and the detailed case study is not the only route. "Nationalism" seemed a key general characteristic and early results suggested that leaders scoring high on this dimension were more "active" in foreign policy behavior, a relationship occurring mostly in closed political systems, and "cognitive complexity" being positively related to cooperative behavior (M. Hermann, 1974). More significant relationships occurred between personal characteristics and foreign policy behaviors for those with little "training" compared to heads of government with more training, but controlling for "interest in foreign affairs" indicated that more significant relationships between personal characteristics showed up in the "low interest" group rather than the "high interest" groups (M. Hermann, 1980: 43). Other findings suggest that a "power motivation" is more associated with a foreign policy style of a confrontational nature, while an "affiliation motivation" tended to a more cooperative and interdependent style of interaction with other nations (M. Hermann, 1980; 1984).

Focusing on variables directly related to leaders' actual behavioral tendencies is one path. A different tack, using "interpersonal generalization theory," suggests that the "direction of disagreement" on force-related issues and cooperative policies "could be predicted by knowledge of individual differences in interpersonal relations":

> personality characteristics of American political elite members in certain situations often have tipped the balance for or against a foreign-policy choice and thus are crucial ingredients in American foreign policy decision-making (Shepard, 1988: 93).

The distinguishing element—our chameleon again—is the dependent variable, which becomes even more specific than the detailed case studies of Eisenhower, Johnson, and Kennedy and their specific decisions on Vietnam: here it becomes policy disagreement/agreement or inconsistency. The independent variables are dominance and extroversion/introversion. The "direction of disagreement could be predicted by knowledge of individual differences in interpersonal relations" (Shepard, 1988: 93).

Confirming earlier accounts (Etheredge, 1978), disagreement, as well as its direction, on force-related issues could be predicted by personality characteristics about 77 percent of the time (Shepard, 1988: 119–120). Elite members who "display high-dominance personality characteristics in their observable behavior are more likely than low-dominance personalities to advocate the use of force in foreign policy debates" (Shepard, 1988: 120). The overall conclusion is more particular: introversion/extroversion "probably does not have an impact on foreign policy decisions pertaining to relations with the Soviet Union and Soviet bloc" (Shepard, 1988: 121), but decisions on the use of force "are partly determined by, and a predictable consequence of, the personality characteristic of dominance." It must be clear, however, that such analyses differ from those attempting to demonstrate distinct links between specific, measurable personality characteristics and specific foreign actions or trends. However, within the broader context of decision-makers' use of "rational" analysis (Chapter Three), the findings take on a broader meaning, even though their specifics might be perceived as disappointing:

> rational analysis is performed by elite members when they make foreign-policy decisions. Yet elite members apparently are not fully aware of how much their personality characteristics shape their thoughts and perceptions. And the conviction of some that

decision-makers make rational choices based exclusively on realistic assessments is itself irrational (Shepard, 1988: 122).

Two key problems perennially plague "agency"-oriented inquiries that attempt specified linkages: the connections between specific independent and dependent variables are by nature loosely drawn, or the dependent variables tend to be constricted. But another avenue originates from a much more primitive theoretical base and thus less refined, but nonetheless intriguing. If personalities differ across individuals, then when officeholders change, and one observes change in behavior for which they are responsible, we can infer that the new officeholder—a different personality—had an observable effect. Should no change occur, the personality change had no effect. The converse is also true: when behavior does shift with no concomitant change in the officeholder, deeply imbedded personal characteristics cannot be a factor causing the change.

Once contemplated in this way—testing personality "indirectly"[2]—a variety of data become grist for the mill. An initial analysis of crude Cold War data from 1946 to 1963 discovered four "watersheds" where observable changes in East-West relations took place along a positive-negative dimension; none occurred when new personalities took over the reins of government, namely, when Eisenhower succeeded Truman and Stalin died in 1953 and when Kennedy succeeded Eisenhower in 1961 (Gamson and Modigliani, 1971). To the contrary, a major shift by the Western allies from nonaccommodative to accommodative behavior occurred in late 1950, another in October, 1956, and a third in November, 1962, none of them at or near the known changes in leadership. More importantly, prominent international crises *were* present at or near those shifts: the Korean War, the Middle East crisis and war of 1956, and the Cuban Missile Crisis all corresponded to major changes in East-West relations.

The variable of "crisis" also emerged in an investigation into the perceptual "definition of the situation." Variations in perceptions of hostility by 19 decision-makers in the pre–World War I 1914 crisis did not appear related to personalities, but rather to the crisis or non-crisis situation: "We have accounted for such a high proportion of the variation in perception of hostility that the 'unexplained' part which might be attributed to individual differences is extremely small" (O. Holsti, 1970: 305). Country (cultural differences) or role (monarch, prime minister, foreign minister, ambassador) also made little difference: perceptions of hostility were almost entirely accounted for by the different situation—crisis or noncrisis (Sullivan, 1976: 37). Perceptions of Egyptian and Israeli leaders during the 1956 war also displayed minimal difference across actors—those serving at the United Nations and those serving the home country—in perceptions of their own country, the enemy, or the United Nations itself (Siverson, 1973: 339). Other studies also showed no significant differences between President Kennedy and Premier Khrushchev on indexes of "conflict-mindedness," little differences along certain key Cold War perceptions among three nonaligned leaders in the 1950s and 1960s, and few differences between Presidents Kennedy, Johnson, and Nixon in perceptions of alleged key issues for the U.S. involvement in the Vietnam War (Sullivan, 1976: 39).

While from a conceptual perspective personality retains a strong attraction, still from a dependent-variable orientation its status remains limited despite protestations of practitioners (Kowert and Hermann, 1997: 630–632). But two central decision-makers have been left stranded: Ronald Reagan and Mikhail Gorbachev. Certainly the "end of the Cold War" could prove an interesting "test case," with great relevance for more recent international politics. Using "indirect tests" with more sophisticated analyses of longer periods of the Cold War confirmed results of earlier probes and found, for instance, despite the fact that "the tenor of US-Soviet diplomatic relations has drifted in and out of periods of detente over the years" and contrary to original expectations, during the "Reagan years" U.S. behavior "conformed reasonably well to [the] average postwar [affective] values" (Dixon and Gaarder, 1990: 166, 170). U.S. foreign policy exhibited a "characteristic persistence that seems relatively immune from the potentially disruptive effects of presidential succession . . . U.S. foreign policy behavior is characterized more by continuity than change" (Dixon and Gaarder, 1990: 170). Conventional wisdom to the contrary, Ronald Reagan "exemplified the standard Cold War pattern better than any other postwar administration," and, with an obvious eye to the skeptic, the authors observed:

> Perhaps our lingering familiarity with the day-to-day diplomacy of the Reagan presidency coupled with the intense rhetorical style that distinguished Reagan from his predecessor have left us with an exaggerated image of the distinctiveness that is unwarranted in the larger context of the entire Cold War era (Dixon and Gaarder, 1990: 173).

Other investigations do unearth evidence *consistent with* individual "agency"[3] although "reciprocity" was the central focus: changes in U.S.-Soviet behavior in the late 1980s "were driven largely by Soviet initiatives" (Ward and Rajmaira, 1992: 343), even though certain statistical models "were not improved by the addition of leadership variables, suggesting that the basic mechanism is one that applies across leadership eras" (Ward and Rajmaira, 1992: 366). While these data indicated marked changes in the Reagan-Gorbachev era, the extent to which those changes represent meaningful deviations from the longer-term U.S.-Soviet relations is not clear.

The picture becomes further confused when other data on "integrative complexity" (I/C)—a perceptual dimension—is analyzed. Few interpresidential shifts occur in I/C, perhaps the one possible exception comparing President Ford to President Carter (Tetlock, 1988: 109–111). To the contrary, during the Kennedy and Johnson years a clear increase in this perceptual property occurred during and after the Cuban Missile Crisis, and while it remained high into the first three months of 1964, it begins to drop; by early 1965 this measure is at about the level it had been prior to the Cuban Missile Crisis. The first two years of Reagan's presidency are low but are consistent with the declining trend underway during President Carter's administration. The one clear deviation throughout the entire 31 years of data occurred with Mikhail Gorbachev, where Soviet I/C started an increase into the last part of 1986 unparalleled by an increase on the part of the United States—a mismatching that had never occurred previously (Tetlock, 1988: 111).

"Indirect" tests are appealing methodologically but by definition forsake direct investigation of personality components. Few have attempted the daunting task of real-time assessments of such characteristics, and one such attempt on Mikhail Gorbachev and George Bush using a complex multifactor evaluation demonstrated the perils. More than a year before the outbreak of the Persian Gulf Crisis of 1990 and War of 1991, the assessment for both individuals was optimistic and concluded, using I/C and other factors, that both leaders desired to be peacemakers, "concerned with development and not prone to seek political ends through violence and war" (Winter et al., 1991a: 237). The year the assessment was published the United States dispatched 500,000 troops to the Middle East. In the authors' view, this did not necessarily invalidate their assessment, concluding in a follow-up analysis that the events in the

Middle East fell—in the scheme of things—into the category of the unpredictable (Winter et al., 1991b). Post–Cold War American reactions in four other international conflicts spanning Presidents Bush and Clinton can only partly be accounted for by differential operational codes, primarily because relatively small differences emerge between the two individuals (Walker et al., 1999).

Clearly, drawing inferences from evidence on personal characteristics is fraught with problems. Specification intricacies do not beset indirect tests, and one tentative conclusion consistent with earlier results is that changes in individual leadership does not appear *systematically* related to changes in major trends of nation-state behavior. The specific—and perhaps unusual—case of Mikhail Gorbachev in the contemporary era may be the exception—and we return to this in a later section—but still no central set of personality characteristics that he may have possessed have been established as having triggered the transformational phenomena often attributed to him.[4] From these findings one might suggest that the input of individual characteristics is little more than residual. Nonetheless, it remains a tantalizing approach, even though at times a bit primitive (White, 1991), and the "Gorby phenomenon" only whets the appetite. We return to it in a later section. Certainly, however, while it is true that popularized notions from Freudian psychology retain a certain currency, they are probably not capable of sustained systematic confirmation beyond illustrative material on dependent variables that tend to be time-, individual-, and situation-specific. Fascinating portraits can still be drawn relating apparent personality characteristics to behavioral tendencies, or even specific events, but such pictures do not confirm an overriding influence of such characteristics.

Internal Dynamics: Immutable "Images"

Personality characteristics reside outside of the realpolitik mainstream. Kenneth Boulding sounded the death knell of realism from a different perspective a generation ago:

> We must recognize that the people whose decisions determine the policies and actions of nations do not respond to the "objective" facts of the situation, whatever they may mean, but to their "image" of the situation. It is what we think the world is like, not what it is really like, that determines our behavior (Boulding, 1969: 423).

Such a viewpoint clashed directly with the fundamentals of realism and "national interest," wherein *perceptual inaccuracies* simply were not part of the lexicon. By the early 1960s, however, cognate disciplines had shown that such arational processes exist, and no mechanical imposition of a realpolitik model could banish them from the international dimension. But images and perceptions run the gamut from simple to complex, from the obvious and "real" to the nonobvious, nonintuitive, and very much "nonreal." In a classic example with reference to the North Korean invasion of South Korea in June of 1950, producing a major crisis for U.S. decision-makers, the "Assistant Secretary of State for Far Eastern Affairs did not expect an invasion, and hence, failed to detect it even when he was confronted with a rather strong signal" (deRivera, 1968: 53). In that same era, "image of the opponent," a primitive conceptualization, suggested that an incorrect image of the Chinese "operational code" and a "deficient concept of what power means in Asia" meant American policy-makers in the 1950s did not accurately gauge Chinese intentions, motivations, and capabilities, with potentially disastrous effects on U.S. relations with Indochina more than a decade later. Contrary to what Washington thought, "the Chinese actually felt their limited aid to nationalist Ho Chi Minh was a low-risk policy option" (Lampton, 1973: 28, 40). A decade later, on the other hand, it is argued that President Kennedy possessed a "relatively sophisticated analysis of Chinese goals and interests," and therefore the "reason he was able to fully use his resources is that the analysis of most components of the ImOP (Image of the Opponent) was largely correct," and thus "perceptual accuracy does matter" (Lampton, 1973: 49).

Almost a half century later perceptual inaccuracies once again emerged along the chain of decisions that led to the Persian Gulf War of 1991, just after the dawn of what was to have been "a new world order." Different cognitive perspectives propose admittedly loose explanations both for the original invasion of Kuwait by Iraq (Hybel, 1993: 37–40),[5] and more importantly for the United States' response, explanations exemplified by the conclusion that the United States'

> principal foreign policy makers reasoned analogically, and that their psychological attachment to certain historical analogies undermined their willingness to consider alternative perspectives or scenarios (Hybel, 1993: 87).

The principal here is simple and obvious: decisions flow from a variety of causes, and momentous decisions can more than plausibly be related to cognitive tendencies.

Such cognitive tendencies, however, have always been related to "big" or momentous decisions; the focus on unconventional perceptual dispositions first emerged with the Cold War. "Mirror images" was a concept originally proposed in the 1950s suggesting that perceptual distortion of American society and foreign policy uncovered in the Soviet Union was only one side of a dual misperception: both sides viewed the other as an aggressor, exploiting its people, having no popular support, being untrustworthy, and fostering a "mad" foreign policy—its "mirror" image. The insight resulted in six mirror and dichotomous images: the diabolical, weak, and evil enemy versus the good, strong, and virile self (White, 1965). Historical analyses found the images before World War I, with Hitler in 1939, and on both sides of the Vietnam War in the 1960s (White, 1968). While certainly intriguing, nonetheless the presence of such images never rose much above historical and anecdotal evidence, unable to confront the problem of *what situations* tend to produce such mirrored images, nor *systematically* testing behavioral consequences from the presence of such images.[6]

The "ideas" and "beliefs" of individuals that have once again emerged (Goldstein and Keohane, 1993) have been part of a long scholarship. These alternative extrarational explanations of behavior were earlier called "belief systems" and "operational codes," the latter referring specifically to Soviet leaders and the former more generally applied. "Belief systems" were employed more as a psychological explanation while operational code contained a political/psychological and somewhat rigid connotation. Belief systems were filtering devices comprising basic philosophical tenets. For instance, Bolshevik or Soviet thinking was thought to see the world as hostile and shrewd, picturing the political universe as one of constant conflict. Yet, possessed with great optimism, the Soviets were thought to see the victory of communism at some future time. As more recently with the belief in "agency," the sense was that man can and does *move* history, therefore adherents to it would tend to see very complicated planning behind events that may have been fortuitous (George, 1969: 204–205).

While all humans possess "belief systems," when these are applied to American leaders, they seem somewhat more inconstant than operational codes, although still implying a certain—almost dangerous—rigidity. John Foster Dulles's belief system had been labeled an "inherent bad faith" model: for him, Soviet cooperative behavior was not sincere but rather a function of their frustration or changing capabilities. Holsti's classic study found Dulles's perception of Soviet hostility did correlate with his perception of their failure or frustration in foreign policy, and with their weakness. However—the key point—his perceptions of decreased hostility notwithstanding, Dulles's evaluation of the Soviet Union in a more general sense remained unchanged. Holsti's results "strongly suggest that [Dulles] attributed decreasing Soviet hostility to the necessity of adversity rather than to any genuine change of character" (O. Holsti, 1969: 547).

A replication on both Henry Kissinger and John Kennedy showed that Kissinger's general evaluation and his perception of Soviet hostility were more positive than the images held by Dulles, and "Kennedy fell almost exactly between Dulles and Kissinger, in a historical continuum from the 1950s to the 1970s" (Starr, 1984: 99). Moreover, while Kissinger did display a similar tendency as Dulles to see the opponent as less hostile or threatening when they are weak or a failure, that tendency was "in a very diluted form" (Starr, 1984: 99–100). Kissinger's operational code or belief system *was* different from Dulles's, but so also was the evolving triadic relationship between the United States, the Soviet Union, and China. "Kissinger's images are *not* congruent with American foreign-policy behavior" and "the centrality of the Soviet Union as America's principal opponent is reflected in the more positive and rewarding behavior directed at China" (Starr, 1984: 142). Thus despite the potential impact of belief systems and operational codes, "Kissinger's belief system could . . . be used to generate hypotheses and explanations of his evaluations of the Soviet Union and China," and yet "Ultimately . . . Kissinger's perceptions of the Soviet Union and China were only indirectly related to American foreign-policy behavior" (Starr, 1984: 159).

The conceptual difference between "operational code" and "belief system" is not necessarily transparent, but the former typically was meant to "refer to those instrumental aspects of Bolshevik beliefs" and therefore to be "related to the strategy and tactics of political action and thereby influence(d) Soviet decision-making" (Walker, 1977: 130), to describe a group's orientation and therefore account for that group's behavior. More specifically, the Soviet elite was viewed as possessing a deviant attitude with respect to international norms and rules of the time accepted by other nations in the system. "Belief systems" more normally applied to specific individuals rather than groups, and focused on the makeup of the individual's "beliefs."

The line between the two is easily crossed, however, and "operational code" serves as a shorthand for beliefs. Henry Kissinger's "beliefs" and operational code affected specifically his negotiations on Vietnam: using George's fundamental questions to generate Kissinger's central philosophical and instrumental outlook,[7] data from Kissinger's scholarly and popular writings have been applied to negotiations in the Vietnam conflict from 1969 through January of 1973. Focusing on a code comprised of the timing of negotiation and the respective use and amount of threats and force, behavior in terms of timing corresponded to Kissinger's instrumental beliefs, while the overall rationale for negotiations was consistent with his philosophical principles as demonstrated in the code. Therefore, "The congruency between this code and his conduct of the Vietnam negotiations implies that a knowledge of Kissinger's operational code is a necessary condition for the explanation of his behavior" (Walker, 1977: 147, 153, 155).

Beyond the specifics of the Vietnam case, the triadic nature of superpower relations suggests Kissinger was "biased positively toward China and negatively against the Soviet

Union—even in the era of Soviet-American detente" (Starr, 1984: 160), and his behavior resembled the Vietnam negotiations: "Kissinger pursued a web of interdependence with the Soviet Union, a dual policy of the use of negotiation as well as force . . . against the United States' single most powerful opponent and the greatest possible threat to world order" (Starr, 1984: 160). Yet despite the draw and potency of belief systems and operational codes, "translating images into foreign-policy behavior (or having foreign-policy behavior faithfully reflect those images) is not a direct and straightforward process" (Starr, 1984: 161).

Such studies deserve classic stature for investigating complex cognitive processes, but lurking in the background are broader systemic transformations, structural changes that come to fruition sometimes one to two decades later, and that cannot be left out of any equation. Nonetheless, despite suggestions of strong belief system influences, still with the much-ballyhooed end of the Cold War, Soviet "operational codes"—and to a lesser extent the belief systems associated with Cold War behavior—appear more as a time-dependent characteristic than when first enunciated in the 1950s to account for apparent non-time-dependent tendencies of Soviet and other leaders.

We now return to the two superstars, Reagan and Gorbachev, for an anomaly arises in the case of superpower arms control negotiations in the 1980s and especially the Intermediate Nuclear Forces (INF) treaty of 1987. On the surface, conventional wisdom hints that Ronald Reagan's belief system, as elaborated at least within the context of acute international crises (Leng, 1984), would not seem in harmony with the signing of a major arms reduction treaty with the "evil empire." Belief systems by their very nature are considered rigid, yet the decade of the 1980s witnessed major decisional metamorphoses, changes that should not have occurred within the context of the belief system normally associated with Ronald Reagan.

One analysis suggests a solution as well as demonstrating the shift in epistemological orientation, from strict hypothesis testing to "a loose form of hypothesis-testing—an 'expectation' is an imprecise form of hypothesis" (Shimko, 1991: 2). With some exceptions—the lack of emphasis on Soviet ideology and the addition of nuclear terminology not used in the 1950s—two of Ronald Reagan's major aides on disarmament, Richard Perle and Caspar Weinberger, possessed "images of the Soviet Union [that] are virtual carbon copies of Dulles's" (Shimko, 1991: 81). Two others, George Shultz and Richard Burt, differed, and this played a role. The conceptualization of Cold War belief systems provides continuity with the destructionist, expansionist, and consolidationist belief systems specified years earlier (Gamson and Modigliani, 1971), which in turn are analogous to the communist expansionism, realpolitik expansionism, and realpolitik defensive belief systems of later vintage (R. Hermann, 1985):

> Hermann's communist expansionist model is similar to the inherent-bad-faith model and diabolical enemy image discussed in relation to Perle and Weinberger. This image does not seem appropriate for describing the views of Shultz and Burt; the realpolitik expansionist model seems more applicable (Shimko, 1991: 100).

The relationship between *these* belief systems and what went on in the world, however, is a bit more complex. Ronald Reagan's second term revealed a

> very slight shift . . . away from the notion that global domination was the primary Soviet objective . . . we see a decreased emphasis on ideology as the source of Soviet behavior beginning in 1985 and an increase in references to personality factors (Shimko, 1991: 107).[8]

But concerning the contemporary functional importance of belief systems, "the nature of Reagan's image . . . is such that a variety of policy positions on most issues could find intellectual support," and determining which policies were consistent with his image of the Soviet Union is enigmatic because

> his image provides us with unclear and occasionally contradictory guidelines. This is a potentially significant finding. The key point is that *if Reagan's image fails to give us guidance, it may not have given him much direction either* (Shimko, 1991: 165).

Thus Reagan's image was not a very well-developed one (a combination of two "uncomplicated . . . mind-sets or belief patterns . . ."),[9] he boasted only rudimentary knowledge of the issues, and his interest vacillated. Those with extensive knowledge and well-grounded beliefs "might be more likely to maintain their beliefs in the face of extensive knowledge that indicates they are incorrect" (Jervis, 1980: 88, cited in Shimko, 1991: 245), and "an uninformed decision-maker may support policies that contradict his or her belief without even realizing it (e.g., Reagan's support for a START proposal that would probably have increased the vulnerability of U.S. forces)" (Shimko, 1991: 245). Ironically, Reagan's belief system—or lack of one—might better explain a major transformation in policy during an administration whose leader's belief system has been portrayed by most conventional (as well as academic [Leng, 1984]) accounts as diametrically opposed to those changes. Others, however, contend that "the direction and scope of the change that took place cannot be explained without reference to the impact of Gorbachev and his representation of the Soviet security problem" (J. Stein, 1994: 156), a key suggestion we return to below. Nonetheless, major change may have resulted from Reagan's shift to an alternative belief pattern, "not a major overhaul of his Soviet image," an interpretation consistent with one analysis of President Wilson's behavior during ratification debates over the Treaty of Versailles, where shifts between different types of belief systems were also observed (Walker, 1995). Perhaps for this reason no dramatic change occurred in the substance of America's arms control proposals:

> The common perception that Reagan's Soviet image had changed substantially during his second term is often accompanied by the belief that US arms control policy also changed.

But:

> Any change was primarily in the realm of intangibles, such as a desire for summits and an eagerness to reach an agreement . . . Neither Reagan's image of the Soviet Union nor his optimistic belief pattern was sufficiently precise or well grounded to provide a high degree of policy guidance. The result was a more upbeat approach to arms control in general—a new arms control stance—without major revisions of policy specifics (Shimko, 1991: 247).

The anomaly, therefore, occurred not so much from change in a fundamental belief system, which we would not expect, but a continuation of established policy covered by a surface appearance of change. Neither individual nor systemic level explanations need be called into play to explain change in policy, since such a change never occurred—at least not to the extent the public was led to believe.

But "perceived" changes in arms control policy occurred concomitant with the broader "end of the Cold War" pattern, a phenomenon we have taken pains to suggest is considerably more complex than conventionally assumed, which raises again the issue of the dependent variable. As noted above, others basically bypass Ronald Reagan and contend that it was the "American peace movement and what became known as the 'freeze campaign' that revived the arms control process together with pressure from the European allies" (Risse-Kappen, 1994: 205), as well as Gorbachev's "new thinking" and reorientation towards the Soviet security problem (J. Stein, 1994: 156). Still, on the American side at a certain point the "intellectual expert community reentered the policymaking process" (Risse-Kappen, 1994: 205), and a shift of power occurred from Weinberger and Perle—whom Shimko sees as the major architects—to George Schultz and Paul Nitze, after which Reagan gave several moderate foreign policy speeches, all before Gorbachev came into office. No one could dispute the assertion that "ideas" are needed "to understand the recent sea-change in world politics" (Risse-Kappen, 1994: 213), but the issue clearly not resolved is whose ideas: those of the freeze campaign, peace movement, Gorbachev, or even Ronald Reagan.

Thus, two problems: are there immutable beliefs or ideas, and what is the makeup of the dependent variable related to these? For the latter, the "end of the Cold War" is certainly a "sea change" but one made up of many specifics, such as the shifts in arms control. "Ideas" can be retrieved plausibly linked to both, but the linkages are much less clear than some would imply. Reagan's belief system was inexact and up for grabs. Mikhail Gorbachev can be given much more credit if his alleged "dynamic learning" proved causal, and the evidence is highly plausible; but even this process is unable to explain foreign policy change and must be viewed contextually in a "highly interactive" process (J. Stein, 1994: 244–245). While others agree that the beliefs of the Soviet leaders stayed relatively unchanged until the emergence of Gorbachev, it is an argument that comes close to a tautology: beliefs remain the same until they change; they

> insulate policy from pressures for change . . . when such pressures became irresistible, beliefs contributed to the peculiar pattern of foreign policy adjustment: sudden, sweeping shifts in strategies (under Khrushchev) or basic policy goals (under Gorbachev) (Blum, 1993: 388).[10]

"Belief system" orientations originally offered an alternative to realism's rigidity, and have now mutated over the course of a generation to more complex nonadversarially-based "images" (R. Herrmann and Fischerkeller, 1995) drawing directly from earlier Cold War-based images (Gamson and Modigliani, 1971), as well as to a more generalized "ideas matter" theme (Goldstein and Keohane, 1993; Wendt, 1994b). But belief systems are "ideas"—John Foster Dulles's "images" were just as much "ideas" as Gorbachev's "new thinking"—and therefore the question has never been whether ideas "matter," but rather which ideas, whose ideas, and, perhaps most importantly, the circumstances under which particular ideas flourish. Recent constructivist work has tended to focus largely on "ethically good norms" such as the stigma against nuclear weapons, the change in norms that brought about the end of the Cold War or the demise of apartheid; "these scholars should give equal attention to the bad things in world politics that are socially constructed" (Checkel, 1998: 339).

One certainly negative component of the original applications of "operational codes" and "belief systems" in international relations was their implied rigidity.[11] The "ideas matter" school suggests that such basic elements do change, an intriguing prospect especially when accounting for the "end of the Cold War." Traveling that road of course shifts the basic, underlying presuppositions of operational codes and belief systems, the rigidity languishes, and whether "strong" beliefs are the driving force behind major decisions comes into question. But it certainly raises the question of the nonrigidity of ideas and beliefs, and the possibility of pursuing "ideas matter" by focusing on more variable specifications.

Mutable "Ideas"

For many years "national interest" was a potent idea, encompassed, as it was, within the power-oriented "realist" school. Later, when the social scientists came along, "definition of the situation" conveyed a false objectivity to what very often was the same "idea." Both have virtually disappeared from serious theoretical consideration. The potency of "national interest" lay in its alleged immutability: it was presumed to be something that *existed*, that people *knew*, and would even *fight for*. We now know that it did change, even though revivals have occurred in recent years (Clinton, 1994; Kimura and Welch, 1998). While "national interest" may still possess currency in the policy community, to use it as an explanatory concept and say countries engage in certain behaviors when their national interest is "at stake" is really to say nothing at all. Nonetheless Morgenthau's original division of the concept into something *inherent* as well as something derived from the *specific contextual situation* was helpful (Morgenthau, 1965: 8, 562–563), and Quincy Wright's definition and primitive early empirical assessment of the presence of "national interest," though subjective, did seem to suggest its relationship to level of hostilities (Wright, 1965). Missed by Wright, and still not well-understood, is that the *use* of "national interest" by decision-makers becomes *itself* an issue. The notion of "issue politics" emerged mostly as a challenge to the realist paradigm (Mansbach and Vasquez, 1981), but that attack failed to see that "issues" were already present in the realist's concept of "national interest," and several analyses of *how* specific images or issues such as national interest actually relate to nation-state behavior existed, none of which challenged realist tenets.

For instance, one theoretical formulation argued that the more general, symbolic, or intangible an issue, the more likely that parties to a conflict will act in an aggressive or hostile way; "The more limited the scope of the issues to be discussed in negotiations, the more likely that a resolution will be attained," and "the more resolutions attained on 'smaller' issues, the more likely will parties be able to negotiate their differences on the broader issues" (Druckman, 1973: 18). One program investigated various stages of World War I, the Cuban Missile Crisis, and the United States' involvement in the Vietnam War and found that in the first and third cases the issues perceived by decision-makers (and also elite newspapers in the third case) changed from more specific and tangible to more symbolic and intangible; such a change did not occur for the Cuban Missile Crisis. An analysis of data on "symbolic commitment" of American decision-makers involved in the Vietnam conflict from 1961 to 1973 suggested that symbolic issues were less prominent in earlier years than during the 1965–1968 period, and that these declined during the 1969–1973 period (Sullivan, 1972; 1974; 1979; 1985). Whether symbolic issues were the cause or the effect was unclear, but the evidence suggested a relationship between the expressed perception of differential issues by leaders and their behavior in a conflict situation.

A closely parallel concept is "integrative complexity," a dimension characterized "at one pole by simple responses, gross distinctions, rigidity, and restricted information usage, and at the other by complexity, fine distinctions, flexibility, and extensive information search" (Suedfeld and Tetlock, 1977: 169). It is a phenomenon descriptive of the individual's perceptions but is also one that changes. Results for I/C have been supportive in a number of empirical domains. The earliest investigation looked at two international crises resulting in war (1914 and 1950) and three settled peacefully (1911, 1948, and 1962), with the first two typified by lower levels of complexity than those resolved peacefully, and—for overtime patterns—decreasing as war approached and increasing as a peaceful resolution approached (Suedfeld and Tetlock, 1977: 182). For the superpower relationship over Berlin, I/C during the period 1946–1962 declined significantly on only two occasions, before the respective 1948 and 1961 "Berlin crises," but increased significantly once the crises began (Raphael, 1982). A more lengthy time-series analysis of U.S. and Soviet I/C from 1945–1986 showed the I/C of the two superpowers through several leaders "tracking"—rising and falling with each other—and that

low integrative complexity was associated with undertaking major military-political interventions in other countries (e.g., Iran, Berlin, Korea, Lebanon, Cuba, Vietnam, Cambodia, Angola); high integrative complexity was associated with the successful culmination of negotiations on issues that had been major sources of tension in the superpower relationship (e.g., the partial test-ban treaty, the non-proliferation treaty, SALT I and SALT II) (Tetlock, 1988: 113).[12]

During the peacefully resolved Cuban Missile Crisis, American decision-makers exhibited increased complexity from precrisis to both crisis and postcrisis periods, although within the crisis period itself complexity was higher during the early, secret deliberation phase than in the later phase (Guttieri et al., 1995: 610–611). I/C in newspaper editorials exhibited higher levels when bilateral relations with other countries were good and lower when relations turned sour (Suedfeld, 1992). During the 1970s, Egypt's Anwar Sadat's cognitive complexity fluctuated with cooperative behavior toward Israel, although the reverse did not occur (Maoz and Astorino, 1992). I/C also relates to the breakdown of negotiations in international crises, although causality remains an issue: "decreasing complexity is probably a sign rather than a cause of the breakdown in negotiations in the Munich and Polish cases" (Walker and Watson, 1994: 19).

The Persian Gulf War of 1990–1991 produced mixed results: between the imposition of diplomatic and economic sanctions (late 1990) and the two-week UN deadline (early January, 1991), both pro- and anti-Iraq Middle Eastern leaders showed a decline in I/C (Suedfeld et al., 1993). Saddam Hussein's I/C was very low immediately before his attack, then increased significantly after his hold had been consolidated. President Bush's score was at first relatively high and then dropped. Hussein's score also dropped immediately before actual fighting broke out, although Bush's scores did not follow that pattern (Wallace et al. 1993).[13] Somewhat less conclusive but still confirmatory evidence was found for Congressional "Hawks" (those in favor of the Congressional resolution for the fighting), who scored significantly lower than "Doves," and heads of government scored lower than subordinates perhaps showing that "the stressful burden of ultimate responsibility borne by those at the very top does indeed have an impact on the complexity of their information processing" (Wallace et al., 1993: 103).

Studies on I/C have clearly established "the impact of the disruptive stress of crisis and war on the complexity of leaders' information process," and even further suggested that "measuring variations in leaders' integrative complexity can on some critical occasions provide an early warning indicator of those leaders' decisions and actions" (Wallace et al., 1993: 104). Further confidence in the generality of the findings comes from remarkably similar conclusions emerging in entirely unrelated investigations—in one instance, of Soviet images of the United States in four different cases—within completely different contexts, and using completely different methods. In the case of Soviet-Ethiopian relations, "the imagery in late 1976 was fairly complex, identifying several national movements as legitimate and the possible solutions as complicated" (R. Herrmann, 1985: 689). As the Soviet involvement increased,

> so did the simplicity of the picture. In 1978 the scene was described in strictly dichotomous terms with the United States pictured as responsible for all of the strife. A similar pattern was found in the conflict among the Yemens and in the Afghanistan case. In each episode, as Soviet involvement grew the regional picture became more dichotomous and the image of the United States more stereotypical (R. Herrmann, 1985: 689–690).

The I/C program has covered diverse behavioral domains, but the research agenda specifically focusing on images drew originally on the Cold War system, for at least operationally in the early years of that era, the idea common to many decision-makers operated under the dictates of a simplified stimulus-response decision-making model. In this model the accepted norm was that communist adversaries would "back down" if only the United States showed the "will" and the "strength" to oppose them. As Cold War battle lines hardened and image analyses became more popular, old-style realpolitik analysis was viewed as not truly reflecting the complex intricacies and dynamics of international interactions. Quite simply, how accurate were components of rational process, stimulus-response decision-making models? During international crises, for instance, how much "congruence" existed *across* that model, and what would happen by imposing a "mediated" stimulus-response model that would consider the *perceptions* nations had of each other?

> The basic problem is this: given some action by Nation B, what additional information is needed to account for Nation A's foreign policy response? . . . If the real world for a President, Prime Minister or Foreign Secretary—and for their counterparts in friendly and hostile nations—is the world as they perceive it, perceptual [or intervening] variables are crucial in a conflict situation (O. Holsti, Brody, and North, 1969: 683–684).

Analysis of the Dual Alliance and Triple Entente leading up to World War I suggested that intensely involved decision-makers are more likely to "overreact" to input stimuli, whereas less involved nations underreacted, but in neither case could "response" be very well predicted from stimulus.[14] For the 1962 Cuban Missile Crisis, congruence across the S-R model was higher. In both cases, however, it did *not* appear that perceptions far outweighed predictive ability in terms of the final response (R).

Cognitive influences insinuating perceptual inaccuracies or misperceptions had long been embargoed from the dominant "focused realist" model, the model implicit in Morgenthau's approach—and Dulles's caricature of it in the policy realm. Evidence from other social sciences had suggested that such a model simply did not correspond with commonsense observation of real human behavior. The generalized cognitive model provided for a revolutionary "cut" into that realist model. But such inaccuracies of a human sort are not entirely absent from the realist framework. One investigation of a limited number of cases wherein both misperceptions and war occurred shows that such misperceptions—primarily of an adversary's capabilities—are important because their impact is felt just prior to a war. Thus the impact is not entangled with other variables, and "in the absence of these misperceptions, it is often possible to infer that war would not occur; and . . . there are numerous historical cases to which these forms of misperception appear to apply" (Levy, 1983a: 99).[15] While concluding that "it is entirely possible that misperceptions lead to war only under a narrow range of theoretical conditions, but that such conditions occur quite frequently" (Levy, 1983a: 99, n. 65), nonetheless, despite such assertions, the empirical evidence does *not* exist across a broad range of intersubjectively tested cases demonstrating under what conditions such misperceptions are more likely to occur.

Perceptions, involving human frailties as well as strengths, would seem to comprise a choice domain for nonrealist analysis. It did serve as a stark break from the realpolitik or "focused realist" model that so many feel had been dominant in the field, and constituted the first antirealist wave (Sullivan, 2000). Results tended to focus—through necessity of research design—on a limited domain within a very small range of behavior, and therefore for all the *interest* that such an approach manifested over the years and for all its apparent potency in calling into question the seemingly simplistic realpolitik model, in terms of accounting for much of international relations, the results too frequently appeared sparse and limited. More complex designs of cognitive studies moving beyond the "enemy image" certainly enlarge the domain on the cognitive part, but do so at the cost of complicating the conceptual apparatus such that linkages between the respective five-part "image" structure are drawn almost idiosyncratically to specific bilateral relations (Herrmann and Fischerkeller, 1995: 439–448).

Ideas, People, Change, and the Cold War

By the time the Cold War had become a settled fact of international life in the late 1950s, it was also a settled fact developed from research in cognate disciplines that decision-making was a complex phenomenon, and by implication that the realities of international decision-making were very unlike those embraced within the realpolitik model. Such recognition issued in the dawn of the cognitive approaches of a generation of scholars, many imbued with data-based research designs. It has been forgotten, perhaps, that many of these projects were spawned by the recognition—and even fear—that decision-making could not be understood by, or left to, the dictates of some mythical, structural, power model so far removed from the realities seemingly witnessed in the everyday crises of the 1950s and 1960s. Those crises themselves, of course, represented a sea change transformation from international politics prior to World War II and the bifurcation of the world into competing blocs. Just over a generation later another sea change set of transformations descended upon the international system, and the debate once again emerged between abstract, structural explanations and those focusing on the individual. In this second "wave" several new code words have become predominant, and all have been noted already: agency, ideas, and constructivism, all in a sense related to one another and yet containing certain nuances. All three still maintain, in agreement with the earlier efforts of the various cognitive revolutions, that to truly understand change requires going beyond the relatively unmoving structural. Just as in the 1950s and 1960s it was felt that one needed the cognitive level to truly understand outbreaks of major wars or the process in "acute" international crises, likewise the 1990s saw the same level of analysis necessary for understanding the new "sea change" in international politics: "Analysis of the individual leader is the critical starting point" (J. Stein, 1994: 182).While other factors may be present, "the direction and scope of the change that took place cannot be explained without reference to the impact of Gorbachev and his representation of the Soviet security problem" especially with respect to the accumulation of events associated with the "end of the Cold War"(J. Stein, 1994: 156).

Now the demise of the very same Cold War that in many ways initiated cognitive approaches to international relations, finds the debates to be similar, yet with instructive differences. On the one hand, both waves were antirealist and used the cognitive model, on the other each possess distinct differences over and above the obvious contrasts in the area of methodology. As for the antirealist stance of both, the original wave simply assumed that realism was inaccurate for certain levels of analysis; in the more recent wave, an extreme antirealism often surfaces. The more interesting theoretical divergence, however, is that the first wave views lapses or inaccuracies in human cognition, which serve as obstacles or impediments to good decision-making, while certain versions of the second wave imply the opposite: that there are positive, reactive perceptions by decision-makers, which frequently assume a much higher degree of accuracy in perceptions as opposed to deficiencies or inaccuracies. It appears that through decision-making seemingly lacking in deficiencies or inaccuracies, and based on an implicit rationality, ideas and norms are mostly viewed in a positive vein (Checkel, 1998), and focus on "ethically good norms" such as global norms of racial equality (Klotz, 1995) and treatment of wounded soldiers or revisions of aid programs (Finnemore, 1996).

While admitting multifactor, complex explanations combining international and domestic variables are all relevant to explaining "the dramatic changes in Soviet foreign policy," during the Cold War, they are nonetheless "underdetermined," and "a satisfactory explanation of the change in Soviet foreign policy must include individual as well as international and domestic variables" (J. Stein, 1994: 155). In fact the individual-level factor is the key ("the construction of meaning becomes a critical rather than an epiphenomenal factor in any explanation for the end of the cold war" [J. Stein, 1994: 160]): "analysis of the individual leader is the critical starting point" (J. Stein, 1994: 182). The problematic chameleon factor remains, however, as the dependent variable is never clearly specified, at one point labeled "dramatic changes in Soviet foreign policy," at another, the "end of cold war."

Agency and "ideas" pose an inviting counter to the abstraction of structures, and the reintroduction of the cognitive level has enjoyed exceptional plausibility, partly at least from the implied model that "ideas" produce good decisions and results. While at times suffering from what has been called an "ambiguity in the dependent variable" (Wendt, 1994a: 1040), they have tended to go beyond cognitive independent variables related to rather limited behavioral phenomena, resulting in a high degree of plausibility with a low degree of predictability.

Conclusion

The "individual" and "agency" have been rediscovered, a generation after their first appearance, in some cases broadened to seemingly expansive metaphilosophical concerns (Dessler, 1989), but ultimately reduced to time-worn levels of analysis issues. Precursors simplistically imbedded within Freudian and other psychological or personality-related approaches enjoyed great popularity, such as the "Great Man" notions of history and interesting though unproductive "psycho-histories." These have seen neither empirical support beyond the anecdotal, nor been related to much more than narrowly drawn, although interesting, independent variables. Early perceptual precursors, such as "national interest," were little more than policy nostrums imbedded within a realist framework which soon saw their own demise. With the recognition that the realist model was just as simplistic as the personality-needs model, other perceptual concepts produced research directly spawned by the concern for decision-making in a dangerous, super-power-dominated, nuclear world. While some, such as "mirror images," proved intriguing but unoperational, the genre focusing on perceptions and images nonetheless established the conceivable role that nonrealist variables render in accounting for admittedly delimited dependent variables.

More recently, with the demise of the Cold War that originally spawned the seemingly novel notion that "ideas matter," the need has reemerged once again to return to the notions of "agency" and "ideas." Transition points seem to demand focused attention on individuals, exhibiting a need to grasp in a tangible way an explanation for something that phenomenologically appears to be happening right in front of one's eyes. Thus the first cognitive wave emerged with the Cold War and the acute international crises, suggesting that misunderstanding and misperception were behind it. The second wave has emerged with the end of such crises and the Cold War, suggesting the "good" thinking and expanded perceptual skill associated with integrative complexity (Rosenau, 1990: 334ff.; Rosenau and Fagen, 1997), Gorbachev's "New Thinking" (J. Stein, 1994), and ideas such as the "liberal, nuclear-freeze movement" (Risse-Kappen, 1994: 204–214) have all become predominant. As noted earlier, ideas have always mattered, but the new focus has shifted beyond the "belief systems" and "operational codes" that were the organizing concepts of the 1950s:

> Cognitive psychology certainly concerns ideas, since it investigates beliefs of individuals about social reality that identify possibilities for action, reflect moral principles, and specify causal relationships. [We are] not concerned with the implications of cognitive psychology for interpretation of reality but with another facet of the role of ideas. We focus on the impact of particular beliefs—shared by large numbers of people—about the nature of their worlds that have implications for human action. Such beliefs range from general moral principles to agreement on a specific application of scientific knowledge (Goldstein and Keohane, 1993: 7).

This could imply that the content of Soviet foreign policy change and the Western reaction were "informed by specific principles and causal beliefs—values and strategic prescriptions" (Risse-Kappen, 1994: 212). For Gorbachev there was "new thinking" and "political learning by doing" (J. Stein, 1994), giving Gorbachev the aura of a new hero. But the issue has always been *which* ideas, in *what* way, and *under what condition* tend to "matter."[16] Learning, for instance, is an attractive but slippery notion:

> It is one thing to say that historical learning often occurs but quite another to specify when certain actors learn what types of lessons from what events, and under what conditions this leads to policy change. The concept of learning is difficult to define, isolate, measure, and apply empirically (Levy, 1994: 280).

But evidence also suggests that in some circumstances ideas don't "matter." Certainly Ronald Reagan's evanescent "belief system" may fall into that category (Shimko, 1991).

The nuclear freeze "idea" of the 1980s (Risse-Kappen, 1994) had several precursors starting in the 1960s, and yet never reached fruition. But in a sense the "ideas" notion constructs a "straw man" argument where the opposite position must be that ideas "don't count," an obvious absurdity. But it is also the case that "ideas are a dime a dozen" and the question remains whether the ideas are "epiphenomenal" and that other structural— or material—factors "bear the causal weight" (Garrett and Weingast, 1993: 203).[17]

Nonetheless, characteristics of the second cognitive wave must be appreciated, for it represents the second of two clear streams of theoretical interest. The similarities and differences between the two waves are instructive. Though they both first posit a pronounced antirealist, and later antineorealist, stance, an important dissimilarity is the reliance in the second wave by and large on the assumption of accurate as opposed to inaccurate perceptions by decision-makers. The third comparative characteristic involves the chameleon, the behavior thought to be explained in the successive waves. The further one moves, as we have seen in the second wave, toward case studies at the cognitive level, the less clear does specification of either independent or dependent variables become and the less clear is the variability of either variable.[18]

Even when variability is not a problem, the behavior itself represents only a very limited range. The escalation of the Vietnam War may have been a fascinating subject (Sullivan, 1972; 1985), as were the perceptual processes in World War I, the Cuban Missile Crisis (Holsti, 1965; 1972), and the workings of Henry Kissinger's operational code (Walker, 1977; Starr, 1984). But such cognitive analyses rarely investigate the large-scale behaviors, the "grand" categories of wars, "global" wars, cycles of wars, broad movements of history such as the very fashionable "end of the Cold War" or long-term evolutionary transformations of the major global powers (Modelski and Thompson, 1996).[19] When they do, they do so with great risk (Lebow and Risse-Kappen, 1995). The "Cold War" certainly falls into the "grand" category, and recent cognitive studies bracket both its beginnings (Larson, 1985) and its endings (Stein, 1994) with a focus on individual-level explanations embracing plausible but certainly nonconfirmatory and nonreplicable evidence, and yet other analyses are capable of suggesting that patterns during the Cold War appeared unrelated to individual-level variables (Dixon and Gaarder, 1992: 173).

The cognitive model's application to "grand" sweeps has been therefore partly facilitated through a change in methodology, and partly a willingness to allow dependent variables to remain relatively unspecified (with some exceptions [Herrmann and Fischerkeller, 1995]). In addition, both waves of cognitive approaches correspond to major transformations in international politics: the first was coincident with the onset, continuation, and criticality of the Cold War "acute" international crises, as well as the residual concern for the effect of certain individuals on the outbreak of World Wars I and II; the primary motivation for the second was the ostensible suddenness of the "end of the Cold War" resulting in the dissatisfaction with structural explanations. Ironically, it was a structural transformation, the original reason for moving away from the individual level, that became grist for the mill as a dependent variable, while allowing the explanations to rest at the individual level. This convergence is not entirely implausible given the evidence presented earlier on the changes in "integrative complexity" (I/C) in the Soviet leadership beginning about the mid-1980s, which were not necessarily reflected within the American hierarchy, and given the finding that Ronald Reagan's belief system may not have provided him with much guidance. Gorbachev and a small group of "reformers" differed substantially from the "traditionalists" on I/C, but as noted already,

I/C scores of Soviet leaders in the aggregate did not, at least by late 1986, exceed the levels they had achieved at earlier points, specifically in 1979, the detente period of the early and mid-1970s, or even in early 1963, subsequent to the Cuban Missile Crisis (Tetlock, 1988: 109–111).[20] As the Cold War was beginning to end, perhaps as early as the 1970s but certainly underway by the mid-1980s, it would be understandable that perceptual phenomena would follow suit:

> The new generation of Soviet leadership confronts a geopolitical and economic environment that, given what we know of macrodeterminants of complexity of thought, places great pressure on them to think about policy issues in integratively complex ways.

Soviet specialists seem to agree that

> increased complexity and resource scarcity are apt descriptions of the recent transformations in the policy environment confronting the Soviet government (Tetlock and Boettger, 1989: 226).

Several "indirect" tests suggested that observed behavior did not necessarily shift when new leaders emerged. While one can tease out *immediate* changes in American behavior toward the Soviets in just about every transition from Eisenhower to Reagan, usually but not always *toward* slightly more cooperation (Dixon and Gaarder, 1992: 163), these shifts were small, and in no case altered the overall trend *across* the presidencies. Other findings suggested individual perceptions as "intervening" variables did not affect trends, levels, and changes in levels of hostility, and that perceptions of stimuli were shown to be quite inadequate in accounting for subsequent action. One deviant case cited was the change in I/C in Soviet leaders immediately subsequent to Gorbachev's ascension to power in the Soviet Union. This could be a powerful supporting argument for the impact of the individual on the transformation in superpower relations, but the caveat must be inserted that, contrary to the contentions of some (Koslowski and Kratochwil, 1994: 247), evidence exists of structural shifts in capabilities taking place beginning in the 1970s and continuing into the 1980s (Park and Ward, 1988: 197–198; Sullivan, 1990: 136–182; Doran, 1991: 72, 225–232; Volgy and Imwalle, 1995: 824) within which must be imbedded any contentions arguing that "analysis of the individual leader is the critical starting point" (J. Stein, 1994: 182).

It was clear almost 40 years ago that the "old realism" was no longer anywhere near as viable a "model" of international relations as it once might have been. The cognitive research agenda that flourished for the next two decades seriously called realism into question, although nowhere matching the crusading spirit of recent vintage. Despite its reemergence, and the accompanying and engaging endeavors to explain recent major transformations, the focus on agency and the individual remains plagued by the standard obstacles typically inherent to this level of analysis. Several have already been noted; two additional ones need to be mentioned. First, serious impediments are inherent in imputing to individuals perceptual constructs imposed by the observer. An early case in point would be the original focus on Soviet operational codes, similar to recent studies on "beliefs." Was it the case that the operational codes of Soviet leaders did in fact change over the years from those originally proposed by Western scholars to the ones implied by recent "New Thinking,"[21] or was it the case instead that the original notions of such Soviet codes were constructed by Western scholars in the first case to explain behavior that at the time seemed bizarre to them? If those operational codes never originally existed, and especially as rigidly and uniformly as often asserted, then they couldn't change as some recent Western scholarship argues. If they did exist, then they must be time-dependent and the research question remains, "what caused them to change?" If it is "New Thinking," then despite the enticingly thorough recent analysis of Gorbachev (J. Stein, 1994), what is to guarantee that this is not little more than an imposition of a competing Western scholarly model?

A second problem is that contrary to the first wave of cognitive model-building, which possessed as its innovative characteristic the introduction of perceptual inaccuracies and misperceptions in a domain that had implicitly excluded them, the second wave has in a sense reintroduced dubious components of realism—namely, the utility-maximizing decision-making model, which assumes accurate perceptions, consideration of alternatives, "national interests," and a host of other implicit and explicit components that had been part of the first wave's reason for rejecting strict realpolitik. An unspecified rationality is reintroduced and while it nowhere reaches the levels of abstraction and robotic character found in debates over rational choice, which entirely steal the life out of international politics, nonetheless in comparison to the first wave of cognitive model-building, which may have overplayed human deficiencies, the second wave represents an outlook that implies a great deal of what approximates cognitively "rational" behavior.

Now that the perennial Pandora's box of rationality has been opened, we turn to this at length in the next chapter. We should not end, however, before noting a remarkable fact about Mikhail Gorbachev, who opened this chapter. According to some recent schemes, Gorbachev played the key role in turning the entire global political system on its head and ought to stand as one of the major movers and shakers of the late twentieth century, managing to harvest apparently single-handedly remarkable feats. Yet he had faded off into such complete political anonymity that when he returned in mid-1996, within a decade of his first ascension to office, to run in a field of ten candidates for president of Russia, he finished seventh with less than 1 percent of the vote, behind an eye surgeon with no previous political experience (Taubman, 1996).

Chapter Three ✿

Real Decisions and Ideal Models

Introduction

In early spring 1995, former Secretary of Defense Robert McNamara unleashed a firestorm of protest with his memoirs on the Vietnam War years, where he admits realizing when he left government in 1967 that the war was unwinnable. This should not have occasioned much surprise, for testifying in a libel suit by General William Westmoreland against CBS News 11 years prior to the publication of his memoirs, he had expressed having come to the view by 1966, "if not earlier," that he "did not believe it could be won militarily." More importantly, however, McNamara expressed amazement during the libel suit at the proposition that either Pentagon or White House bureaucrats might have actually deceived him on key aspects of the war, displaying an astonishing optimism about *how* decisions are actually made, even at the highest levels of government: "No responsible military officer would ever hold information from a superior that conceivably could bear on the superior's rightful decision-making power."[1] Such optimism has not been widely shared by all who examine such foreign policy decisions, but it is an optimism that in certain odd and subtle ways seems to be returning.

The picture drawn by McNamara conforms with certain underlying tenets of what has come to be called rational choice decision-making. The realist paradigm, in which the "national interest" is alleged to play a central role in the making of decisions, has been established as one guiding prototype directing *how* decisions are and ought to be made. For many, these guiding assumptions remain a forceful part of the thinking about how foreign policy decisions are still made. They serve in one fashion or another as the theoretical underpinnings of an approach often considered in recent years to be the closest to "rational choice," namely, "expected utility." "Rational choice" borders at times on tautology, however, and both "rational choice" and "expected utility" may be nothing more than "national interest" warmed over: nations become engaged when their "national interest" is involved or when their "expected utility" is high. Although admitting the complexity of issues, the trade-offs and linkages potentially involved across policy issues and the desire to distinguish such approaches from neorealism, nonetheless the consistencies with realist theory are recognizable (Bueno de Mesquita and Siverson, 1995: 843, 852–853).[2] Despite provocative research over the past three decades seriously calling into question such processes embedded in a realpolitik model, it nonetheless *lives*. Tracking the history and attitudes toward decision-making approaches reveals a great deal about the discipline, international relations theory, and decision-making itself.

The Perennial Tug of War:
"Rational" vs. "Reality"?

Decision-making as a distinct form of analysis in international relations came into its own in the 1950s. Traditional explanations, which flowed from extensive, detailed description in case studies, proved unsatisfactory in a social science groping for explicit theory. The revolutionary notion was that foreign policy decisions were only a *type* of behavior or process, and despite differences among specific decisions enough comparable similarities existed across decisions that meaningful comparisons could be made. The earliest foreign policy decision-making "model" represented nothing substantively new, but established explicit dimensions along which decisions were to be compared and explained, and not— as had been the case—"evaluated" according to normative or political criteria (R. Snyder, 1958; Sullivan, 1976: 67ff.). The three variable "clusters" viewed as determinants of decision-making behavior would be fairly standard "first cuts" at theory-building in the 1990s. The "spheres of competence" cluster looked at the *characteristics* of the decision-making unit (formal or informal, susceptibility to change, level of bureaucratization). "Communication and information" focused on who communicated with whom, how they communicated, the amount of information from outside the unit, and flexibility of the unit in accepting it. "Motivation" focused on the norms and values of those within the unit, but—mimicking Morgenthau—was referred to as a "ball of snakes."

Rather than providing a parsimonious tool, however, the primitive model in fact required the collection of enormous amounts of historical data for any given decision, resulting in a return to the traditional "case study."[3] The model *did*, however, orient attention toward decisions as the outcome variable, and was to some degree outside the simplistic realist paradigm: individuals do not necessarily maximize goals, but rather "satisfice" them, a process of considering alternatives sequentially or incrementally until one appears to meet certain basic requirements. Subsequently, Charles Lindblom questioned what he labeled the "rational comprehensive" model: in the real world of decision-making, he argued, individuals do not isolate goals, consider all alternatives, decide on the one alternative that will best reach their goal and then pursue it (Lindblom, 1959).

Lindblom's alternative, the "successive limited comparison" model—popularly known as "muddling through"—was not aimed at foreign policy decision-making, but when transposed to that arena, proposed the revolutionary idea that goals of nations were not separate from means but affected by them. Goals changed when means sometimes became untenable, and that the "best" policy was not necessarily the one that "achieved" the goal but the one everyone agreed to. Information is limited, often ignored, and, as many others have proposed since, decision-making *in groups* produces odd effects on those within the group. Decisions are also *costly;* as a result they may be put off or avoided. Contrary to the realist model, high information and numerous alternatives may cause human "overload." Contrary to the caricature of the realist paradigm, even foreign policy decision-makers may not see long-range implications of making small, incremental decisions they face every day. In sum, decision-making may *not* correspond to the dictates assumed by rational models imbedded in the realist paradigm.

Over a decade later, Graham Allison's classic study appeared, focusing more specifically on foreign policy decisions through a case study of the Cuban Missile Crisis (Allison, 1971; Allison and Zelikow, 1999), brandishing the contrast between the accepted, traditional model and two alleged competitors, explicitly laying out the underlying parameters and assumptions that had always been in use but rarely set out in the clear, rarified form which justified its "*classic*" stature a generation later after much criticism. The "rational process" model resembled Lindblom's rational-comprehensive model—the "normal" or realist model—with the usual underlying elements: important events have important causes, monolithic units like nations "exist" and perform large actions for big, important causes; large-scale *purposes or intentions* must be present that call for explanation. A sufficient explanation of a state's decision consists in showing what goal the state was pursuing through its action; important actions do not merely "happen" (Allison, 1971: 32–35; Allison and Zelikow, 1999: 23–26).

The first competitor, "organizational process," viewed governmental decisions as a function of organizations, which possess fixed sets of procedures and with a propensity to retain tendencies and routines in order to reduce uncertainty—in everyday language, Standard Operating Procedures (SOPs), which enable organizations to maneuver through uncertain environments, resulting in behavior *today* not much different from the way they behaved *yesterday*. Organizational SOPs thus narrow decision-makers' alternatives. The second competing model, "bureaucratic politics," recognized political decision-makers as bargaining and compromising politicians, with each "player" possessing different perceptions and priorities, each vying for power, promotion, and retention of position *after* the current crisis or decision situation has ended (Allison, 1971: 78–97; Allison and Zelikow, 1999: 163–185).

"Revisionist" decision-making models enjoy a strong appeal for three reasons: their explicit or implicit criticism of rationality and the "rational process," their appeal to common sense, and the recognition of the often very strong, at times *negative*, impacts organizations have. However, it is well to remember—as a later critique of Allison reminds us—that Herbert Simon had viewed SOPs as *positive* rather than *negative*, as "enabling" rather than "constraining":

> Habit performs an extremely important task in purposive behavior, for it permits similar stimuli or situations to be met with similar responses or reactions . . . Habit permits attention to be devoted to the novel aspects of a situation requiring a decision (Simon, 1947: 88; in Bendor and Hammond, 1992: 313).

Simon's observation places organizational impact in a very different light; the conventional implications drawn from Allison's model applied to the Cuban case stressed its constraining effect, whereas Simon had suggested the innovative possibilities for organizations. A key point, often overlooked, especially when considering organizational impacts in the context of foreign policy decision-making—which was *not* Simon's concern—is that the early organization literature emerged *before* the onset of the "acute" international crisis. Simon notes that strict organizational routines are essential for success in certain settings: athletic teams such as football, fire-fighting organizations, and even businesses. But while SOPs might be splendid in such settings, in the context of acute—especially nuclear—international crises, they could stymie the creativity needed, and could even be dangerous.

Nonetheless, the revisionist view exemplified in the Cuban Missile Crisis case study remains fashionable even though an extensive reanalysis concluded:

> what is often taken to be a major lesson of *Essence of Decision*—that rational choice explanations of policy-making are weaker than those of Models II or III—lacks foundation.

Whatever their ultimate worth, rational choice models were not given a fair test (Bendor and Hammond, 1992: 319).

Still, *at the time,* Allison's critique provided an important and provocative counter to the then-prevalent view that the decision process and outcome in that situation represented classic thoughtful, "rational" decision-making, advancing serious questions about underlying traditional assumptions of decision-making based on realism.

Following on the heels of that singular case study, came development of the "Groupthink" phenomenon (Janis, 1972; 1982). Centered in social-psychological processes observed operating in group decision-making settings, "groupthink" was added fuel for those resisting realism's decision-making strictures. Eight "symptoms" characterized groupthink[4] which were thought to be more likely in cases of decision-making fiascoes as opposed to successes. Unlike Allison's concern with the "political" aspect of organizations and bureaucracies, Janis fixed on social-psychological processes that emerge and develop in groups. His compelling case studies of fiascoes certainly capture—although do not test—the subtle influence that variables such as group uniformity, pressure on dissenters and feelings of invulnerability can produce in a small group. These processes can appear to take on a life of their own within the group, interfering with what we normally associate with "rational" decision-making.

Groupthink was not without its critics, especially with regard to the issue of case study methodology and the grouping of cases into groupthink and non-groupthink categories (Fischhofff and Beyth-Marom, 1978; t'Hart, 1991). Nonetheless, evidence adding support to the basic proposition emerged beyond the early case studies. Utilizing "integrative complexity" (I/C), Tetlock (1979) showed that discussion of policy issues along the simple-complex dimension differed between groupthink and vigilant decision-makers. In a later study (Tetlock et al., 1992), data from ten historical decision-making episodes produced support for Janis's earlier groupthink and vigilant categories, though less so for the causal model of groupthink. Groupthink episodes indicated greater Leader Strength, less Factionalism, more Rigidity, greater Conformity, and less Task Orientation. Democratic Accountability and Pessimism did not differ between the two groups (Tetlock et al., 1992: 412). "The current study provides the clearest evidence to date that Janis's . . . classification of decision-making episodes is not idiosyncratic (as some critics feared) but rather captures a broad coṅsensus of historical opinion" (Tetlock et al, 1992: 416).[5] Two cases of failures not investigated by Janis (the American rescue of a captured naval vessel in 1975, and the American attempt to rescue hostages in Iran in 1980), "more closely resemble[d] . . . vigilant cases than they [did] . . . groupthink cases" (Tetlock et al., 1992: 413). Janis's early conclusions of universal support thus gave way to a "probabilistic" outcome (Tetlock et al, 1992: 419). Specifically,

> In both the Mayaguez and Iran rescue decisions, policy-makers displayed many more symptoms of vigilance than of groupthink. They were generally alert to trade-offs and contradictory information and willing to tolerate considerable dissent. Nonetheless, the outcomes in both cases were disappointing and embarrassing (Tetlock et al., 1992: 419).

"Groupthink" developed a substantial following, appealing to an intuitive grasp of what takes place in group decision-making, engaging because of its "sound intuitive sense" (Schafer and Crichlow, 1996: 428). It may also have served as a post-Vietnam salve, accounting for "bad" decisions with a view very much in contrast to realpolitik and rational process. Like the organizational and bureaucratic models, it colorfully challenged the mechanical-like features of realism, and served as a healthy antidote to simplistic models. But an almost forgotten element within the "groupthink" popularity was the fact that decisions can at times be successful. After heady apparent success from an overemphasis on fiascoes, the tide turned. Despite that "it is generally recognized by experts on decision-making that a 'rational actor' model is inadequate both as a descriptive and a normative theory for improving the quality of policy-making" (Herek, Janis, and Huth, 1987: 203), 15 years after "groupthink" was proposed, it was argued that it does not

> preclude the possibility that the most effective policy-makers engage in careful search for relevant information, critical appraisal of viable alternatives, and careful contingency planning, exercising caution to avoid mistakes in making important policy decisions (Herek, Janis, and Huth, 1987: 204).

This in turn served as an antidote to "a dominant trend in present-day discussions of management science and political science . . . of emphasizing the relative *unmodifiability* of policy-making processes" (Herek, Janis, and Huth, 1987: 223; emphasis in original).

An analysis of 19 decisions from 1947 to 1973 focusing on key variables related to several of the "groupthink" characteristics[6] concluded, in a spirit markedly different from earlier implications and contrary to much of the tone of Allison's case study, that "policy-makers use analytic decision-making procedures at least some of the time . . . when [they] use such procedures, they tend to make decisions that better meet their goals . . . quality of the decision-making process *is* related to the decision outcome" (Herek, Janis, and Huth, 1987: 218). In other words, "effective" decision-making is possible, and when it does occur it results in "good" final decisions.

Critiques focused again on methodological issues of data collection and evaluation, producing the periodic testy disputes (Welch, 1989; Herek, Janis, and Huth, 1989), but the decisive notation to be made is that by the late 1980s earlier potent critiques of rational decision-making were (1) coming somewhat full circle in admitting the possibility of "intelligent" decision-making and (2), more importantly, focusing on the key variables thought to distinguish those "good" or "effective" decision-making situations from the "fiascoes." A rational process tone at times intruded; an analysis of American decisions on the Jordanian civil war and the October 1973, Middle East war, despite concluding that "process quality, policy quality, and outcome success are interrelated" (Haney, 1994: 939–940), still seemed to assume that social-psychological mechanisms can fade when decisions are actually made, and that good decisions and favorable outcomes can occur "by taking the structure of an advisory system seriously before crises occur, and by encouraging [decision-makers] to do their work" (Haney, 1994: 956). Others suggest that the antecedent conditions posed by Janis take a back seat to those like the creation of a "proper" decision-making environment prior to a crisis (Schafer and Crichlow, 1996: 429), even though isolating such factors does not provide answers about how to produce them.

"Realism" had implicitly held sway on how decisions are made until Snyder's protomodel of decision-making cast the first doubts, followed by the perceptual elements proposed by the early cognitive models [Chapter Two], later by Allison's critique of "rational process," and then the social-psychological approaches only exemplified by "groupthink." But once the bloom of "fiasco-producing" models had worn thin, a focus turned to whether in fact effective and "good" decisions were ever made at all; while the answer to the latter question seems to be in the affirmative, and certain factors related to "good" decisions seem to have been isolated, how to produce the desirable scores on those factors remains elusive.

What had slowly been evolving was to become the center of a hotly contested debate pitting "rational choice" against arational processes, both in their own ways at the time constituting responses to structuralist explanations. Ten years after *Essence of Decision*, "rational choice" components remained in systemic analyses: "A state will attempt to change the international system if the expected benefits exceed the expected costs (i.e., if there is an expected net gain)" (Gilpin, 1981: 10). Contemporaneously, a tantalizing reworking of earlier rational choice models focused on the one singular dependent variable of the decision to go to war (Bueno de Mesquita, 1980; 1981), spawned an agenda concluded over a decade later that:

> We have proposed a theory of the reasoning process that might account for foreign policy choices and have found that theory supported by the record of history. From this, we infer that international interactions follow a path of reasoned judgment. Even war is waged "with reason" rather than without it (Bueno de Mesquita and Lalman, 1992: 265).

Thus it seemed states do compare costs and benefits, reason prevails with respect to war, and perhaps Allison's comparison of models was such that rational choice had never been given a chance (Bendor and Hammond, 1992: 319). Yet sandwiched in between, and almost epitomizing the schizophrenic nature of the debate, others concluded, "it is evident that recent decades have witnessed growing uneasiness about the utility of retaining the rationality assumption" and "few today would accord it more than very limited utility, at best, even while mourning its disappearance" (Ferguson and Mansbach, 1988: 143). But the problem may continually lie, however, in the chameleon influence as much as in theory directly; distinct dependent variables are often at the center of what are thought to be contending explanations of the same phenomenon, as the analysis noted above of Allison's three "cuts" into the Cuban Missile Crisis so clearly suggested: the dependent variable was not the same across all three models.

Expected Utility

Such a critique does not apply to the research agenda specifically subsumed under "expected utility." Here alternative dependent variables over the years related to a relatively unchanging conceptualization of the positive characteristic of "expected utility." Expected utility has consistently referred to the similarity of interests between two sides: the utility for one side of, for instance, initiating war against the other in a bilateral situation: "one nation's utility for another nation is a direct, positive function of the degree to which they share a common policy perspective . . . utilities are determined by the congruence of policy ends between states" (Bueno de Mesquita, 1980: 918). In a multilateral situation, these calculations figure into the likelihood of additional states entering on behalf of one side or the other: the greater the similarity of interest, the more likely one nation will aid the other. And utility, the key concept, has usually been *measured* by a comparison of four types of military alliances. It would seem, therefore, that, simply put, low utility is equal to a low similarity of interest with the other party.

"Expectations" are derived from structural relations:

A foreign policy position adopted by a nation is assessed according to the array of formal defense commitments it has undertaken. The utility terms are measured as a function of the similarities in international accords . . . When two nations hold similar foreign policies, there is little to be gained by one's challenging the other. Conversely, greatly dissimilar policies provide an incentive, though not necessarily the requisite capability, to challenge those policies. The combination of both the incentive for a change and the capability to achieve that change forms the basis for a decision maker's expectation of a gain in its welfare (Bueno de Mesquita and Lalman, 1988: 17–18).[7]

Estimation of the "subjective expected utilities" consist of data "drawn from characteristics of national behavior" that are based

on the notion that military alliances are revealed-choice indicators of preferences. National leaders add new alliances or terminate old ones in part as *expressions of their likes and dislikes among the foreign policies of other states.* National leaders are assumed to select some tradeoff between pursuing policy objectives that they really want and choosing policy objectives that enhance national security.

Alliance formation and dissolution is a costly signal about foreign policy preferences because alliances are highly visible declarations of commitment under specified contingencies (Kim and Bueno de Mesquita, 1995: 59; emphasis added).

Failure to live up to alliances can "damage a nation's credibility." As such, "the correlation of alliance portfolios *probably* captures an important element in the revealed interests of each pair of states under the then current leadership" (Kim and Bueno de Mesquita, 1995: 59; emphasis added).

Expected utility is classic rationality—realpolitik—but even though the inference is that "something" is occurring at the individual decision-making level, evidence of any individual's actual perceived utilities, expected or otherwise, is lacking. Despite the implications concerning decision-makers' perceptual realities and inferences drawn concerning actual decision processes, in fact all data almost uniformly apply to the systemic level; no actual individual level data on psychological outlook or perceptions of utilities exist.[8] Despite the "consistent efforts by Bueno de Mesquita to portray his expected utility approach as quite different from realism or neorealism . . . it is still quite possible to argue that the similarities between BBDM's approach and the interaction game in *War and Reason* (1992), and realism or neorealism, are more important than the differences between them" (Ray, 1995: 38). The approach is essentially "based on an assumption about the fungibility of military power, in the manner of a realist or neorealist, that reaches impressive proportions" (Ray, 1995: 39). Although similarities in alliance patterns can be noted, nothing can be said about real—not "inferred" from alliance behavior—expected utilities: "it is arguable whether the convergence between two countries' utilities is properly measured by [BBDM's] indicator of similar alliance patterns" (Wayman and Singer, 1990: 258).[9] This problem also applies to another major variable—probability:

The variables used as indicators of the two basic concepts of utility and probability, namely agreement in alliance patterns and relative capability, could perfectly well be used in their own right and without interpretation in decision theory terms (Nicholson, 1987: 357).

To do so is "to draw attention to the fact that these are decision processes, that is, mental processes on the part of someone somewhere, if only in an idealized form. This is a large step" (Nicholson, 1987: 360). Moreover, one does not *have* to interpret it in such a way:

> A theory could perfectly well have been stated entirely in terms of capability and alliance patterns without imposing these further interpretations on them. Thus a generalization that "the product of relative capabilities and a measure of alliance similarities is a good predictor of war initiation" would be perfectly acceptable as a statistical hypothesis, be an interesting comment, and be admirably attested to by the evidence (Nicholson, 1987: 366).

Inferred "utility," some might say, is "a big step." But that variable is on one side of the equation. A second key element for evaluation is that the scope of the dependent variable was limited for a time primarily to whether a nation is an initiator or opponent in a war. As a result, it focused only on war *initiation* excluding other possible variables—outbreak, onset, or nation-months of war. Certain critiques of the measurement of that specific variable (disputes about definitions of initiators, opponents, and winners of wars, judgments that might be affected by a mere matter of days or even hours [Thompson, 1988: 11; Majeski and Sylvan, 1984]) could be critical for the results.

But the statistical success of the agenda is evident in the wide variety of empirical-temporal domains covered as well as numerous discrete dependent variables, from war initiation and successful deterrence (Bueno de Mesquita, 1980; 1981) and likelihood of war (Bueno de Mesquita and Lalman, 1988; Kim and Bueno de Mesquita, 1995) to European Community decisions (Bueno de Mesquita and Stokman, 1994), the debt cartel in Latin America (Kugler, 1987), and decisions concerning the future of Hong Kong (Bueno de Mesquita, Newman, and Rabushka, 1985). The continuously strong statistical support and broadening scope of the outcome variables, especially those related to various war-related behaviors, leads to the previously noted conclusion that decisions flow from "reasoned judgment" (Bueno de Mesquita and Lalman, 1992: 265). This implies a certain level of rationality, that costs and benefits do appear to be taken into account by something more or less akin to a unitary actor (Bueno de Mesquita and Siverson, 1995: 843). While critiques have been leveled at the statistical analyses, they seem to hold up consistently across this impressive array of dependent-variable domains. The vexing problem is whether the major variable, "expected utility," is actually measuring utilities of decision-makers or some other, structural, variable, where the data originate. The broader the scope and domain of dependent variable behavior accounted for by a single independent component—"utilities," usually measured by alliance structures—the more the conclusions rest on inferences from those measures, and determine whether systemic measurements provide calculations of "perceived utilities" or whether, perhaps, they more closely relate to a "theory of alliances."

In addition to problems of inference, the broader rational choice agenda has consistently been targeted, especially with respect to originality and empirical validity (Walt, 1999). Nonetheless, the Expected Utility (EU) research agenda does possess attractive internal characteristics: strong consistent statistical findings, relative simplicity, as well as inferred "rational" decision-making. The essential operating concept in EU is "utility." Less appreciated is risk: whether a nation is risk averse or risk acceptant, the latter being the case of a state which "expects to derive positive expected utility against fewer states than expect to derive positive expected utility from attacking it" (Bueno de Mesquita, 1980: 926), and is crudely measured by alliance configurations (Bueno de Mesquita, 1981: 122–124). One "leading alternative" to EU is prospect theory (Levy, 1997: 105), a theory of choice under risk. Here, all elements—the options, outcomes, probabilities, and, most importantly, "framing"—are given (Levy, 1997: 100). EU views utilities as defined subjectively by the individual based on risk-acceptant and risk-averse propensities: if utility for an option is high enough, the decision-maker chooses it. For Prospect Theory (PT), how the decision is "framed" determines whether the actors are interested in changes in assets or overall net assets (i.e., relative over absolute). In other words, gains and losses are viewed from a reference point. Experimental subjects tended to prefer less risky options when problems are "framed" as gains (from an already established point), and more risky options when framed as losses (from the reference point).

State leaders should then take more risks to maintain current positions than enhance them and after losses, greater risks should be taken to get them back (Levy, 1997: 93). Applications to international decision-making have been few and thus the evidence is sparse (Farnham, 1992; McDermott, 1992; McInerny, 1992). A case study of Japan's decision for war in 1941 found support for PT: "recommendations for war, the high-risk alternative, were associated mainly with reference-point-related arguments involving Japan's unmet aspirations and the aversiveness of the status quo" (Levi and Whyte, 1997). In addition, PT was deemed preferable to EU simply because Japanese decision-making processes seemed to lack basic characteristics of the EU process, especially in terms of estimating subjective probabilities (Levi and Whyte, 1997: 809). Difficulties in assessing reference points can be illustrated in the complex situation of Saddam Hussein's behavior in 1990, in which two different situations—precrisis and postcrisis—could both equally serve as valid "frames" (Levy, 1997: 99). Survey data of public opinion towards different types of interventions suggests those options considered protective received higher positive opinion response, although results are more ambiguous in terms of Congressional resolutions (Nincic, 1997).

However, PT faces problems because, contrary to one assertion, national leaders in fact do *not* "confront risky decisions on a regular basis" (Kowert and Hermann, 1997: 611), and, while PT addresses individual decision-making, international relations often rely on group decision-making. Very often here the decision process does not have alternatives already framed and specified, but requires the generation and framing of alternatives. While attractive, the disjunctures occur because the origin of PT in an experimental laboratory situation complicates its transfer to real-world decisions.

Both EU and PT demonstrate the continuation of successive shifts in emphasis about appropriate models for explaining decision-making, which have proven over the past 40 years to be alternately stimulating and frustrating. From cognitive-oriented, nonrational, unkempt organizational processes and bureaucratic politics models, on the one hand, to the simplicity and rationality of "expected utility" on the other, one is reminded of President John Kennedy's comment after two advisors from the Departments of State and Defense had tendered their widely divergent presentations on the status of the Vietnam situation in 1962: "You two did visit the *same* country, didn't you?" One is often left with the feeling that investigators have visited separate domains or minimally are talking about entirely different phenomena—the chameleon—when they investigate respective decision situations with alternative models.

Nonetheless, President Kennedy's quandary in the early 1960s indirectly exemplifies the predicament in analyzing decision-making. On the one hand, neat, orderly, and understandable interpretations can be proffered that display "reasoned judgment." On the other hand, we find the unkempt and the untidy. To this point, no model has explicitly focused on "incremental" processes and although implied in so much of the arational approaches (especially Lindblom), it defies formalization. Attention is now turned to a single case in recent U.S. foreign policy that more than any other not only embodies so many of the issues raised here, but does so because it spawned many of these issues. The Vietnam case still haunts the American public. Very few early investigations were made into these questions (Ellsberg, 1972; Sullivan, 1974), but even in those early probes the central questions raised here were pivotal. What emerges satisfies no one, a brief case study that may serve only as an antidote to the pristine nature of "rational choice" models, but at the same time might be the ultimate demonstration of realpolitik and rationality.

"This War Had Such Promise"[10]

> On 30 April, 1975, as American diplomats and Marines were being hastily lifted off the roof of the American embassy in Saigon into waiting helicopters under heavy enemy fire, an era in American foreign policy was ignominiously coming to an end. The United States was exiting South Vietnam in the most undignified manner possible—short of military defeat in 1973 (Sullivan, 1985: 1).

The Vietnam War was a pivotal event both for contemporary American foreign policy and international politics more generally, and was also one factor instrumental in spawning the debate over "rational process." Aside from the release of the *Pentagon Papers* in 1971, and a few other scattered publications (Gelb, 1970; Ellsberg, 1972; Sullivan, 1974), the issue of the original American involvement in Vietnam did not generate systematic scholarly notice for several years. Those few beginning studies, with preliminary data, drew only hesitant conclusions.

More than a generation later, the debate continues, the same questions are asked in different ways, and despite more evidence, the controversy still returns to the early decisions moving the U.S. toward the Vietnam involvement.[11] What follows is the unfolding of the intellectual debate over decision-making through the prism of a real-world case to see what conclusions about that war, American involvement in it, as well as decision-making models in general can be derived. We have already set the stage with the tension between "rational choice" and its competitors.

A more specific controversy on Vietnam has centered directly or indirectly on the intriguing question, "Would Kennedy have gotten the United States out of Vietnam?" It is a highly charged debate, with those taking the affirmative presenting a very romantic, certain, sure picture of the world, implying that national decision-makers make clear decisions and take clear positions. It is a picture of almost pure rationality and a novel of epic proportions—in the Vietnam case, the prince who could have saved the country from a disaster but for an assassin's bullet. *JFK*, the popular movie of the early 1990s, presented just such a picture. It is certainly a possible description of what transpired; it is also very possible that it is completely wrong. The debate pits those who contend Kennedy had every intention of getting out against those saying that he most likely had every intention of living up to the many (including his own) American statements about the importance of Vietnam—in the rhetoric of the time, that he would "stay the course." Or generally that decision processes do not follow the neat and easy steps of a "rational choice" mechanism, that incremental and other processes exert their influence leading to further escalatory decisions. But one important factual point remains: the United States *did* get involved in Vietnam, and that involvement did escalate, and therefore we are interested in why the

U.S. did what it did and *not* why the United States did not do what some people claim certain leaders wanted to do but never did, namely, abandon the enterprise. This empirical fact can often get lost in the contending debates, a process related to "counterfactual" theorizing, which we turn to below in further consideration of Vietnam.[12]

Throughout the Vietnam debate, a first cut might suggest that decision-makers did perceive a big problem called "Vietnam," which they reacted to in a "big" way—as demanded by the rational process model.[13] The *Pentagon Papers* saw the Truman administration's early aid to France as "directly involving" the United States in Vietnam and "setting" the course—as noted, a favorite phrase in this model—of American policy in Southeast Asia (*Pentagon Papers,* 1971: p. xi). When a 1954 National Security Council paper outlined the American position in Vietnam, "'American policy toward post-Geneva Vietnam was drawn.' The commitment for the United States to assume the burden of defending South Vietnam had been made" (*Pentagon Papers,* 1971: 15). Kennedy did not want to upset "the whole balance of power and fabric of the security structure of the region, where so many countries had based their policy on continued American involvement" (Hilsman, 1968: 420). After Kennedy's assassination, Johnson was portrayed as not wanting Vietnam to go the way China had. "The tragedy of Lyndon Johnson . . . was set in motion barely 48 hours after he had taken the oath [of office]" (Wicker, 1968: 205). Some argued from the outset that the infamous 1964 Tonkin Gulf resolution had been prepared before the alleged "attack" on American ships and that bombing targets were placed on Johnson's desk the day after his election victory in 1964 (Wicker, 1968: 225; Halberstam, 1968: 20–21), all of which strongly suggests a rational process model at work.

One analysis presented as the war was still in high gear cited "high objectives" as the driving force behind years of United States' planning and action: "Statements about the vital importance of Vietnam to United States national security are a matter of the yearly public record" (Gelb, 1970: 11). In 1948, the State Department asserted that the objective in Southeast Asia was "to eliminate so far as possible Communist influence in Indochina." Sixteen years later President Johnson said, "We seek an independent, non-Communist South Vietnam." When the rational process model argues decision-makers see big stakes, support is found in the Taylor-Rostow mission in 1961, with its recommendation to provide minimal assistance to Vietnam "but with the significant warning that much greater troop commitments were likely in the future" (*Pentagon Papers,* 1971: 85). With less than 1,000 Americans in Vietnam in 1961, Secretary of Defense Robert McNamara said, "I believe we can assume that the maximum United States forces required on the ground in Southeast Asia will not exceed . . . 205,000 men." (*Pentagon Papers,* 1971: 149).

The *Pentagon Papers* noted that in the summer of 1965, with the commitment of 44 battalions, the

> choice was viewed as winning or losing South Vietnam . . . Final acceptance of the desirability of inflicting defeat on the enemy rather than merely denying him victory opened the door to an indeterminate amount of additional force (*Pentagon Papers,* 1971: 416–417).

In November 1965, as the American troop buildup ballooned, McNamara noted, "The odds are even that we will be faced in early 1967 with a 'no decision' at an even higher level" (*Pentagon Papers,* 1971: 466). Such evidence insinuates Vietnam occurred because of a large-scale goal going back many years, decision-makers clearly assessing the stakes, and "by implication, their decisions resulted from a rational process in attempting to achieve their goals" (Sullivan, 1976: 76). Decision-makers faced a large-scale problem, possessed a long-range goal, and the final decision was viewed as the path toward that goal, all along with the faith that a rational process of considering many alternatives and information would produce the "right" alternative.

Such a picture of decision-making is always compelling—almost too compelling. In early analyses with limited data, we asked, If Vietnam was as vital an issue as the rational process model demands, why did President Kennedy ask the very key, blunt question in November, 1961: "was it important to save South Vietnam and Laos?" President Johnson later asked the CIA virtually the same question in 1964. And yet "all the evidence visible at the time, and much testimony gathered since, suggests that, in 1964, Johnson was not deeply concerned about Vietnam" (Wicker, 1968: 229). Senator Richard Russell, far from a shrill dove on foreign policy, concluded and forwarded to Johnson the observation that Vietnam "is by no means a 'vital' area of U.S. concern" (Barrett, 1993: 36). Then there is the oft-told story of George Ball's warning to Kennedy about further increases in advisors and Kennedy's response—"George, you're crazy as hell!"—certainly opening the possibility for an incremental interpretation to early decisions.

Such incremental decisions, moreover, do solve political problems: to ignore long-term objectives and to concentrate "almost exclusively upon the aim of minimizing the short-run risk of anti-Communist collapse or Communist takeovers" (Ellsberg, 1972: 105). What Buchanan and Wagner concluded about governmental spending bears a striking resemblance to the way decisions on Vietnam can be analyzed: "Politicians themselves have, for the most part, short time horizons. For most of them, each election presents a critical point, and the primary problem they face is getting past this hurdle" (Buchanan and Wagner, 1977: 159). Once that hurdle is past, however, whether concerning domestic spending or foreign policy commitment issues, the situation has been changed by those very decisions thought to solve the immediate problem.

No sense of time-imposed crisis necessarily existed affecting major decisions of early 1965, following attacks on American bases. There was an

> opportunity for a reasoned assessment of the administration's goals and means of attaining them. Instead, the choices Johnson and his associates made in Vietnam seemed like a *caricature of the incremental process of unplanned decision making that Charles E. Lindblom describes in his classic account "The Science of Muddling Through" of how leaders commonly operate* (Burke and Greenstein, 1989: 174; emphasis added).

In mid-1965, at a point of major escalation, Ambassador Taylor cabled Washington: "I badly need a clarification of our purposes and objectives" (*Pentagon Papers,* 1971: 445). Concerning the bombing campaign, the *Pentagon Papers* remarked, "the decision to go ahead with [it] seems to have resulted as much from the lack of alternative proposals as from any compelling logic in their favor." (*Pentagon Papers,* 1971: 344). Maxwell Taylor's deputy in Saigon, U. Alexis Johnson,

> capture[d] the unevaluated moves from increment to increment that marked the transition from bombing to ground combat by American troops. He and Taylor had hoped that the initial retaliation and the move to sustained bombing would halt the pressure for use of American ground forces, but "ironically, it was the decision to start bombing that indirectly led to deploying the first American ground forces" (Burke and Greenstein, 1989: 175).

The incremental process could not have been clearer:

> We had no real choice but reluctantly to permit the Marines to send another battalion to guard the missiles that were protecting the base. This immediately generated a cable from the JCS for a plan to send an entire Marine Expeditionary Brigade of more than 5,000 men, carrying its own artillery, tanks, and fighter aircraft. Max [Taylor] and I were appalled and refused to approve this grandiose scheme. *It went far beyond anything we envisioned or the military requirements could justify* (Burke and Greenstein, 1989: 175–176; emphasis added).

And, "looking back at the quick introduction of the Marine landing team, Maxwell Taylor reflected on how an extraordinarily consequential step had been taken without focused attention" (Burke and Greenstein, 1989: 176).

Contrary to the ritualized formality of rational process models and the constraints of "choice" models that assume "instrumental rationality," even evidence on Vietnam available fairly early, along with later analyses using a larger set of documents, suggests a picture very different from stylized "choice" models. In May 1967, Robert McNamara suggested changing the entire rationale for U.S. presence in Vietnam and intimated that the stated anti-Communist purpose, an "independent non-Communist South Vietnam" should no longer necessarily be the rationale. The Joint Chiefs of Staff (JCS) noted on May 31, 1967 that this would "undermine and no longer provide a complete rationale for our presence in South Vietnam or much of our efforts over the past two years." (*Pentagon Papers,* 1971: 538). The incremental model fits even the last decisions before the dramatic turnaround in March, 1968. When another request for troops arrived in early 1968, after the disastrous Tet Offensive, "several insiders later suggested that a smaller request, for 30,000 to 50,000 men, would probably have been granted and the Administration's crisis would have been avoided or at least delayed" (The *New York Times,* March 5, 1969: 14).

While decision-making models do *not* provide the systematic guidepaths one would like for research, competing models do provide an antidote to the "normal" model with its realpolitik assumptions. The more narrow question of whether President Kennedy would have extricated the United States from Vietnam seems hopelessly confined, and yet it has produced extensive public debate about the decisions in those early years, about the later accuracy of Hollywood movies, and also generated continuing exchanges among authors, academics, and former government officials, some of whom had been involved in Vietnam decision-making. What actually happened, what individuals' motivations and "utilities" might have been at the time, and what might have been the case had a "counterfactual"—no Kennedy assassination—occurred: all have been central to the debates.[14]

As for Kennedy's "decision," one analysis unequivocally concludes that Kennedy "had already made up his mind against troops" (Newman, 1992: 129–130). In November 1961, after the Taylor-Rostow mission and recommendations, Kennedy according to this view decided *against* combat troops, not when the situation was ambiguous, but

> when the battle was unequivocally desperate, when all concerned agreed that Vietnam's fate hung in the balance, and when his principal advisors told him that vital U.S. interests in the region and the world were at stake (Newman, 1992: 138–139).

While the overly pessimistic picture of the situation in 1961 was not nearly as drastic as portrayed, even this depiction notes that "Kennedy deepened the American commitment . . . considerably . . . without any adequate discussion of the problem" (Newman, 1992: 139), and later, in March of 1963, "[he] had figured out—exactly when is unclear—that the success story was a deception" and "[his] program was a failure—in his heart he must have known that" (Newman, 1992: 321).

Even within this sympathetic analysis infused with implicit rational process decision-making, evidence of obvious incremental processes surfaces. Wrote William Colby:

> I . . . gave more thought and effort to ensuring that the station would receive permission to continue the small—but, I thought, promising—project we had started than to outlining my fundamental strategy for Vietnam . . . this was the attitude of most of the other participants . . . [Kennedy] had not articulated any very solid expression of his own ideas or strategy. Consequently, we had produced an agglomeration of the preferences of all the agencies involved, devoid of any strategic concept or inspiration (Newman, 1992: 139).

Even discussion of withdrawal by Newman—a partisan—is characterized by ambiguities: it assumed the insurgency would be under control in three years, that during that time "extensive" support would be needed, and that funding ceilings could be changed (Newman, 1992: 287). The coup against the South Vietnamese leadership, which resulted in an unexpected and unplanned assassination, further encapsulated Kennedy, and yet not much thought appears to have been given to the possibility of an assassination. Once that unplanned event occurred, it radically changed the course of events for the United States in Vietnam.

But the most cardinal tenet of the belief in Kennedy's plans to extricate from Vietnam rests on the infamous 1,000-man withdrawal that Kennedy was said to have backed, an option itself fraught with risky political considerations, namely, the potential "criticism from conservatives that would be unleashed if it were carried out against the backdrop of a collapsing battlefield situation" (Newman, 1992: 360). Even within the confines of that specific policy decision, incremental processes loomed, for "the fine print in the plan . . . meant that only half of the 1,000-man withdrawal would actually be units[?]" (Newman, 1992: 364). A symbolic issue was involved, since units carried more impact than individuals. However, a question remains as to whether Kennedy actually *decided* to implement the 1,000-man withdrawal at a specific point. Newman claims: "The fact is that he did. That McGeorge Bundy forgot to mention this detail in the minutes of the meeting that he drafted two days later is only a *minor nuisance for historians*" (Newman, 1992: 409; emphasis added).

Even after the coup against Diem, his subsequent and unwanted assassination during the course of the coup, and in the context of continuing U.S. casualties, Kennedy intended, according to this account, to pull out. But what *really* happened? According to the *Pentagon Papers*

> It proved essentially an accounting exercise. Technically, more than a thousand U.S. personnel did leave, but many of these were part of the normal turnover cycle, inasmuch as rotation policy alone, not to mention medical evacuation or administrative reasons, resulted in an average rate of well over a thousand returnees per month (*Pentagon Papers*, Gravel edition, vol. 2: 191–192, cited in Newman, 1992: 433).

It came down to slowing down the "replacement pipeline" temporarily, and

> Incredibly, after all the meetings, memos, plans, approvals, and a Presidential National Se-
> curity Action Memorandum (263), the much vaunted 1,000-man withdrawal was carried
> out by a couple of personnel clerks who accomplished it by just delaying replacements of
> individuals for a few days. Even this did not work fully, and the December strength dipped
> by about 800 men instead of 1,000 because of "additional deployments approved since
> September." This was a pathetic end to the bold and determined effort that Kennedy had
> engineered in NSAM-263 (Newman, 1992: 433).

Despite mountains of contradictory evidence, still it is nonetheless concluded:

> Kennedy would never have placed American combat troops in Vietnam. He did, never-
> theless, make a commitment short of that, giving into the urgency of the situation and to
> the pressure from his advisors (Newman, 1992: 453).

Ironically, in an analysis claiming clear evidence of Kennedy's decision to keep the
United States out of deepening involvement in Vietnam, a form of "counterfactual" ar-
gumentation, which if true would lend support to a rational process, "choice," utility-
maximizing approach to decision-making, the actual evidence points clearly to
incremental, bureaucratic, and organizational factors playing pivotal roles. To recall a
key empirical observation: during the 33 months of the Kennedy presidency, the American involvement in Vietnam *did* escalate. Regardless of any counterfactual exercise or
"experiments" one might think up, that remains a reality.[15]
However, contradictory analyses of the Vietnam involvement have been legion.

> Almost from the onset of the conflict till its denouement nearly thirty years later, American
> officials of six presidential administrations viewed events *in a remarkably consistent way.* They
> supported the principle of gradual decolonization and the transfer of power to non-Com-
> munist Vietnamese (Schaller, 1985: 152; emphasis added).

A 1946 State Department document is cited noting the worst eventuality would be a
"Moscow-oriented" state in Indochina. Both assertions appear to imply that a planned,
consistent policy existed for 30 years—the infamous "stage was set" reasoning. Yet, 500
words later we learn that "During 1947 and early 1948, the colonial war expanded while
America's policy continued to drift" (Schaller, 1985: 153; emphasis added). Likewise, Policy Planning Staff (PPS) memorandum 51, generated sometime around 1949–1950,
"formed the basis of Asian containment policy for the next two decades" (Schaller, 1985:
159), painting the most dire picture of the "fall" of Southeast Asia, especially after the
"fall" of China, and yet

> Given the poaching on bureaucratic turf inherent in PPS51, the policy paper aroused stri-
> dent controversy within the State Department. Most Europeanists (and a few Asianists) ob-
> jected both to Kennan's conclusions and his presumptuousness in discussing questions over
> which they had a say (Schaller, 1985: 160).

Despite intense bureaucratic infighting, "these two features *locked* American policy in step
behind French colonialism" (Schaller, 1985: 161; emphasis added), a picture that speaks

of continuity in policy-making. Yet at the same time "almost all American diplomats expressed private misgivings over the phony grant of autonomy to Bao Dai and admitted there seemed 'little chance the agreement would appeal to Vietnamese nationalists,' and they despaired over the lack of acceptable alternatives" (Schaller, 1985: 161).

In sum, whether focusing on the grand sweeps of early American involvement in Vietnam or the more specific decisions that propelled it, beginning in 1961 and lasting until at least the Tet Offensive of 1968, the contrasting models run the gamut from the very "rational"-appearing to extreme illustrations of incrementalism. The reason for this partly rests on the "chameleon" factor once again: because the dependent variable can shift between perspectives, "Vietnam decision-making processes" are susceptible to being modeled and U.S.-Vietnam relations calibrated into either an "expected utility" framework or, as we shall see later, into other larger data sets of warlike behavior of nations. But using the very selective "case study" cut presented here provides a strikingly different—and for certain purposes more real—picture.

Despite later conventional perceptions of Vietnam, for many *at the time* that war *did* hold out much "promise." As many have pointed out, the individuals involved *felt* they were utilizing the most recent formal game theoretic models to rationally analyze the unfolding conflict, and were motivated by the highest ideals of a young president: nation-building for the furtherance of economic development and democratic expansion. It seems to have been forgotten that those "ideas" were a central, driving force behind U.S. foreign policy of the time, supporting, incidentally, recent proposals directed at how "ideas" do serve as causal factors directing policy (Goldstein and Keohane, 1993) despite that the specific ideas backing U.S. involvement in Vietnam at that time may not have been those of most contemporary advocates of "ideas" perspectives. The "decision to go to war" *can,* it is true, be modeled in an unadorned, rational way, but once one delves into the specifics, it takes on a complexity missing from the more formal models; still at issue is which more accurately reflects reality, or whether—once again—we are talking about different realities.

The rationale for focusing on this specific analysis of Vietnam decision-making was noted earlier, and while this inquiry appears point-specific, the processes are not singular to that involvement. The United States in the early 1980s interjected itself into a realpolitik venture in the Middle East and enthusiastically assisted the government of Saddam Hussein for almost a decade before Iraq's invasion of Kuwait in the summer of 1990. Even behavior undertaken by the Iraqi leader in the early 1980s that violated the grossest of human rights standards did not sway the United States, which looked the other way, using the "enemy of my enemy" strategy (Jentleson, 1994). Decisions were made without contemplating the consequences of the ultimate outcome, all in an attempt to impose a simplistic realpolitik framework on a complex situation, involving ponderous risks of "becoming trapped in a process of escalation it [the Reagan administration] could not control" (J. Stein, 1988/89: 148, cited in Jentleson, 1994: 67). Even decisions after the invasion of Kuwait by Iraq may not have resulted from maximizing utility or even "satisficing," but rather were "decisions . . . made based on the rejection of undesirable alternatives on the basis of one, or at most a few, criteria" (Mintz, 1993: 595). In such a noncompensatory strategy, "in a choice situation, if a certain alternative is unacceptable on a given dimension (e.g., it is unacceptable politically), then a high score on another dimension (e.g., military) *cannot* compensate/counteract for it, and hence the alternative is eliminated" (Mintz, 1993: 598), and the decision to use force against Iraq thus "followed a noncompensatory strategy of elimination by aspects" (Mintz, 1993: 614).

Case studies of specific decision-situations cannot shed light on formal models of decision-making, but this brief case study of Vietnam decision-making, while not rebutting any formal modeling endeavors, does serve as an illustrative rejoinder to implied rational processes contained in certain models. It is true that formal models do not necessarily insist that "decision-makers actually sit down and make the calculations precisely as described by the theory," which implies some leeway for all the influences and processes found to be present in the Vietnam case. But if the models are merely suggesting that "decision-makers will behave *as if* they had made such calculations" (Ray, 1998: 139; emphasis in original), then of course the alternate suggestion may be just as feasible: that decision-makers did *not* make such calculations, and certainly evidence from and later analyses of the Vietnam case would lend great credence to that interpretation.[16]

From Crises to "Rationality"

A generation ago the American involvement in Vietnam did have "promise": the "ideas" prevalent at the time about international politics and the capacity to make decisions were characteristic of the period. While Vietnam became a long-term crisis, it rarely possessed the characteristics of the acute international crises that had also become of great concern to both policy-makers and decision-making theorists. We found in Chapter Two that crises are related to major, long-term break-points in international politics, often more systematically than other factors, such as individual-level variables. But crisis has also played an important role in terms of structural impacts on the very process of decision-making over and above any influence on broader international trends, and the transformation of crisis analysis has undergone very instructive adjustments in the contemporary era of rationalized decision-making.

By the late 1950s and early 1960s, at least three different conceptual strands were unfolding revolving around crises. The first was the focus on the "acute" international crisis as a new phenomenon that would prove to be a defining characteristic of the international system for the Cold War years. "Tracking" such events produced the influential "events data" movement concentrated on the patterned behavior exhibited in such crises (McClelland, 1961; Leng, 1984; 1993b; Goldstein and Freeman, 1990; Schrodt, 1994). The second strand focused on the impact of crisis on decision-making processes, viewed as a potential independent variable as opposed to a process itself to be studied (Holsti, 1965; Holsti et al. 1969; Brecher, 1993; Brecher and Wilkenfeld, 1991; 1997). The third analytical perspective, the "crisis cube," remains one of the most succinct analytical descriptions of the components of crisis in international politics (C. Hermann, 1972). Much of the conceptual work surrounding crises as static observable phenomena flows from that third diagrammatic exposition.

While the study of the crisis phenomena itself served as an unobtrusive measure of the onset, peak, and then culmination of the broader Cold War, the major conceptual insight, brought to international relations from cognate disciplines, concerned the *effect* of crisis on decision-making. It also served as one more early and powerful nail in the coffin of stylized realism. That is, assorted theoretical formulations suggested that crises are more likely to produce hasty, quick, perhaps temperamental decisions—the opposite of the ideal of carefully processed information and calculated responses. The classic 1914 crisis study suggested that "high stress" periods (i.e., July 1914) induced more concern or perceptions about "time," especially "current" time, than low stress periods, with participants more likely to view themselves as faced with "closed" or "necessity" alternatives while opponents had a "choice" (Holsti, 1965: 371).

A generation later (Brecher, 1993), a more comprehensive Unified Model of Crisis (UMC) posited a much more complete, multiphased, nuanced analysis combining sundry structural with process variables, a view of crises in their entirety (a dynamic whole which requires an integrated model" [Brecher, 1993: 506]) not through a narrowly defined interpretation of them as singular independent phenomena impacting the decision process. Ironically, after drawing extensive specific conclusions and inferences from propositions and hypotheses related to the UMC (Brecher, 1993: 358–403, 500–519), all of which involved complex focus on the multilevel and multiphase component of the overall research design, Brecher returns to the "continuing 'war' between political psychologists . . . and the proponents of rational actor behavior" (Brecher, 1993: 520) and presents an extensive, comprehensive summary of the effect of crisis on decision-making (Brecher, 1993: 522–526; 537).

With 19 hypotheses evaluated across 17 crises, nine were strongly supported and four disconfirmed. Contrary to assumptions of dysfunctional characteristics in stressful situations, the picture drawn from this comprehensive assessment shows decision-makers actively searching for more information in crisis, relying on past experience, and moving that information to the "top" of the decisional pyramid, with more consultation with those outside of the group and using extraordinary channels of communication. Alternatives were *not* necessarily evaluated less carefully during crisis, premature closure was not prominent, nor was there an inadequate assessment of consequences. In sum, high stress—crisis—did not appear systematically across these 17 cases to be dysfunctional: "The evidence uncovered here points strongly to the need to be much more sanguine about the human capacity for effective crisis management. The traditional view is, simply put, scientifically incorrect" (Brecher, 1993: 537).

As astonishing as those cumulative findings are when compared to earlier considerations and speculations of the "political psychologists," nonetheless they do not necessarily equate with support for rational choice or expected utility formulations. Nonetheless, crises have lost much of their appeal as a focus of scrutiny in the contemporary world, increasingly perceived to consist of orthodox, non-"acute" international harmonization and interactions enveloped in an implied migration toward instrumental rationality. The same fate has been accorded the function of organizations. Terms such as SOPs enjoyed street parlance long before Allison's classic Cuban Missile Crisis study popularized their impact on foreign policy decisions. But illustrating organizational effects and carrying those illustrations over into hypothetical effects on decisions are uncomplicated tasks. More complex is demonstrating their effect in a systematic, empirical fashion, a task which seems outmoded in an era apparently dominated by economic rather than political, concerns, in which organizational processes are often ignored or overridden by the instrumental rationality implied by economic concerns.

Few systematic tests on organizational-bureaucratic influences have been conducted, and those supporting organizational influences have been limited to defense issues [Chapter Nine]. One investigation found the rate of acquisition of naval weapons systems in four countries relatively constant over long periods of time, with changes in acquisition related to external "shocks"—factors outside the organization (Dennis, 1974). Another concluded that "bureaucratic momentum" was the single most important determinant of defense spending in European states and the Warsaw Treaty Organization (WTO) in Europe from 1950 to the early 1970s (Rattinger, 1975: 593), and yet a third found little support when comparing a simple action-reaction model against an organizational politics model (Ostrom, 1977: 258). Even though one review concluded that by the early 1980s bureaucratic factors seemed to be taking precedence in most findings, especially when compared to action-reaction models (Moll and Luebbert, 1980), and even though, as noted above, illustrating organizational effects in specific situations can be relatively effortless, systematic attempts face numerous hurdles. By the late 1980s critiques began to question certain, perhaps misused, statistical analyses (Anderton, 1989), especially when involved with stimulus-response models [Chapter Nine].

Separating out the third from the second model—bureaucratic from organizational—has always been difficult, but the specific test of the former within the limited domain of relative force postures within different sections of the United States Navy did not support the effect of "bureaucratic politics" on outcomes. In fact, "intraservice bureaucratic parochialism" (Rhodes, 1994: 20) did not predict which segments of the navy would be favored in procurements, and bureaucratic affiliations appeared to have no effect on the navy procurement budget, ship construction program, or annual shifts in fleet composition (Rhodes, 1994: 30). To the contrary, an alternative images model based on general beliefs about naval warfare and images about foreign policy appeared to more accurately impact on the posture of naval force.[17]

Organizations and crises would seem to occupy the opposite ends of a single continuum, yet they have both received attention from those who felt their presence impacts on decision-making in ways questioning traditional rational process realpolitik models. However colorful and obvious certain illustrative assessments of organizations' impacts on decisions may seem, they lack systematic confirmation, especially outside the narrowly defined area of defense-related issues. More importantly, for the contemporary era, the movement to a world of rationality would appear to relegate both unpredictable crises and very predictable organizations to merely background variables.

Conclusion

John Kennedy is said to have warned of the Cuban Missile Crisis, "Any historian who walks through this mine field of charges and countercharges should proceed with some care" (Allison, 1971: viii; Allison and Zelikow, 1999: xiii). In the heady days of more than a generation ago, a foreign policy endeavor held much "promise" for many but then turned into a war. One of the main players in that drama later conceded that, contrary to his model of decision-making, subordinates might actually *withhold* pertinent information from superiors. Along the way, academic analysis of decision-making in some ways has come full circle, though more than one circle seems to be involved. Quantum shifts have occurred in the transformation from strict historical descriptions to analytical categories proposed in the primitive decision-making models of the 1950s and again to the elaboration of those models that attacked the rational process assumptions of realpolitik. In terms of breaking down that realpolitik model, the assaults by the early 1970s seemed to sound the proverbial death knell for the "unitary actor" assumption.[18] However, the full turn has finally been completed by the more recent resurrection of utility maximization and "rational choice" suppositions, a not-so-transparent return to dubious aspects—such as the unitary actor—of the realist perspective: "To state it crudely: national leaders wage war when the expected gains minus the expected costs for doing so outweigh the net expected consequences of alternative choices" (Bueno de Mesquita and Lalman, 1992: 250).[19]

If cumulation of knowledge is to be found, it rests perhaps in the minimal recognition of a variety of quite distinct models compared to the previous dominance of an exclusive one. And yet decision-making in international politics remains intractable for a variety of reasons. A continuing tension persists between rational choice or utility maximizers on the one hand, and incrementalists who investigate the internal messiness of how decision-makers really make decisions; between those who view decisions as if through the lens of a mythical economist on a remote island with only an unopened can of tuna for food (solution: "Assume a can opener"), and those viewing decision-making from what they feel is a much more "realistic" perspective—real human beings grappling with sometimes intractable issues without the luxury of prior assumptions.

Moreover, these are not idle speculations removed from the real world. Concerning the use of rational choice models,

> some of the policy implications . . . are a cause for concern as they may give rise to unwarranted complacency about dangers in the international system. If we assume rationality in foreign policy and international relations, the threat of nuclear war—the epitome of irrationality—is largely reduced to a non-problem because it is almost impossible to construct scenarios by which such a conflict might result from rational decision processes . . . Exploring the limits on rationality and the constraints on rational choice faced by individuals, groups, organizations, and governments may lead to far more interesting and significant problems (Holsti, 1989: 387–388).

At the same time, in a different policy arena and time period, post–World War II, which appears more and more for some to be relevant to the contemporary era, we find illustrations of a new form of "choice," "belief," or "utility" approach:

> I argue that a transatlantic group of economists and policy specialists, united by a common set of policy ideas and a shared view that past economic failures could be avoided by innovative postwar economic arrangements, led their respective governments toward agreement by identifying a set of common Anglo-American interests that were not clearly seen by others (Ikenberry, 1993: 59).

When nuclear war is no longer viewed as a problem in a "new world order," then "common Anglo-American interests"—although drawn from an earlier historical era—hew nonetheless conceptually and operationally close to "national interest." Is this genuinely "rational choice"? As with realism and other labels, what is in the symbol is often in the eye of the beholder. Once "rational" creeps into the dialogue, considerable accompanying—at times even burdensome—baggage comes along with it. Some prefer "choice models" or "instrumental rationality": the first finesses the issue of "rationality" while retaining the attraction of "choice" and thus agency; the second implies that when "rationality" does enter the picture, it is clearly limited to a specific domain, perhaps even a clearly specified dependent variable.

The theoretical and the methodological cannot be separated, however, and the lure of the detailed, in-depth case study can become traditional historical analysis as well as an unwitting return to the implicit coloring of "rationality." *Theories* of decision-making do not fare well in such an environment; case studies and analysis of "models" require many "bits" of historical information, with the unwritten implication that all the bits add up to the explanation of the decision. What has always plagued the historian also plagues the "reconstructivist": no criteria exist denoting what information is to be left out and what to be included, what is merely background "noise" and what is important.

The American involvement in Vietnam accompanied by Allison's classic study brought consideration of these models to the forefront of both scholarly as well as popular analysis, yet few *systematic* efforts have addressed the validity of the respective models. An earlier attempt (Sullivan, 1976: 94–99) to set out evaluative criteria concerning decision-making models applied to the Vietnam case investigated their underlying assumptions. One assumption of the rational process model is that large-scale phenomena, such as the Vietnam War, do not just "happen"; their occurrence in a tautological way, confirms the model. A second assumption, that evidence for the existence of "importance" can be deduced from the historical record, can again be confirmed, although in the case of Vietnam the record also suggests that it was not that important or "vital" early in the process.[20]

Rational process also offers implications concerning leadership capabilities, and the Vietnam case places those arguing that Kennedy was intent on withdrawing—a "rational process" decision—in a very difficult bind. The main protagonist for Kennedy's rationally having decided to "get out" argues that Kennedy did *not* wish further involvement, the opposite of numerous advisors who favored further involvement in Vietnam (Newman, 1992). And yet in terms of actual decisional outcomes during the January 1961 to November 1963 period, it would appear that Kennedy loses at almost every turn in the road—including, as noted above, the debate on the infamous "1,000-man withdrawal." Chomsky even contends that in the transition to Johnson, evidence suggests that Kennedy's advisors supported what came to be Johnson's position on the war, and that this policy was a *continuation* of what they felt had been Kennedy's policies (Chomsky, 1993: 89–90). Kennedy gave to Johnson "the doctrinal framework" that considered victory significant, perhaps because Kennedy "had apparently given little thought to the matter altogether, and it was regarded as of marginal interest by those closest to him" (Chomsky, 1993: 110). Concerning the role of the advisors,

> Newman's basic contention seems to be that JFK was surrounded by evil advisors who were trying to thwart his secret plan to withdraw without victory, although unaccountably, he kept giving them more authority and promoting them to higher positions (Chomsky, 1993: 128).[21]

Moreover, to concur with the more positive portrayal of Kennedy insinuates that he was unaware of the potentially devastating effects of incremental decision-making; even the key story retold time and again as "proof" that Kennedy intended to extricate American troops—his comment after meeting with Senator Fulbright that he would extricate the United States but only after the 1964 elections—suggests a casual discounting of the pull of such powerful incremental tendencies, the recognition that decision-making—unlike what any "rational" model says—is a dynamic *process*.

Moreover, such a view inadvertently confirms one key assumption of an incremental model in political decision-making: do anything to survive the next election. Ellsberg noted years ago that the "quagmire" model implies that decision-makers should be optimistic at key decision points, and each new, small commitment should be perceived as promising to "do the job"—in contemporary parlance, "send the right message." Ellsberg raised doubts about these assumptions on Vietnam and evidence shows that particular decisions at the time were *not* met with optimism (Sullivan, 1976: 96). Proposed solutions would not necessarily solve the problem, with certain options weakening strategic U.S. forces, involving American prestige, and creating pressures for further commitments (*Pentagon Papers,* 1971: 141). Rarely in internal documents do sustained discussion of ultimate goals or long-range plans take place. In fact, quite the opposite occurred, as numerous analysts have confirmed:

> As far as the record shows, they held no session devoted to re-examination of the engagement they had inherited in Vietnam, nor did they ask themselves to what extent the United States was committed or what was the degree of national interest involved. Nor, so far as appears in the mountains of memoranda, discussions, and options flowing over the desks, was any long-range look taken at long-range strategy. Rather, policy developed in ad hoc spurts from month to month (Tuchman, 1984: 283).

The process describes the continuing decision-making:

> Johnson did not press for alternatives or question incisively the direction in which his administration's policies were headed . . . there is no evidence that Johnson searched beyond the range of policy options presented by the small group of advisors he relied upon, or closely examined the strengths, weaknesses and trade-offs in the varied positions of his advisors (Burke and Greenstein, 1989: 144).

Decision-makers are constantly divided between optimism and pessimism, but to focus only on pessimistic observations is misleading, for that can ignore the very fact of the decisions themselves. The incremental model, simple and unsatisfying as it may be to the theoretician as well as the ideologue, nonetheless often provides a reasonable, although not very parsimonious, explanation for an assortment of decisions. The major drawbacks are multiple: its lack of theoretical sophistication, the inability to ascribe culpability, as well as its complete inability to satisfy any need to find "rationality" in decisions.

Much skepticism was expressed in the analysis completed many years ago on decision-making in the Vietnam case about "rational process" or "rational choice." Nothing in the interim has suggested a different view, and while this analysis in no way directly questions "choice" models, getting into the trenches where decisions are actually made yields a very different picture than that produced by more abstract formulations. But that "transatlantic group of economists and policy specialists" referred to above did operate in the trenches, and yet the picture of that group differs greatly from that provided in our case study of another group of "specialists" facing different problems. Political actors often gravitate toward the short term, and despite the many arguments that can be made about what *might* have been done, the powerful incentive of short-term political factors was a strong motivation for decisions in the Vietnam case at several points: for President Kennedy, until the election of 1964; for Johnson, the elections of 1964 and originally 1968; and for Nixon, the election of 1972. But each time, the situation was altered every day, week, or month that passed in which decisions continued on the same path. Had Kennedy not been assassinated and been reelected, then those same pre-November 1964 motivations to consider continuing on as a valid option would become more powerful the closer he came to the midterm election of 1966. Not one of the Kennedy apologists addresses how Kennedy would have dealt with his own party subsequent to 1964, had it become known that he was entertaining plans of extrication, especially if the opposing party made an issue out of Vietnam.

As atheoretical as it might seem, decision-makers view their decisions as possible solutions *for the time being*. Kennedy's 1961 decision to send two top policy counselors to Vietnam contributed to the later incremental increase in advisors—noted by few at the time as an "important" decision. Johnson's immediate response to the Tonkin Gulf incident in 1964 and subsequent early bombing decisions in 1965 were directly characteristic of Lindblom's "muddling through" (Burke and Greenstein, 1989: 174). Were these "large" decisions? At the time, perhaps not. Ellsberg isolated several "large" decisions, such as Eisenhower's increase of advisors in 1960 and Johnson's inauguration of bombing in 1964. Other decisions, such as Kennedy's increasing the number of advisors or Johnson's increase in the troop commitment after 1965, are "merely quantitative," according to Ellsberg. Such a procedure imposes by fiat one of the requirements of a "rational policy" model. To assert that there *are* large and small decisions stacks the cards in favor of a model that relies on the existence of "large" decisions. But no decisions occur in a vacuum, and therefore all are intertwined with one another.

As compelling as the above story might seem, it still represents a single case study, and as such possesses all the faults of that genre and the risks of depicting an aberration. Yet a generation later in the Persian Gulf, early American support for Saddam Hussein in the 1980s against Iran—cast within a realpolitik model not unlike that which hypothetically drove Vietnam policy—might have inadvertently set the stage for later activities in the region. In many ways the key lesson of Vietnam—dangers of incrementalism—had already been forgotten by the mid-1980s, for that decade-long U.S. commitment to Iraq and attempts at power-balancing between Iraq and Iran had unwittingly set the stage for Iraq's perception of the advisability of an attack on Kuwait. The American decision in the spring of 1990, to refrain from involvement in the border dispute between Iraq and Kuwait, continued the earlier alliance with Iraq. Ultimately, of course, with the invasion of Kuwait by Iraq, there developed a sudden need to take decisions against Saddam Hussein. Subsequent to that decision, conventional wisdom suggested the decision represented—through the medium of a much-vaunted UN coalition—many characteristics of a "rational" choice. Yet over a decade later, military forces—admittedly of a lower magnitude—were still in the region, and regular air attacks were being carried out by British and American forces ten years after the original imbroglio.

But time's numbing effect takes its toll on memory of decision-making. Public support was high for the United Nations' coalition ranged against Iraq in the Persian Gulf, another "lesson" taught during the Vietnam War. Of the many things about the American involvement in Vietnam that have been forgotten, however, was that public opinion data of the time showed that the American public supported that war also; only near the end of peak American involvement did the public turn against the war. Who did and who did not support the war along class and age differences has also been forgotten (Sullivan, 1985: 109–121). The "responsible elite" most likely now remembers only their own opposition to the war *at some point* in the process, but to read analyses of the time paints a very different picture about this "informed elite":

Reaction to President Johnson's decision . . . on July 28, 1965 was generally favorable, even among some of his critics. Walter Lippmann, a very influential columnist, who had been strongly critical of Johnson's Vietnam policy, called the decision "realistic." "As a result," he added, "the American position is strengthened and improved." The *New York Times* said that despite the implications of the fact that the war could go on for years or even decades, "few Americans will quarrel with President Johnson's determined conclusion to hold on in Vietnam" (Gibbons, 1987: 32–33).

Conventional wisdom has often put the blame for "failure" in Vietnam on the Fourth Estate. But one of the most detailed analyses of the role of the press in Vietnam depicts a very different picture: "News coverage in the later years of the war was considerably less positive than in the early years, but not nearly so consistently negative as the conventional wisdom now seems to hold" (Hallin, 1986: 10). Aside from a fleeting awareness of the Buddhist crisis of 1963, "Vietnam probably entered the consciousness of most Americans for the first time in August, 1964" (Hallin, 1986: 15), and that early in the war the "responsible journalist" did not give credence to "communist propaganda," but by and large gave passive attention when the leader of the "Free World" said that "aggression" had occurred: "These were core symbols of the journalists' world view, just as deeply held as they were for anyone else in the political establishment" (Hallin, 1986: 25).[22]

The Vietnam case holds no prominent importance for many in the contemporary world, perhaps because in some ways this world possesses characteristics of the heady atmosphere of more than a generation ago, when another group of optimistic decision-makers held sway. The possibility of nuclear war seems remote; to some even the possibility of major war is equally so (Mueller, 1989; Mandelbaum, 1998/99). There is also the resurgence of rational choice models, a controversial agenda with its critics (Walt, 1999) and its ironies.[23] Still, Vietnam undeniably imprinted policy-makers as well as the conceptualizations of world politics drawn by academics, but that impact may be wearing off. It remains an interesting case study—with all the many pitfalls of that methodology—and one that sharply contrasts respective decision-making models. Regardless of its fading impact, and beyond the question of the suitable application of models to decision-making in general, is the question of the utility of applying contrasting models to understanding decisions undertaken by an adversary. Regardless of the conclusions drawn about the veracity of respective models' applications in *explaining* decisions, observations noted years ago concerning inferences about adversaries still seem applicable; the "warning" not only had relevance at the time, but to more recent incidents:

> Be suspicious of explanations that depend on the assumption that one can reason back from detailed characteristics of specific behavior to central government intentions . . . Recognize that in most cases the full range or behavior exhibited by a government was not intended by a single participant (Allison and Halperin, 1972: 70).

Whether similar "rational" processes occur within an adversary's decision-making bureaucracy is hard to assess. For the Cold War, few systematic analyses to date exist of Soviet and Chinese internal documents, which have only recently been coming to light. These could be a test of the adversaries' goals in Indochina. As for the American side, internal position papers that have been seen as "setting the course" for Vietnam policy over the long term might have carried no more importance than the many, often ignored, position papers for other areas of the world during the 1950s and 1960s, with similar, also ultimately ignored, goals.

This chapter opened with poignant comments by a former American secretary of defense and "player" in the American involvement in Vietnam, and has followed a somewhat circuitous route, primarily because the analysis of decision-making itself has followed such a route. The era that saw that involvement as holding "such promise" was an American phenomenon that has passed, and a new one—globalization—has allegedly emerged, presenting new issues that must be decided with new foci and perhaps addressed by new players. Subsequent chapters suggest the potential role for international institutions—NATO and the United Nations certainly appear as promising possibilities for collective peacemaking. Perhaps ironically, however, one of the very justifications for that American involvement—"democracy"—has resurfaced as an "'enabling' norm" for the "collective ordering of power" to facilitate the "construction" of security in post–Cold War Europe (Flynn and Farrell, 1999: 512). A blunt but cogent observation by a scholar little interested in assessing decisions or "utilities" concerning Vietnam concludes with this analysis:

> One of the great puzzles for historians of this period, if the threat of communism was the leitmotif of U.S. foreign policy conduct . . . was why the United States would expend such a pitiful effort at the Bay of Pigs in ridding the Hemisphere of communist dictatorship sixty miles off American shores, while it would fight a ten-year war thousands of miles away in Vietnam for the same purpose. The answer is only found in the irrationality of foreign policy decision making . . . In neither the case of Cuba, nor the case of Vietnam, was the territorial security of the United States *per se* at risk. In each case, however, the political freedom of a people was being mercilessly denied. But so before, and so since, in places as diverse as Cambodia, Ethiopia, and Afghanistan, the political freedom of peoples was subverted, yet the United States would not send troops to save them. In fact, the corruptness and ineptness of the Diem regime and its successors made South Vietnam a questionable choice for the high-minded pursuit of the defense of free people. What was special about Vietnam? Nothing (Doran, 1991: 197).[24]

Unless of course one imposes a type of "ultimate" realpolitik, rational process scheme to the Vietnam case, which might admit that American decision-makers made mistakes, behaved incrementally, and that Vietnam could be considered correctly in the short term as a failure, but that in fact the larger war—the Cold War—which has been broadly interpreted as having been "won," proves that there was something "special" about Vietnam. Even though at the microlevel incrementalism may have ruled, at the macrolevel Vietnam was part of larger macrolevel processes. But the decision-making at that level gets lost, as in any macrolevel model, and the effect of those processes on ultimate, larger decisions also gets lost. This process occurs in all macro models, whether it be realpolitik in the ultimate, as suggested here, or in neorealism, liberalism, neoliberalism, liberal institutionalism—or whatever broad macrodesign is imposed. Unfortunately, lives are lived at the microlevel, and at that level, Vietnam, contrary to Doran's implications, meant everything—and therein lies the tragedy.

Chapter Four ✺

The Nation-State:
Cause, Curse, or Cure?

What to Do with "the State"?

Revolutionary events coincident with the fall of the Berlin Wall and the reformations sweeping through Eastern Europe, the Soviet Union, and elsewhere profoundly affected political actors as well as the scholars who study them. "Democracy" became the catchword, producing a fortuitous outcome for political leaders and scholars as well. The makeup of governments—the "state," the "within" traditionally essential to what political scientists study—had become lost in the rush toward systemic theories. For so long conventionally accepted, the state was in the process of denigration as little more than a necessary evil or a mental construct unrelated to reality, or an entity—contrary to strict "realist" thought—always very much in transition.[1] But now it emerged again as the focus of attention. In the late 1980s, just as Eastern Europe and the former Soviet Union were convulsing under unparalleled transformations away from controlled economic and political systems, a wave of research had reemerged involving the relationship between democracy and war, and the implications of those phenomena for world politics. The mundane world of the research scholar was interfacing with daily events, providing a real-time laboratory. Other forces were also at work suggesting the decline of the nation-state, perhaps at odds with the promising and perhaps pacifying effects of "democracy." While the former is frequently positively heralded,[2] nonetheless nationalisms new and old can produce potentially negative results.

The debates became tethered to broader issues involving realism and neorealism, and the contrasting views of the "within" school versus the "without" school—reduced often to the question of "what do we do with 'the state'." Ironically, for all the clamor suddenly in the 1990s for the importance of domestic sources, few scholars had systematically investigated attribute changes in those states swiftly becoming the focus of such interest (Moynihan, 1993). Attributes were mutating with little regard for what was happening in the broader international arena and prior to the most recent calls for the focus on "domestic sources."

Contrary to those heralding a "new" focus on domestic sources to counter the narrow systemic neorealists, the "state" and "domestic sources" had always been there, quietly existing and transforming. Investigation of their influence, however, has a checkered history. Just as personality characteristics shape individuals' behavior, so national characteristics had been viewed as the "personality" of nations, distinct from the individuals within it as well as from the surrounding system, as if both were exogenous, controlled variables (Sullivan, 1976: 102–141). The internal cannot be divorced from the external, and the nation-state is certainly in flux. But a totally holistic analysis of all levels, contextualized to the *n*th degree, results in case studies; analysis of specific levels is thus justified, and despite much conventional thinking the fate of the nation-state is not yet decided. National attributes do not annihilate agency; they work only as *constraints* on decision-makers and not as *direct* forces on foreign policy; the theory asserts only that states *tend to be constrained in similar ways* if possessing similar attributes.

National Attributes, Domestic Sources, and "the State"

To focus on nation-states through their attributes presents not only a changing discipline, but also distinct and portentous continuities. The most traditional national attribute was geopolitics, a concept that underwent radical changes and definitions as its popularity waxed and waned. Once declared extinct only to be resurrected by the very events of international politics that, it was thought, other theories had declared unimportant, geopolitics of one sort or another has retained its hold.

> For most things, geography still matters. That is why Canada is the biggest trading partner of the United States, why America is Mexico's biggest partner, and why the countries of the European Community trade more with each other than with anyone else.[3]

Traditional scholarship held geographic location, climatic conditions, and availability of natural resources as decisive factors, but their assumed linkage with *realpolitik* cast them in a hopelessly traditional role as the Cold War and modern technology compelled them into apparent irrelevancy. Yet, whether it be Mahan's view that naval capabilities bestowed more "power" on nations, or Mackinder's famous "heartland" thesis that whoever ruled the "heartland"—central Europe—would rule the world, or the effect of borders and their mutations, all have been resurrected in one form or another in modern contexts (Modelski and Thompson, 1988; Midlarsky, 1995; Starr and Most, 1978; Siverson and Starr, 1991; Starr, 1991a; 1991b).

Traditional geopolitics, however, proposed few *systematic* linkages with nations' behavior, and thus remained theoretically amorphous. When "transnationalism" first became the prevailing buzzword, national boundaries became even more of a relic. But historically, borders *do* change: 775 border changes occurred between 1816 and 1980; 59 new states emerged between 1946 and 1965, with a total of 372 "new" borders; contiguous homeland borders changed from 166 to 412 between 1946 and 1965 (Siverson and Starr, 1991: 30).

> These territorial changes, involving any gain or loss of a territory, were clearly associated with international conflict, both before and after the changes. By illustration, the Six Day War (1967), which resulted in Israel's annexation of territory from Egypt, Syria, and Jordan, radically changed the geopolitical context of the Middle East; these changes reverberate even to this day (Siverson and Starr, 1991: 30).

New borders came into existence in rapid fashion after 1989, and the ongoing controversy concerning "democracy and war" also returned to these basic, elemental, "environmental" factors (Midlarsky, 1995).

Lenin's theories of imperialism suggested equally traditional and significant impacts of national variations on behavior:

> as capitalist economies mature, as capital accumulates, and as profit rates fall, the capitalist economies are compelled to seize colonies and create dependencies to serve as markets, investment outlets, and sources of food and raw materials. In competition with one another, they divide up the colonial world in accordance with their relative strengths (Gilpin, 1987: 39).

Capitalist economic systems thus escape the crisis and class revolt, predicted by Marx, by expansion, supposedly propelling those nations into wars more often than noncapitalist countries. Events subsequent to 1989 provide great contemporary relevance for assessing the validity of such predictions, including those related to the ultimate demise of capitalist systems.

A third focus for nation-state attributes derives from governmental type: traditional liberal-democratic notions that democratic states are more peaceful. A review of the argument four decades ago suggested that liberal "democratic" polities were "good" because they provided decentralization, economic well-being, participation, rationality, and harmony. War should become an anachronism as more states achieved democratic status, settling their differences in peaceful, logical discourse (Waltz, 1959: 101). The "liberal democracy" belief boasts a long but checkered history, recently traveling within less than a generation from ridicule to a reputed "law" of international politics. The "democratic peace" has amassed many believers, but such has not always been the case, and the systematic research has proved both theoretically and empirically rocky. At the height of the American involvement in Vietnam, the world's leading democracy exhibited in many observers' eyes a policy clearly affirming the folly of "democratic theory."[4] Whether "political correctness" of the time demanded philosophical allegiance in the academic community (Ray, 1995b: 344), or whether the conclusions produced were strictly "scientific" is not a question to be decided here, but three decades later the picture is decidedly different. Today's widely accepted wisdom is the exact opposite of earlier accepted wisdom: the lack of wars between democracies has been declared by some an empirical law and the policy implication stated and restated numerous times in multiple ways: the Kantian "perpetual peace" seemed potentially to be on the horizon, only to be "grasped" (Russett, 1993).

These three traditional strains—geopolitics, imperialism, and democratic theory—continue to reflect contemporary thinking, but one excluded element relates to the contemporary world and addresses not only the makeup but the viability of nation-states at the end of the century. That factor is of course "nationalism." As with "motivations" at the individual level, nationalism has perennially produced problems at the state level. National or ethnic identity as a key mobilizing and unifying factor received a boost after World War II with the rising tide of new nations; while the number of independent nation-states had risen from less than 50 in 1870 to just under 70 in 1940, they then ballooned to almost 140 in the next 30 years. But by the late 1960s, the surge had crested, accompanied by reverse phenomena. One "antinationalist" force was the growing popularity of the "transnational" view, in which distinct nationalisms would fade and antagonisms between nationalities slowly die out. Another was the, by then, 50-year-old communist revolution, wherein cultural, religious and national differences should slowly fade as the communist revolution's goals were achieved throughout the world.

Events in recent years have questioned both views. The Soviet empire is dead, and nationalism as a driving force has resurfaced there, in Eastern Europe, and elsewhere, both between and within traditionally defined nation-states, producing both positive as well as negative effects. Positively, reemergence of national identities carries with it spin-offs such as security and identity. Negatively, ethnic diversities produce intense conflict. Before the final breakup of the former "nation-state" of Czechoslovakia, Czechs and Slavs battled each other, ethnic Moldavians in Romania demanded more autonomy, and before his departure from Russian politics, Mikhail Gorbachev warned against the real possibility of civil war. The secessionist war in Chechnya became Russia's Vietnam, followed by similar problems in Dagestan. Yugoslavia remains tension-filled and divisive over a decade after its breakup, causing repeated international intercessions and peacekeeping operations, and finally the war in Kosovo in the spring of 1999, where NATO forces bombed Belgrade, the first bombs dropped in Europe in 54 years. This list does not include the many other areas subject to the same processes (Gurr, 1994; Carment and James, 1995). Nationalism, thought unimportant in the modern world because of emerging "globalism" and "transnationalism," has reemerged in force.

When telescoped, however, perceptions appear more significant than they actually are; the long-term effect of recent changes on attribute theory are much less clear. States' differences and their effect on behavior has always served as a background variable, but imbuing them with the rigidity and impermeability required to categorize them systematically and measure them empirically emerged only at mid-century. The first two major data-sets exemplifying this approach[5] were empirical manifestations of such thinking about the relationships between attributes and behavior, with the empirical dovetailing nicely for a time with the more conceptual. The upside was its systematic and empirical orientation, while the downside—emerging clearly in the critiques to follow—was its attempt to investigate what many came to feel was a rigidified "entity" that no longer existed in the way the data implied. When the broader issue of sovereignty intrudes, and the possibility emerges that sovereignty is "neither fixed nor constant," and changes over time, possessing a juridical content in one era different than sovereignty derived from nationalist sentiments in another (Barkin and Cronin, 1994: 128), then perceptions and definitions of what constitutes a "nation" also thereby change.

Such issues were not of great concern at mid-century: nations were considered "known" entities, and by the 1960s the data necessary to allow numbers to represent these concepts was becoming more readily available. On the conceptual side, Rosenau's "pretheory" summarized traditional thought distinguishing nations by their attributes, with the two most prominent variables being "governmental" and "societal." The former referred to

> those aspects of a government's structure that limit or enhance the foreign policy choices made by decision-makers. The impact of executive-legislative relations on American foreign policy exemplifies the operation of governmental variables (Rosenau, 1966: 43).

More broadly, the governmental variable referred to the distinction between open and closed systems utilizing the simple linkage noted above: open systems are less free to act in foreign policy, their policies should be more stable, they may be less capable of using internal disruptions as an excuse for fomenting external conflict, and therefore may exhibit less external conflict. Closed, autocratic, or totalitarian regimes, it was thought, possess more flexibility, are more capable of rapid changes of policy, and are less dependent upon domestic support for their decisions. They may even view conflict as a more feasible and preferable alternative. While these differences and the behavior thought to flow from them have been extensively elaborated over the years, the essential arguments remain.

The societal variable referred to nongovernmental aspects of a society, including value orientation, unity, degree of industrialization, size, level of economic and social development, all of which can "contribute to the contents of a nation's external aspirations and policies" (Rosenau, 1966: 43). Large, developed nations would more likely be active in foreign affairs, have more international interests, and be involved in more conflicts as well as more cooperative behavior such as alliances. They may also—given the relationship between size and military capability—seem more militaristic in their foreign policy. Smaller countries, were they to engage in conflict, would more likely rely on less extreme types of verbal behavior rather than major threats, or minor sorties across borders rather than full-scale invasions.

Early empirical analyses, while not uniform, produced some congruence on comparing nations that coincided with the theoretical work (Russett, 1967; Rummel, 1969b; 1969c).[6] Three general categories seemed to distinguish nations at the time: size and economic wealth, type of governmental system, and political or social unrest or strain. All had dominated the theoretical literature, and the empirical research supported the first two as distinct dimensions. The third variable—domestic unrest or strain—presents a very interesting and continuing anomaly. Myriad hypotheses had been consistently generated over the years and an enormous effort was expended testing those hypotheses from the late 1950s through the early 1970s. Domestic unrest was repeatedly cited in the traditional literature, popular in journalistic accounts, and was used by policy-makers as a facile explanation of other nations' intransigent, testy foreign policies during the Cold War; and yet over the years, until recently, it simply failed to stand up when subjected to systematic empirical analysis (Levy, 1988a).[7]

Brushclearing

Early tests of national attributes, while considered groundbreaking at the time because of the heavy reliance on data and adherence to an overarching framework, are now viewed as little more than brushclearings, essential for establishing a base and certain parameters (Sullivan, 1976: 106f.). More importantly, they *failed* to confirm certain widespread notions and hypotheses in traditional literature, such as that just noted concerning domestic unrest, and in doing so laid the groundwork for subsequent analyses that have reoriented certain hypotheses.

Larger and more economically developed states are more active in the international system because they have more at stake. No consistently strong ties emerged between economic development and conflict-related behaviors, although indicators of low-level conflict—protests, expulsion of low-level diplomats, troop movements, and accusations—did tend to correlate moderately with certain indicators of size and development. Other conflict-related behaviors, such as war, number killed in foreign actions, foreign demonstrations, and so on tended to have few relations with economic or other size-related variables. A pattern emerged where larger states tended to protest and accuse more (verbal acts), and take up arms (war acts). Wealthy or developed states, however, tended *not* to protest, accuse, or partake in troop movements, but did tend to expel lower officials. While smaller and less developed states participate less, they tend to sever relations more often than the more wealthy states (Sullivan, 1976: 110ff.). Other patterns included high economic development being associated with high cooperative behavior (trade, common international organization membership, and diplomatic exchanges), and smaller and less developed states using more offensive verbal conflict such as accusations, demands, warnings, and threats (Sullivan, 1976: 113).

Later results showed that using proxy measures for size, such as per capita revenue other than trade and per capita governmental transfer of payments, showed relationships to alternative outcome variables such as trade policy and openness of trade (Bates, et al, 1991). The larger and more industrialized developing nations attract more Foreign Direct Investment (FDI), as do those with close political and military ties with the U.S. (and those with stronger central governments) (Chan and Mason, 1992). Conversely, "the smaller, less industrialized, and nonaligned African, Asian, and Latin American countries have been largely ignored by Western investors." A time series analysis from 1967–1987 for four countries (Kenya, Indonesia, Mexico, and South Korea) provided "selective support" for those patterns, and results

> tend to be generally congruent with both neoclassical and statist interpretations of FDI. Neoclassical interpretations stress theories of product cycle, oligopolistic rivalry, and comparative advantage . . . Yet the state appears to be an important actor in attracting FDI (Chan and Mason, 1992: 229–230).

Size also relates to tariffs, even though results have differed: earlier analyses suggested little or no clear relationship between size and tariffs in the early 1970s (Conybeare, 1983: 459–460), but later data for the mid-1980s suggested a rather strong relationship between size and nontariff barriers (Mansfield and Busch, 1995: 746–747).

Overall, though certain early empirical findings were mixed, patterns still existed. They did not provide the level of statistical and predictive ability hoped for at the time, and often differed depending on the outcome variable analyzed—overall conflict compared to different types of conflict, or total conflict compared to the proportion of total behavior. Nonetheless, these explicitly empirical designs certainly changed the perspective, although not the central focus, on nation-states, for they had always been the principal locus. Perhaps the data-sets of that period served as a necessary prelude for the theoretical evolution since their extreme rigidity provided the opening for critiques which questioned that construct, and proposed that both transnationalism and contemporary nationalisms might actually be tearing down the revered entity of the state embodied in the rigid quantification.

Nonetheless the national attribute studies of an earlier generation set the stage both conceptually and theoretically, systematizing much theoretical work that had been scattered. Furthermore, despite potential incipient transformations, as long as the important actors that currently seem to matter the most—essentially, nation-states and their leaders—continue to act *as if* the nation-state remained an important entity, then the construct itself remains useful, which itself suggests several ironies. First, certain traditional linkages, such as the prized one between internal unrest and external relations, have not been sustained—perhaps questioning the division between the internal and the external, while at the same time the "liberal peace," relying almost as heavily on the notion of a rigidly bound nation-state as an entity—at least conceptually—has achieved a remarkable consensus. A second irony has already been noted: just at the point when for some the nation-state was taking on a measurable, quantified reality, for others events were overtaking such theoretical and empirical finery and the state's traditional mold was in the process of breaking down. A final irony, as we will see, is that the ongoing attribute studies that continue despite the theoretical onslaught against the state revert back to the domestic variables of very traditional interest to political analysts. Especially with type of government, the emphasis becomes so extreme that it reaches beyond singular linkages thought to exist over the years to a much broader umbrella: "the final conclusion is that d*emocracy is a general method of nonviolence"* (Rummel, 1995: 25; emphasis in original). This certainly constitutes a conversion both from a generation earlier as well as from those contending that the hegemonic "nation-state" as an entity is a "curse."

Governments: From Curse to Cure—
"the Democratic Peace"

The "democratic peace" constitutes an indisputable ten-year wonder, and the acceptance of this basic, simple hypothesis extant for so long in the literature certainly stands out in the annals of the sociology of knowledge. Undoubtedly the "end of the Cold War" and the onslaught against "realism" has helped, for the importance of democracy and the "liberal" peace has become harvested as part of the antirealist school.

Political Scientists focusing on nations as the unit of analysis would logically start with type of government, but in the Cold War–Vietnam era no groundswell erupted for what has become known in the contemporary era as the "liberal peace." Empirical studies either found no effect or were only minimally supportive of the traditional hypothesis. One of the earliest systematic investigations was quite conclusive: "the degree of totalitarianism of a government has little relationship to its foreign conflict behavior" and, further, "the values of a nation have little relationship to its foreign conflict behavior" (Rummel, 1968: 207, 211). Needless to say, things have changed. The theoretical component was revived and acquired refinement, extension, and further specification, and the level of empirical data and complexity of designs expanded. The evidence has taken a very different turn, and a veritable cottage industry sprang up as the Cold War ended, which has painstakingly investigated a hypothesis considered virtually moribund 20 years earlier.

Implications concerning world politics have been no less than astonishing, but the confluence of this research revival with events in the world—the end of the Vietnam War and the end of the Cold War primarily—while not calling into question the subsequent research, certainly strikes a note in favor of caution concerning the relation between social science research and changing conditions in the world under investigation. A chronological listing of "democratic peace" research products shows the bulk emerging just after key events marking the so-called "end of the Cold War" and the advent of a "New World Order" defined as the flowering of democracy and "rule of law." General comparative patterns describing the research agenda have already emerged (Chan, 1997: 82–84), and we eschew that at this point to present some generalized findings.

While recent years have seen a variety of elaborations and refinements in both research designs and data-set utilization, the basic theoretical links were for some time relatively straightforward; refinements have emerged in the second wave beginning in the 1980s and 1990s, in some cases emerging from critiques of the "liberal peace" hypothesis. One description, set down years before the growth of the cottage industry and utilizing extant formulations of the time, serves as a starting point: "democratic systems" permit a certain type of freedom within government that tends to inhibit leaders of these systems from using their position to trample over other countries in foreign affairs. If we assume people do not like war, then systems where the leaders are accountable to the people are much less likely to become involved in wars (Sullivan, 1976: 117).

Abbreviated and unadorned, it reflected the times. Extensions and refinements emerged from Doyle's influential reenergizing of Kant's basic notions (Doyle, 1983) and revolve around the three general formulations: public opinion, noted above, making Kant's "republican states" more cautious in the use of force and respective of similar states; the tendency for such states to engage in trade and commerce (a more truly relational and not attribute variable); and—most often followed—the notion of a "pacific union" among democracies (Chan, 1997: 74–75). Other categorical schemes begin by distinguishing the "structural" from the "normative" or "cultural" explanations. The first contends that democratic systems comprise structures that produce checks and balances and a diffusion of power, and within those systems decisions will be made less often to go to war because of those very checks and balances. Leadership mobility patterns in democratic systems socialize leaders toward different ways of resolving disputes and conflicts. Debates within a democratic system involving "the people" might slow the decision process moving a country toward war; other, non-war alternatives would be more likely to emerge in such systems.[8]

The cultural or normative explanation suggests leaders internalize the "norms" defining democratic systems: belief in diversity, liberties, and processes for the resolution of conflicts distinct from socialization processes in "nondemocratic" systems. Compromise and nonviolence mark the central characteristics of these political systems:

> One fundamental democratic norm is the willingness to accept compromise solutions to contentious public issues. If we extend this norm to the international arena, then it becomes reasonable to expect democratic states to adopt compromise solutions to international problems as well (Dixon, 1993: 43).

A somewhat extreme variant of this position might contend that leaders in nondemocratic systems as a matter of course rely on violence and coercion and expect others to do so.[9] Certain reformulations present similar arguments under different umbrellas; a microeconomic theory of the state might suggest that *all* nations possess a certain "imperialistic bias," but that bias is lowest in democratic states where the costs to society of controlling a state are relatively low compared to autocracies (Lake, 1992). Disincentives for war and dispute behavior may hypothetically exist within democratic systems relating both to elite survival and the effectiveness of communications made by democratic systems—all analyzed in an operational sense independently from public opinion (Bueno De Mesquita and Siverson, 1995; Schultz, 1999).

The theoretical elaborations have taken multiple specific paths, some deriving from Kant's respective notions of public opinion and the more broadly conceived "Pacific Union"; some from more narrowly construed formulations such as the "libertarianism" of Rummel (1983); and others generating formulations on norms and culture partly related back to Kant. This sheer variety almost confirms the lack of consensus on what it *is* about democratic regimes that allegedly produces the respective outcome variables (Thompson, 1996: 171–172), and the multiple specifications of independent and dependent variables has produced many subtle measurement distinctions and design decisions that have served to produce very differing results over the years. The admittedly first-cut inquiry—are democracies more peaceful—has been expanded to many more specific questions about whether democracies go to war with one another, whether they *ever* fight one another, whether they ever get into *conflicts* with each other, what types of conflicts democracies might engage in, and, finally, of more recent vintage, whether democracies *resolve* their conflicts differently than nondemocracies.

The plate has been a full one, and the continuing abundant empirical results reflect this, from the first, relatively primitive attempts through the later "rush" of democracy-war findings beginning in the late 1980s. Early, forgotten research supported the democracy-war link without the fanfare accorded later work (Babst, 1964; 1972), but the conclusion—30 years before the democratic peace "law"—was certainly straightforward:

> the existence of independent nations with elective governments greatly increases the chances for the maintenance of peace. What is important is the form of government, not national character (Babst, 1964: 14).

The most often-cited findings, however, were those showing variables associated with type of government strongly unrelated to foreign conflict (Rummel, 1963; 1968; Tanter, 1966), while others found "centrist" countries exhibiting just slightly more foreign conflict than would be expected by chance, and "polyarchic" exhibiting less, with stronger differences occurring when focusing on specific types of conflict (centrist countries exhibiting more warlike behavior, for instance) (Salmore and Hermann, 1970: 28; Zinnes and Wilkenfeld, 1971: 208). A measure of "national support for world order" (NSWO) was related to several attribute variables, including economic development and "freedom," with the implication that nations should try to "foster worldwide development and open countries" (Sullivan, 1978b: 116). Thus, despite a small number of early systematic findings supporting the pacifying effects of "democracy,"[10] the research agenda withered until an influential two-part conceptual analysis (Doyle, 1983) and a single empirical investigation of questionable validity (Rummel, 1983) spurred this moribund area. Ten years later many had accepted a new "law," and a hypothesis virtually discarded as hopelessly naive at the peak of democratic America's involvement in the Vietnam War had been transformed.

The most expansive extension was the reintroduction of the Kantian "perpetual peace" within a broader dissection of the role and varieties of liberalism, with the strong suggestion of an apparent absence of war between liberal states for almost 200 years (Doyle, 1983; 1986). The "joint freedom" hypothesis, more limited theoretically, focused on "libertarian" states, viewed as less violence-prone, and when interacting with other libertarian states "this inhibition becomes a mutual barrier to violence" (Rummel, 1983: 28); data covering 1976–1980 as well as the Correlates of War (COW) war data-set supported the hypothesis, but the conclusion was subsequently supported only in the monadic and not the dyadic design (Chan, 1984), and for the COW data the finding held only for the more recent rather than distant past, and only if colonial wars were excluded. Cross-sectional analysis failed to support the results, while a longitudinal one did:

> if we compare Britain during the nineteenth century with Britain during the twentieth century, it has obviously become freer as well as more pacific (measured in terms of frequency, but not the intensity, of wars). On the other hand, if we compare nineteenth century

Britain with other countries during the same period (an approach used in this analysis), it was clearly more war prone even though it was also freer (Chan, 1984: 643).

Rummel's findings proved replicable only for the narrow 1976–1980 period, and he was even castigated for contradicting the "consensus he helped create 15 years ago. Whatever Rummel's message was in 1969, in 1983 it is as clear as it was back in 1968, but it differs radically in substance" (Weede, 1984: 650).

By the late 1980s, replications and reinterpretations poured forth, with stronger support for no relationship at the *monadic* level (in fact, democracies "disproportionately initiate against, and are targets of disputes initiated by other regime types" [Maoz and Abdolali, 1989: 31]), but with a significant one present at the *dyadic* level: "democracies" rarely clash with each other and never fight one another in war. At the *system* level, the proportion of democratic dyads in the system had a *negative* effect on wars in the system and on the proportion of disputes that escalate to war. Most significant was evidence that findings were dependent on the specific outcome variables and regime types utilized, and all were subject to significant cross-time variations (Maoz and Abdolali, 1989: 31–32). The overall conclusion was that "results . . . are generally mixed . . . [and] . . . not sufficient to win the scientific war on this issue" (Maoz and Abdolali, 1989: 31). Others concurred with respect to "decisional constraints":

> Had [our] analyses uncovered strong, statistically significant relationships linking high levels of domestic political constraints to a low probability of war, we would have clear support for our theoretical argument. On the other hand we could confidently reject the argument had the results been indicative of random noise. That the vast majority of the coefficients, though weak and insignificant, were in the predicted direction, suggests that the argument might have some merit (Morgan and Campbell, 1991: 206–207).

Thus, contrary to Doyle's facile findings, the growing evidence was that relationships that did exist were much less straightforward, especially in the debate between the structural and normative explanations (Morgan and Campbell, 1991: 210). The latter contended that the more "deeply rooted are democratic norms . . . the lower the likelihood that disputes will break out or that disputes will escalate," the former that "political constraints" affect executives (Maoz and Russett, 1992: 627). In one extensive analysis, both were related to less war, but the normative seemed to be more robust and significant, although a microscopic analysis of certain specific elements suggest a less strong conclusion.[11] Nonetheless, support does exist for "structure"—"democracy seems to inhibit war at the dyadic level to a greater extent than does the existence of constraints on executive decision-makers" (Morgan and Schwebach, 1992: 317). Despite support for the effect of culture, structures present a constraining influence on the belligerent impulses of state leaders

> by creating additional barriers through which decisions for war must pass. The effect is felt through a reduction in the probability that the state will opt for war and does not appear to depend on the domestic structure of the opponent (Morgan and Schwebach, 1992: 317–318).

For the initiation and escalation of violence within crises, democracies seem less likely to initiate crises with all other kinds of states, but once in a crisis they are less likely to initiate violence only against other democratic states (Rousseau et al. 1996: 527). Extensions beyond the war/conflict variable furthers the norm-based argument, suggesting democracy's even greater efficacy. Data on interstate disputes for the limited 35-year period, 1945–1979, suggested that democracies were more amenable to intercession by third parties attempting conflict management: the "norms of dispute resolution . . . integral to the democratic process" suggest that "democracy does carry the systematic positive influence on the probability of conflict management expected of it" (Dixon, 1993: 64).[12] Similar findings were reported for 206 dyadic disputes for the longer 1820–1965 period (Raymond, 1994), and for 1,580 disputes between 1816–1992 (Mousseau, 1998). Other dependent variables are also effected by democracy: democratic states appear to incur fewer battle deaths in war than nondemocracies (Siverson, 1995), and disputes initiated by democracies were less likely to result in reciprocation than those initiated by nondemocratic states (Schultz, 1999).

Testing multiple variables also suggests support for the general proposition. Using all wars between 1816–1965 showed democracy ranking fourth out of seven variables (Bremer, 1992), and having more impact on reducing *wars* than in reducing *disputes,* suggesting that democratic dyads tend to keep conflict levels low rather than veer away from conflict (Bremer, 1993). Within the heavily used and more limited temporal Cold War domain of 1946–1986, the "freedom" hypothesis received support even when including alternative variables, although it was also suggested that political stability "rather than or in addition to regime type, may account for the low rate of disputes between democracies" (Maoz and Russett, 1992: 262). However, while the general results were supportive, the lowest "observed" (compared to "expected") frequencies occurred in all three "similar-regime-type" cells (democracy-democracy, anocracy-anocracy, autocracy-autocracy), although the biggest deviation—fewer disputes than expected was in the "democracy-democracy" cell (Maoz and Russett, 1992: 253). Other data indirectly confirm this (Werner and Lemke, 1997: 543–544): more disputes than expected occur with democracies as initiators and anocracies and autocracies as targets.[13]

As the agenda drew more adherents, democracies became even more daunting. They seemed to prevail more in wars with autocracies, suggesting that they were more "powerful": as noted earlier, a microeconomic theory of the state suggested that differences in imperialist bias and differential internal relative costs of controlling the state produce systems more supportive of the government in democracies and thus more "powerful" (Lake, 1992). Democratic leaders seem to select wars that have a lower risk of defeat than authoritarian leaders do (Bueno de Mesquita and Siverson, 1995: 852), and, both as initiators and targets, are more likely to win wars than other states (although less statistically significant as targets) (Reiter and Stam, 1998b), even though the advantage seems to pass to autocratic states during longer wars (Bennett and Stam, 1998), and the positive benefits to democracy would appear to be from initiative, leadership, and morale as opposed to any greater desire to fight for the democracy *per se* (Reiter and Stam, 1998a). Those systems with higher executive constraints are more likely to achieve a victory—rather than defeat or stalemate—in an international crisis (Partell, 1997: 519–520; 523–525), and they are more likely to prevail in disputes and less likely to back down (Partell and Palmer, 1999).

The growing consensus and continuing analyses and reanalyses unearthed further support, especially for the Cold War period (Oneal and Russett, 1997; Oneal and Ray, 1997), and, when combined with the other elements of the "Kantian peace"—trade and international organizations—suggests that each makes an independent contribution to reduction of conflict, at least for the Cold War years (Russett et al., 1998). Fragmentary evidence also began to resurrect a linkage thought discredited, namely, that democracies in a *monadic* sense fight less than nondemocracies. For some, the relationship was weak and only noted in passing (Morgan and Schwebach, 1992: 319, n. 3), but others, while confirming the strong relationship dyadically, began to unearth monadic effects under certain specific circumstances when investigating the escalation of international crises (Rousseau et al., 1996: 525, 527),[14] and a more directed reanalysis using earlier data-sets covering the 1960s and 1970s with different statistical techniques[15] supported the monadic pacifying effect: democracies were less likely to be involved in international wars than less free states (Benoit, 1996: 654). They also appeared less likely than other states to engage in diversionary behavior (R. Miller, 1999: 394–399). Attempting cross-links between the monadic (national), dyadic, and systemic levels suggested definite confirmation of the pacifying effect dyadically, contradicted the study just noted at the monadic national level (but in doing so recognizes the inflating effect of democracies' tendencies to ally more), and speculated that at the system level over the 1816–1994 period democratization seemed to be associated with increasing violence between states but more recently this relationship had reversed (Gleditsch and Hegre, 1997: 307–308).

The beneficial effects of democracies emerged in alternative periods, empirical domains, and outcome variables. Similar processes were found among the Iroquois nations (Crawford, 1994); democratic states' alliances with each other appeared to be more durable than nondemocracies (Gaubatz, 1996), and crises between democracies appeared to go through fewer "phases," suggesting they are better able to communicate intentions (Eyerman and Hart, 1996). Focusing on "interventions" limited to the short 1974–1988 period confirms that "free" states tend to militarily intervene less than expected in other "free" states, while "not free" intervene in their counterparts much more than expected (Kegley and Hermann, 1995: 11).[16] Even including cultural factors such as ethnic, religious, or linguistic similarities does not appear to dampen the overriding effect of joint democracy (Henderson, 1998: 474–480), which also impacts strongly and positively on dyadic trade (Morrow et al., 1998). One of the few skeptical analyses focused on cooperation as the outcome variable and found that for the Mercosur nations during the 1947–1985 period, democratic pairs of states, while more likely to cooperate than other pairs of states, exhibited a relationship that disappeared when controlling for other variables (joint GDP and trade interdependence) (Remmer, 1998).

At what point continuing statistical regularities becomes solidly convincing evidence is unclear in most fields, but certainly, contrary to the thinking of the previous generation, at some point it became clear that "democracy" might pack some wallop as a crucial causal factor. Although certain patterns suggested in one lengthy review (Chan, 1997: 82–84) have not all been confirmed with multiple independent inquiries, consensus had clearly formed. However, the singular argument that democracies rarely—"if ever"—go to war with each other had unfortunately reached extremes in convoluted manipulations of historical evidence in order to demonstrate that such an event *never* happens (Ray, 1993), including utilization of an exceptionally loose criterion for democracy that manages to squeeze much in under the guidelines (Ray, 1995a: 89–102). For others, the "democratic peace" had become something to be "grasped" (Russett, 1993) as part of a Kantian "tripod for peace" (Russett et al., 1998), and yet others referred to it as the "insignificance" of the liberal peace (Spiro, 1994).

Parts of the acrimony of the debate can be traced back to the first reopening of the issue in the early 1980s, when an unfortunately rigid theoretical stance was established, suggesting that *no* violence can occur between "libertarian" states (Rummel, 1983: 29),[17] a claim later labeled as an "absolute one" (Spiro, 1994: 62), and producing the need to make wars between democracies not only "rare but nonexistent" (Ray, 1993). That narrow absolutism led to the equally narrowly construed question of whether the "zero observation" at times observed in the "wars between democracies" cell of empirical presentations is in fact truly significant (Spiro, 1994); resolving that issue rests on differing statistical models, but the claim did lead to attempts to find exceptions, an interesting exercise.

More systematic critiques suggest that the "democratic peace" may be an artifact of the Cold War, a period when democratic dyads were aligned against a common enemy. Even within this empirical critique, however, the probability of war and low-level disputes between democracies is lower even outside the post-1946 period, during the World War I period (for wars) and the World War II period (for low-level disputes). The relationship also seems to be significant for the lengthy 1817–1913 period (for low-level disputes) (Farber and Gowa, 1995; see tables 2, 3, and 4). (Still, the pattern of democratic dyads engaged in disputes in the nineteenth century might also be a function of two long-term "rivalries" [Britain-France and Britain-U.S.] [Thompson and Tucker, 1997a: 438–439]).[18]

One path of the debate therefore has been the potential Cold War-based time-variant nature of the hypothesis. Another intriguing departure suggests that the dynamic process of *moving toward* democracy seems to be associated with a *greater* probability of war behavior (Mansfield and Snyder, 1995), a finding contradicted by others (Enterline, 1998a; 1998b: 824–825), and one which has been seriously questioned by a contrary finding noting that *any* change is more likely to be related to war (democratizing *or* autocraticizing, compared to stable states) (Thompson and Tucker, 1997a: 443).[19] The bulk of the evidence seems to support the democratization-producing-less-war hypothesis, and a complex design focusing on the amount of polity change and the specific process of transition suggests a more complex picture: the larger the shift toward democratization and the more it involves increased executive constraints—only one aspect of democratization—the less the probability of war for the new regime (Ward and Gleditsch, 1998: 57–59).

Equally troubling to the time-invariance issue and possible reverse causality between democracy and conflict is the one of potential spurious relationships. Numerous studies have noted that alternative variables do not impact the basic relationship, but an intriguing candidate as a background factor for the genesis of democracy itself is a confluence of geopolitics and economic development: "the important influence of environmental factors on the genesis and sustainability of early democracy" should be considered. "Aridity" and "land borders" share a common dimension—"a threatening environment for human populations that can give rise to rigid controls in the form of despotic political organization" (Midlarsky, 1995: 254). Both factors are strongly related to a political rights index, which suggests their important influence in terms of the genesis of democracy. "Geopolitics" and reverse causality also enter in when considering the "zone of peace" notion, the hypothesis that "the diminished probability of certain types of conflict is less a consequence and more an antecedent of the development of democratic states," and that four case studies of Scandinavia, revolutionary France, North America, and Taisho Japan suggest that in France and Japan fledgling democratization processes were suppressed by efforts to attain regional hegemony. In . . . [Scandinavia and North America] democratization was facilitated (and war between democracies made less likely) by situations in which the pursuit of regional hegemony was either exhausted early or constrained by extra-regional circumstances (Thompson, 1996: 142–143).

While perhaps not as alluring as the "democratic peace," and while not calling into question the basic linkage within the spatio-temporal domain of most such studies, it is ironic that traditional geopolitical national attributes, long considered essential but in decline for years, potentially play a plausible and perhaps antecedent role.

Such contextual variables add to the several distinct "waves" that present a singular research thread embellished with extensions, debunking critiques, and resurrections with competing, contending findings—in some ways the classic normal science pattern (Chan, 1997: 85). The diverse products clearly demonstrate the relevance of the "chameleon" factor in terms of what democracy can and cannot explain (Chan, 1997: 66–68), and demonstrated the centrality of the "state" as a defining concept as well as assisted in the resurrection of two of the most traditional of state variables— geopolitics and governmental type. In some ways, the transformation has been total, from 30 years ago, when "democratic peace" results were met with ridicule, to the accepted "law" of the democratic peace 20 years later—in which, some argue, *no* democracies ever go to war with each other and "the final conclusion is that *democracy is a general method of nonviolence*" (Rummel, 1995: 25).

Nonetheless, findings have not been completely uniform, and certain questions do arise. Evaluation of alternative variables seems at times minimized, thus enhancing the role of the democracy share in terms of explained variation.[20] The itch to root out deviant cases contradicting the "no wars among democracies" thesis (Ray, 1993: 271; Russett, 1993: 16–23) appeared inconsistent with the growing elaboration of complex multivariate research designs functioning with an assumed probabilistic basis, and reduces the issue to disputes about specific cases as if the entire structure rides on these (Spiro, 1994: 60–62).[21]

What appear to be quite consistent findings—even if not as strong as the proponents contend—cannot nonetheless assuage certain ponderous thoughts colloquially summed up by the label "it-all-sounds-too-good." The theoretical linkages have a long history and high intuitive plausibility, and the sizable body of large-n empirical results present convincing data, yet enough contrary empirical evidence also exists within the theoretically narrow democratic-peace relationship to nurture at least minimal doubts. This would also seem to be the implicit thrust of certain rebuttals either of a strictly theoretical nature (Gowa, 1995) or those presenting contradictory evidence (Farber and Gowa, 1995; Thompson and Tucker, 1997a; 1997b), especially when doubts injected theoretically contend that the "something else" that might be involved turns on traditional variables such as alliance patterns, "interests," and geopolitics. These would seem, if only implicitly, to be questioning the necessary concatenation of forces whose occurrence seems almost either too good or too ominous. It would seem almost "beyond" idealism to contend that internal myriad structural and normative forces are being discovered as such potent explanations just as the Cold War is winding down, "democracy" seems to be flourishing throughout the world, authoritarian systems are on the wane, a rule-orientation imbedded within regimes seems to be spreading internationally—all working more or less in just the way traditional democratic theory suggests. A central observation is that the groundswell of support for the democratic peace materialized during a transforming era in international relations itself, a very short slice of time including the most recent neoidealist or neoliberal vision of the world, and can be viewed as one factor contributing to that vision. The broader concerns so dominant during the same period about realism dovetail nicely into the growing consensus about the democratic peace.[22]

This raises the challenge of the discovery and explanation of empirical regularities (Thompson, 1996: 171–172). Granting for a moment the accuracy of the empirical regularities, still multiple explanatory variables have been proposed. One analysis suggests the broad categories of the Kantian rationale; interests, norms, and structures; and the rationalist approach (Chan, 1997: 74–82), only one of which embodies the "liberal" argument as generally proposed. If one focuses on elements of the Kantian rationale as well as traditional normative and structural linkages, certainly one finds it incorrect to argue that "there is little about democracy that helps us to deduce why one would never fight with another" (Spiro, 1994: 81). But to date no compelling analysis has suggested which of the many explanations it might be. Beyond the "liberal" thesis is the possibility that

> there is clearly something to the notion that liberal regimes fight to protect (i.e., to spread) the values of democracy and freedom, and this might imply that like nations would ally in the liberal cause (Spiro, 1994: 81).

But "shared norms across nations"—such as through alliances[23]—not only reverts to potentially non-liberal variables but also changes the level of analysis: it is a relational characteristic between two countries and *not* the presence or absence of the attribute characteristics *within* separate countries that produce the expected outcomes (Sullivan, 1976: 120–121). However, "shared norms" would imply that any tabular cell containing dyads "sharing" the same norms—such as autocratic or totalitarian governmental systems—would also contain few entries. Such has occurred (Maoz and Russett, 1992: 253; Hermann and Kegley, 1995: 518; Chan, 1997: 82–83), suggesting a very different proposition than the narrow "democratic peace" hypothesis.

Implications from the liberal view, however, dominate the compelling policy-related connotations about the state implicitly as "cure." But governmental makeup is only one of several distinct attributes that had been isolated a generation ago as worthy of systematic study. No other single variable in the theoretical arsenal has had to bear such a burden, and while the extreme position—democracies never fight one another—has receded somewhat, perhaps its very exposition should be suggestive of a very tendentious and powerful underpinning contained in the original theoretical formulations. It would be naive to assume, moreover, that the recent rebirths and multiple investigations result solely from theoretical reformulations, new data, or different statistical techniques. The rebirth of the "democracy" variable has also patently occurred in an era receptive to it, and in some ways seems to have become a litmus test of views about realism and the role of democracy in the "New World Order." However, there is no assurance that democratic processes are always accompanied by the requisite underpinning of liberalist ideology (Zakaria, 1997), and when the two diverge, policy implications become suspect. More complexity no doubt exists underneath the surface of "democratic operations," some of which may perhaps relate to another time-worn attribute variable that became lost in the shuffle many years ago and that, to some, is "obviously correlated with democracy" (Maoz and Russett, 1992: 262): political instability.

The "Weak" State:
From "Diversions" to Ethno-Nationalism

While the democratic peace genre has dominated the terrain, still just over a decade ago one extensive review declared that *at that time* no other national attribute had probably received as much theoretical and popular attention and yet so *little* support in systematic, empirical research as domestic instability (Levy, 1988a; 1989), a variable as celebrated at one time as "democracy" has been recently. As typically proposed, leaders in trouble focus attention on an external enemy—the classic "internal-external" hypothesis associated with Georg Simmel and refined by Lewis Coser, a hypothesis possessing broad theoretical applicability across several levels of analysis. It rests on the assumption that conflict with an "out-group" is a *defining element* of the "in-group" (Simmel, 1955; Coser, 1956).

The theoretical linkages have taken distinct routes. Conflict with another group may serve to lessen in-group conflict, but that does not necessarily mean internal conflict will drive leaders toward seeking foreign conflict to reduce that domestic unrest. Societies undergoing internal strain may simply respond differently to external situations than societies with basic domestic harmony. Thus, one hypothesis views leaders rationally reacting to their internal problems—an "agency" perspective—while the second implies an explanation not relying on "agency." The theoretical predictions are roughly the same and equally logical, although greater interest has focused on the first, wherein decision-makers actually respond to unrest within societies.

In the contemporary world "domestic unrest" has taken on a new face, and for some may portend an entirely new phenomenon. A "new ethnonationalism" or what some refer to as "ultranationalism" (Gurr, 1994: 361) has emerged, a phenomenon viewed not only as a desire by indigenous groups to claim their perceived rights to "separateness," but also as a factor impinging on international politics. Regardless of the effect of systemic, structural changes on internal ethnopolitical conflict, the phenomenon nonetheless constitutes a process internal to nation-states, often provokes responses by those states, and has been potentially linked with increases in international conflict. While certainly manifesting distinct characteristics compared to traditional "domestic conflict" variables, it generally can be grouped under that broader rubric and poses potential problems for the international system comparable in importance to traditional processes of domestic unrest.

Evidence over the years, however, despite the widespread attraction of the theory, has not been forthcoming in support of the underlying hypothesis (Sullivan, 1976: 121f.). Sorokin claimed to have found no relationship across countries and empires through several centuries (1947: 484), but a reanalysis of his data showed that "internal disturbances" were declining in European countries from the 13th to the 18th century while casualties and army strength were increasing.[24] The first—and classic—contemporary cross-national study concluded that "domestic peace occurs whether or not foreign conflict is present" (Rummel, 1963: 23), and early replications confirmed these results (Tanter, 1966; M. Haas, 1968; Zinnes and Wilkenfeld, 1971), a blow to accepted wisdom. Subsequent analyses, however, found the opposite: moderate support for the original hypothesis (Burrowes and Spector, 1973). Other designs controlled for regional or cultural factors by focusing on a single region (33 African countries) and showed very high correlations between the domestic and foreign dimensions, with nonviolent behaviors being the "best" predicted (negative communications, closing borders, expelling foreigners), and the "best" predictors being actions against the populace as opposed to citizen activity against the government (Collins, 1973).

A longitudinal analysis of China during an important era of its contemporary history suggested that—contrary to conventional wisdom—China's "belligerent" foreign policy may not have been a function of its need to produce domestic harmony, despite anecdotal suggestions in the popular press. For the 1950–1970 period only a very moderate relationship occurred (Onate, 1974), and most interesting was that when lagging domestic and foreign variables against each other, domestic conflict seemed more strongly associated with foreign conflict in *previous* time periods. Others found that foreign conflict seemed overwhelmingly related to *previous* levels of foreign conflict (supporting an internal, organizational process), with one exception: with no foreign or domestic conflict, or medium levels of each, the tendency is to remain at the lower level of foreign conflict. However, when domestic conflict is at a high level, the situation changes:

> When domestic conflict becomes extremely intense it would seem more reasonable to argue that there is a greater likelihood that a state will retreat from its foreign engagements in order to handle the situation at home. Given that a state had been involved in foreign conflict at level two, if the domestic conflict situation reaches level two one would expect an attempt to retreat to at least level one of foreign conflict behavior (Zinnes and Wilkenfeld, 1971: 184).

Still, early results concluded that "domestic conflict in general appears to be only minimally related to foreign conflict behavior" (Wilkenfeld, 1972: 298).

The "diversionary version" of the internal-external hypothesis reemerged within an antirealist framework—domestic politics, it was argued, *does* count—but findings remained mixed and limited mostly to the American political system. For the United States during the 1949–1976 period, domestic factors measured by popularity and "misery," indices related to "use of force" (Ostrom and Job, 1986). A more extensive replication suggested that an international indicator of severity[25] proved predictive of the U.S. use of force in addition to three domestic factors (presidential popularity, presidential success, and a weighted "misery" index) (James and Oneal, 1991: 323–327). Within the shorter time frame of 1953–1976, the United States "has been more prone to initiate aggressive foreign policy actions when the president was faced with a loss of support among his partisans" (Morgan and Bickers, 1992: 49). A "modified version" of the diversionary notion "captures the dynamic leading from domestic political problems to foreign conflict better than have previous versions of the theory" but the relationship only applies to relatively low-level uses of force as the outcome variable (Morgan and Bickers, 1992: 49). The results contradict the earlier internal-external findings, but seem to confirm others that find economic decline and international conflict related with specific time lags when including type of government and internal repression as controls (Russett, 1990).

Discounting low-intensity/low-risk uses of force for the 1945–1984 period, there becomes only "an indirect linkage between the economy, Presidential approval, and the uses of force" (DeRouen, 1995: 683 and 689). Others are even more dubious. In one case, the effect of presidential popularity, electoral period, and the misery index was considered "overstated" (Meernik, 1994: 136). Later findings suggest that for an outcome variable specifically defined as "the opportunity to use military force" (Meernik and Waterman, 1996: 581) for the 1953–1988 period, only the "misery index" emerges as an important domestic predictor; no domestic variables appear as predictors to "moderate use" of force during international crises, and only "partisan popularity" is weakly related to the yearly frequency of international crises (Meernik and Waterman, 1996: 582–583, 586). For decision-making within a crisis, "domestic political factors such as the electoral cycle, economic difficulties, and presidential support in Congress affect crisis decision making" (Wang, 1996: 92). American presidents for the 1954–1986 period select more intense responses

> when the economy is doing badly, when they are in the later states of the electoral cycle, and when their general support in Congress, at least in terms of party membership, is high (Wang, 1996: 92).

The outcome variable of the *number* of major uses of force by the American president between 1949 and 1994 seems to be proportional to high unemployment, strong investor confidence, wartime presidential election years, and the absence of ongoing wars; a relationship which is mitigated by the Vietnam War experience (Fordham, 1998b), and an activity apparently more attractive for Republican presidents when unemployment is high and for Democrats when inflation is high (Fordham, 1998a). However, for longer periods of time, 1870–1992, U.S. recourse to force was unrelated to domestic factors (Gowa, 1998), but U.S. intervention had an apparent positive impact on democracy if under the auspices of that intervention the United States promoted free and fair elections (Peceny, 1999).

Relationships clearly depend on the type of and—in some cases—the specific measure of the outcome variable. The same complexities found at the domestic level for American politics, with similar caveats, hold cross-nationally. For 18 advanced industrial democracies, 1952–1988, no pattern exists to either initiate more disputes or show or use force more often during times of poor economic performance or when elections are approaching. In fact, the intriguing suggestion is made that during such times *other* nations might in fact tend to make fewer demands on those countries (Leeds and Davis, 1997: 831–832). This receives some confirmation for 830 militarized disputes from 1820–1992: democratic leaders especially appear not particularly prone to engage in diversionary behavior (R. Miller, 1999: 399). Likewise, intervention in international crises seems less likely in situations where leaders are likely to *win* an upcoming election—a "positive" domestic situation, where presumably the opposite, a projected loss, would be related to intervention (Huth, 1998: 765).[26] Contrary to most results, cross-sectional findings on the use of force in 180 international crises during the Cold War suggests that the "diversionary initiation of force" is in fact "generally a pathology of democratic states" (Gelpi, 1997b: 277): democracies were more likely to initiate force under conditions of domestic unrest, findings that restrict at least the monadic version of the "democratic peace" (Gelpi, 1997b: 278–279).

In sum, four decades of research has produced remarkably disparate results on a central formulation. Perhaps it is deficient theory, "a classic example of the futility of rigorous empirical research that is not guided by adequate theorizing" (Levy, 1988a: 670). Over a decade ago the problem was summarized succinctly:

> Although most of these studies refer explicitly to the scapegoat hypothesis based on group cohesion theory and present their empirical studies as a means of testing that hypothesis,

they fail to recognize that the scapegoat hypothesis or diversionary theory of war is not the same as the relationship between internal and external conflict. Consequently, operational models of domestic-foreign conflict linkages are often not congruent with the hypothesized theoretical relationships supposedly being tested (Levy, 1989: 283).

In addition, many particular methodological critiques plagued this area (Levy, 1989: 265–266, 268, 273).

Conventional theory prior to the systematic wave—even when bolstered by compelling illustrations—was also deficient for not denoting specific variables and their potentially convoluted interactions. Empirical studies testing the hypotheses remedied that weakness but still failed to uncover the relations as broadly spelled out in conventional theory. However, lackluster empirical findings appear so only if expectations are extremely high; in fact, the broadly based and mainly negative generalized conclusions from early attempts actually hid statistical correlations of, admittedly, very moderate proportions, and more recent evidence suggests scattered evidence of a positive nature. Ironically, consistent *failure* to unearth strong and widespread links between internal and external phenomena could be seen as supporting those who contest the realpolitik view of single, unitary decision-makers calculatedly utilizing internal troubles to foment foreign conflict, an implication apparently lost on critics. Such a strong link could reconfirm the existence of and—in the process—continue to "reconstitute" the state as an objective entity. The *failure* to find such systematic relationships would suggest that other, nonrealpolitik factors operate.

The "new nationalisms" of the last decades of the twentieth century may change all of this, of course, and produce novel depictions concerning the externalization of internal conflict. Nonetheless, the research over the past 40 years has raised doubts about traditionally potent explanations for foreign conflict behavior, even though recent findings have unearthed some positive relationships cast within the more broadly defined "diversionary" theory. Whether empirical studies will demonstrate that "new nationalisms" exert a different or more clearly systematic effect on external relations is unclear. Certain evidence does point to the impact of nationalist and ethnic factors on war, but in one extensive analysis they tended toward the "low impact" side (K. Holsti, 1991),[27] and in another, ethnic, cultural, and religious elements, while related to war and conflict-relevant behavior, were not necessarily of recent vintage (Henderson, 1997: 664–666).[28] New nationalisms have been linked to the "breakdown" of nation-state types, but certainly decolonization itself appears to have exhibited cyclical as well as secular trends (Strang, 1991: 443–444), suggesting that the "processes producing decolonization are primarily external rather than internal to the dependency" (Strang, 1991: 429). While the intensity of foreign policy crises seems to be related to the presence of an "irredentist element" (Carment and James, 1995: 103), irredentist strife itself has been associated with international "system transition" (Carment and James, 1995: 85). The evidence is not yet clear that recent phenomena claimed as novel for the 1990s have either new effects or permanency.

In sum, the multiple domestic factors enumerated under the "unrest" dimension do not appear to exert systematic influence beyond the confines of the nation-state—raising again the question of whether those "confines" remain "constitutive" of reality. This conclusion in turn raises the issue of the degree to which a factor thought central to the realist approach and which has received much attention because of its alleged demise—nation-state borders—continues to assert any influence.

Realpolitik Redux: Borders

Any truly realpolitik model should include borders—"the essence of geopolitical analysis is the relation of international power to the geopolitical setting" (S. Cohen, 1963: 24)—and yet it has recorded remarkably little continuing systematic attention. Beyond the confines of diplomatic history and with the exceptions of Quincy Wright's and Lewis Richardson's early investigations, and several more recently, borders have in fact been ignored by many—realists included. Despite assertions that realism reigned throughout the Cold War period, the focus on borders plummeted to such a degree that it became one of several variables—like the "state" itself—that had to be brought "back in" to the study of international relations (Starr, 1991b: 1; O'Loughlin and Anselin, 1991: 29).

Subsequent empirical work treated geography as a general facilitating "condition" or direct "source of conflict" (Diehl, 1991), or as a "treatment" or opportunity (Siverson and Starr, 1991). Straightforward, rather obvious findings emerge for geography as a general condition: borders clearly serve as "sources of conflict," providing for disputes over their configuration (Diehl and Goertz, 1988: 120). A "propensity for territorial change(s)" tends to "prompt future conflict between the same states" (Diehl, 1991: 23); geographically contiguous nations seem to be more crisis-prone (Brecher and Wilkenfeld, 1997: 769–773); and a large number of wars seem to occur in "shatterbelts" (Kelly, 1986), regions "whose internal, geographical, cultural, religious and political fragmentation is compounded by pressures from external major powers attracted by the region's strategic location and economic resources" (S. Cohen, 1982: 226, cited in Diehl, 1991: 23).

Results have been rather consistent especially with respect to the outcome of war. Richardson unearthed links between the number of borders and the number of external wars (L. Richardson, 1960: 176–183). An expanded data-set distinguishing between six different types of borders (Starr and Most, 1976: 588–595) produced respectable correlations for the 1946–1965 period and for various subperiods during those 20 years (Starr and Most, 1976: 607; Starr and Most, 1978: 451, 456), and groups with high "border scores" exhibiting higher levels of war behavior (Starr and Most, 1978: 453–454). While the later evidence suggested less uniform support for Richardson's general finding of "more borders lead to more wars," evidence did support the argument that "more homeland borders tend to lead to less war, and that more colonial borders tend to lead to more war" (Starr and Most, 1978: 461).

The data seem both compelling and obvious, perhaps producing the lack of interest in borders in the contemporary world. But clearly a state's borders proves to be a powerful attribute, increasing significantly both the probability that wars occur more for the possessor and that those states with many borders will join ongoing wars: "Both bordering states that were at war and alliance partners that were at war increased the probability that states at peace would become war participants" (Siverson and Starr, 1991: 93). Moreover, borders in conjunction with alliances are more potent than either singly. Further specifications suggest that distinctions be made between diffusion effects *across space* from those *across time*: "over and above the interactive effects found . . . alliances had a greater impact on the spatial dimension of diffusion while borders had a greater impact on the time element." In terms of the original decision to join wars, alliances ("willingness") seemed to have the greatest effect, whereas borders ("opportunity") seemed to have the greater effect on the timing of entry into an ongoing war (Siverson and Starr, 1991: 93).

Outside of the diffusion context, an extensive dyadic analysis showed that contiguous dyads (1816–1965) had a 35 times greater chance of war than noncontiguous dyads, and when evaluated against six other variables, contiguity placed first in terms of predictive capacity for war (Bremer, 1992: 327). It did not account for the "relative lack" of conflict between democratic states (Maoz and Russett, 1992: 261–262), but retreating further back in the causal chain, an intriguing investigation shows that the number of sea borders is not only strongly related to a standard political rights index thought to measure democracy, but the relationship also retains its strength when compared to other independent variables (Midlarsky, 1995: 243–244; 247–248). Contiguity has also been found related to whether nations allow disputes to be referred to arbitration and whether that arbitration be binding or not (Raymond, 1994: 34–35), and whether enduring rivalries go to war: when noncontiguous rivals do go to war, it is usually when they join an ongoing war (Vasquez, 1996: 541–553).

The evidence confirms that borders are clearly important and that certain patterns are systematic, yet the conventional wisdom tells us borders are breaking down, and are not in fact as rigid as the traditional geopolitical "border" reality suggests. In fact, states defined by their borders are really nothing more than "organizing devices"—useful for distinguishing between people, territory, ideas, and religions. Borders themselves only reflect or facilitate that organizing principle. Whether that is good or bad is beside the point—the reality is that is what people do, not only between nations but between all manner and sorts of groups. It is, in other words, the most routine—but not trivial—of human traits. A derivation on this theme impacts on the border-war relationship, in which borders may not serve as truly "independent variables," but rather should be viewed "instead as an expression of social and political realities," and by doing so borders do act not so much as the cause of things like wars but rather: "they do not even, in themselves, increase the likelihood of conflict, rather a border simply signals the existence of previous conflicts" (Kirby and Ward, 1987: 308).

As with all such devices, they are not perpetual; any division scheme will, and periodically does, break down. At those points, new perceptions of the boundaries occur, and we have a shifting of nationalisms. From one perspective, these "new nationalisms" are nothing more than a rearrangement, a new organizing device, and the strengths of these new divisions—or organizing devices—as well as their historical continuity, is likewise not going to be perpetual. The historical record suggests that the process of in-grouping and out-grouping "variation" will continue, with the greatest "variation" across traditional nation-states and the lesser variation "within." Once that pattern shifts, of course, then the traditional organizing lines are indeed breaking down and what constitutes an "in-" and an "out-" group is truly changing. Whether the systematic patterns already uncovered based on traditional boundary lines will change merely because the lines themselves move is not necessarily a foregone conclusion.

Nonetheless, "borders" suggest a finality and certitude about them; in a sense, that is—as noted above—their function. But the historical evidence contradicts that: borders change and those changes have meaning. In fact, the very modern era—defined narrowly as post-1989—has probably witnessed as many border changes as any other comparable period of history. Perhaps the "new nationalisms" are as much a result of border fluctuations as they are of ideological leanings. But as perceptions of borders change, international norms change, and perceptions of the nation, the state, and the relationship between the two also change (Barkin and Cronin, 1994). All of this suggests intense flux, but two facts remain: first, borders still exist, are recognized as facts, therefore constituting a real-world national attribute—for good or for evil; second, continuing evidence suggests that that solitary attribute has emerged as an extremely important predictor toward, but not limited to, warlike behavior.

Conclusion

The debate over state attributes has evolved into a broad reinvestigation touching upon the role, position, and even the existence of the "nation-state" itself, casting it within the broader debates over larger paradigms. Waltz himself laid down the gauntlet:

> It is not possible to understand world politics simply by looking inside of states. If the aims, policies, and actions of states become matters of exclusive attention or even of central concern, then we are forced back to the descriptive level; and from simple descriptions no valid generalizations can logically be drawn (Waltz, 1979: 65).

A critique certainly meant to apply to foreign policy studies, and more concerned about chasing after the chimera of a general, broad theory, it did not have much validity beyond that sterile quest, especially with regard to systematic attribute studies, which are far from idiosyncratic "descriptions." But the broader issue—especially in the post–Cold War world—has become the very existence, relevance, and makeup of the units being studied—the "nation-states." But bypassing that broader issue for the moment, one point stands repetition: long-held seemingly simple and theoretically obvious beliefs about the linkages between nations' attributes and external behavior that had remained as accepted truth for such a long time have not been broadly confirmed with systematic research. While Waltz was not dead wrong—looking inside states is productive—the relationships are more complex.

Economic development (wealth), size, political stability, and type of government were at one point the dominant influences in the theoretical literature, usually in that descending order. The first two remain the strongest influences across much international behavior, and have received empirical support, so much so that they now serve mostly as background or intervening variables. Nonetheless, while large and developed states have contributed their share of tragedy to the world community, in terms of total output they also tend to be proportionally more cooperative than smaller, less-developed states.

However, a *generalized, broadly supported* link between internal conflict and foreign policy still remains without systematic empirical support; despite conventional wisdom, it remains suspect as a *broad-based* explanation of international behavior. Critiques (Levy, 1988; 1989) provided plausible reasons for much of the failure to find broad relationships, and the reinvigoration of the agenda in the more general "diversionary" model, while unfortunately limited in terms of empirical and geographic scope, nonetheless has suggested some evidence of linkages. But certainly in terms of broad, solidly consistent significant empirical findings, generally speaking conventional wisdom has stumbled.

The situation, however, is not such with type of political system. A generation ago it was concluded that "the role of the political system has not been as extensively researched as either size and wealth or internal conflict," and yet the "evidence that does exist lends credence to the argument of democratic theorists who see 'good' flowing from open, democratic systems" (Sullivan, 1976: 136). Such a conclusion places more recent effervescent judgments about the role and efficacy of democracy in a broader historical context.

To be sure, earlier evidence was only grudging and limited, while more recently a different era witnessed the same finding take hold with such tenacity that it became for some a law and a rallying point about the entire future of international relations. If as powerful as some advocates maintain, the hypothesis not only calls into question Waltz's denigration of domestic factors, but also holds the promise for world peace in its hands. Even within the complexity of contextual systemic factors to be noted in a later chapter, the democracy-and-war findings are often used to illustrate what appear to be implications so straightforward that the contextual complexities disappear:

> Focusing solely on the tripolar structure of the emerging post–Cold War system, one is tempted to predict increasing systemic instability, possibly culminating in general major-power war . . . however, the huge increase in the number of democratic states, and the fact that, unlike the interwar system, all three poles of the post–Cold War system will be democracies, should greatly mitigate the destabilizing effects associated with its volatile tripolar structure (Schweller, 1993: 99–100).

The extraordinary serendipitous results for the "flowering" of democracy unravel just a bit when one investigates the findings as a totality, goes beyond the specific claims of single pieces, or even draws many of those claims together. The empirical findings mostly apply to a relatively short, and recent, time period. Imperial activities of democracies are virtually ignored, and the strength of the findings derives in some cases from a tortuous process of elimination of "deviant cases" (M. Elman, 1999: 102–103). Other methodological questions have been raised about several of the more impressive findings (Ray, 1995a: 34),[29] and alternative explanatory variables tested to see if they can *discount* the impact of democracy are not as weak a set of explanations as certain adherents contend. Finally, normative expectations also would be one of the normal suspects rounded up in terms of the perceived consistent results within the democratic-peace research agenda:

> I am not confident that all the current conflicts involving democratic and quasi-democratic states will be resolved peacefully. I am confident that if and when one of these conflicts does escalate to war, defenders of the democratic peace proposition will be quick to insist that one or both of the participants are not "really" democratic states. I will probably be among them (Ray, 1995a: 212).

The "democratic peace" constitutes a "normal science" research agenda, but its popularity may also rest in its consistency and kinship with corresponding formulations comprising an optimistic neoidealism, itself conceivably part of a passing preoccupation, or even fad.[30] Regardless, the national attribute of "type" of political system, most recently the specific "type" of choice is "democracy," emerges as a consistently important but also changeable entity, the one attribute having unquestionably witnessed a major metamorphosis. As such, other attributes are taking a secondary position in recent times, and the type of government is enduring. Challenges to the standard, traditional attributes over the years have included "state of mind" (Burrowes and Spector, 1973: 316), and "density" or "crowding" of nations (Bremer et al., 1973), and while some attain short-term popularity, they have rarely endured. The concept of "role," conceptualized theoretically as a relevant factor a generation ago (K. Holsti, 1970), was then expanded to role-taking by nations specifically within the United Nations (Volgy and Quistgard, 1975). But the role categories as originally proposed were enormously unwieldy in number (K. Holsti, 1970: 260–273), and when related to actual foreign policy produced results reminiscent of patterns found with attributes more readily measured: the more active nations possess a larger number and organization of role conceptions (K. Holsti, 1970: 283, 288); nations with leaders projecting "dominant" roles are more active in international affairs; those with roles displaying competition or "high policy" are more likely to exhibit hostile behavior (Wish, 1980: 544–549).

One popular contender already noted in the contemporary era is "ethnonationalism," an emerging force potentially capable of countering traditional state constructs and power. Historically, however, the state has proven to be a resilient entity. The admonition to contemporary theorists—"they would do well to abandon the notion that the state is the state is the state. The national state that emerged in 1900 was a fundamentally different entity from its predecessor" (Thomson, 1994: 149)—is relevant but not necessarily meant to suggest the impending demise of the state. In Thomson's analysis of an earlier era the delegitimation of non-state violence was carried out not by domestic political actors but by system-level statesmen (Thomson, 1994: 105). Even though the state may have been reluctant to exert authority and control over non-state violence, those actions were the result of unintended consequences of a series of ad hoc actions by various states (Thomson, 1994: 143, 145). And even though sovereignty is very far from a "fixed" entity (Thomson, 1994: 151), this is not equivalent to claiming the end of the state or its power, but rather its shifting character and role in world politics.

Dealing systematically with state transformation proves difficult when assessing issues such as "state capacity" in the political economy dimensions of the contemporary era, even when applied to a limited dependent variable—reaction to embargoes (Ikenberry, 1986: 137). But economic behaviors such as embargoes, while important, may not necessarily require novel predictors. Fascinating case studies of telecoms, insurance companies, international crime syndicates, and other new actors may illustrate that states can no longer make the exceptional claims they once did, and that they are just one source of authority (Strange, 1996: 73). But the question now is how much of that change is perception rather than actuality: perhaps states have never had the supreme power and authority conferred upon them by "decline-of-the-state" critiques (Krasner, 1999).

Nonetheless, the reemergence of nationalism and the incorporation of ethnicity and ethnonationalism under that umbrella seem capable on the surface of tearing apart the neat conceptual schemes that had come to dominate traditional paradigms, raising questions about whether states are enduring entities or in the process of receding, whether they can make the claims and demands they once did, or are merely one more actor (Strange, 1996: 73). Is the nation-state and the paradigmatic system that goes with it facing extinction just as the paradigm was becoming empirically grounded? The emergence of relatively strong findings concerning democracy and the significance of borders suggests that traditional distinctions for nation-states appear to have much staying power; the intuitive "feel" of alternative attributes has failed to translate into consistent, systematic research, and the nation-state, for good or for evil, is a resilient entity. The specific attributes of note describing states may be shifting from "political" to "economic" modes, but they may be describing the same basic unit.

With respect to policy, extant research some time ago indicated that large, developed countries, providing most of the funding for international organizations, tended to be the most negative about the role of international organizations (IOs) (Sullivan, 1976: 140). After the People's Republic of China was admitted to the United Nations in late 1971, the United States seriously considered reducing the size of its future UN contribution. This specific issue of funding has continued into the 1990s, with relations between the United States and the UN at times worse even than during the 1980s (Miller, 1999: A6). Problems concerning the UN Law of the Sea Conference (UNCLOS), as well as the continuing funding quandaries, confirmed that the UN was to be persistently hobbled, despite the popularity of the short-lived UN coalition against Iraq in 1990 and Libya in 1992. The precarious relationship between the developed nations and the UN continues at century's end.

Recent interest in policy implications drawn from the "liberal peace" has mostly been positive in nature. Such implications have some history, although not nearly as popular as in recent times: preliminary findings years ago showed "rather consistently . . . open democratic systems to be more cooperative and less conflictual" (Sullivan, 1976: 140). The policy advice proposed then used a slightly different construction compared to the currently fashionable form, suggesting that "the support that countries such as the United States give to small, closed systems may in the long run be one factor adding to international tension" (Sullivan, 1976: 140).[31] Postdictions, especially of a point-specific nature, risk being superficial, but the case study cited in the last chapter concerning the United States' relations with Iraq during the 1980s constitutes the archetypical illustration of the above prediction: the United States for ten years supported a small, closed, autocratic nation only to have it disrupt the entire international system in 1990 resulting in a war and tension continuing for at least a decade. Needless to say, opinions concerning democracy in "policy" statements were not at all dominant a generation ago—unlike the very changed atmosphere of the 1990s.

Research has not only extended the empirical findings, but also grounded the policy implications, making them ultimately more controversial—because the operative causal factors are still disputed. The broadest concern with respect to policy advice revolves around whether the more realist (state "interests" and alliances [Farber and Gowa, 1995; Thompson and Tucker, 1997a, 1997b]) or liberalist factors (norms, internal structures, and normative orientations [Russett, 1993; Dixon, 1993; Russett, et al., 1998]) ultimately hold sway. For the former, traditional precepts prevail: "Building bridges may serve U.S. interests far better than building polities abroad" (Farber and Gowa, 1997: 456). Within the latter, both "culture" and "structure" suggest generally similar paths: a world of democracies should be peaceful, which provides an incentive to create such a world and

> increases the price we are willing to pay to accomplish this end . . . many proponents . . . advocate, or justify, particular policies (including the use of force) on the grounds that they will spread democracy and ultimately lead to a more peaceful world (Morgan and Schwebach, 1992: 309).

Still, some "dismiss the political culture argument on the grounds that democratic states have shown no disinclination to use force against nondemocratic states" (Ray, 1995a: 30, citing Bueno de Mesquita and Lalman, 1992). More broadly, despite impressive statistical findings, there is little to suggest that the "political culture" alleged to exist in democracies makes individuals within those political units any less willing to use brutal force, as has occurred on many occasions (M. Haas, 1995; Chan, 1997: 83). And if it is the case that nondemocracies also face decisional constraints, it may be "the *level of decisional constraints* on national leaders and *not* regime type or democracy that has a pacifying impact" (Ray, 1995a: 32; emphasis in original). Such results would affect "policy decisions regarding, for example, how much support to give to democratic factions within other countries or how willing we should be to fight for the spread of democracy" (Morgan and Schwebach, 1992: 309).[32]

Policy-related conclusions, more often cryptic and implicit as opposed to obviously explicit, do not come unfettered. If interests, alliances, and geography are not the operative variables, then regardless of whether one holds with the "culture" or "structure" thesis, implications still assume that in a systematic way the positive benefits from democratic cultures and structures in fact work themselves through all the many individual, organizational, and decision-making layers operative in the real world. Positive, morally uplifting liberal processes such as compromise, "bounded competition," and the effect of accountability (Sullivan, 1976: 117; Dixon, 1993: 43; Dixon, 1994: 15–16) implied within the "democratic peace" hypotheses must wend their way through many levels of domestic political processes, organizational restraints and influences, as well as human diversities, and do so across a large number of cases across many years in order to become finalized in the ultimate outcome—multiple and widespread joint foreign policy actions producing the "democratic peace."[33]

The implication beyond all the correlations and an unwritten common theme in the genre is that democracies are "better," and at that point the scientific positivist posture desists. The extreme contrary case argues that "the claim that democracies do not fight one another is not about democracies *per se*"; rather,

> it is better understood as a claim about peace among countries conforming to a subjective ideal that is cast, not surprisingly, in America's self-image. Democracy is "our kind," and the coding rules by which it is defined are but the unconscious representations of current American Political values (Oren, 1996: 294).

An underlying sense of "fair play and the rule of law"—compromise and bounded competition—underlies much of the democratic peace agenda, as it does the broader mood of neoidealism; while the focus in the scientific products has been in some cases on detailed and systematic critiques calling into question certain theoretical or research design flaws, fewer have noted that instances abound even in the very recent, contemporary era (post-1950) where democracies in fact have engaged in absolutely horrific behavior (Haas, 1995). To answer, "still, they 'don't go to war' with each other," may be technically correct but highlights even further the limited slice of international relations—the outcome variable—the literature has tended to cover. Despite the defense by some (Huntington, 1982), it was not too long prior to the popularity of the "democratic peace" that one thrust of U. S. foreign policy, implicitly or explicitly, involved suppressing democracy and democratic movements in other countries. If democracies normatively are seen to prevent or militate against war, then why does one find so often in the actual inner workings—the messy decision-making of the previous chapter—of the principal "democracy" in the world, so many policy decisions the end result of which was to wittingly or unwittingly suppress democracy, sometimes with massive force?[34] Investigation of inner counsels within democracies might unearth discussions with an underlying tone very much different from those presumed to be taking place by segments of the democratic peace literature. If the divergence between liberalist ideology and outward democratic practices can be seen in certain "emerging" democracies (Zakaria, 1997), no reason exists why similar processes might not operate at times in "developed" democracies.

Nonetheless, until just recently a broad consensus viewed the attribute of democracy as the wave of the future. Certainly compared to its position less than a generation earlier, when it was relegated to the farthest corners of the discipline, ignored and even scoffed at, the promise of democracy for some has become the most recent panacea. In such movements, of course, always lurks the danger of a new crusade:

> as democracies search for the means of preserving peace in the next millennium, there thus is ample reason for them to take seriously the proposition that the diffusion of democratic governance can allow democracies to use intervention to contain violence rather than to wage war (Kegley and Hermann, 1995: 15–16).

The focus on nation-state attributes may seem anomalous at a time when that traditional creature seems under assault from so many quarters, and perhaps doubly ironic that the breakdown of the state theme fashionable in certain niches of the neoliberalist's terrain should appear to be in direct contrast to other junctures of that domain—the democratic peace—which seems to necessitate constructions that clearly distinguish democratic from nondemocratic state systems.[35] Despite antagonism toward states for all the evil they do produce, the empirical fact remains—as noted several times—that most of international politics continues to operate *as if* nation-states still exist as entities, are important, and possess substantial enduring attributes. As long as that remains the case, then the operative behavior in international politics can be analyzed with states taken as a given. *Which* attributes are the most important in a direct sense and which may serve merely as ambiguous background factors may still be disputed, but certainly at a time—the mid-1990s—when one nation in the system was able single-handedly and against enormous voting odds to oust the secretary general of the United Nations, preclude major agreements at an international environmental conference in Kyoto, and forestall a key nuclear test ban treaty,[36] it would certainly be well to consider the background variables of size and power as retaining a high level of—admittedly, perhaps inexact—importance. While the major focus has been on the fashionable democracy attribute, other traditional background factors, and their dynamic changes, may ultimately play as important a role. But a mystical aura seems to have descended concerning the focus on "democracy" and its effect, and despite some evidence suggesting transitions *to* democracy can lead to greater conflict, there seems to exist a broader, assumed, foregone conclusion that movement *toward* democracy itself constitutes an inexorable mechanism, involving an assumed linear progression, with rarely a thought given until recently to the possibility of reversion or consideration of the possibility that states might regress toward "undemocratic" status (Mearsheimer, 1990: 50; Ray, 1995a: 204; Zakaria, 1997). Attribute studies appear by and large to support the liberal peace linkages. Yet not entertained is the possibility that the key variables in the next generation may be those thought a generation ago to be unmoving, but which in the interim have been the most observably changing: wealth, size, and population. Combine these with the attribute of political stability, fused in some analyses with democracy, and perhaps embodied in new processes of ethnonationalism, and the focus on the state, which some see as having entered a new theoretical as well as empirical era, may prove more vigorous than many have thought.

Chapter Five ❀

Systems: Chaos and Anarchy, or Organized Complexity?

How Does It All Work?

Thomas Schelling once wrote, "if you are in a mood to be amazed, it can amaze you that the system works at all" (Schelling, 1978: 21). Schelling was of course ruminating about social behavior within market settings: "all of the activities seem to get coordinated," he noted; there's a taxi to get you to the airport, food on the plane (including "decaf" if you prefer); refineries to make the fuel, cement for the runways, electricity for the elevators; "and, most important of all, passengers who want to fly where the airplanes are going" (Schelling, 1978: 20). All is not rosy, of course: "there is never a taxi when you need one in the rain, or . . . you can fly 3,000 miles more comfortably than you can fly 300, and flights are occasionally overbooked." And the system can break down: holidays happen with regularity with their predictable disasters, and unions have been known to go on strike. But nonetheless, even though to the observer waiting in the terminal Dallas–Forth Worth, JFK, Orly, or Narita may appear to be entirely chaotic and "turbulent," if one wishes, one can be truly amazed, for those "systems" do work.

The conventional view of daily international politics is not unlike the view of the impatient passenger waiting at Gate D48 at Dallas—everything seems random, chaotic, unpredictable, on the surface the opposite of the world Schelling was so amazed with. Troops are abruptly mobilized without apparent warning and—it seems—appropriate justification. Two old foes are suddenly toasting each other in an ancient, decorated conference hall. Rifts, crises, and confrontations seem to erupt suddenly. New "detentes"—or tensions—leave the lay person whirling. Perhaps no other single event in contemporary times more epitomizes such a view than the American President's visit to China in 1972, an event that "suddenly"—or so it seemed—rearranged the world's political map. And less than two decades later, after 40 years of what seemed to be an interminable and unending but nonetheless *known* and familiar "Cold War," suddenly in the short time-span of 26 months the Eastern European communist regimes overthrew their rulers; the Berlin Wall was destroyed; East and West Germany were reunited; and finally, in December, 1991, the Soviet Union expired, the Cold War was declared "over," with the West the winner and Ronald Reagan the hero. Just over a half decade after those events, the long-heralded economic "Asian miracle" was teetering on the verge of disaster, one of the economic bulwarks of Asia—Malaysia—was in the throes of revolution, and the U.S. and China were in an on-again, off-again crisis mode reminiscent of the 1950s.

For many, the ending of the Cold War and the sudden reversal of both economic and political fortunes in Asia were like the chaotic and unpredictable view from Gate D48, confirming the belief that international relations are truly "turbulent." But though it does all look hopelessly complicated from that standpoint, nonetheless international politics—as Schelling noted—"works." Much of the contemporary controversy lies in determining what picture or "system" most accurately describes those turbulent "workings." "Complexity" and "chaos theory" have taken hold in some quarters in recent years, with the colorful image of that ubiquitous little butterfly flapping its wings over the South Pacific, and—through long, complex causal processes—having a hand in causing a tornado over Kansas six months later. But while everyone knows the butterfly has little direct effect on the tornado, the question still remains: How can random-appearing, perhaps "turbulent" events (Rosenau, 1990) be understood? Everyone also knows that we are not dealing with truly chaotic or anarchical phenomena, and the only truly interesting questions concern which organizing devices are the most personally appealing while at the same time most conceptually and empirically accurate. Finally, of course, the purpose for which a system is constructed will dictate its format and style.

But instead of being amazed at the fact that the system—international relations—"works" at all, the panoply of systems or organizing devices that have been proposed to understand these "workings" has of course produced the expected battles concerning, first, whether it is possible to put order into all the seeming chaos, and second, which might be the most productive picture to capture the apparent diversity. The controversies among protagonists of different systems can derive as often from ideological sympathies as they might from disputes about empirical reality.

Thus, thinking in systems terms has a long, controversial, and yet productive history beginning in a formal fashion with General Systems Theory in the 1950s and making a comeback again in a somewhat formalized way 40 years later (Snyder and Jervis, 1993). But throughout the period self-conscious efforts to exploit the "systems" perspective for international analysis have continued, constituting an integral part of the enterprise, as it would of any theoretically disposed discipline. The only valid issue, as already noted, is not whether "systems" exist, but rather the most fruitful means to conceptualize them as manifested in international politics, or *which* systems apparatus or perspective is the most useful for which specific research question, raising again the specter of the chameleon. The variety of system apparati is rivaled only by the diversity of the subject.

What should emerge from this and subsequent chapters is that just as Richard Nixon once said, "We are all Keynsians now," so also we find that much of contemporary theorizing revolves in one way or another around debates concerning the appropriate "systems" of analysis. While true that the 1950s witnessed the first attempts to use "systems" analysis in an explicit, self-conscious way, and the focus on formally defined systems in a vacuum certainly held sway for a period of time, in fact most analysts exploit—in one way or another—some form of systems armor, one that many see as undergoing a resurgence in the 1990s (Snyder and Jervis, 1993). Despite attacks throughout the past half century,[1] its utility has been quietly under development and expansion since those early days of the 1950s.

Within the context of systems strategies popularized 40 years ago, it is true that no consensus as "to what constitutes the fundamental 'structure' of that system or its subsystems, or what lies behind change within it" ever existed (Ferguson and Mansbach,

1988: 197). But within that critique was one of the fundamental errors of early attempts: the assumption that using a "systems" strategy implies a single, specific, given international system, which fails to see the possibility—which theoretical formulations since have amply provided—of a wide variety of different pictures of the international system and therefore the possibility of a wide variety of "international systems" that might exist. These multiple systems might exist coincident with each other, or theoretically be in contention with one another, but the latter does not have to be the only option. To critique the systems perspective for not presenting an agreed-upon view of what *the* international system consists of fails to recognize the possibility of going beyond *competing* system structures to a picture that admits the diversity of numerous international systems, many of them operating at the same time, perhaps at different levels, maybe even imbedded or nested within one another. Obviously such a suggestion is in contradistinction to and goes beyond the notion of a "single" logic encompassing the interstate and world capitalist systems (Chase-Dunn, 1981).

There was, however, indeed a time when a vapid, simplistic view of "systems analysis" did impose its way into theories of international relations, developed a following, and then met its critics. While providing a framework for some useful descriptions, abstract models, and as a "gloss for some highly inductive work," nonetheless it was an accurate critique to note that "systems analysis" "has not yet generated any impressive lawlike assertions pertinent to international politics" (Young, 1978: 241). Such critiques, although certainly premature, in a sense hit the mark, but did not recognize that many standard, traditional, historically grounded works were also fashioned on a form of systems analysis. Manifestations of newer analyses—such as regimes, for instance, or later "globalization" or even allusions to the emergence of "collective identity" (Wendt, 1994b), possess clear, systemic components because systemic properties cover a broad panoply of specific theoretical approaches. Critiques limited to the most general and formalized or stylized metatheoretical views of "systems analysis," ones so general that they fail to apply to any useful specific conceptualizations of international politics, were correct. But much has happened in the intervening period, and suddenly, as we have noted, "everyone is a systems analyst."

Stimulating advances in the multiple fashions in which international systems can be conceptualized have occurred, and the following sections paint a selective picture of the modes of thought felt to be most productive over the past 40 years from the *consciously* systemic perspective, a history of contemporary theorizing through the development of respective systemic approaches. An inherent problem remains in all such attempts, however: the difficulty of moving from the *concrete* level of real-world actors to an *analytic* level of aggregation, a process requiring fertile, perceptive, and creative imagination in order to rise above specifics to conceptualize "systems" that one cannot touch. The difficulty complexifies, and the imagination stretches further when, as noted above, the possibility arises that *multiple* systems might exist, perhaps describing very different patterns, structures, or forms of behavior, or perhaps in competition with each other to describe the complexity of the same concrete system. In other words, critiques of almost two decades ago were correct when applied to the narrow and flat domain known as systems analysis of the 1950s and 1960s. They do not apply to the developments that have ensued since, and the point made above deserves repeating: it was those early attempts at "systems analysis" that paved the way for the conceptual sophistication we will see briefly noted in the next section and played out at greater length in subsequent chapters.

Much of this has gone unnoticed, however, partly because of the ideological sympathies underpinning both realist and liberalist views of international politics, which have been allowed to dominate much of the debate. Nonetheless, by the 1990s, despite earlier criticisms, the system appeal has come to define much of the field. Regardless of whether the issues revolve in a specific sense around *which* system accurately describes contemporary international politics, or whether the systemic, structural approach is to be considered superior to subsystemic theories considered in earlier chapters, the end result is a ubiquitous focus on "systems."

From "Systems" to Chaos to "Systems"

The introduction of unabashedly self-conscious "systems" to political science tantalized a discipline that had hitherto focused on the discrete and idiosyncratic with the novel notion that what appeared to be disparate, different, and hopelessly complex and muddled in the "political" could be usefully compared by constructing generic political systems and utilizing concepts appropriate to all systems: investigating system "structures," recognizing that all systems have "inputs" and "outputs," that complex "feedback loops" operate and so on, all implying an underlying assumption that complex systems imply "unintended consequences" and complex nonlinear processes. Exactly 40 years later the same defining concepts introduced a latter-day version of systems and complexity, wherein we are reminded once again that systems analysis does *not* imply straightforward effects, one-way, linear, or simple additive relationships (Jervis, 1993: 25–26).

Such concepts were meant to make differing political systems amenable to cross-system analysis. Humans were seen as operating within social systems that could be generically defined, and that such interactions occurred within the context of certain functional requisites, hypothesized to occur regardless of the specific context of any given system. While a central notion was the "equilibrium" of social systems, related to both "stability" and "maintenance"—two concepts recently imbued with inherent conservative biases in terms of social change—it has also been forgotten that change and learning were also components of these first sociological approaches. That is, when social systems "operate in response to the environment, they are in the performance mode" but when they "operate in response to a significant change in their own structure (that is, a morphogenetic change), they are in the learning mode" (Modelski, 1990: 8). In other words, social systems at the most general level can be compared, they "learn," and therefore they change.

Early systems analysis was very generalized and formalized, with close ties assumed to broader themes of "systems" to be found, for instance in *General Systems Yearbook.*[2] Somewhat less formalized and more specific to international relations was the introduction of six explicit, distinct prototypes of international systems (Kaplan, 1957) along with the rules that nations either *automatically* follow within those systems or *choose* to follow in order to maintain the system. The central concept was power, imbedded in the very names of several of the "systems" (bipolar, balance of power) as well as constituting a key element of the behavior of the nations within those systems. Kaplan distinguished *between types* of systems, the *rules* within those systems, and the *transforming processes* that describe the potential movement from one system to another.

Such "power systems" were to hold a central position in structural analyses for decades (Sullivan, 1976: 169–176), but an often forgotten element in discussions of international systems at the end of the century is that earlier, at mid-century, about the time Kaplan first proposed a systems analysis with a strong conceptual reliance on the central notion of power and its utility for distinguishing between and analyzing international systems, a radical alternative was also on the table to analyze or "picture" international systems, namely, that they be conceptualized along *integrative* rather than power—or potentially *disintegrative*—lines (Deutsch et al., 1957). Rather than power and the "balancing" of power, conceptualizing systems as composed of units engaged in transactions and communications on a variety of diverse and complex dimensions meant that international systems could be viewed in terms of multiple streams of potentially cooperative communications or transactions. Rather than seeing nations as fused to rules related to alleged power relations among the actors, the Deutschian "sociocausal" perspective implied a much more benign progression toward larger and potentially more *integrated* international systems. Some might be tempted to see the latter as more successful as an analytical tool because of the many strides made toward European integration since the 1950s—the major focus of study of early integration work. Still, it is also the case that the processes described as operative in this model still functioned within a "system" framework, with all of the assumptions and implications that perspective implies: the notions of complexity, unintended consequences, nonlinear processes, phenomena perpetually operative in the real world, but cyclically popular in academic frameworks.

Nonetheless, in the conceptual contest, "power"—whether associated with realism or not—has in one form or another held the dominant position over the past half century, as well as long before self-conscious theorizing about international behavior. But for all the theorizing that had occurred for so long about power, balance of power, and their alleged relationship to behavior, and for all of the talk a quarter century later about "neorealism" and later "structural realism," it was in fact Kaplan's early work that set out structural realism in the first systematic attempt to fashion the arguments theoretically. Subsequently, following early pioneering work (Richardson, 1960; Wright, 1942), major data collection efforts provided the first *accurate* system-level descriptions of the behavior thought to serve as the predominant dependent variable of interest, namely, war (Singer and Small, 1972). Imposing a "system" orientation implied that war would be subject to system-level variables.

Recent thought has suggested that such "systems" are "socially constructed," an assertion very much in contention. Nonetheless, systems do propel the focus *away from* the idiosyncratic, those interesting, point-specific, sometimes very individualized factors that have traditionally been considered the true or "ultimate" explanations.[3] Unfortunately, since social construction does play a role, "systems" do not come unencumbered. "Power" systems have been interpreted in recent years as sustaining negative ideological connotations, and have been seen as a causal factor in preventing the international system from moving toward more cooperative and less power-oriented directions (Lebow, 1994: 277). Deutschian and later regime "systems," as we shall see, deriving from liberal preconceptions, impart much more positive connotations—no doubt accounting for their continuing popularity and reincarnations in institutionalism and neoliberalism.

Ironically, a very different view of the international system sidesteps certain ideologically related issues, eschews the construction of systems as units with capabilities and aspirations for power, and yet has not received the accolades accorded neoliberal or regime systems. This alternative view sees the *interactions* between the units conceptualized and structured as "systems" (McClelland, 1961). While taking many forms over the years (Bull, 1977: 10; Onuf, 1997: 8–12), a set of assumptions needed to "picture" this type of "system" first set out more than a generation ago still reveals the differences between constructing systems based on units with capabilities versus units in interaction. The first assumption is that "organized complexity prevails" (McClelland, 1968: 6); what often appears to contemporary observers as nonpatterned or "turbulent" behavior (Rosenau, 1990)—modern terminology favors the oxymoron "chaos theory"—in fact may conform to organized, though complex, patterns. Second, "repetitive patterning and deterministic processes" mix with "accidental, idiosyncratic, and random elements" (McClelland, 1968: 6). Thus, interactions between units constitute a "flow of events"; while nations as the major actors perform many acts, the most important ultimately find their way into some public record of events, producing a sequence or chronology or flow of events or interactions between units. While historians may choose among events thought to be important, the "stream-of-events" analyst ideally records all publicly recorded event interactions between the actors, producing a much more complete—although certainly not *total*—chronology of the stream of events. This becomes a "picture" of the international *system* or, for certain analytical purposes, of smaller *subsystems*, providing general patterns and shifts in events between actors, including various theoretically interesting *structures* of interaction patterns during international crises (Leng, 1993a: 66–90; Schrodt, 1994: 43–46), patterns of East-West bloc bipolarization during the Cold War (Rapkin et al., 1979), conflict-cooperation patterns of major protagonists of the Cold War (Dixon and Gaarder, 1992), or any number of other potentially interesting "interaction systems." Streams of events do not constitute the *only* pictures of the international system; these coexist side by side with the types of system described above utilizing realist or liberal conceptualizations. While systems analysts may insist on the superiority of *their* system as the dominant one, the reality is more likely that diverse systems exist side by side, perhaps operating independently from other systems.

Just as "power systems" and processes operate at other levels of human interaction, so also does "events" analysis have generality beyond nation-states: interaction and sociometric studies have long been a staple of small-group analyses. Moreover, while originally developed to focus on the "high politics" issues, it can just as easily apply to "low politics" economic issues; in terms of the "global system of transnationalized microeconomic links," for instance, it has been more recently suggested that a "nonterritorial 'region' in the world economy—a[n] . . . integrated space-of-flows" exists alongside more traditional structures (Ruggie, 1993: 172).

The events/interaction approach remains controversial, and certainly seems much removed from perennial normative questions of "order" and anarchy (Bull, 1977: 65–74), but more than a generation after its inception it possesses staying power, potentially useful even for analyzing very contemporary issues (Goldstein and Pevehouse, 1997). Unlike the well-known system models built on power attributes, this system artifice requires a facile imagination because it transcends the "known": power and traditional structural images. Instead, it imagines a world of "pure interactions," perhaps related to power but not necessarily, a sociometric analysis that finds beauty, interest, and pattern solely in the interactions between units, and therefore does address the "order" question indirectly through the patterning of interactions.[4] Power and balance of power systems were in a sense obvious and had been spawned by the clear perceptions of such behaviors over long periods of time, although some of the most popular of these conceptualizations may have applied to only a relatively short time-span (Cederman, 1994: 503–507). The "events" focus was spawned by an interest in even shorter time-frame phenomena, the "acute" international crisis (McClelland, 1961), a substantive interest generated by the occurrence of the many "acute" international crises starting with Berlin in 1948 through at least Cuba in 1962. Given the structure of the larger Cold War system and the presence of nuclear weapons, these phenomena carried implications potentially never before seen in history, but by the early 1970s such crises, while still important, had become to one degree or another "routine," and recognition of other phenomena in international politics had begun to emerge almost unrelated to the Cold War, national security, and "acute" crises, which in turn generated other "pictures" or systemic conceptualizations.[5]

"Systems" proposed between the mid-1960s and the mid-1970s were more traditional than "event interaction" systems, and reflected the emerging interest in sociological and economic dimensions (Galtung, 1966; 1971; Wallerstein, 1974), although subsequently regrounded in more traditional international political dimensions (Modelski, 1978). Social rank and status—"topdog" and "underdog" were the chosen terms—produced one of the first systemic contributions to regard polarization of the East-West system as representative of underlying patterns of political relations (Galtung, 1966). In this scheme, "imperialism" imposed "structural violence" on components of the international system, implying that "imperialist" international structures—not merely nations that were imperialist—induced violence simply as a consequence of the structure itself. To the Cold War depiction of the East-West international system, therefore, was added the alternative picture of a North-South system with important *economic* consequences such as concentration of trade partners and commodity concentration as implicit contenders to traditional "power" relationships (Galtung, 1971). Policy implications, while certainly possessing a strong ideological component, rested not only on the accuracy of the systemic descriptions but also recognized that facile recommendations would no doubt be futile unless the underlying structural dimension itself were changed:

> Our point of departure is once more that the world is divided into have's and have-not's, in have and have-not nations. To decrease the gap, one aspect of the fight against structural violence, redistribution by taking from the have's and giving to the have-not's is not enough: the structure has to be changed. The imperialist structure has inter-national as well as intra-national aspects and will consequently have to be changed at both levels (Galtung, 1971: 108).

The "world capitalist system" sustained many of the same conceptual underpinnings, but broadened the picture to a larger historical time-frame, asserting the existence of a complex, multi-level *world* system, grounded in capitalism, markets, forms of production, the exchange of goods, and resulting economic—as well as political—relations among the units within that system. In this picture a "core" dominates the "periphery," and the respective cores rise and fall as peripheries shift. But the essential relations—or systemic interactions—remain:

> the only totalities that exist or have historically existed are minisystems and world-systems, and in the nineteenth and twentieth centuries there has been only one world-system in existence, the capitalist world economy . . . which we define quite simply as a unit with a single division of labor and multiple cultural systems . . . there can, however, be two varieties of such world systems, one with a common political system and one without. We shall designate these respectively as world-empires and world-economies.

It turns out empirically that world-economies have historically been unstable structures leading either towards disintegration or conquest by one group and hence transformation into a world-empire (Wallerstein, 1979: 4–5)

The focus now shifts, therefore, from relatively simple systems to more complex ones, with numerous levels, and including recognition of historical change. In addition, however, the causal relationships posited between international systems defined or constructed as "imperialist" or "world capitalist" and structural violence are not specified. Finally, at least in the original, this formulation of systems does not readily entertain the possibility of multiple other systems necessarily existing either cross-cutting in conjunction with or conceptually in opposition to and in competition with the existence of a world capitalist system. Comparisons do exist, however:

> Dependency and world systems writers see the *capitalist world-economy* as part of a single *world system* defining the place of a state within the hierarchy of nations. This hierarchy is divided in terms of *level* (rather than the form) of development into the categories of *core*, *periphery*, and *semi-periphery*. This roughly corresponds to the realist concept of the inter-state system (Gill, 1990: 38–39; emphasis in original).

"Realism" and "world systems" thus entertain several similarities. "The dominant interpretation in each approach to the question of international order is roughly the same" and "both approaches view historical levels of conflict in cyclical terms" (Gill, 1990: 38–39). A third similarity—and criticism—

> relates to the inability of the world systems approach to really get to grips with the problem of international change. This weakness stems from a combination of its state-centric conception of international relations, a basic economism and an essentialism akin to that of realism. Indeed, despite the polemical hope that left-wing forces will triumph, the basic logic of the Wallersteinian approach leads to deeply pessimistic conclusions for socialist forces (Gill, 1990: 41).

Nonetheless, the panorama of a "world system" turned attention to a longer time-span and broader scope than the familiar, traditional, power-oriented theories, and also suggested the dominating influence of economic factors as opposed to the strictly political ones of the narrow post–World War II "realist" school. The reintroduction of explicit power relations into a longer-term analysis of the international system, originally propounded by the cyclical school of historians, was brought about through the medium of "long cycles" of international politics, a cycle defined as "a recurrent pattern in the life (or functioning) of a system," and the "global political system" as "the institutions and arrangements for the management of global problems or relations, or alternatively as the structure for the management of global interdependence" (Modelski, 1978: 214). Following growing conventional periodization, this "system" was seen to begin about 1500 and is still with us.

A lengthy and tantalizing "descriptive account" of this global system and the nation-state within the mechanisms of the long cycle employed the economic analogy:

> The underlying logic of this argument is identical with familiar explanations of periodicity in economic activity. Long-term business cycles in particular are commonly seen as pro-

moted by fluctuations in the rate of capital accumulation. The structure of a world order may be regarded as a form of capital asset and as the product of innovation and investment; if so, changes in the rate of build-up and decay in structures of world order may be seen to lead to (possibly accelerated) changes in the rate of political activity (Modelski, 1978: 225–226).

In this scheme five global orders existed from 1500 to 1980, each one possessing four properties: the role of global wars, the power monopoly the orders rested on, the functional specificity each global order represented, and the "drift into territoriality that they seemed unable to avoid" (Modelski, 1978: 226). The link with traditional analysis results from the notion of phases of the long cycle and their relationship to war, with a global war resulting in the emergence of a new "world power," followed slowly over many years by the delegitimation of that power, in turn followed by deconcentration of power, producing a global war once again. Central to the long cycle "system" was the notion of change, an element thought absent in realist analysis: the latter "tend to see the realm of international relations as a static one, the enduring realm of the permanent laws of power politics" (Modelski, 1990: 2), whereas the long cycle is "a process of structural change—that is, the creation of form. Its product is the emergence of new forms of order, such as the emergence of global leadership and world powers that can resolve critical global problems" (Modelski, 1990: 10).[6] "Long cycles" presented a fused picture of the international system, its widespread popularity resulting no doubt from its combinatorial characteristics, reintroducing the traditional notions of "power" (without the narrowness of much of traditional "realism") as well as the perennial draw that any formulation based on cycles or cyclical notions possesses.

At about the same time, traditional realism reemerged in what would become known as neorealism, proposing another type of repetitive, although not cyclical, picture of the international system—resurrecting an old and familiar vision with strong ties to Kaplan's formulations of two decades before. While directing attention toward a "market" description of "systems" but purposely eschewing any manner of specific and directed economic explanation as "reductionist," Waltz (1979) set out a three-pronged structure. This structure consisted of contrasting the ordering principles of anarchy versus hierarchy, specifying the differentiation of nation-states as the necessary units, and setting the focus specifically and solely—even simplistically—on the distribution of capabilities across units. "I have now defined the two essential elements of a systems theory of international politics—the structure of a system and its interacting units. In doing so I have broken sharply away from common approaches" (Waltz, 1979: 99). While his revolt will be contested below, Waltz did provide the advance team for fixating on the bipolarity-multipolarity debate through his lengthy discussion of anarchical and hierarchical systems (Waltz, 1979: 111–116), the problems of counting poles and measuring power, the utility of small vs. large systems, and issues of interdependence. Bipolarity-multipolarity certainly proved a relevant and interesting, but somewhat narrow topic for the time.

However, these "neorealist" pictures of the world, further elaborated in the next chapter, had by the late 1970s become rather standard and should not have generated as much controversy, given the theoretical work that had preceded them during the previous two decades as well as the empirical work that had been in process for almost that long. Certainly Kaplan's "systems" and structural analysis had already laid out the terrain, and the Deutsch-Singer "interaction opportunities" model (1964; 1969), the bipolar–multipolar debate (Rosecrance, 1966), the suggestion for distinguishing in a self-conscious way between "dyadic" and "systemic" power relations (Sullivan, 1976: 164–176), as well as earlier work by Waltz himself (Waltz, 1959) all had demonstrated the continuous interest in the preceding two decades in systems, structures, and the distribution of capabilities. Thus, in reality, the soon-to-be-labeled "neorealism," instead of breaking away "sharply" from "common approaches," dovetailed nicely into ongoing approaches, although that is not how the debate would unfold in the subsequent two decades.

However, the attempt to self-consciously distinguish—simply for analytical purposes—between dyadic and systemic perspectives on the role of "power" (Sullivan, 1976: 164–176) can take on any number of specific formulations. The "cycle of relative power" constitutes one, focusing on the power relationships specifically within a given dyad of nations, with key turning points indicative of times when the "relative power" can be dangerous for the two nations involved (Doran and Parsons, 1980). On the other hand, a "theory of hegemonic war" rests on notions of equilibrium and change in the international system at the system level (Gilpin, 1981), resembling long-cycle formulations but lacking the sense of rigidity embodied in the imposition of the notion of "cycles." Theories relative to hegemonic ascension and decline paint a picture rising above the dyad: the entire system is the focus of analysis and while specific countries—the major powers—may play a role similar to that played in the "cycle of relative power," the unit is more clearly the system than the dyad.

But *power* need not be the central or only conceptual center. Economic foci added one system view already (Galtung, 1971; Wallerstein, 1974); a related "picture" of the international "system" involved the inheritor of the earlier Deutschian socio-causal paradigm, and would be called over time interdependence, "regimes," and "neoliberal institutionalism" (Grieco, 1988). Given not only several historical events of the era and processes slowly surfacing, the view emerged that a more accurate picture of the international system must place less emphasis on traditional realism's focus on war and conflict, with its nation-state orientation, and also go beyond the necessarily state-dependent view of earlier Deutschian models, and recognize that other processes were looming, namely, "complex interdependencies" that could involve the organizational or legal parameters of what would be called "regimes" (Keohane and Nye, 1977). This "picture" opened up a multiplicity of issues over which nations might contend, as well as the means through which they could achieve their ends, which hypothetically could include behaviors and strategies at times thought to be completely outside of the "realist" or "neorealist" paradigms, and also hold out the possibility of a more norm-oriented international system structure.

Linked with the growing interest in emerging economic issues, "regimes" and "interdependence"—like events analysis—required the analyst to undertake an imaginative task of picturing the world as a system very much *unlike* those drawn in the past and especially those generated by a vista composed of nation-states as careening billiard balls, in which each of these "meaningful" units in the system were incessantly embarked on a rigid and narrow definition of achieving the "national interest." In this alternative depiction, complexities rather than simplicity abound, but nonetheless produce a "picture" of the international system as plausible, valid, and perhaps as reliable as any others but consisting of very different elements. In this new picture, actors other than states were emerging, those new actors—as well as traditional nation-states—were focusing on newer issues, the system was moving toward greater interdependence, and war and national security issues were fading as central concerns

(Sullivan, 1978a; 1990: 21–56). In addition to these components, states themselves—and therefore decision-making—were no longer viewed as unitary and entailing centralized actors, and, perhaps most important as these new pictures were emerging, international institutions of a wide variety were perceived as occupying a new and central position (Grieco, 1988: 487–490). Such a view has proceeded down diverse specific paths, even to the point of including the proposal that a Waltzian-type structural analysis be applied to international monetary relations, suggesting that "the constraints imposed on states by capital mobility are structural in nature, or at a minimum can usefully be construed as structural" and therefore the "degree of international capital mobility systematically constrains state behavior by rewarding some actions and punishing others" (Andrews, 1994: 197).

"Systems," it is true, may be socially constructed, but those constructions appear to be the best way to address the possibility of a disparate, multifaceted, and rich theoretical terrain. Unlike contentions made by each adherent along the way, it is possible that no one, single international *system* exists, a view often overlooked. Therefore no single theoretical conceptualization of international politics exists; the imagination must wander across numerous and varied conceptual lines and perspectives. The pull of realism and realpolitik resulted in systems defined in terms of nation-state power, and the developing bipolar, Cold War system after World War II propelled that conceptual thrust into the forefront. But World War II itself also had a major impact on the opposite development, which viewed nations not as units lusting after and demonstrating power or crashing about in a billiard-ball setting, but rather as communicating, "transacting," and interacting with each other, a model far removed from power and power relations. But realism reemerged in the form of "neorealism" or "structural realism," which have ebbed and flowed in popularity, while regimes, interdependencies, and then liberal "institutionalism" emerged to replace Deutsch.

Utilizing systemic pictures requires imagination. Realist, power-centered "systems" have dominated and, for some, have stifled the imagination needed to picture the system in alternative and perhaps multiple ways. However, to entertain alternative models to the power-dominated ones that have generated and continue to generate such criticism does not mean that the latter are no longer valid, but only that they may be more accurate for understanding only a certain limited range or type of behavior, or answering only certain types of questions, or have applicability to only certain—perhaps short—periods of time. Diversity should not necessarily produce confusion; any moves toward unnecessary cloture on the "correct" image or picture of the system narrows the types of questions that can be addressed. Unfortunately, each successive wave of "new" system approach covets cloture on *it* as the final, most comprehensive one.

"States" and "Systems"

Once upon a time, states and the "state system" were taken as given realities. A generation ago they were the subject of inquiry but in essence given a clean bill of health: the state system was not in decline, nor was it "dysfunctional in relation to basic human purposes," provided the "element of international society in it could be preserved" (Bull, 1977: 318–319). Since then, "states" and the "state system" have again come under great scrutiny; coincident with the volatile issue of "inside vs. outside," their essence has been strongly contested. They are central to any discussion of international systems, system types, and system transformation, since—as the last section demonstrated—almost all "system" models rely heavily on the "nation-state." For better or worse, as we concluded in the last chapter, the nation-state remains the actor of utmost immediate empirical reality, despite broad attempts to dislodge it from that reality. With the emergence of the interdependence school in the 1970s, and the reintroduction of neoidealist notions in the *de rigueur* rhetoric of transnationalism, globalism, and globalization, the underlying hypothesis was that these new theoretical contenders—namely, systems describing the "new reality" as one of interdependence and globalism as opposed to the independent sovereignty of the state system—were wreaking havoc on that traditional nation-state system, that the latter no longer described reality, and therefore theoretical orientations based on that assumed reality—such as realism—were outmoded.

"New thinking" is always more fashionable than "old thinking," and, to be sure, many observable changes were interpreted to be in line with this "new thinking." The surge in numbers of intergovernmental organizations, the increasing role of multinational corporations, the perceived emergence of non-state terrorist actors, the increasing rapidity and breadth of international communications and travel, and especially the emergence of economic issues were cited as evidence of this new, changed "system" (Sullivan, 1978a; 1982; 1990). The state and the traditional state system based on power, as described in the realist school, were allegedly on the way out. While widely evident to many and argued vociferously through the 1970s and 1980s, despite several observable setbacks to be noted below, the same argument was widely perceived even into the 1990s:

> The ensuing analysis self-consciously breaks . . . with the "state-is-still predominant" tendency by positing a *multi-centric* world as having evolved independently of the one in which states function, a world in which actions and reactions originate with a multiplicity of actors at diverse system levels . . . (Rosenau, 1990: 97).

Unfortunately, as for many such arguments going back a full generation now, heralding a "new beginning" is easier than demonstrating its empirical reality and exact content. That is, systems change, but such change is sometimes hard to see. Anecdotal evidence has flourished, but systematic evidence has been less frequent. For much of the 1970s and 1980s the empirical data that was analyzed (Thomson and Krasner, 1989; Sullivan, 1990) did not necessarily support the anecdotal views that had been developing during that period. Moreover, certain events during the very period of heightened perceptions of "new interdependencies" suggested in fact the exact opposite. The Soviet Union's invasion of Afghanistan and the American hostage crisis in Iran were only the beginning of a series of deeply troubling and dangerous events for those entertaining a non-state-centric system. These were followed by the beginning of the Iran-Iraq war, which was to continue for ten years. Throughout the 1980s incidents continued to intrude on such a view: the United States' dispatching of troops to Lebanon in 1983, the invasions of Grenada in 1983 and Panama in 1989 were only two such incidents. With the fall of the Berlin Wall in 1989 and the Soviet "empire" two years later, the "new thinking" received another positive boost and much promise for hope, but within short order the world in the summer of 1990 saw Iraq follow through on a threat to invade Kuwait, resulting with more than half a million American troops in the Persian Gulf War—equivalent to Vietnam in 1968—joined by numerous forces from the broadly based UN coalition. This war—casualties estimated at perhaps 100,000—was followed by the reemergence of nationalism in numerous parts of the world, and by the middle of the last decade of the century the world was focused once again on events in the very city where 80 years before World War I had been launched with a terrorist assassination—Sarajevo. This resulted in agreements and an occupation still ongoing at century's close with no end in sight. By the spring of 1999, nationalist eruptions produced the crisis in southern Serbia, in Kosovo, resulting in the bombing of Belgrade by a newer, expanded NATO. Elsewhere in the mid-1990s internal disruptions in Rwanda resulted in the major civil war in neighboring Zaire three years later. Few of these events were to have been in the cards if at least one variant of the model of an interdependent, transnational, and globalist world system suggested in the 1970s and the early 1980s had proved largely accurate.

More recently, markets and globalization have enhanced the attacks on the state. Certainly in-depth case studies of telecoms, organized crime, insurance and accounting firms, cartels and international organizations (Strange, 1996) demonstrate that multiple centers of power are plausibly different in the 1990s than in the 1950s, that power no longer resides solely with state "officials," that markets may both define and exercise power, and that the authority that flows from power therefore no longer solely comes from states. How definitive and substantial the impact on the favored "constructions" of international system structures will be remains somewhat in the speculative phase.

People become attached—and some antagonistic—to the system they inhabit; familiarity can breed solace or contempt. Normative and ideological considerations influence the types of systems we perceive, construct, and—perhaps more importantly—the systems we want and don't want. Certainly this may well be the case with nation-state-based models. The same might apply to alternative constructs. Conceptions of an interdependent, globalist, transnationalist system intimate a positive sense of the international system; conceptions of power and hegemony, based on rivalry, competition, and "difference," connote a radically different view. In the broader world of international politics, the interdependence of the 1970s and the globalism of the 1980s implied idealist notions reminiscent of the 1920s."Triumphant liberalism" is a phrase describing one view of the most recent feelings about American foreign policy. Even Huntington's early 1990s view of the emerging post–Cold War world, while controversial because it contradicted those growing idealist notions, nonetheless constitutes a systemic "picture" of the world:

> During the Cold War the world was divided into the First, Second, and Third Worlds. Those divisions are no longer relevant. It is far more meaningful now to *group* countries not in terms of their political or economic systems or in terms of their level of economic development but rather in terms of their culture and civilization (Huntington, 1994: 121; emphasis added).

"Groupings" therefore can change; nation-states have produced the nation-state "system," with its fault lines, fissures, and very distinctive groupings. But just as nation-states as individual entities come and go, so also might the larger structure based on them transform and change. Separating out evidence on such transformations that meaningfully demonstrates the shift to new realities from anecdote or normative desires that favor a change (Cox, 1997: 170) has been difficult. Groupings will remain and the systems "constructed" will reflect those groupings. As we will see unfolding, the tensions surrounding these issues continue to serve as the underlying point of departure for seemingly different theoretical explanatory models, tensions that have persisted for decades.

Conclusion

Weather "systems" existed long before humans could actually "see" them on the evening news satellite downloads from space. Stock "markets" are many things and can go up or down or sideways; just because they are not as observable as visual weather systems does not mean they are any less a "system." The same applies to international "systems." The latter may exist or they may not, but regardless, constructing such systems is not meant to *reify* them. They are simply constructs utilized to organize what often appear as unrelated turbulence and random behavior, thereby representing organized complexity rather than "turbulence." The fact that many "systems" happen to be conceptualized by so many different people in different ways either means they each are actually describing different realities, or viewing the same reality in different ways; in the latter case, the conceptualizations may then be in competition with one another for accounting for the same reality.

Nation-states, as well as other actors, operate within these systems, are affected by and also serve to bring them about. "Agency"-oriented theorists may object to certain implied deterministic underpinnings, but certainly recognition of the dual directionality of causality appears to be dawning:

> System organization is both a product of states' initiatives and a factor conditioning their behavior: it is the manifest aspect of that latent attribute called structure by the system theorist. States contribute—with different roles, capabilities and aims—to the making of organizational rules and institutions and are conditioned by the existing rules and institutions even when acting to change them (Attina, 1991: 318).

Personalities, images, belief systems, decision processes—all play a manifest role in understanding international politics; few have had the audacity to suggest that such factors may produce only minor or even random perturbations on international behavior, depending of course on *how* that behavior is defined. Even those operating solely at the system level do not do so: "systems do not choose to go to war; national leaders do" (Pollins, 1996: 104). The return of the "agent-structure" debate, which is at bottom in some ways a modern variation of the free will vs. determinism rift (Onuf, 1997: 9), reveals that a subtle trap had been unintentionally set: "agency" theorists appearing to cast individuals and ideas as somehow "counting" more than something else, and system theorists seeming deterministic. Moreover, the tendency seemed to be to cast agency against realist or neorealist systems. But consistency demands that agency also be set in opposition to all systemic approaches, including world systems, regimes, interdependence, "globalization," or any other systemic construct of interest. To pit "agency" against realism or neorealism is limiting and misleading: "The international system is, indeed, an overdetermined system and it is not possible to solve the agent-structure problem by providing evidence of the ontological primacy of either the actors or of the structure" (Attina, 1991: 318).

The primacy of neither one leads of course to the notion of "co-constitution" (Wendt, 1987: 358–360; Onuf, 1997: 7–8). Few analysts—constructivists or not—would disagree, but the debates often descend to attempts at casting one or the other in a superior role. Subsystemic explanatory factors have already been demonstrated to be compelling in order to understand certain specific segments of the behavior defined as international relations, but those factors may also produce only minor effects or even random perturbations. Analysis of "systems," despite certain very real limiting characteristics, does have the distinct advantage of removing the stultifying chains of the momentary interests and attention spans of crisis-oriented policy-makers and newspapers, as well as rising above the simplistic calls for "multivariable" nuanced explanations. It requires a very different mental attitude, and forces the observer to shift away from the specifics of daily events and specific crises. As simplistic as such a position may seem, it nonetheless has fostered much controversy.

Despite a checkered and questionable history, analysis of "systems" not only thrives, but in terms of the focused central issues of concern to so many analysts one could conclude that in recent years systems analysis dominates in one form or another. Almost two decades ago the paucity of systems research beyond the "early" pioneers, including Kaplan, Luard, and Rosecrance, was cause for lamentation (Zinnes, 1980). Such grief was unfounded. It is true that early, stylized adherence to a general form of systems analysis was not necessarily productive, but the time-line briefly sketched here has demonstrated the broad extent of types of international systems and the diversity of approaches. Despite the attacks based on the "end of the nation-state" argument, and the more recent attention given to the transformation to a new, post–Cold War "globalized" system, these very changes demonstrate that analysis focused on descriptions of international politics in systems terms and hypotheses of multiple effects of differential system structures remains not only healthy but perhaps, even if only implicitly, dominant. The continuing vigorous debates concerning the viability of the nation-state in the contemporary world, the demise of one of the two major hegemonies, the possibility of the emergence of a new multipolar system, the ostensible unification of Europe, the emergence of a new, reunified, and perhaps more powerful Germany, and the transformation of Asia into a new "bloc" or "actor" in the system, have caused systemic approaches to take a central place in the attempt to assess these many changes. While disputes continue on how adequately respective approaches can handle such transformations, certainly it would be incorrect to continue to assert that transformation of the international system(s) is not on the agenda. Yet, it is the very question of *transformation* that has caused so many of these disputes:

> Like Newtonian mechanics, conventional international structural approaches are simple, powerful, elegant, and useful for many things. But just as Newtonian mechanics does not have much of a grasp on transformation of the palpable forces in nature—because the universe comprised by the theory presupposes their stability—so too it is with conventional structuralism in international relations. As a result, the processes of international transformation are among its voids (Ruggie, 1989: 32–33).

One reality will unfold over the next several chapters: much of the difference between initial works of the 1950s with their limited focus provided by simple, realist, power-oriented "systems," and the newer types of systems suggested for analysis of contemporary change are differences in extent, scope, and sophistication. Certainly the recognition of differences between structures is *not* among the field's contemporary voids, and many of the modern conceptual structures have been built in response to a direct need to focus on the empirical, observable transformations that have occurred in world politics. The problem may still exist, however, even when utilizing structural descriptions aimed at understanding what is perceived to be a transformed system, with the movement or transformation from one system to another. That, however, is not a condemnation of the analysis of systems itself.

World systems, long cycles, hegemonic stability, and cycle of relative power do tackle the issue of transformation. Deciding whether such theories constitute a theory of *change* we leave to those who know what a theory of change would look like. It is true, however, that these approaches are "simple, powerful, elegant" and therefore very parsimonious, but they are also thereby very seductive, for they appear to be all-encompassing. So much of empirical observation made through the lens provided by several of these approaches "fits." Broad sweeps of history and international political relations, as well as very sweeping contemporary changes can be "understood" with the assistance of the world system, long cycle, hegemonic stability, and especially world history contextuality. However, while on the one hand the data "fits"—broad general similarities in patterns and trends do appear to exist at a certain level of systemic abstraction—the fit breaks down naturally when the analysis attempts to deal with specifics.

Moreover, the preponderance of system-level pictures of the world owe their heritage in one way or another to what has been called the "realist" school. What happens when idealism reemerges, as it does from time to time—perhaps most recently in the last decade of this century—and system constructs are proposed with its basic tenets? One clear result is that the systems pictured within the confines of those structural constraints become dominated by concern over institutions more oriented toward cooperative relations. The manifestation of idealism occurring in the last two decades of the twentieth century has taken the form largely through the concept of "regimes," which are thought to exist and their presence or absence thought to explain international political behavior. But regardless of whether the focus is on power relations, anarchy, integration, interdependence, development, or "regimes," (Ferguson and Mansbach, 1988: 186–194, 198–211), all nonetheless imply a structural approach and a focus on "systems." Despite that the picture resulting from each of these respective approaches will certainly look different, employ different assumptions, and produce different implications, they are all "systems." Critiques that had become rampant in misinterpreting realism, power, and power relations (Sullivan, 1990) resulted largely from perception of a newly interdependent system allegedly unlike any preceding one. What seemed to be missed in so much of that burgeoning literature—correct as far as it went—was that interdependence exists in addition to the ways it had been conceptualized by the interdependency "school." Interdependencies can exist along almost any line the analyst wishes to focus on—for a variety of purposes and reflecting a variety of theoretical approaches—and represent a certain form of system construct.

Previous chapters have examined more discrete theoretical approaches, usually with concomitant limited purviews and domains. More broadly conceived theories have generated continuing controversy since their formalized inception almost half a century ago, partly because they manifest the polar opposite of those assumptions implicitly contained in less "grand" theories, and because of a residual distaste for the very notion of "system." This is chiefly manifested in the philosophical or metaphysical opposition to "imposing" socially "constructed" theoretical systems, especially when dominance, hierarchy, or difference—as contained in many of the structural models—is implied. Whether the analyst using systemic constructs imposes such "realities" is among the many controversial issues; whether other structures or systems different than those fashioned by theorists might not be preferable and even potentially achievable, a position espoused by critical theorists, is even more controversial. Here a key point is that more than one "system" may exist at any one time: systems may in fact be "nested" within one another. While it may be that "the state system and the capital accumulation process are part of the same interactive socioeconomic system" (Chase-Dunn, 1981: 21), it is equally plausible that a "world capitalist system" could very well be operating at the same time as a "multipolar political system," and the former may very well be continuing to operate as the multipolar system slowly undergoes transformation to a bipolar political system. Nested within both of these "grander" systems might in turn be other dynamic systems operating coincidentally with them: shifting bipolarity and bipolarization in the Cold War (Rapkin et al., 1979); the dyadic U.S.-U.S.S.R. conflict system (Dixon and Gaarder, 1992); diffusion of democratic regimes (Starr, 1991); short-term shifts in status inconsistency (Volgy and Mayhall, 1995); "regimes" flourishing in certain specific policy domains (Muller, 1993; Young and Osherenko, 1993; Nayar, 1995). In other words, while the "grand" systems—bipolarity vs. multipolarity, world systems, hegemonic stability, and world history—appropriate the bulk of the attention, nested within these grand schemes are multiple potential additional "systems," which are not necessarily competing with the larger, host system. Even where debates have become so heated with the assumption that only one system can be consistent with reality,[7] the question that should be addressed is not solely whether one system exists *rather than* another, but whether also it is possible that multiple systems are operating.[8]

Given the diverse and multiple levels and dimensions of behavior manifested in international relations, it is not surprising that multiple varied interests and potential conflicts might be reflected in multiple complex systems. In some ways Schelling was right: it does all "work." When one considers the possibilities the world might face if one were to creatively generate "counterfactuals" that might occur in a truly "anarchic" world, and compares that to what does actually happen, where things often seem, in comparison, to be very ordered, one can, in other words—if one wants—be truly amazed.[9]

Chapter Six ❀

Realism's Circuitous Route: Realpolitik to Structures and Back

What's in a Name?

The United States' alleged inability to exert its power in Southeast Asia in the 1960s provided the first of many purportedly nonanomalous illustrations demonstrating the declining role of "power" as an explanatory tool in the modern world. A second instance two decades later involved Panama: whereas "United States–Panamanian relations were thought to provide an exemplar of a dominant, powerful regime . . . directing with considerable accuracy the actions of a much weaker, subservient client regime, Panama," by early 1989 the roles had reversed, prompting the question,

> Is Noriega's regime more powerful than the United States? Is the United States *powerless* in the face of a much "weaker" opponent? . . . Is there such a thing as power? Is God no longer on the side of the larger battalions? (Ward, 1989: 121).

Such assertions appeared consistent with the case of Vietnam in 1969 and 20 years later in Panama. Yet, in 1989, the United States invaded Panama, captured Manuel Noriega, and brought him back to the United States for trial; today he languishes in a south Florida jail. Yet with the end of the Cold War, systemic concepts of power and "neorealism" have again been undermined: bipolarity ended neither according to neorealism's precepts of hegemonic war, differential alliance patterns, nor to a gap in military capabilities.

> [A]ccording to neorealist assumptions, the United States should have taken advantage of Soviet weakness with an aggressive foreign policy and efforts to compound Soviet difficulties so as to make the Soviet Union as weak as possible (Koslowski and Kratochwil, 1994: 220).

Instead, according to this interpretation, the United States extended offers to the Soviet Union to join multilateral institutions and offered financial assistance. And yet by the mid-1990s the United States vigorously pursued NATO expansion almost to the boundaries of the former Soviet Union, and by 1999 a U.S.-led NATO alliance was bombing Belgrade.

The debates over the role, function, and utility of "power" have continued, producing a cottage industry devoted to criticizing power, realism, and neorealism (Sullivan, 2000). Some see the Cold War as evidence of the United States having "balanced" formidable Soviet power, and others view the entire enterprise of power balancing and structural realism as outmoded—and perhaps even dangerous—concepts. But "classical realism" consists of little more than a series of assumptions about nation-state behavior; an alternative path is to purge the baggage from traditional realism and focus on dyadic and systemic conceptualizations using extant theoretical literature based on one or more structural views of the world (Sullivan, 1976: 155–179). Whether labeled "neorealism" or "structural realism," it eschews certain traditional assumptions of "realpolitik." Instead it makes assumptions concerning structural constraints on behavior as well as how behavioral regularities themselves often produce recognizable structures.

Assaults on "power" analyses often confuse classical realism as well as structural realism, and the potential explanatory utility of both, with a desire for a peaceful world (Sullivan, 1990). Such critiques can produce caricatures of classical realpolitik, a picture of the world few people thought truly reflective of the way nations interact.[1] Yet despite endless assaults, "power" persists as an analytical approach, but nonetheless carries with it multiple human emotions—accounting both for its staying power as well as the cottage industry critiquing it. Despite polemics toward and stereotypes about the evils of power, it remains a focus of interest, and has been reconstructed over the past half century in quite intriguing ways.

The Beginnings

The story takes many forms, but most would agree that Hans Morgenthau started it all, playing a monumental role in the emergence of contemporary realism; his ideas have been a central target down into the 1990s. But perhaps almost as important as understanding what Morgenthau *was* saying—and the times from which he was speaking—is to know what he was *not* saying. At the most basic level, his cardinal assertions are well-known: humans possess an inherent "lust for power," a desire for control over others; aggregated into states, humans behave as a function of this basic drive:

> It is sufficient to state that the struggle for power is universal in time and space and is an undeniable fact of experience. It cannot be denied that throughout historic time, regardless of social, economic, and political conditions, states have met each other in contests of power (Morgenthau, 1965: 33).

The essentials of this "model," referenced by friend and foe alike, are also well-known: the international can be separated from the domestic; the former is a struggle for power in an anarchic environment; gradations exist between nations in capabilities, but all possess legal equality or sovereignty; objective rules of human nature dictate behavior; statesmen think and act in terms of interest defined as power; no nation's moral principles are to be equated with universal principles. The problems of the world result not from depravity that can be fixed or evil abolished, but from "forces inherent in human nature," which consist of the "drives to live, to propagate, and to dominate." In the satisfaction of those drives, power is centrally important. Motivation and ideological preferences become unimportant:

> Even if we had access to the real motives of statesmen, that knowledge would help us little in understanding foreign policies . . . knowledge of the statesman's motives may give us one

among many clues as to what the direction of his foreign policy might be. It cannot give us, however, the one clue by which to predict his foreign policies (Morgenthau, 1965: 6).

The most famous phrase in all the realm of realism was Morgenthau's assertion that international politics is a "struggle for power . . . whenever [nations] strive to realize their goal by means of international politics, they do so by striving for power" (Morgenthau, 1965: 27). Nations retain, increase, or demonstrate their power, the first supporting the status quo, the second producing imperialism, and the third involving displays of military force or other influence (Morgenthau, 1965: 38–85).

Such is Morgenthau's "theory"; while variations, permutations, and extensions abound,[2] all hark back to these tenets. He was not alone. Organski wrote, "One of the most important characteristics of a nation is its power, for power is a major determinant of the part the nation will play in international relations" (Organski, 1968: 101). World politics was the "doings" of the major powers; "it is not much concerned with relations between Iceland and Liberia or with the latest twist of foreign policy in Paraguay" for "they are simply less powerful." Deutsch asked, "Who is stronger and who is weaker? Who will get his way . . . [this] leads to rank lists, such as the rankings of baseball clubs . . . of chickens in the pecking order, and of great powers in world politics" (Deutsch, 1969: 257). These traditional bases say only that something called power exists, it is central to international politics because it means bigness, which equals influence, which means affecting other people. Violence and force are central "because power equals the ability to be violent and impose one's will on others" (Sullivan, 1976: 157).

The Doubts

Leaving aside for the moment the empirical question of exactly how *much* of international politics consists of force and violence—the actual "pool" of behavior related to power—*explanations* of behavior using power were becoming less satisfactory by the mid-1970s. Assumptions were becoming either questionable or at least "wither[ing] away as a valid *explanatory* theory of international behavior," namely, that some states are powerful and some are not, some increase their power and some do not, states influence one another, and power is "complex" (Sullivan, 1976: 163). National interests, power, accumulation of power, and balancing of power—all can "explain" virtually all nation-state behavior. Systematic, cumulative theory, however, does not flow from saying only that some states with certain attributes are more powerful than others, and that some states increase their power; that power means force and force is important in international relations; that some nations balance and others do not; and that power is so complex that no single entity or index can measure it.

It was further becoming clear that "theories" such as "power politics," "balance of power," or "interest defined in terms of power" were limited or tautological. Haas's and Claude's classic critiques of "balance of power" (E. Haas, 1961; Claude, 1962) appreciated the problems. Balance had been used as a *situation,* a *policy,* and as a *system.* Also it has been used to describe a process of "power politics," an equilibrium, hegemony, or a universal law. But to say states will always balance is like "saying that there will always be *weather* (good or bad, hot or cold) on the earth" (Claude, 1962: 28, emphasis in original). Diplomatic history is a succession of stories of alliances and balancing tactics, but the empirical phenomenon itself cannot be equated with a "theory," nor necessarily a normative decree that states *should* play the balancing game. Merely describing a series of balancing acts says little about the circumstances under which states act in a "balancing" fashion, under what conditions they refrain, nor what impact on international behavior various balancing systems have. Waltz later wrote:

> Balance of power is seen by some as being akin to a law of nature; by others, as simply an outrage. Some view it as a guide to statesmen; others as a cloak that disguises their imperialist policies. Some believe that a balance of power is the best guarantee of the security of states and the peace of the world; others, that it has ruined states by causing most of the wars they have fought. (Waltz, 1979: 117)

Not surprisingly, the debates that first surfaced in the 1950s were echoed again 40 years later in a lengthy exchange weighing the merits and demerits of realism, neorealism, and especially balance of power (Vasquez, 1997; Elman and Elman, 1997; Schweller, 1997; Walt, 1997).

Nonetheless, in the 1970s, power and related concepts were usually equated with the "classical" realism of Hans Morgenthau, and its complexity and atheoretical nature dictated a shift toward thinking "in terms of power *relations* or *distances* (not influence relations), and power *distributions* or *systems*" (Sullivan, 1976: 163–164). "Balancing" as a central focus received less attention. Such suggestions occurred ironically after one of the major events in world politics of the last half of the twentieth century—the American "opening" to China—which was certainly consistent with balance of power terminology. Nonetheless, the long-heralded pitfalls in "balance of power" as traditionally formulated warranted a full-scale focus on clearly structural elements, taking precedence over what later was labeled "irrelevant diplomatic lore" (Waltz, 1997: 914).

The Cold War and Theory:
Bipolarity Vs. Multipolarity

Focusing directly on observable structures and eschewing the prior assumptions of "classical" realism ("power as a 'drive' or 'lust' or automatic 'balancing' system . . . have not been given attention here" [Sullivan, 1976: 200]), moves consideration to the sociological or structural.

> Individuals make choices and act in a world of rules and norms not entirely of their own making. Moreover, these constraining rules and social structures cannot be reduced wholly to self-interest; in many cases individuals can even be viewed as behaving in ways opposed to their self-interest (Gilpin, 1981: x).

Waltz stated it only slightly differently later in the decade:

> Some states may hunger for power for power's sake. Neorealist theory, however, shows that it is not necessary to assume an innate lust for power in order to account for the sometimes fierce competition that marks the international arena. In an anarchic domain, a state of war exists if all parties lust for power. But so too will a state of war exist if all states seek only to ensure their own safety . . . (Waltz, 1989: 43–44).

But structures had been around long before the 1980s and the emergence of neorealism. Kaplan's six classic models—balance of power, loose bipolar, tight bipolar, universal, hierarchical, and unit-veto (Kaplan, 1957: 21–53)—may have only had three historical referents, but each described differential reality and proposed rules required of each system for self-perpetuation. The balance of power, for instance, "required" that nations oppose the predominance of one actor or bloc, increase their capabilities in order to do this, negotiate rather than fight, and if compelled to fight, stop doing so before destroying an essential participant. Thus a balance of power system *describes* a given international system, but nations *must* follow those rules to retain the system (Healy and Stein, 1973: 40). The system exists because states behave in certain specified ways, and states behave because the system exists and therefore constrains them. Predictions also abound: a balance of power system should produce short-term and very specific alliances, which will "shift according to advantage and not according to ideology (even within war)" (Kaplan, 1969: 295), and should result in limited wars because nations do not want to eliminate an essential actor. Tight bipolar systems should permit less powerful countries more freedom of action, resulting in numerous small wars; major actors contend with each other on the peripheries. The loose bipolar system, on the other hand, should have alliances that "tend to be long-term . . . based on permanent and not on shifting interests, and to have ideological components"; wars under such circumstances, except for the fear of nuclear devastation, "would tend to be unlimited" (Kaplan, 1969: 297).

Kaplan's systems set the stage, and while debates evolved, the focus was clear: shifting from viewing power as a usable attribute providing nations with the influence thought to be associated with power or as an element toward which nations "strived," towards a structural view defining either the number of actors or units in the system, their structural relations based on power, or other structural attributes. In the process, two tendencies emerged: first, structures could be specified regardless in some cases of "power capabilities" of specific actors, and, second, the "rules" for different systems began to recede. Subsequent debates recognized the limits of "traditional" balance of power while at the same time not entirely extricating the dialectics from the ideological dimensions, especially—as we will see—with respect to the Cold War contest.

As the bipolar, Cold War international system became imbedded in the realities of international politics (Cox, 1986: 211), the first sustained structural-theoretical focus came to be known as the bipolar/multipolar stability issue: which systems are more stable, bipolar or multipolar? While the dangers of a bipolar—and nuclear—system had focused attention on the *individuals* who make the decisions and the realization that those decisions need not necessarily follow dictates of rational, realpolitik models, those dangers could be compounded if the structure of the international system—a rigid, bipolar one, now without all of the simplifying constraints of realism—was itself also a danger.

The theoretical formulations of the time did not produce necessarily sanguine results. Deutsch and Singer's presentation provides a historical benchmark for contending arguments, although several years would elapse before empirical research shed light on the arguments: "As the system moves away from bipolarity toward multipolarity, the frequency and intensity of war should be expected to diminish" (Deutsch and Singer, 1969: 315). Using the domestic analogy of the "pluralistic" model, incompatibilities between states tend to be amplified if they all run along the same lines or divisions, resulting in fewer "interaction opportunities" between opposing groups. The contrary situation of multiple interaction opportunities "would seem to favor social stability and to inhibit social cleavage" (Deutsch and Singer, 1969: 317). If some minimal level of interaction is needed between two states before they can have anything to conflict about, an increase in the number of actors, decreasing the amount of attention any one actor can pay to any other actor, "is likely to have a stabilizing effect upon the system" (Deutsch and Singer, 1969: 321). While those viewing bipolar great power nuclear systems as inherently dangerous may see them as intellectually enticing as well as normatively attractive, stability could also flow from a bipolar system: the two poles are clearly delineated, no realms are open to possible aggrandizement by either party, and the overriding interest would be the continuation of a stable system. A later summary of the arguments concluded:

> Because only two major powers are present, and they are the most powerful, each side knows that any move will result in an equal and opposite reaction by the other side. The preponderance of the leaders of the blocs means that shifts that do occur are not of decisive significance. One knows who one's enemies are, and mutual spheres of responsibility can be clearly delimited (Sullivan, 1990: 82).[3]

A small multipolar system might be optimum, but as the number of parties grows, each member has less incentive to maintain it: greater surveillance is called for in the increasing number of parties, and "so does the difficulty of predicting and detecting deals that other parties may make to one's own disadvantage" (Waltz, 1979: 136). Multipolarity could produce advantages, however, such as dampening arms races: a state's increased armaments against one other state in the system will have less effect if there are more states in the system. Multipolarity could also provide flexibility: "the availability of alternative major partners for alliances . . . lends the system suppleness and capacity for rapid adjustment" (Modelski, 1974: 18). Twenty years later the arguments remained: multipolarity brought flexibility, presence of greater interaction opportunities, thus less attention devoted to specific countries, as well as risk aversion from the difficulty of appraising relative capabilities (Kegley and Raymond, 1994: 51–53). It might also lessen caution among nations, increase statistically the probability of more powerful nations coming into conflict with one another, increase uncertainty, engender serious and potentially growing inequalities, all the while lacking the essential simplicity of a bipolar system (Kegley and Raymond, 1994: 48–50).

The bipolar–multipolar controversy strode the high theoretical plateau, but the divisions and related tensions of the Cold War intensified the gravity of the debate, and the theoretical realm cannot be divorced from realities of international politics of the 1960s and early 1970s. While the tensions of a rigidly bipolar nuclear world have receded, it was alarming for those living through it and attempting to analyze and forecast events. Thus normative concerns may have played as much a part in the assessments of the relative stability of bipolar and multipolar systems as any abstract academic concern for theoretical rigor, accuracy, or behavioral predictability. While Waltz's focus revivified the debate (Waltz, 1979), thus continuing to focus the discipline on those categories, they had been widespread for some time. Ironically, the later debate over "neorealism" that derived so much from the bipolar-multipolar debate emerged just as the bipolar system itself was beginning to break down. By the early 1970s the most recent and sweeping of several "detentes" was in full swing, the Vietnam War was ending, and tensions were increasing in other areas, producing concern over growing shifts in power relations in the world more broadly: the "oil shocks" of 1973 and—for America—the growing sense of trade imbalance with Japan were only two very specific events suggesting the beginning of dynamic changes in structures of international power relations.

From Cold War Systems to
Parity, Preponderance and Transitions

The bipolar–multipolar debates possessed a long history, and while integrally absorbed with the Cold War were not the only arena of structural dispute. All the structural permutations, including bipolarity and multipolarity, parity and preponderance—as well as others—can be interpreted in terms of "balancing," but need not be. In fact, several linkages drawn between "balancing" and state behavior under parity or preponderance situations produce the problems for which the balancing is supposed to be the solution. Traditionally, it was thought that under certain conditions a state will act to increase its power when another increases its potential:

> Further increases on the part of one side will always bring corresponding increases on the part of its competitors, so that in effect a rough equality of power potential will always prevail, a factor which may make for either open conflict or induce fear of refraining from hostilities (E. Haas, 1961: 165).

Thus, a balance that produces equality is more likely to result in conflict than balancing that produces inequality. Equality means each side thinks it may win; it may also mean each side fears what the other may do. However, "confrontation with approximately equal power will deter a state from undertaking aggressive adventures" (Claude, 1962: 56). If either side has an equal chance of winning, it also has an equal chance of losing. Combining these produces a relationship between power equality or inequality and conflict that may be curvilinear: the more equal two units are, the greater the probability of conflict, *except* that at some point the opposite process begins to operate: high equality stifles aggressive tendencies because of the 50–50 chance of losing (Sullivan, 1976: 166).

The above argument—which some may see as perversely anachronistic in the contemporary era—is a version of "power transition," a "theory" that lay dormant for many years but became repopularized with numerous variations (Organski and Kugler, 1980: 13–63; Doran and Parsons, 1980; Gilpin, 1981; Houweling and Siccima, 1988; 1991; Doran, 1991). The distinction drawn between dyadic and systemic structures (Sullivan, 1976: 164–176), which imposed the simple differentiation of "dyads" versus "systems" as the unit of analysis, was not very sound because dynamic transition processes could operate at both levels. That is, transition processes can operate between two nations in a dyad as well as units other than nation-dyads. Organski's original presentation grafted comparative politics onto international processes, distinguishing between nations with potential power, where productivity is low and industrialization has not begun, from those in the transitional growth stage and those that have reached power maturity by having become fully industrialized. Transitional nations were the key for the original power transition because sudden changes in power were felt to upset previous distributions or "balances." When *transitional* nations, dissatisfied and already powerful, begin to increase their power, they become a threat, causing instability in the system to increase. When first elaborated, power transition focused on the major powers, then generalized (Sullivan, 1976: 164–169) to all potential dyads, and later reformulated so that not only was transition important but also the rate of change: "The faster one nation overtakes the other, the greater the chances for war" (Organski and Kugler, 1980: 62).

Transitions can apply to all dyadic units. "Hegemonic transition" (Gilpin, 1981) was a reaction both to the bipolar–multipolar debate within the context of the Cold War and the possibility of a declining American hegemony. It reoriented the spotlight not to the static distribution of bipolar or multipolar power but to

> the dynamics of power relationships over time. It is the differential or uneven growth of power among states in a system that encourages efforts by certain states to change the system in order to enhance their own interests, or to make more secure those interests threatened by their oligopolistic rivals. In both bipolar and multipolar structures, changes in relative power among the principal actors in the system are precursors of international political change (Gilpin, 1981: 93).

While predictions about why hegemonic war is unlikely in the modern era may be the same—belief in the relative stability of the bipolar system in the 1980s (Gilpin, 1981: 234–235)—nonetheless the key element in understanding "hegemonic war" are the dynamic changes occurring in the system rather than static structural characteristics, despite differences between traditional empires and the "modern pattern."[4]

The "cycle of relative power" constituted a more particular form of hegemonic transition (Doran and Parsons, 1980) focusing on the major powers:

> At critical points during this cycle where change is most rapid and disruptive of past trends, namely at the inflection and turning points, the probability is highest of major power initiation of extensive war (that is, of wars which escalate beyond the level of those initiated at other times) (Doran and Parsons, 1980: 952).

The first articulation had directly focused on nation-state dynamics (Doran, 1971): a state's changing absolute growth relative to the system produces differential acceleration and deceleration wherein states gravitate toward "hegemony" only at certain points along those curves, producing instability potentially leading to war. The "cycle of relative power" expanded the methodology and specificity of those earlier suppositions.

Transitions can actually be distinct variations of what may seem to be similar processes. In "elementary" transition theory, "a rising challenger contests a dominant state for position at the top of the international hierarchy, initiating war to change the status quo." Hegemonic stability theory is characterized by "a hegemon facing imminent decline initiat[ing] preventive war in an effort to prevent its subordination by a challenger and eventual decline." However, "the crisis of a critical point is in no way equivalent to either a power transition or hegemonic decline as has sometimes been asserted" (Doran, 1991: 11). Fine points certainly, since the data are not so finely drawn, but undoubtedly intriguing refinements contrasting differing explanations by the "cycle of relative power," "simple," or "hegemonic" transitions (Doran, 1991: 121–125).[5]

Thus, despite diverse formulations, when dominant countries start losing their power, the *expectation* is for growing instability resulting from fear over losing status or the risk that an adversary will wait until its power has become further diminished. Extending this suggests that *any* unstable power relation is more likely to produce instability than a stable one. Power transition goes beyond simple "balance of power" or stultifying notions of power as a natural lust in favor of a focus on differential structural processes, a clear set of theoretical formulations amenable to empirical testing. While those relations were usually meant to apply to major or hegemonic powers, regardless of whether it be called power transition, hegemonic transition, or cycle of relative power, its generalized form applies to any two nations, groups of nations, or indeed, to any two units.

But What Chameleon Are We Talking About?

While realism in a traditional sense was mostly fading, terminology mutating, and disparate structural formulations proliferating, the problem of the chameleon remained. As noted almost two decades later,

> The first step in theory-building is to determine what is to be explained. This sounds simple enough, but . . . a loosely stated or poorly conceptualized dependent variable can create tremendous problems . . . scholars sometimes accuse theories of failing to meet a particular test when in fact they do not purport to explain the phenomenon in question . . . Do theories of world politics that are rooted in domestic sources and those rooted in structural realism seek to explain the same phenomenon? (Kapstein, 1995: 757).

One observable, empirical reality had unfolded: the lack of major power war during the Cold War years, despite the tensions and presence of nuclear weapons. While viewed as empirical support for the stability of bipolar systems, lost in the subsequent uproar over neorealism's defense of a hegemonic bipolar system was the fact that "stability" so defined was a limited dependent variable, which raises the issue of the empirical *domain*, not only related to "neorealism" in general, but to any structural formulations. "No major war"—or no "hegemonic" war—could be one such dependent variable, but still be limited, representing only one domain of behavior. Each side of the bipolar–multipolar debate had marshaled convincing arguments. Those favoring bipolarity's stability were right, though in a limited sense: the specific Cold War bipolar system had been stable insofar as a major-power war had not occurred. But it had already been demonstrated (Zinnes, 1967) that similar-appearing dependent variables—such as international peace or the status quo—may be quite different. Once less-limited measures of stability were proposed, the picture looked much different (Brecher et al., 1990; Brecher and Wilkenfeld, 1991). Stability could also represent only low-level war or mean no war at all. At the time, little concern was paid to this, but "Predicting peace from a balance of power situation is quite different from predicting simple maintenance of the status quo" (Sullivan, 1976: 172).

Moreover, as the debates shifted from balance of power to bipolarity versus multipolarity towards issues of parity, preponderance, concentration, and transitions, and—as we shall see—cyclical hegemonies, the major focus of the dependent variable also shifted: from traditional measures of war to only those wars which themselves produced major dependent variables:

> The number of participating states, the number of people killed, the number of years fighting, or even the geographical scope of the fighting—all of which are likely to be considerable in systemic wars—retain some relevance, to be sure. *Yet they must take second place to the fundamental reordering consequences of the war. Such an approach is restrictive, but it is a restriction that is done intentionally* (Thompson and Rasler, 1988: 341; emphasis added).

Thus an entire range, from "stability" to point-specific indicators such as casualties, years of war, nation-months of war, and finally the "reordering consequences" of war, is open for investigation. But even within the last category, diversity thrived: "hegemonic war" was a "realignment" war to see whose interests would be best served in the new system, while "global" and "general" war produced a new leadership structure.

Wallerstein's "world war" and "systemic" wars were over serious and fundamental issues and both drew in all of the major actors as combatants (Thompson and Rasler, 1988: 337–338). Varying nominal definitions produce different lists of "Big Wars": four "world" (Wallerstein) or "systemic" (Midlarsky) wars compared to ten "general" (Levy) wars (Thompson and Rasler, 1988: 343); 12 "most severe" wars compared to five "global" wars (Thompson, 1988: 7, 216); or ten "peak wars" (Goldstein, 1988: 240–241). One analysis indicated that only two out of 11 wars—the French Revolutionary Wars/Napoleonic Wars and World War I—were included in seven "general war" studies (Goldstein, 1988: 146).

Thus, multiple dependent variables operate both specifically within balance of power, parity/preponderance, or transition models as well as across them. Limiting "stability" to the question of war, especially "great power," "hegemonic," or "system transforming" war is a constraint, and could result in the simplistic but incorrect conclusion that presence of a system level structure such as bipolarity and absence of major war implies causality of structure and peace. That may be so, but limited to only one outcome variable. It is therefore not particularly surprising that the very period Waltz viewed as exceptionally stable was in fact marked with successive periods of extreme instability (Brecher and Wilkenfeld, 1991; Brecher, 1993).

Nonetheless, by the 1980s the fashion in which the theoretical arguments were proceeding related directly to differential specification of the dependent variable, not surprising given the general trend toward distinguishing two general models of the world, which we can call here BOP vs. COP. Traditional Balance of Power (BOP) painted a picture of the international system viewed horizontally, imbuing nations with billiard ball-like qualities, careening around bopping each other in sequential fashion (i.e., Organski and Waltz). Core over Periphery (COP) viewed the system vertically, with a Core, Hegemon, or Maximum Leader in one way or another subjecting the rest of the system in various fashions to its will (Galtung, Wallerstein, Keohane, and Modelski/Thompson). Manifestly disparate models see different empirical worlds. Thus, another elaboration on alternative pictures of the world saw the emergence once again of the persuasion that recurrently produces wonder in advocates and abhorrence in opponents—the enduring, cyclical favorite, "cycles."

Cycles Come and Go

Essential to many structural theories, especially "transition" variations, is the rise and fall of nations and the enduring subject of cyclicality. But the focus on that process itself goes through repetitive cycles, and it is perhaps noteworthy that in cyclical terms it was exactly one generation between the publication of Toynbee's *Study of History* (1954) and the emergence of the next wave of cyclical analyses 25 years later (Modelski, 1978; Organski and Kugler, 1980; Doran and Parsons, 1980; Gilpin, 1981).[6] Cycles in international behavior have proved captivating, stemming from the widespread belief that nations rise and fall, propelled in cyclical fashion, and popularized from Toynbee to Kennedy's *Rise and Fall of the Great Powers*. Cycles offer a link between apparently observable—and fascinating—behavior, and complex theory, although the link with warlike behavior is spelled out more clearly in "hegemonic" and "long cycles" compared to "world systems" approaches (Boswell and Sweat, 1991: 130).[7]

Cyclical models were reinvigorated with the growing orientation toward quantitative measurement and as power-structural theories became more intricately elaborated. Evidence over the years on international violence has been contradictory (Levy, 1983b: 136–144; Sullivan, 1985: 139–143; Goldstein, 1988: 102ff., 239–244; Sullivan, 1990: 52–55; Beck, 1991; Goldstein, 1991a), with one analyst noting

> the absence of empirical support in the literature for hypotheses of cyclical trends in war . . . confirmed by a visual inspection . . . There are no hints of any cyclical patterns in either the occurrence of war or in any of its other dimensions (Levy, 1983b: 137).

At the other end of the spectrum: "The great power war severity times series . . . strongly suggests fifty-year cycles" (Goldstein, 1988: 239).

Some differences are attributable to time-period: COW data for 1815–1975 show only barely minimal cyclicality at about 26 years,[8] while the longer 1495–1975 period shows a peak at about 50 years (Goldstein, 1988: 244–245). Different expectations also produce different interpretations: some expect definite, "real," prescribable cycles while others only look for "linkages" between variables that illustrate cyclical regularity with other behavioral regularities (Beck, 1991; Goldstein, 1991). While concluding that "As for long war cycles, we are unlikely to find them, even if they exist" because data do not go back far enough, nonetheless it is noted that

> Fortunately, the issue of cycles in single time series and the univariate analysis of time series should be of little interest to political scientists. The issue for us is the interrelationship between series . . . We have seen that the cross spectrum can show positive findings on the relationship of war and the economy. Empirical analysis of others has shown that in the short run war is associated with increased inflation, at least for the last two centuries (Beck, 1991: 471).

More important for the story here, however, is the reemergence of cycle appeal. Coming a generation after Toynbee, a facile explanation might be simple: cycle fascination itself runs in cycles. A second and more substantive interpretation would be the belief in a "declining" world hegemon, reflecting a much more dynamic picture than prescribed by the rigid bipolar model, or the one normally imputed to Waltz's neorealism. A third reason would be that, quite simply, cyclical analyses could—if we let them—explain a great deal parsimoniously, although in reality rarely explaining anything at all in a specific way.

Different cyclical formulations propose distinctive periodization, thereby reflecting different aspects of "neorealism." Modelski's "long cycle" (Modelski, 1978)[9] runs to a 100-year duration, and a decade after its first presentation was declared "fully vindicated, with an accuracy that is just short of astonishing" (Modelski, 1987: 5). Gilpin's hegemonic wars related more to a simplified model of international political change (Gilpin, 1981: 12–13) involving uneven growth and other processes (Gilpin, 1981: 93–96), but implying nonetheless some sense of cyclical change, even though the "cycles of empires" (Gilpin, 1981: 110f.) differed from more recent periods because of the triumph of the nation-state as the major actor, sustained economic growth, and the emergence of world market economy (Gilpin, 1981: 116–144). Cycles certainly reside in Gilpin's notion of successive hegemonies, although he views a 100-year cycle of war and peace with caution because "no mechanism is known to exist [that] can explain them," and therefore the idea "must remain speculative, albeit interesting" (Gilpin, 1981: 205).

Doran's cycle of relative power is less grandiose and more particular to two-nation dyads (Doran and Parsons, 1980; Doran, 1991); whereas hegemonic stability and long cycle see world order as controlled from above by a dominant state, Doran contends that power cycle theory asserts that

> the mechanics of world order are neither devised nor maintained by such hegemonic dom-
> inance . . . the dilemma of peaceful change can have no resolution unless order mainte-
> nance is recognized as a shared responsibility. Only thereby can a just and stable
> equilibrium prevent a collapse into world war during systems transformation (Doran,
> 1991: 14; emphasis in original).

These most recent sets of cyclical formulations played a forceful role in theory development in the 1970s and 1980s, but controversy remains both about their empirical
veracity and potential prognostications. One analysis concluded that the "long cycle correlations between economic and military events do not hold for the 20th century"
(Rosecrance, 1987: 301), but another asserted that "several trends in the current era" appear to have the potential to "alter" what appears to be the "dynamic of recurring war,"
and that certain "globalizing influences" might support "a shift to a new world order
based on common security rather than power politics" (Goldstein, 1988: 369). Never-
theless even the most extensive analysis of the roots of the cyclical controversy (Goldstein, 1988: 100, 124), reasons for its most recent resurgence, and analysis of extensive
data related to what appears to be convincing evidence of cyclical trends, and that sees
the 1893–1914 period as the most likely historical precedent to the contemporary era
(Goldstein, 1988: 361–364) concludes,

> The transition to a "postwar" world order—be it through global cooperation or global
> suicide—is inevitable. But how that transition occurs, and where it leads, is up to us to
> choose (Goldstein, 1988: 376).

Structural theories are parsimonious, and cyclical underpinnings possess the sense of
observable generational change. Of note, however, is that once time frames of previous
cycles begin to look suspiciously like recent cycles, and the "end" of the cycle appears to
be drawing near—an end at which, one might have argued from previous cycles, is likely
negative—the attractions of cyclical theories begin to lose their lustre (Goldstein, 1988:
369–376; Modelski, 1990: 24). At that point, "new" phenomena—as outlined in the
previous paragraph—begin to emerge. Thus, in addition to problems well-elaborated in
the cyclical literature,[10] and despite their fascination, "cycle theory" possesses practically
its own built-in doomsday artifice in which predictions drawn from it are too inauspi-
cious to warrant attention.

Is There a "Real" in Realism, or
How Do We Know Power When We See It?

The rapidity with which the "end of the Cold War" seems to have been accepted as established empirical fact (Gaddis, 1992/93: 5; Little, 1995: 64) ironically contrasts with
the continuing disagreements over the meaning and measurement of essential concepts
potentially related to that very phenomenon. The ceaseless bedevilment with which international relations has dealt with the definition and measurement of power is a long

story in itself. As with the link between measurement of any outcome variable and theory-building, so also we see here that the conceptualization and measurement of power are inextricably linked.

For instance, a trivial example of "power" opened this chapter: Manuel Noriega's relationship with the United States throughout the 1980s, which hypothetically demonstrated "power's" inability to account for contemporary international political relations: Noriega, it was implied, was more powerful. Such, of course, was not the case, as ultimately became very clear. A trivial illustration, perhaps, but so also are many debates about power, where questions asked in certain ways do not relate to power as reflected in extant theories. Many critical questions can be addressed by relatively good measures of power, provided the questions are specified precisely. These issues have been revisited periodically, plaguing the discipline a generation ago and more recently resurfacing with the end of the Cold War.[11] Still, despite the many protestations, significant groundwork has transpired producing measures reflective of key structural concepts. Early work on bipolarity and multipolarity (Modelski, 1974) retains its utility (Volgy and Imwalle, 1995), and some convergence can be found for certain concepts using slightly different measures (Kugler and Organski, 1989; Park and Ward, 1988; Sullivan, 1990: 110–123; Ward, 1989).[12]

Measurement implies empirical analysis, and while the attitude toward empirical evidence may still be ambivalent, an equally troubling problem is the notable lack of consensus on the categories into which empirical findings should be located, especially since the findings are driven by widely recognized theoretical venues. Findings reported relevant to one set of hypotheses—parity/preponderance, for instance—at times appear related to alternative sets of hypotheses—transition theory, for instance. Several different taxonomies have been used by those attempting to bring order to this domain (Sullivan, 1976: 179–200; 1990: 124–135; Kegley and Raymond, 1994), but only one has explicitly used a taxonomy based on four key structural elements most often used by structural realists: system polarity, concentration, alliances, and polarization (James, 1995: 183). Since no one scheme is satisfactory because of the above-noted intermeshing of the theoretical dimensions, and all represent certain arbitrary elements, the attempt here has been to use as many disparate and seemingly discrete theoretical foci, while recognizing the lack of agreement in this area.

Structural Realism: Empirical Assessments

Balance Of Power

Balance of power "theory" has been considered the *central* theory of international relations (Waltz, 1979: 117),[13] and scholars have arrived at far from clear results concerning the workings of "balance of power" systems. Claude (1962: 40–87) cited both Herz, who concluded that although balance of power systems had managed to prevent one-power hegemony they had failed to prevent war, and Morgenthau, who contended that "balance of power systems" after the sixteenth century had safeguarded the independence of small countries. Morgenthau did find periods of stability, one beginning in 1648 and the other in 1815, but both were preceded by elimination of small states. Thus, balance of power exhibited a "poor record" with respect to the prevention of war or helping weaker states. Others saw certain periods—from the Treaty of Vienna to World War I—as peaceful times aided by the balance of power (Claude, 1962: 67–70).

And E. H. Carr, says Claude, argued that it was British supremacy, rather than equilibrium, that kept Europe stable during that century (Claude, 1962: 71).

Traditional historical citations are no less conclusive than empirically generated data, but the latter can be evaluated more cumulatively, and data utilizing alliances, traditionally linked to balancing mechanisms, have been an important starting point. Pioneering work (Singer and Small, 1968) found more alliances in the nineteenth century related to less war, and the reverse in the twentieth century, but later refinements on the design suggested that only a very weak relationship existed between formal alliances and war (Thompson et al., 1980). If balancing was occurring with alliances, it was not related to war. Confirmation is found in data covering a longer period, 1495–1975: high levels of balancing seemed to be associated more with peace than with war, but the findings were moderate, depended on whether the alliances were "offensive" or "defensive," and there was a strong possibility that the relationship was spurious (Levy, 1981: 610–611). Major powers in alliances seemed to be more often initial war participants than did major powers without alliances, although for minor powers the relationship was reversed (Siverson and Sullivan, 1984).

In sum, balancing exhibits more complex relationships at least with warlike outcomes than traditional theory seemed to suggest. Such complexity is also demonstrated when transforming "balancing" to the dependent variable. One analysis compares the balancing carried on against the USSR during the Cold War to the lack of similar behavior against Napoleon a century and a half earlier; system structure was unable to account for the differences in balancing between the two periods. In fact, a coalition of Great Britain and Russia did ultimately restrain Napoleon (Rosecrance and Lo, 1996: 482); perhaps the real question is why balancing was not applied earlier than it was. Thus, while claim is made to contest the "theory of the Balance of Power," what actually happened is merely that "balancing" occurred later than an observer might expect, namely, "when Napoleon had been weakened militarily" (Rosecrance and Lo, 1996: 497).

The question therefore remains: what is the status of "balance of power," does alliance behavior "represent" or "cause" balancing, and do either relate to war? The thrust seems to be that "balancing" as reflected in alliances seems more complex than traditional theory suggested, and thus "traditional" balance of power theory has not received overwhelming support from alliance studies. The utility of using "alliances" as a surrogate or measure for "balancing" behavior, however, can be questioned, perhaps because alliances "do not fit as neatly within the structural realist paradigm" (James, 1995: 194). It is perhaps for this reason that while multiple empirical studies utilize alliance behavior (James, 1995: 193–197), the direct link to "balancing" is not always essential. Confusion over "balance of power" has not been assisted by empirical studies because the original concept itself is so malleable.

Bipolarity/Multipolarity

Bipolar–multipolar issues picked up intensity first as the perceived dangers of a Cold War nuclear world increased and then as ideological debates unfolded, pitted a "hegemonic" two-power world against a more cosmopolitan, multicentered, multipolar world. Alliances and balancing continued in the classic Singer and Small (1968) analysis, which claimed to show bipolarity—greater number of nations in alliances (less interaction opportunities)—related to war, with alliances covarying with the occurrence of war negatively in the nineteenth century and unrelated to war in the twentieth century.

M. Haas (1970) found that all systems witnessed war, but multipolarity produced higher scores on several war indicators, and bipolarity fewer but longer wars (Sullivan, 1976: 196; James, 1995: 186). Two slightly different curvilinear relations showed, first, that war was more probable at very *low* and at very *high* levels of polarization and minimized at moderate levels (Wallace, 1973: 597) and, second, a more dramatic increase in war occurred in the shift from one to two poles compared to changes to more than two poles (Midlarsky, 1974: 427). Yet another curvilinear finding showed the probability of war moderately larger with two poles than with three, but then increasing with the emergence of a four- or five-pole system, and then declining again at six poles (Ostrom and Aldrich, 1978: 762).

Measuring polarization by the *patterns* of cooperation and conflict (rather than power distributions) showed that cooperation decreased when one moved from strict unipolar to strict bipolar, and loose bipolar to loose multipolar structures (Hart, 1974: 239). With alliance-related measures of polarity, "the greater the shift toward a multipolar system, the greater the amount of war that can be expected to begin during the subsequent five years" (Bueno de Mesquita, 1975: 206). An increase in the number of poles in the system related to increase of probability of war, as did an increase in tightness of the system (Bueno de Mesquita, 1978: 258–259). Despite these findings, later results suggested structural variables of tightness and number of poles were secondary compared to individual-level variables of "expected utility" (Bueno de Mesquita and Lalman, 1988).[14]

In the Eurocentric system, "bipolar systems have historically been more stable than multipolar systems, while unipolar systems have been the least stable," but at the same time Great Power wars have been less frequent in multipolar systems but those wars were more serious than wars in bipolar systems. The overall conclusion suggests again a possible curvilinear relationship: stability is lower at the ends—unipolar and multipolar—and higher in the middle bipolar range (Levy, 1985: 58–59). Wayman (1985) also found multipolar years to be slightly less war-prone, although 75 percent of those wars were of high magnitude: multipolar years seem to have fewer but more intense conflicts. Thompson's analysis (1988: 218–223) concluded that "bipolarity can, at times, be just as destabilizing as multipolarity" (Thompson, 1988: 220), but nonetheless presented as a general pattern that

> less warfare than would be expected is found to be associated with the first three types of capability distributions: unipolar, near unipolar, and bipolar. Nearly twice as much warfare as anticipated is associated with multipolarity. Furthermore, the weighted warfare means rise as the polarity distribution ladder is descended into the less concentrated capability patterns (Thompson, 1988: 219).

Midlarsky's analysis focused more on purely theoretical derivations combined with historical referents and case studies—with a more generalized dependent variable rather than quantitative indicators—but also concluded:

> multipolar systems engender serious inequalities under conditions of scarce international desiderata. Bipolar systems do not suffer from this limitation, allowing for equality of distribution under all conditions (Midlarsky, 1988: 66).

Even defining the dependent variable as crisis occurrences, systems manifesting either multipolar or "polycentric" characteristics were the least stable (Brecher et al., 1990;

Brecher and Wilkenfeld, 1997: 742–759). "Polycentric" systems, a hybrid combining characteristics of bipolarity and multipolarity, were the least stable (i.e., largest number of crises), and strictly multipolar systems only slightly more stable than bipolar systems. Excluding the World War II period, the fewest percentage of crises occurred in the interwar—multipolar—(1918–1939) period, followed by the bipolar (1945–1962) period, with the greatest percentage of crises in the "polycentric" (1963–1988) period (Brecher, 1993: 76).

For the brief 1495–1559 period, strategic beliefs concerning the offense–defense balance questioned Waltz's predictions concerning polarity and stability (Hopf, 1991: 487); however, other interpretations of the same evidence find bipolar systems "marginally less warlike" (James, 1995: 186).[15] Adding the contextual variable of "scarcity" suggests that other periods subsequent to 1559, especially the seventeenth century and the period before World War II, furnish support for the relationship between multipolarity and instability under conditions of "significant scarcities" (Midlarsky, 1993: 175).

For the outcome variable of "mean number of wars begun per year," two different data sets show bipolar systems are more warlike than multipolar when considering *all* wars (Mansfield, 1994: 50, table 2.3), but when considered with other variables the mean number of *major power* wars begun per year is slightly greater in multipolar compared to bipolar years (Mansfield, 1994: 64). Multipolarity may produce these effects, however, mostly under conditions of hegemony (Mansfield, 1994: 108; 236). Bipolarity has no effect on a dependent variable defined narrowly as "end of interstate rivalries" (Bennett, 1996).

The empirical evidence does not solve the bipolar–multipolar debate,[16] but does suggest some degree of truth to what many have taken to be Waltz's original formulation concerning the potential positive outcomes in a bipolar world.[17] Unfortunately, the original exposition and ripostes fostered more than debate merely about empirical regularities related to structural characteristics; they became imbedded in normative assessments concerning the "Cold War system," which many saw Waltz as favoring because of its alleged stability. The two—the debate over empirical regularities and the normative associations—unfortunately became inextricably intertwined. The empirical evidence, although possessing the usual multivoice characteristics, does tend to show certain relatively consistent regularities.

Parity/Preponderance

Bipolarity and multipolarity share intellectual borders with parity and preponderance, and thus similar conclusions apply to this domain. In addition to findings in the previous section relevant to parity/preponderance questions, other specific findings relate more directly to the parity/preponderance issue, both at the dyadic and the systemic level.

Early studies found only moderate and inconsistent relationships relating parity to higher conflict (Rummel, 1966; Sullivan, 1974a), and only with limited dependent variables (Rummel, 1972: 102), usually below the level of war. Extensive reanalyses of several data-sets from Ferris (1973) clearly showed relationships between parity/preponderance at both the dyadic and systemic levels. However, these were usually modest, mostly with cooperative behavior and not conflictual, and had a hint of curvilinearity (Sullivan, 1976: 181–184).

By the mid-1970s evidence seemed to favor the preponderance-results-in-peace argument. Two small studies (Garnham, 1976: 391; Weede, 1976) further supported that position, despite problems with missing data, statistical manipulation, and construction of indices (Siverson and Sullivan, 1983: 479–482); these results were confirmed later for 66 border disputes between 1945 and 1974 (Mandel, 1980). Differences occurred between the two centuries as well as more complex results than earlier (Singer and Small, 1968; Singer, Bremer, and Stuckey, 1972), but, at least for the 20th century, parity and movements toward parity seemed to be more dangerous (James, 1995: 192). Controlling for system size seemed to dissipate the results (Ostrom and Aldrich, 1978). Organski and Kugler found no statistically significant relationship between equal/unequal power distributions and war (Organski and Kugler, 1980: 50) until "transition" was taken into account (see following section); despite the lack of statistical significance, however, the raw data slightly supported the preponderance-results-in-no-war hypothesis. Bueno de Mesquita and Lalman likewise concluded that "when balance-of-power theory and power preponderance theory have diverged in their hypotheses, the theory supported, if either, tended to be based on the notion that a preponderance of power encourages peace" (Bueno de Mesquita and Lalman, 1992: 198).

Parity/preponderance was also unrelated to war behavior when using total capabilities, but "static conditions of preponderance and parity—when measured by military capabilities alone—indicates war as approximately twice as probable with rough equality of military power as with preponderance" (Geller, 1993: 189). Lemke and Werner confirm a weak relationship between [static] parity and war (Lemke and Werner, 1996: 251), with the strongest relationships occurring when the less-dominant nation has 70 percent—as opposed to 80 percent or 90 percent—of the more-dominant nation's power. Ranges in power parity from 1/1 to 3/1 are more likely to increase probability of conflict than preponderance situations (3/1 to 9/1) (Huth, 1996: 115, table 10). Shifting the dependent variable to success or failure of peaceful territorial change suggests a modest correlation between an asymmetrical power distribution and success, and a symmetrical distribution of power and failure (Kacowicz, 1994: 246). For crises as a dependent variable, parity seems linked to violent crisis "triggers" whereas preponderance is linked to nonviolent crises (Brecher and Wilkenfeld, 1997: 846–847). However, for major power interventions on behalf of a target state in international crises, such interventions were less likely to occur under situations of preponderance of the target over the attacker than situations of relative equality between target and attacker (although relative weakness of the target was almost a necessary condition for superpower intervention) (Huth, 1998: 758–759).

A growing consensus had developed on parity and war, although several studies raised doubts. Parity in the ratio of military forces played a secondary role compared to competing variables in accounting for "dispute initiations" within enduring rivalries during the 1948–1982 period (Huth and Russett, 1993: 68–69, tables 2 and 3). Another study found that "power preponderance is up to twice as likely as parity to predict war" (Schampel, 1994: 1), a finding itself disputed for having relied on simple bivariate designs and contradicted by data showing no statistical relationship between parity/preponderance and war—although, interestingly two separate tables in the critique itself suggest patterns at least consistent with a preponderance-results-in-no-war hypothesis (Gochman and Hoffman, 1996: 22–23).

On balance, however, although unsavory policy implications can be deduced from these results, structural situations of preponderance appear more likely to be related to peaceful situations and outcomes than parity. The patterns are broad and general, and although not exceptionally strong, they do present a high level of consistency.

Concentration

Power "concentration" has taken on changing specific meanings to accommodate different theories over the last generation, not unlike balance of power. Singer et al. (1972) interpreted data for the nineteenth century to mean that the more "concentrated" the system the greater the incidence of war, with the reverse pattern in the twentieth century. Changing the research design (Healy and Stein, 1973) produces less significant results (Sullivan, 1976: 193–194), but others also found war more likely when resources were highly concentrated and when the proportion of capabilities held by "revisionist" states increased (Stoll and Chapman, 1985). Adding a dynamic, perhaps "transitional," element suggests that "decreasing capability concentration" is necessary for contender power transitions to trigger war: "A growing systemic diffusion of capabilities . . . apparently is required for dyadic power transitions among contender states to create the . . . conditions for war initiation" (Geller, 1992: 280).

A very small proportion of the variation in war can be explained by concentration in a pattern involving "an inverted U-shaped relationship . . . between the concentration of capabilities and the frequency of wars involving major powers" (Mansfield, 1994: 87); wars were lower when power was *least* and *most* concentrated, and higher at the midpoint of concentration, with results differing with different sets of war data. The impact of concentration, however, is not a simple one: it might be considered both as the number of major powers as well as the relative inequality of capabilities among the major powers; the influence of each depends on the level of the other:

> the impact of increases in the number of major powers on the number of wars per year depends on the coefficient of variation of capabilities among the major powers. These results provide additional evidence that the actual relationship between concentration and war is much richer than either balance-of-power or power preponderance theory implies (Mansfield, 1994: 108).

Concentration has a similar, U-shaped effect when considered with levels of international trade and their combined effect on war (Mansfield, 1994: 127–149): concentration—measured both as the number of major powers in the system and the relative inequality of power among them—"is strongly related to the incidence of wars" involving major powers according to the inverted U-shaped relationship described above (Mansfield, 1994: 228–229).

Clearly, traditional formulations do not find a clear match in many of the most extensive analyses of concentration. Not unlike polarization hypotheses, concentration appears to play a more complex role in accounting for warlike behavior, and is subject to various nonlinear relationships. Concentration in the system appears to be neither completely propitious nor completely deleterious.

Transition

"Transition" theories provide a dynamic element, and one early analysis to which others have responded suggested few relationships between static equal/unequal power distributions and dynamic "overtaking" situations except where "contenders" were isolated for analysis: peripheral and central/major powers showed no relationships between parity and war, but when contenders are isolated "equal *and* overtaking" situations seemed to be associated with more war (Organski and Kugler, 1980: 50–52). Subsequent analysis of within-cell observations questioned whether the findings did not in fact do little more than "explain . . . parts of World War I and World War II" and therefore perhaps "portray the history of thwarted German expansionism" rather than producing an "abstract, useful theory of international war" (Siverson and Sullivan, 1983: 487).

The findings were not idiosyncratic, however: other data suggested power transitions among great powers as a potent predictor to the outbreak of war (Houweling and Siccama, 1988) and that

> a power transition in dyads of major powers, together with the passing (by at least one of the nations concerned) through a critical point on its capability trajectory, is a complex sufficient condition of warfare in these dyads: No pair of great powers that meets this complex condition remained at peace in the period of observation (Houweling and Siccama, 1991: 655–656).

This condition was not *necessary* for war (seven dyads wherein the complex condition was not met did in fact go to war) but suggested an advancement beyond the earlier results, which had focused—perhaps too narrowly—on *contenders*. Replications produced slightly weaker results but nonetheless confirmed and expanded on them: while dependent on the different measures of power utilized (COW index vs. GDP) as well as cases analyzed, basic findings confirmed that war was more likely when nations were equal and a transition had occurred (de Soysa et al., 1997: 516, 525–526).

Organski's transition model has been characterized as a one-step process in which a "dissatisfied great power improves its capability position to some impressive although unspecified extent and challenges the relatively declining strength of the system's leader" (Thompson, 1988: 240). Applying long cycle notions to transition processes indicated "some utility as a guide to unraveling the capability changes that precede periods of global war" (Thompson, 1988: 240), but that guide proves to be a rough one. Graphical presentations of transition (Thompson, 1988: 235–239) unearth no clearly transparent pattern of similar transition processes across all five cases of global war, thus Organski's model was labeled insufficient to capture the "full complexity of the transition process" (Thompson, 1988: 240) because it is the "threat of transition," and not its accomplishment, that "creates a crisis for the global political system" (Thompson, 1988: 241). Further findings on the "cycle of relative power" suggest 10-year and 16-year "critical periods" of transition, which, compared to all the remaining periods, produce longer, more severe, and larger wars (Doran, 1991: 114). It has already been noted that adding a transition element to concentration shows that decreasing capability concentration tended to "trigger war" (Geller, 1992: 280). However, power "shifts" are more likely to be associated with war than power transitions: "power shifts *toward* parity rather than away from rough equality show the strongest linkage with war" (Geller, 1993: 189). Other graphical evidence of one illustrative case—the Iran-Iraq war—suggests that the capabilities of the two sides displayed a clear transition toward relative equality just prior to and at the outbreak of war in 1980 (Kugler and Arbetman, 1989: 272–273). Expanding the original Organski model to include the pre-1816 era in addition to the nineteenth and twentieth centuries and adding alliances "as an alternative means by which nations augment their power," thus assisting an "overtaking" situation, suggests that "major war is most likely when the challenging great power, supported by its allies, catches up with the dominant power" (Kim, 1992: 171). Using major wars as the dependent variable "supports Organski's contentions that rough equality of the sides and more dissatisfied rising states increase the chance of war," while transitions themselves have no effect on the probability of war. Injecting risk-averse vs. risk-acceptant attitudes suggests that a choice-theoretic model not only builds on Organski's power transition theory, but "where our model agreed with power transition theory, both are correct. Where they disagree, the evidence supports our model" (Kim and Morrow, 1992: 917).

A model focusing on five global wars (Rasler and Thompson, 1994: 13) suggested a more complex process "that is most important for global wars involv[ing] an ascending regional leader catching up to a declining global leader," wherein the latter sees the former as threatening its global interests and the former sees the latter as a barrier: "The repeated outcome has been acute conflict, consistently won by the coalition organized by the declining global leader to contain the threat of regional expansion" (Rasler and Thompson, 1994: 157).[18] A model employing multiple hierarchies found "power parity and challenger's commitment to change [extraordinary military buildup] have a positive, significant, and generally sizeable impact on the incidence of war in such dyads" (Lemke and Werner, 1996: 257), a relationship applying to major as well as minor powers. Finally, "high velocity change" within dyads was a preceding condition for wars whereas "low velocity of dyadic change strongly approaches a sufficient condition for peace . . . irrespective of nation size, contiguity, and century" (Schampel, 1993: 405). For a sample of enduring rivalries, 1948–1982, the probability of initiation of a militarized dispute increases when a power transition is present (Huth and Russett, 1993: 68–69).

The empirical domain of transition tests encompass both limited time-space dimensions as well as broader, macro pictures modeled after the larger "transition" paradigms (Gilpin, 1981: 186–210). The former receive somewhat higher levels of empirical support, perhaps because this "micro" representation, as opposed to the "grand" systemic, might be more amenable to transition processes: "Since power transition theory refers to national comparisons and not to systemic properties, we can only conclude that our logical extension of the theory to the world level is not supported" (Boswell and Sweat, 1991: 143). Regardless of the level of application and specifics of the findings, overall it appears transition processes are structurally more dangerous situations.

Hegemony

In addition to theoretical and testable dimensions, "hegemony" also embraces normative and ideological implications. Because it bears close similarity to concentration and relates to transition, these paradigms might also be incorporated into this section, as well as "hegemonic stability theory" [Chapter Eight], which compounds the issue even further. In a word, "hegemony" is not a well-defined theory with clear parameters, on which the majority of analysts agree. Thus, where investigators have claimed to be looking at "hegemonic" hypotheses, in fact we are assuming they have done so, although alternate labels might be applied.

Broad-sweep historical analyses of hegemony with much historical description (Goldstein, 1988: 239–249) are common, and such investigations have suggested that major hegemonic-style wars, long waves, and cycles seem to be generally linked with the presence of hegemons and hegemonic activity in one form or another and associated—albeit loosely—with wars during those periods (Goldstein, 1988: 281–286; 309–313;

326–327; 345–346). Even though such findings may find "resonance" in earlier work (Wright, 1942, and Doran, 1971; see Goldstein, 1988: 284), specific empirical linkages are not spelled out and have been called "descriptive" (Boswell and Sweat, 1991: 124).

More strictly empirical analyses utilizing data sets covering diverse time-spans present a seemingly complex array of findings, but on balance generally conclude with respect to hegemony's relationship to an outcome variable defined as "wars begun," that

> hegemony does not seem to be associated . . . with either a decrease or an increase in wars with major-power participants, although it does appear to be strongly associated with a greater incidence of all types of war (Mansfield, 1988: 44–45).[19]

Later reanalyses confirmed this (Mansfield, 1994: 49), and although results differ depending on the data-set utilized (Mansfield, 1994: 130–133), still for *all* interstate wars the presence of a hegemonic power seems to be related to more wars (Mansfield, 1994: 50–51, 88–89;),[20] although when adding the dynamic aspect of transitions from one state to another—hegemony vs. nonhegemony—results are not conclusive (Mansfield, 1994: 52).

In addition to receiving minimal support, and extension, these findings also show some counterindications from a study of British hegemony for 1815–1939. With a predictor variable of overtime *levels of British hegemony*, less wars occur in periods of higher levels of British hegemony and more wars when hegemony is lower—"the results generally support Gilpin's contention that systemic instability is inversely related to the magnitude of a hegemon's relative military and economic capabilities" (Spezio, 1990: 179)—a relationship more significant for *all wars* as opposed to great power wars. The relationship itself was stronger while Britain was declining as opposed to rising, but little difference between the two periods in terms of wars occurred (Spezio, 1990: 177), although a period of systemic instability did occur near the end of Britain's hegemony, which "flies in the face of Gilpin's assumption" (Spezio, 1990: 179).

Comparing four hegemonic-like approaches to analyze initiation-onset-per-year for the 1816–1976 period shows that none is clearly superior, that all achieve respectable statistical significance, but that a "coevolving" model combining both long wave and world leadership (hegemony) proved the most significant (Pollins, 1996: 112–113). Specifically for "hegemony," it appears that "the British and the American periods were associated with significantly less new conflict than times when no hegemon was present" (Pollins, 1996: 113). For a longer period, 1496 to 1967, similar results emerge suggesting a negative relationship between hegemony and war intensity, but in using different measures of hegemony to reflect four different theoretical perspectives, the expected negative relationships also produce numerous complexities (Boswell and Sweat, 1991: 143–144). More consistent results came after 1790—"the deterrent effect of hegemony after the industrial revolution is strongly supported" (Boswell and Sweat, 1991: 146)—compared to the previously more complex interpretations. While hypotheses formulated for sweeping historical time frames should not also be expected to operate during shorter periods, some evidence from 35 years of the Cold War suggests that possibility:

> reductions in hegemonic capabilities correspond to dramatic increases in wars . . . hegemonic share of capabilities continues to demonstrate a significant relationship to both crisis and foreign policy events . . . :as the hegemon weakens, crises and foreign policy activity increase. Decreases in hegemony correspond to exponential increases in both crises and foreign policy events (Volgy and Imwalle, 1995: 829).

Hegemonic theories have always been popular. Having gone through a resurgence beginning in the 1980s, the limited number of such investigations seems to lean toward hegemony's being related to lower conflict. At the same time, the findings make it very clear that "hegemonic power . . . does not account for an impressive share of the variation in the frequency of international conflict" (Spezio, 1990: 179), but given the theme outlined so many times concerning multiple causalities such a conclusion is not surprising—nor necessarily devastating in terms of the utility of this specific structural approach. While findings are certainly mixed, hegemony does appear to exhibit beneficial effects.

Competing with Structures

A crystal clear picture does not emerge from findings on structural "neorealist" impacts most frequently cited in the theoretical literature. Highlighting contradictory findings in no way discredits the endeavor. As with other such synthetic attempts in recent years (Kegley and Raymond, 1994; James, 1995), these undertakings move toward a greater appreciation of what areas of investigation such empirical results can, and cannot, support. Thus, to note that realist theory "'explains' a comparatively small number of the behavioral patterns in international politics" (Fozouni, 1995: 505) is an assertion consistent with a central theme throughout several preceding chapters.

Following, of course, upon the growing popularity of empirical structural analyses came attempts to deride them, especially within the context of growing debates pitting subsystemic against systemic explanations, as if one might serve as *the* only satisfactory model. Expected utility approaches have been viewed as a strong head-to-head competitor, with the conclusion that "domestic imperatives, rather than international considerations alone, play a prominent role in foreign policy choices" (Bueno de Mesquita and Lalman, 1992: 266). The compelling statistical results, however, do not alleviate already noted concerns that expected utility variables derive from structural measurements.

In other cases, design issues limit the range of competitors. For instance, a dependent variable notably limited to the U.S. president's use of major levels of military force in the Cold War period is accounted for by domestic political considerations such as popularity, "success," and the widely used "misery" index of domestic economic conditions. The one "realist" factor isolated—severity of the international situation—does not compete, but that hardly merits the conclusion that "only with considerable effort" could a realist theory of America's use of force be "sustained" (James and Oneal, 1991: 327), since it is likely that nonrealist factors would normally relate to the one restricted outcome variable of yearly fluctuations in "use of force."

An outcome variable more broadly defined—the escalation of deterrence encounters among great powers, 1816–1984—presents a broad test of structural realism against deterrence hypotheses suggesting that the latter receives considerable support compared to the former: "structural theories may provide some insight into the initiation of great power disputes . . . but they do not explain decisions by state leaders to escalate such disputes" (Huth et al. 1993: 614).[21] In sum, evidence suggests that differential findings result from the structure's impact depending upon the definition and measurement of the dependent variable, and whether in fact large-scale structural factors were ever meant to predict to the specificity, for instance, of the escalation that occurs in situations of "deterrence encounters."[22]

Finally, a "modified" realist model incorporating domestic factors receives support, but illustrates the obstacles in categorizing hypotheses into international or domestic levels (the latter being the "modified" part of the realist model). Three domestic factors illustrate the problem: prior unresolved dispute for the challenger, prior loss of territory by the challenger, and support for decolonization when the target is a colony or overseas dependency, all nominally "domestic" but certainly carrying international residues (Huth, 1996: 70). Two others are the prior military conflict and level of democracy (Huth, 1996: 65). All but the last demonstrate the difficulty of establishing which factors are necessarily domestic and therefore truly "nonrealist," an assessment crucial to appraising structural versus contending explanations. In sum, challenging results do not necessarily constitute an unabashed elimination of structural realism.[23]

Conclusion

The concept of "power" has traveled far in the past generation. Over three decades ago, Charles McClelland concluded:

> with rare exceptions, the users of power explanations of international politics have only a misty notion of what they are talking about. Power is an arousing and poetic symbol capable of evoking a wide range of feelings, fears, satisfactions, and discontents in people without contributing, however, to any genuine understanding. Under hardheaded and clear-sighted scrutiny, the concept of power is diminished from a commanding theoretical resource to a very modest abstraction for which an occasional legitimate use can be found in theory and research (McClelland, 1966: 82).

Power still evokes the same emotions, but conceptual formulations have moved from simplistic assumptions about how decision-makers behave, or "ought" to behave, to certain empirical findings coalescing around observed patterns. Results are consistent with earlier evaluations but many have contravened them (Sullivan, 1976: 201–202). In certain quarters, however, much of this has been ignored, substituted instead by the same old debates. Disagreements over definitions and measurements of power persist, and the apparently universally accepted wisdom of the "end of the Cold War" provides an apparent death knell for "structure," bipolarity, and neorealism.

The road, however, has been an interesting one. Morgenthau's realism became transformed into elaborate debates over the merits of bipolar or multipolar systems as well as sustained attempts to test for the effects of power concentration vs. deconcentration on the system. The effects of narrowly defined dyadic or more macro-oriented systemic power "transitions," and the transitional cycles that nations and systems undergo, has received consistent attention in terms of effects on international behavior. The term "hegemony" emerged and often replaced "power" in the ongoing debates, but the wine within the bottles was frequently the same although a slightly different vintage. While so many of the debates have revolved around the "neorealism" allegedly proposed in Waltz (1979), the more interesting theoretical formulations and empirical evidence were clearly those that transcended and expanded on the rudimentary structural depictions contained in that version of neorealism and the many earlier formulations.[24]

But what do "realism" and "neorealism" mean and imply for change in the contemporary world? For all the debates, few bother with what Morgenthau actually said. The preface to his third edition notes that "the chapter on peaceful change has been expanded in view of . . . recent developments," and, lamenting the fact that he had been criticized for ideas he had not held, concluded:

I am still being told that I believe in the prominence of the international system based upon the nation state, although the obsolescence of the nation state and the need to merge it into supranational organizations of a functional nature was already one of the main points of the first edition of 1948 (Morgenthau, 1965: Preface).

Gilpin has noted concerning the subsequent tendentious debates:

> I read Morgenthau as simply saying the following: if the nation-state is to disappear, as in the case of earlier forms of the state (empires, city-states, and absolute monarchies), it will do so through age-old political processes and not as idealists would wish through a transcendence of politics itself (Gilpin, 1984: 299).

The debates are too often removed from the real world; dealing with that real world requires focusing on the behavior to be explained, and one of the refinements has been the attention devoted to setting out clearly defined and well-developed outcome variables in great and measurable detail. Ironically—despite the virulent rhetoric—power, realism, and neorealism are ultimately meant to be meaningfully applicable in a strict sense to only a very small portion of international behavior.[25] In certain circumstances, as suggested above, realism has been discounted as an explanatory variable or framework despite the fact that the specific behavior in question may never seriously have been thought amenable to any realist or neorealist analysis in the first place.

Thus two general orientations have dominated in recent years. One has focused on abstract underlying assumptions of realism and its offspring neorealism and the potential differences between neorealism and structural realism (exemplified by Buzan et al., 1993: 12–23, 48–62); placing realism within the broader historical and philosophical context of the realist–liberal debate (Doyle, 1997); and evaluations against realism from a postmodern perspective (Beer and Hariman, 1996). Mostly removed from direct reference to the "real world," this stream infrequently and reluctantly makes reference to elements and "applications" (Buzan et al., 1993: 61–68) that belong mostly in the second stream. This second stream has taken a much more derivative theoretical direction explicitly using the distinction between dyadic and systemic analysis to generate specific and well-defined research questions spanning the bipolar–multipolar debate, the role of "concentration" or hegemony, or the impact of parity-preponderance or "transition" phenomena on the actual empirical reality of what is happening in international behavior.

"Schizophrenic" might be an apt descriptor, for while the broad paradigmatic ideas continue to unfold,[26] within the confines of the empirical research agenda the theme has been for greater specification, producing another irony that while the broad paradigm addresses generalized behavior, in the trenches only very small portions of international behavior end up being accounted for by realism, neorealism, and power.[27] Even though most emphasis has remained focused on traditional behavior—war—more specific measures both broadened and more finely tuned the potential empirical domain. The distinctions between measures of war itself (length, casualties) as well as different types of wars—global wars, for instance—have opened up the possibility of more finely tuned results that go much beyond rudimentary linkages. Such findings may seem confined to a narrowly defined substantive domain, while the power and realism of Morgenthau seemed so expansive. But the latter, in seeming to account for so much, might have been accounting for very little in terms of specifically understood behaviors.[28]

If realism embodies from one perspective a limited domain, and if the end of the Cold War is accepted fact, one might inquire at this point, "what has happened to the venerable 'balance of power' and the 'rules' that Kaplan laid down so many years ago?" Is it still the case that "the balance of power is the very heart of Realist strategy in world politics" (Doyle, 1997: 161), or is it a "degenerating paradigm" (Vasquez, 1997)? The rules, implying to some degree agency, virtually disappeared from the ongoing discussion, but Kaplan's traditional rules might serve as the linchpin within the much-vaunted and dubiously named "agent-structure" debate. Claude noted many years ago that

> Some writers . . . stress the automatic or self-regulating character of the balance of power system, while others insist that it is a system wholly dependent upon manipulations carried out by shrewd statesmen (1962: 21).[29]

Decision-makers—or agents—do follow rules when they behave; whether that means they follow Kaplan's "rules" or someone else's, or simply their own decision-making "rules," is almost irrelevant. Kaplan's rules do make a great deal of sense *if* decision-makers wish to continue the existence of a specified system. Failing to follow those rules, as Kaplan noted, risks transforming the system, and therefore decision-makers may consciously do so or (unconsciously) fail to follow them; if so, the system becomes transformed, and we have at least the locus for an explanation of "change"—even though that locus may not be at the structural level. In this sense, such balance of power rules can serve both "constitutive" and "regulative" functions (Dessler, 1989: 454–458).

Whether Richard Nixon and Henry Kissinger, in opening relations with China, were breaking or following the rules is almost irrelevant, because the system transformed, but in terms of the agent-structure issue it is important to remember that diverse measures suggest the system had already been undergoing change before those two specific agents became operative and before the momentous point-specific changes of 1971 and 1972 (see Rapkin et al., 1979; Doran, 1991: 71–72, 196ff.). Since the system was already undergoing major transformations, possibly including the early signs portending the "end of the Cold War," were they playing "balance of power" or were they pawns in the structure's grasp? Perhaps the loaded phrase "balance of power" should itself be banished, for it implies that states must act in power-political terms. As Claude noted with Morgenthau's theory of balance of power, what starts out as an iron law of politics—states act in terms of power politics—turns out to be Morgenthau's prudent rule of diplomacy (Claude, 1962: 35).

Nixon and Kissinger's behavior was certainly consistent with "balancing"; what impact conscious agency had is unknown. But nations historically *have* "balanced," frequently do engage *as if* they were balancing in a self-help system, and act *as if* their preservation were at stake. "Preservation" seems still to involve much more than "merely" economic statecraft: the Soviet invasion of Afghanistan, the Iran-Iraq war, the U.S. invasion of Panama, the Persian Gulf War of 1990–1991, the Kosovo War of 1999, the Chechnyan War of 1999–2000—all have certain elements of preservation, although the stories of several of these can also be told with other, more institutional, and less "realist" perspectives. And nothing could be more traditional than China's behavior toward the island of Taiwan in the spring of 1996, and again from mid-1999 through mid-2000—offshore military activities strongly reminiscent of the Cold War crises of the 1950s.

But balancing and "balance of power" have always been fluid and thus open to continual "emendations," a major motivating factor in the move toward more strictly "structural" formulations. Findings relevant to structural approaches often have nothing to say directly about "balancing." Much has been made, however, of superpower behavior at the end of the Cold War as having "undermined" neorealist theory (Koslowski and Kratochwil, 1994: 217). One interpretation suggests that realism's mandate directs the United States to take advantage of the Soviet Union's weakness; instead, the fact is the United States extended help, even if realists argued that aid was consistent with an attempt to prevent the opening of a power vacuum. The latter line of argument could be faulted because it "contradicts the neorealist postulate of power maximization and that of relative gains concerns" (Koslowski and Kratochwil, 1994: 220).

However, a half decade after the Soviet Union's demise, it was a bitter pill for Russia to swallow to accept the United States' zealous drive for NATO expansion into countries that had, a mere six years earlier, been members of the former Soviet bloc itself. Accept it Boris Yeltsin did, but he was not alone in resisting it; the originator of containment itself opposed it, labeling it "the most fateful error of American policy in the entire post-Cold-War era" and asking

> Why, with all the hopeful possibilities engendered by the end of the cold war, should East-West relations become centered on the question of *who would be allied with whom and, by implication, against whom* in some fanciful, totally unforeseeable and most improbable future military conflict? (Kennan, 1997; emphasis added)

By the spring of 1999, U.S.-led NATO was bombing Belgrade. Thus, observable superpower behavior by the late 1990s undoubtedly could be consistent with balancing precepts. Domestic political objectives and dancing visions of future democracies and enhanced stability throughout Europe may have been the clarion calls, but the behavior was also consistent with realism.

What might be observed about the rules of balance of power from these historical incidents is ambiguous. Deriving policy implications from empirical findings is likewise risky business. Nonetheless, so much has been made of the link between realism and policy[30] that it is certainly relevant to ask within the context of a generation of empirical studies: what has been unearthed with relevance to policy? "Balance of power" remains a confusing orientation, perhaps because the original concept itself is so malleable, which in turn may explain its continuing popularity in extraempirical realms and the attacks on it as a "degenerating" research program (Vasquez, 1997). Effects of "balancing" through alliances has not emerged as clearly as traditional formulations suggested; alliances can have a pacifying effect, but seem to be related—either directly or indirectly—to warlike behavior.

The evidence on bipolar versus multipolar systems suggests the former as more stable—with the clear recognition that "stability" has been defined in diverse and multiple ways. Multipolarity is far from the benign structural system once implied (Deutsch and Singer, 1964). Disparate empirical designs have tended to point in the same general direction, and such findings do not resonate well in certain quarters; the same applies to the general thrust of results in the parity vs. preponderance debate, perhaps because nowhere do such findings more seriously relate to potential policy issues concerning foreign relations. The traditional implication thought to have been drawn from realism, that parity balances and deters while preponderance leads to conflicts, certainly gets little support from a variety of discrete research products: parity may constitute—in general—a much more dangerous structure than preponderance.

Theories involving concentration, transitions, and hegemonies produce less consistent findings. High and low levels of concentration appear in some cases to be more stable than midlevels of concentration, and transitions are usually structural conditions more prone to war or other conflict behaviors; findings on hegemony and hegemonic status are mixed, but lean closer toward supporting—as opposed to disconfirming—hegemonic propositions that view the existence of a hegemon as a positive factor.

Translating empirical findings into specific policy is a much different enterprise than unearthing the findings themselves.[31] First, because systems change, the analyst is caught amidst complex, elusive, dynamic processes, producing the "forests-vs.-the-trees" dilemma. Second, a repetitive critique of realism and especially structural realism is that "findings" might be hopelessly out of date in the "post–Cold War" era, findings that would, insofar as they relate to neorealism and what has been referred to as "the ideological form abstracted from the real historical framework imposed by the Cold War" (Cox, 1986: 211), be hopelessly time-bound. And that may be the case. But that assumes that the changes currently underway reflect quantum transformations in the very underlying political processes at work rather than a manifestation of the results of those very processes. Once structural realism is extracted from its alleged reliance on the bipolar Cold War system for its framework, then the idea of a neorealist "model" based on an aberrant period becomes irrelevant. The events of a very short period of time—1989–1991—while certainly of import, should not then be taken necessarily as earth-shatteringly momentous in a causal sense. This is especially the case when the end-of-the-Cold War theme is taken as a message concerning not only structural analysis, but also the viability of the nation-state system. Neorealism need not account for the emergence of the state-system or for the rise and fall of specific states. The neorealist era has been cast as the "consolidationist" phase of "power politics" (Cederman, 1994: 504) following on what has been labeled the "contraction phase" during a longer period itself referred to as the focus of "dynamic realism." In this time line the "consolidationist phase" associated with neorealism covers a longer time span than the Cold War, further questioning the inference that neorealism and the Cold War are intertwined. Despite neorealism's inability to answer the question, "from where these great powers arise" and "lacks a convincing theory of institutional change" (Cederman, 1997: 72, 74), the processes involved in structural neorealist systems hypothetically extend back much earlier than—and therefore might outlive—the Cold War.

However, one cannot discount the possibility that the "end" of the Cold War, recognized by so many as momentous fact, has established a novel structure with a new set of "rules." Such assertions, however, need confirmation. Perhaps a "multipolar peace" with three factors—concentration, alliance behavior, and norms—has emerged in such a way that their interaction *this time* will produce different outcomes (Kegley and Raymond, 1994).[32] Nations, we are told, can rise above the processes of the past and—contrary to Michels's notion of history being successive waves breaking endlessly on the same shoals ("they are ever renewed")—this alternative construction suggests the successive waves eventually erode the shores,

thus altering the landscape and their own patterns . . . great powers at the late twentieth and early twenty-first century are not doomed to repeat the failed methods of the past. They can be masters of their collective fate (Kegley and Raymond, 1994: 235).[33]

This view requires the emergence and strengthening of democracies and the development of free market economies, both combining into a "neoidealist moment" (Kegley, 1993), all of which can imply agency at the nation-state level.

Propelling the debates about the system, which have produced more sophisticated and complex models, has been the serious defect contained in the Waltzian view of basically static orientations. Advancing dynamic analysis, however, suggests knowledge about the transition between systems and the recognition that systems are not only ranged somewhere between ideal types, but that other system-types exist. The multiple processes that transform a system from one stage or type to another reside at least partly at that nation-state level, and no one seriously questions that;[34] ultimately, while the transformations are manifested in one form or another at the system level, they often originate elsewhere, are slow moving, and difficult to track.

Venturing predictions concerning system change is fraught with difficulties. Gilpin predicted stability for the bipolar system for the foreseeable future at a point when evidence suggested it was already on the way to breaking down (Gilpin, 1981: 235),[35] and Kennedy was certain about the future of the Eastern European puppet regimes, predicting no retreat by Soviet forces in Eastern Europe approximately two years before they began retreating (Kennedy, 1987: 477–478). Sweeping hypotheses concerning system transformation characterize a broad interpretive history of international systems of the ancient Middle East, but only broad implications are drawn about contemporary systems: ultimately, individual agency—"people's ideas, values, and inventiveness"— seem to control the fate of larger systems (Kaufman, 1997: 205).

None of this means, however, that the systemic enterprise is doomed, or suggests that balancing or power parity effects will cease to exist, or that future shifts among bipolar, multipolar, or other systems might not produce effects already uncovered empirically, nor that transitions might not also have their effects. But—following Cederman to some degree (1997)—they need added complexity. Dyadic analyses especially in terms of power transition, for instance, have mostly been carried out in isolation, in which the unit of the analysis is the two-nation dyad, with the assumption that transition processes operate within dyads in relatively similar ways. But transition mechanisms themselves might be affected by the characteristics of the larger system. Bipolar or multipolar systems might affect transitions in different ways, and the cycle of relative power might be differentially affected by whether the various tur..ing points occur within bipolar, multipolar, or mixed systems. These linkages in turn can become more complex when considered within the larger possibility of a "world system" model that would incorporate the idea of a "single logic versus political and economic subsystems" (Chase-Dunn, 1981: 41).

Systemic, structural models fail to consider many complexities, but "structural realism" merely relegates decision-making (realism) to another level, recognizing that it occurs within the context of structural constraints. This approach does not eradicate detailed and colorful descriptions of how structural constraints that decision-makers faced during specific historical eras might have appeared to them, and how those constraints might affect the decisions they were being called on to make (Doran, 1991: 125–132; 1995: 5–9), a world in which perceptions and expectations play decisive roles in the many discrete situations concerning their own and other nations' actual and expected decisions. Structural constraints that decision-makers *most certainly* were acting under become to them alive and real elements in these accounts. For the decision-makers in this world, systems of power do not resemble the abstract entities academic scribblers may construct many years later, but are nonetheless the same systems. Concerning the pre–World War I era, for instance:

> Did Britain and France know of their impact upon the German collective political psyche? Why were they seemingly unable to alter their foreign policy conduct? In the early years, forced onto a declining trajectory by Germany's rapid growth, they were unwilling to "move over." The problem was not so much that they failed to understand their predicament, nor that they could not fathom the result of political inaction. The problem was that they started too late to make adjustments in terms of style and international political comportment (Doran, 1991: 131).

The theoretical progression and empirical evidence demonstrates substantial transformation compared to the circumstances just over a generation ago. Realism, realpolitik, and neorealism, perhaps because of the excessive attention to Waltz's variation of structural analysis, became associated equally with the Cold War, the existence of what many felt was a "hegemonic" and perhaps dangerous bipolar system, and—more broadly—with a perceived irresponsibility that "pursue[s] policies that perpetuate destructive old orders," a view that says that "if *realpolitik* causes the very conditions to which it is a response," then "to the extent that realism counsels *realpolitik,* therefore, it is part of the problem," and therefore to be opposed "if we care about the well-being of future generations" (Wendt, 1995: 80).

The implication of such charges is clear to some: "realists like me are irresponsible and do not care much about the welfare of future generations" (Mearsheimer, 1995: 92), but such debates merely hurl charges or shoot the messenger. They do not advance the modifications to structuralism capable of meshing competing realist with liberal explanations, which have always been nearby but witnessed a post–Cold War resurgence especially in their direct competition with either the realist or neorealist perspective. Combining specific parameters from the structural power approaches to the liberal views would advance theoretical progression and bypass the ideological debates. Whether this "current intellectual movement away from the starker, more rigorous, neorealist model of international politics toward the richer analytic framework of traditional realism" (Schweller and Priess, 1997: 23) means a complete reversion to traditional realism awaits the next generation of empirical research.

Chapter Seven ◉

Integration, Liberalisms, and Balance: Tales of Two Theories

Introduction

Hope springs eternal, even in the region of the world where the most intense wars in modern history have occurred. The conviction quickly grew after the second of those wars that peace could prevail, and later, even during "periodic spells of gloom" in the European Community, when headlines shouted, "Europe's Hopes of Unity in the Dust," "seasoned observers were reportedly convinced . . . the impetus for integration will return."[1] Despite the pessimism generated by the cynical view of realpolitik so often used to characterize models of realism and neorealism, a broad strain of "liberal" thought, always present, has once again come to play a growing role in the development of contemporary views of world politics.

This broad strain, referred to as "a succession of terminological incarnations in opposition to realism" (Nayar, 1995: 139) has included idealism, functionalism, "neofunctional regionalism," interdependence, liberalism, "neoliberalism," "institutionalism," and "liberal institutionalism"—as well as the broadly encompassing and popular concept of international "regimes." The entire aggregate re-energized with the end of the Cold War, while a second strain of structural thought, structural balance theory—originally considered as loosely related to liberal thought if for no other reason than it carried only minimal realpolitik implications but also a sense of integration among those with an external enemy—never quite succeeded in capturing the imagination. Both in different fashions generate hope opposed to the pessimism of un-ending conflictual anarchy one might take away from structural realist formulations, and yet both have followed very different paths.

Early theories of international "integration" resting on both hope and the theoretical have been succeeded by the richer formulations listed above, all the while retaining a positive "liberal" undertone. Theories of "structural balance" were more accurately grounded in simple observations of human behavior, but also the equally-liberal hope that conflict might derive not from deeply-rooted ideological or power-driven antagonisms, but simple deficiencies in mankind, correctable through the sheer recognition of the repetitive structural patterns these deficiencies produced. Each has fared differently, the first metamorphosing into numerous clones, and the second slowly fading from the scene with few remaining adherents.

Integration: The Liberal Tradition

Liberal theories cover a broad terrain.[2] "Cognitive" and "republican" liberalism have already been analyzed [Chapters Two and Four] at individual and state levels; sociological, interdependence and institutional liberalisms all operate at the systemic level. The beginnings of the modern focus arose from the reaction to World War II and the emerging gloom of the realist perspective, with hopes for integration in the very geographical region that had spawned two massive wars within a half century. But it boasts a long history underpinning debates between the realists and neorealists, on the one hand, and the liberal internationalists, on the other, and "reproduces, with up-to-date materials, the Seventeenth century challenge presented by the civil philosophy of Hobbes to the natural law theory of Grotius" (Cox, 1996: 130).

The Grotian view that reemerged after World War II primarily focused on Europe and possessed at least three attractions. First, it countered the growing influence of Morgenthau's "realism," and even though it did not take it on as bluntly as later critiques, it clearly recognized that much popular wisdom and a growing body of social science theory were proposing that nations did not necessarily always—as some later erroneously thought realism dictated—"act in terms of power." Second, it reflected the growing interest in international organizations, partially spawned by the new aura and moral commitment surrounding the United Nations—highlighted by its action in Korea—and by the fact that it was seen as an important "end product" to be achieved in international politics. Third, early liberal formulations imbedded in integration theories were viewed as the opposite of conflict, and, based on the sociological "transaction" model, cast a positive light, addressing important questions in political theory of how to achieve integration, consensus, and shared values without deference or force.

The focus on integration continued after its immediate post–World War II popularity in the early 1950s as a major research orientation into the 1960s, when it was replaced in policy and academic discussion by "interdependence," transnationalism, and later "regimes" and "neoliberal institutionalism." The early research on European integration, which constituted a major agenda from the mid-1950s to the late 1960s, did not resurface until the late 1980s, and then focused more on "EC92" as a historical moment rather than "integration" as a long-term sociological transaction process. In fact, despite receding academic interest in favor of more trendy notions, the actual integration of Europe had progressed to such a degree that in 1993 the *Economist* noted that the European Community still had flaws, but the "flaws" referred to consisted of the absence of a European trademark office and the continuing restrictions on road-haulage—which were seen as "little more than irritating oddities."[3]

Thus, Western European integration, begun with moderate enthusiasm, was matched with elaboration of theoretical propositions meant to track, understand, explain, and perhaps prod and expand the process elsewhere. "Integration studies were one of the most exciting and dynamic areas within . . . international relations . . . in terms of theoretical developments within the discipline, this work represented a clear and important challenge to state-centric realism" (Smith and Ray, 1993: 7). Nonetheless, by the 1970s academic interest had waned and become "dominated by skepticism and pessimism, which, until very recently, was replaced by boredom and an almost total lack of interest" (Smith and Ray, 1993: 20). Ironically, concrete, genuine, real-world integration in Europe, after witnessing a desultory decade in the 1970s, continued with remarkable progress, while theoretical interests had shifted to somewhat more amorphous phenomena such as interdependence and "regimes."

Integration: Elaborating Liberal Theory

Standard histories note that World War I spawned the League of Nations and related organizations as well as theories of functionalism and hope for Intergovernmental Organizations (IGOs)—all premised on loyalty transferring from the nation-state to other entities at the system level or to specific IGOs. World War II spawned the United Nations and related organizations, and while functionalism held a strong pull emotionally and theoretically, it was tied to organizations. Given the experience of the League, the view that integration of nation-states is achievable through organizations changed with the revolutionary intellectual movement after World War II that visualized the theoretical importance of increased transactions and communications. Formal organizations are, after all, only human creations with all the built-in defaults of human decision-making. Transactions and communications, however, are simply normal by-products of the human condition, but by-products reflecting behavior and interactions—as well as containing the seeds of later "liberal" thought.

The "Deutschian communication" model departed radically from previous views (Sullivan, 1976: 208–213). While later organizational formulations posited greater sophistication by suggesting that institutions initiate structure in the anarchical international system as well as produce other orderly by-products that may go beyond the original substantive motivations for the specific organizations, early organizational approaches were more bare: nations formally integrated with one another would behave differently than less integrated units, international systems exhibiting integration would by definition be—on the whole—more peaceful, and that integration could be equated with interactions within organizations. The Deutschian intellectual ferment shifted the focus from organizations *per se* to transactions and communications that occur repeatedly between groups and nations, introducing concepts partly found later in interdependence, regime, and neoliberal institutional models.

The long forgotten "Deutschian steps," rarely referred to as "liberal," nonetheless link early and later forms of liberalisms. A series of nominal definitions described the process of integration: a "security community" was a group that had become integrated, the attainment of a "sense of community" and of institutions that could assure dependable, peaceful change, and implied agreement on at least one point: that common problems must be solved by "peaceful change." The final stage was that "peaceful change" consisted in the resolution of social problems, normally by institutionalized procedures, without resort to large-scale physical force. The first step meant "communication of some type must exist"; groups or nations in communication constitute social "systems." Second, "something of interest must be present for two parties to communicate about," an "identification" of interest. The result is mutual relevance; communication defines the presence of relevancy (Cobb and Elder, 1970: 8–9). The standard hypothesis that served as the basic assertion of the Deutschian model has been long-held by policy-makers, namely, that "the one thing which is unlikely to accompany a high level of transaction is continued high tension and conflict" (Deutsch, 1964: 67). Later hypotheses would posit that such interaction develops patterns that can become institutionalized; standard procedures can then culminate in formal organizations.

The communication model struck a positive chord; mistrust of traditional institutional approaches, negative reaction to Morgenthau's power-based model, as well as a postwar optimism similar to that after World War I combined to provide a ready following. Components of this influential communication approach did not recede in the elaboration of its most direct offspring, interdependence and transnationalism, but subsequently did so when the turn was made toward "regimes," although the latter focused on what was seen as the by-product of the early communication linkages, namely, institution-building. As later with regimes, the communication model had strong antecedents in international law:

> In proportion as men in different groups *communicate* with each other regularly and abundantly they tend to form a public opinion . . . in the long run synthesizes the values and technologies of the communicating groups into a *common culture* and value system . . . [participants] tend to become aware of that culture . . . to formulate in legal rules the standards, interests, and goals that culture implies, and to *cooperate* . . . Such cooperation stimulates the acceptance of common policies and an *organization* to enforce the law and to achieve the policies (Wright, 1966: 84–85).

Deutsch first explicitly spelled out the implications of communications and transactions, and Wright's analysis established it also as a key to the development of laws. But "political" elements remain, and "neofunctionalists" emerged to expand upon the functionalist approach that had emerged earlier in the century, which had argued that because political problems between states are often intractable, social inequities can only be dealt with on a social and economic level; joint nonpolitical problems might be dealt with cooperatively whereas political matters could not. Functional processes could hypothetically then be transferred to organizations. Neofunctionalists did not view the process in automatic terms, for political variables cannot be extracted. "At the core of both approaches, however, is the process of spillover, wherein certain procedures and behaviors occurring in the communication process spill over into others" (Sullivan, 1976: 212).

Thus by the 1960s, three processes were in motion. Neofunctionalists had expanded upon earlier and somewhat simplistic functionalist ideas, the transaction-communication school was drawing in adherents more tuned to observable phenomena of integrative tendencies, and multiple conceptual developments had burgeoned. At one point seven different "process" mechanisms and four "conditions" essential to consideration of the integration process were proposed. Another scheme involved ten "variable properties." While suggestive and exciting in an era when theory development was often associated with extensive elaboration of "factors," "variables," and "processes," conceptualizations approached the complexity of Snyder's decision-making "models" of a decade earlier, producing an overdetermined "closed" system. The only casualty was parsimony.

Very few continuous tests were carried out on the later processes and changes occurring in Europe through the 1970s and into the 1990s, but early attempts highlighted the major tensions between communication approaches and traditional, standard institutional or decision-making explanations. Not that traditional views were not present. Etzioni's model of the formation of international communities, for instance, concerned the locus of power, arguing that "a new community is formed . . . when a nation more powerful than the other potential members 'guides' the unification process." While these conceptualizations later reemerge in the guise of hegemony operating within "regimes" (Levy et al., 1995: 310), at the time Etzioni's formulations were outside the more popular "transactional" communication approach.

Despite their popularity, they remained hampered by definitional and operational problems, a similar fate, interestingly enough, that has persistently plagued later formulations on international "regimes." Such problems have chronically troubled the "liberalist" agenda—even down to current renditions. The fairly obvious question of "What is integration?" depended on whether the phenomenon was seen as an end or as a process. Integration as *level or situation* that nations reach differs from integration as an ongoing dynamic process. For some, integration was a well-defined "point" established most assuredly by the formation of a union. For others, the *process* of integration consisted of the fluctuation of numerous transactions, wherein integration was viewed as constantly oscillating, perhaps even unrelated to a formal union.

A further distinction that more clearly emerged with regimes was whether integration was an independent or dependent variable. Some predicted *to* high levels of integration from high levels of communication, others *defined* integration *as* high levels of transactions or communications, and still others were concerned with whether integration was a unidimensional or multidimensional phenomenon (Sullivan, 1976: 213–217). While trade was the first widely used measure of integration, subsequent research established potential drawbacks in such a simple, although readily available, measure. Broadened empirical measures encompassed economic, political, and social variables, the unification of elites or masses, and a wide variety of phenomena. The question never was resolved, however, and, as with others, returned to haunt successors.

From Theory to Data

The better part of a half-generation devoted attention specifically to the "integration" of nation-states, especially Europe, but hopes of the early theoretical work were not borne out by corresponding empirical work (Sullivan, 1976: 216–221). Investigating a small portion of that data in light of the major integrative strides made since then is instructive, especially given the often swiftly changing views about both contemporary European and international integration more generally. Deutsch concluded very early, and prematurely, that no "unequivocal trend toward more internationalism and world community" was occurring, and the closer to modern times, he concluded, "the more difficult it is to find any instances of successful amalgamation of two or more previously sovereign states" (Deutsch et al., 1966: 4). In those very early studies, several variables traditionally thought to have been related to "pluralistic security communities" actually turned out to be relatively unimportant: a previous administrative union, ethnic or linguistic assimilation, strong economic ties, and foreign military threats. A key variable appeared to be a "core area" or country capable of playing a leading role in the community—a factor already noted (Etzioni, 1969: 348) of later formulations (Levy et al., 1995: 310) and a role, interestingly, that contemporary analysts felt might characterize a new, reunited Germany in further efforts toward European integration in the 1990s.

But at a time when hope ran high concerning European integration—the 1960s—empirical evidence suggested caution. Trade in Europe had reached the "highest level of structural integration it has ever reached" in the 1957–1958 period. While Europe certainly was more integrated then than between the wars or before World War I, "from about 1957–1958 on, there have been no further gains" (Deutsch, 1966: 355). Coming at a time when great hope had been placed on integrative possibilities in Europe, Deutsch's findings were a bombshell.

Trade was not the sole indicator contradicting the conventional wisdom. An analysis of elite newspapers indicated that interest in an Atlantic Alliance decreased in French, German, and British newspapers, remaining high only in the *New York Times*. Concern in the newspapers with internal as opposed to external supranational questions was the same in the mid-1960s as it had been a decade earlier (Deutsch, 1966: 356).

Similar trends occurred in mass opinion. While European unity as a goal had surfaced, by 1966 Deutsch reported "no clear image in mass opinion as to what these steps should be, or how far they should go, nor is there any sense of urgency about them" (Deutsch, 1966: 357). Later data supported those findings: "the period of all-western European partnership is over . . . There has been as much economic *dis*integration in Europe since 1951 as there has been integration" (Alker and Puchala, 1968: 315). Members of the Common Market were no closer economically in the early 1960s than they were in the early 1950s, and Franco-German integration was not always marked by increases: confidence, amity, and cooperation between the two countries did expand from 1954 to 1965, but the 1963–1965 period had shown a drop in cooperation, and the establishment of bilateral institutions generally leveled off after 1959. By the mid-1960s a "strain" or "load" had been put on Franco-German relations (Puchala, 1970).

Such evidence in the contemporary context may be little more than a historical footnote, using empirical evidence of less relevance to current concerns, covering only a very short period of time a generation ago, and focusing on units—nation-states—that many view as growing anachronisms. Nonetheless at the height of the early integration movement, it proved a bombshell for those who held out hope that "integration" was a process that could be tracked, understood and ultimately used to produce more peaceful international subsystems. The warnings about failure proved to be very much wide of the mark—or at least as the evidence available in the mid-1990s would suggest. But it is also true that even into the 1990s, with what appeared to be indisputable evidence of further integrative moves marked by the Maastricht Treaty, EC92, and the move toward a European Monetary Unit, doubts and reservations persisted, as evidenced by quotes from the popular press noted earlier.

Deutsch's "socio-causal paradigm" or "social assimilation" model was not without its critics. One analysis used actual decisional outputs of the European Community (EC), and the European Coal and Steel Community (ECSC), and found that political assimilation *increased* in Europe at the point that Deutsch claims social assimilation decreased (Fisher, 1969), demonstrating the tension between an interaction model and institutional conceptions, whether transactions, attitudes, or institutional decisions more accurately reflected integration. But still other evidence generated in the 1960s suggested that the European Economic Community (EEC) was a "weakly integrating social system," with limited responsiveness on the part of other components of the EEC. While certain indicators suggested integration—Germany's exports to the EEC and the number of political decisions and regulations adopted by the EEC had become greater—changes in certain time series did not uniformly respond to experimental events. Thus "European integration" seemed to be increasing in terms of certain indicators—growth of intra-EEC trade and decisional outputs—but not in terms of "responsiveness" of one component to another (Caporaso and Pelowski, 1971; Sullivan, 1976: 220–221).

The role of international organizations was also confusing from both theoretical and methodological perspectives, as well as the level at which they were thought to operate. Findings on the effect of regional organizations on regional integration and cooperation certainly were not overwhelmingly positive for the role of specific organizations, including for the UN (Nye, 1971: 131, 171, 175). At the more clearly systemic level, a higher *creation* rate of IGOs seemed to occur at the *end* of warlike periods, but no relations emerged between IGOs during one period and the pattern of war in later periods (Singer and Wallace, 1970: 540). Inverse relations were found between number of IGOs, INGOs, and their formation rate and various conflict-related dependent variables: armed force levels, battle casualties, number of wars, and arms races (Wallace, 1972: 66; Harf et al., 1974: 240).[4] Later investigations found joint IGO membership related to lower incidents of militarized disputes, with a potential "virtuous circle of reciprocality" operating because absence of militarized disputes appears related to subsequent readiness to join IGOs together (Russett et al., 1998: 462).

Despite widely noted problems in the early research, hope still rested on integration as a phenomenon capable of occurring, from which would flow community formation and ultimately sustained and continuing cooperative/collaborative behavior. Whether the original theoretical hypotheses truly withstood the empirical test of time is unknown; even though certain subsequent system-level behavior in Europe is consistent with predicted outcomes in a general sense, the original models were never submitted to persistent, systematic, rigorous tests. Moreover, the popularity of certain theoretical tenets did not appear to weather the test of time:

> The putative development of a "we-feeling" among individuals or states in a security community was something hard for Karl Deutsch to demonstrate and explain, and it would remain hard in Europe today (Weber, 1994: 37).

Nonetheless, the amalgam of normative hopes and theoretical propositions was a less than explicit precursor to the more recent "liberal" program, even though liberalist assumptions that contrast it to realism—to be noted shortly—were rarely enunciated in the earlier formulations. Deutsch's pluralist security community, Haas on the uniting of Europe, as well as others, are all recognized as having constituted part of this complex (Grieco, 1988: 486; Keohane and Nye, 1989: 247). These "transnational coalition opportunities" focused "very directly on the political processes of learning and the redefinition of national interests, and on the ways that institutional frameworks and regimes foster such processes" (Nye, 1987: 373). The general historical linkage of this lineage is certainly correct, although the evaluation of respective theoretical potency is certainly open to interpretation, namely, that:

> the development of regional integration theory outstripped the development of regional communities. Predicted changes were slower than expected. This discrepancy may account for the decline in academic interest in the subject during the 1970s (Nye, 1987: 373–374).

The mere occurrence of an outcome variable consistent with the predicted outcome of earlier theories does not itself constitute a rigorous test of the linkages involved. The lack of interest in the early 1970s has been in fact attributed, not to the theory running ahead of itself, but rather because "it was becoming increasingly clear that the predictions of the neofunctionalist model were not coming to pass" (Smith and Ray, 1993: 30) and "from the perspective of the mid-1970s, the gloomy assessments found in the scholarly literature of both the past accomplishments and future prospects of the European Community seemed no doubt well-justified at the time" even though "from our current perspective those assessments seem strangely pessimistic" (Smith and Ray, 1993: 20).[5] A simple measure of trade by the early 1970s shows very clearly: there were unmistakable linear increases in integration—intra-EC exports—for the previous 13 years (Smith and Ray, 1993: 26). It would not be perhaps until the late 1980s that the "stalemate," at least as far as *European integration*—defined by trade—had set in (Downs et al., 1998: 411). A variety of subsequent trade data were to demonstrate that between the early 1960s and the early 1980s "integration" of a very clear sort was occurring (Garrett, 1992: 538).[6] Moreover,

> especially in institutional terms, and most especially during the ten or fifteen years before the passing of the Single European Act, that is, during the era of "europessimism," and at a time when the Community was largely ignored, the EC nevertheless experienced dramatic growth (in membership), important developmental advances, and corresponding increases in its influence and importance (Ray and Smith, 1993: 25).[7]

The fact that integration occurred at some point later in time—1980s or 1990s—does not imply that prior "regional integration theories" have been confirmed; a convenient argument, perhaps, but disingenuous, for the empirical studies do not confirm which ones or which components of those prior theories are correct. It is accurate, however, that "the transformation of Western Europe into a pluralistic security community is real" but it is less obvious—to jump ahead in our story a bit—that "many insights from integration theory transferred to the growing and broader dimensions of international economic interdependence in the early 1970s" (Nye, 1987: 374). It is more accurate to note that during the 1970s and 1980s little continuous, systematic effort was given to applying and tracking the earlier integration conceptual apparatus, and that even into the 1990s no extended systematic effort was being made to assess and handle the many oscillations in the observable integration that was occurring along the lines of integration theories of a generation earlier.[8]

From the historical perspective of the 1990s, with a flourishing integration movement in Europe, the evaluation and understanding of where that putative movement stands with respect to its potential academic progenitors remains uncertain. Several conclusions, however, are warranted. Integration "theory" was one of the first anti-, or certainly a-, realist movements in international theory, and was largely databased. It was structural and contained theoretical explanations. What it spawned operationally or explained theoretically in the real world of political integration in Europe and elsewhere is still open to question, but offers a radical departure for international theory. It also began a theoretical movement that in several different reincarnations influences structural explanations and anchors part of one side in the realist-liberal debate. That viewpoint, however, has undergone numerous transformations.

Interdependence, Transnationalism, and "Regimes": Same Tunes, Different Drummers?

Research on international integration as opposed to discord, conflict, and anarchy—and the "gloomy" prognosis some see as the outcome from one strand of "realism" (Nye, 1987: 371–372)—was constituted of multiple threads and had multiple causes. From the early, large-system transaction/communication models to later, more refined ones on regional integration, the endeavor promoted complex categorical schemes as well as much hope (Cobb and Elder, 1970; E. Haas, 1970; Puchala, 1970; Nye, 1971), but as noted the popularity peaked in the early 1970s, and conceptual development shifted, and, to some degree, empirical development and cumulation along previous lines declined. A tracking of the multiple lists of factors, phenomena, and variables designated essential to integration theory could have tested whether the theory had done its job and was running ahead of itself, or whether failures emerged. But alleged "new" transformations in world politics appeared, and other conceptual notions surfaced in the wake of the post-Vietnam period (Sullivan, 1990: 21–72).

These transformations manifested themselves in numerous specific episodes. Between 1971 and 1975 a new detente emerged more extensive and substantively meaningful than the two brief previous excursions in superpower peacemaking in 1955 and 1959, exemplified in President Nixon's dual visits to Peking and Moscow. The Bretton Woods system ceased to exist, the world financial and economic system was devastated by the first oil embargo of 1973, and the major focus and byproduct of the Cold War—the Vietnam War—ended. By the mid-1970s concern had shifted to the notion that in this new post-Vietnam, tri- or multipolar oil cartel-dominated world, major transformations were underway. It had also been roughly 20 years since the world had first become dominated by the continuing, oppressive superpower tension embodied—it was thought—in realism, and it was time for a refreshing change. If the hope for Europe had leveled off, it was time to look elsewhere. Once the international system either begins to change in reality, or if perceptions or desires change, many immediately assume that old models must be cast adrift and different ones exploited to understand this "new world." Just as realism played that role after World War II, and began to fade as the above events unfolded, it became logical to propose another model appeared to be more in line with the unfolding world of the early 1970s. The broad concept to emerge was "interdependence," encapsulated within a narrower notion by one influential work as "Complex Interdependence" (CI), and linked with yet another concept emerging from the tradition of international law: "regime." The first, as we will see, fades quickly from the scene, while the second, for many, becomes the new silver bullet.

In light of subsequent developments and elaborations of the larger genre, two observations are warranted. First, the basic underlying presumptions and assumptions spelled out in these formulations were largely reactive to opposite presumptions contained in realism—and debates continue to the present on these. Thus, second, the originators of "complex interdependence" did not propose it as a theory, "but as a thought experiment about what politics might look like if the basic assumptions of realism were reversed" (Keohane and Nye, 1989: 254). The direct challenge to realism, one variation of which assumed "nations" establish goals, which then become the national interest, which then serves as the impetus for behavior, was contained in the three characteristics of CI: state policy goals are *not* arranged in strict hierarchies; *multiple* as opposed to *singular* channels of communication exist between societies, limiting the control governments can exercise; and "military force is largely irrelevant" (Keohane and Nye, 1989: 255).

"Complex Interdependence" (CI) can be seen as reflecting aspects of the reality of the mid-1970s to some degree, but *especially so when compared to a picture drawn using a caricature of the traditional realist model.* CI was an "exercise," *not* a theory, an exercise done "as if" the tenets of realism were reversed. The four case studies analyzed in great detail elaborating CI (the substantive issues of money and the oceans and dyadic cases of U.S.-Canada and U.S.-Australia relations) illustrate the world as a very complex place indeed, complete with the intricate multiple interdependencies that would be expected and are capable of being introduced in highly nuanced case studies. But as accurate as such a picture can be at the multiple levels the model dictates, nonetheless with the in-depth case studies this approach demands, the underlying model—much in contrast to more parsimonious ones such as Deutsch's transaction approach—sometimes seems to read almost something like, "Things change a lot, multiple variables are involved, and decision-makers are intertwined at multiple levels. In other words, a lot of things happen."

Following complex interdependence came transnationalism, globalism, and, most recently, globalization—each perhaps with specific nuances concerning descriptions of the contemporary world. Ironically, complex interdependence was left at the church, and the second concept virtually took off, and for a time becomes the central part of the story. As later noted,

> The alacrity with which the concept of international regimes has been accepted in the international relations literature contrasts sharply with the relative neglect of complex interdependence. The concept of international regimes has proven its value, identifying and clustering together the important phenomena to be explained (Keohane and Nye, 1989: 257).

Regardless of lineage, by the early 1980s an entire issue of *International Organization* was devoted to "international regimes" (Krasner, 1982a), and five years later it was proudly noted that "Indeed, 'regimes' seem now to be everywhere!" (Keohane and Nye, 1987: 740). Six years afterward, the concept was christened "regime theory" (Rittberger, 1993), which, it was asserted,

> has tackled—more successfully than other approaches—the puzzles of international co-operation and of international institution-building in a world of sovereign states . . . [and] filled analytical gaps which other theoretical approaches either did not address at all (such as Waltzian neo-realism) or proved ill-quipped for (such as integration theory) (Rittberger, 1993: xii).

But regimes can serve in one form or another to fill almost any gap, and the broad and loose conceptual umbrella does not necessarily equate with specific empirical findings, which are less amenable to such strong evaluations.

Not unlike its predecessor—integration theory—of a generation earlier, "regime" analysts faced a sticky, murky area, a morass even when it came to basic definitions. Even early on, one proponent of the approach noted in introducing the parameters of regimes:

> grappling with the problem of trying to describe and explain patterns of order in the anarchic world of international politics, scholars have fallen into using the term "regime" so disparately and with such little precision that it ranges from an umbrella for all international relations to little more than a synonym for international organizations (A. Stein, 1982: 299).

An early and fascinating but linguistically unmanageable definition has—perhaps for the obvious reasons—been ignored; regimes refer to:

> The degree to which and the manner in which agreement on joint purposes is expressed in and unilateral volition is constrained by institutionalized collective behavior (Ruggie, 1978: 388).

Ultimately, most definitions revolve around similar descriptions and use similar terminology, and in the aggregate exemplify the broad generality of regimes. That is, regimes "constrain and regularize the behavior of participants" and involve "principles, rules, and norms" (Sullivan, 1990: 186; see Jervis, 1982; Puchala and Hopkins, 1982) or "sets of implicit or explicit principles, norms, rules, and decision making procedures around which actors' expectations converge in a given area of international relations" (Krasner, 1982b: 186). These "sets of implicit or explicit principles, norms, rules" are "applicable to specific areas of international relations" (Keohane, 1993: 778), such as Bretton Woods, air transport and telecommunications, and nuclear weapons:

> the concept of international regime helps observers to describe the rapid increase, since 1945, in the number of multilateral arrangements through which states cooperate to regulate transborder activity. Most international regimes include at least one formal international organization, with the tasks of providing particular services, monitoring members' compliance with rules, and serving as a forum for negotiations (Keohane, 1993: 778).

Regimes have been called "collective arrangements . . . designed to create or more effectively use scientific and technological capabilities" (E. Haas, 1975: 147), involving "organizational energies and financial commitments, which have been accepted by a group of states" (Ruggie, 1975: 570). For others, regimes constituted participants' "understandings" of appropriate behavior, including decision-making procedures, major principles that the regime "upholds," perhaps including a set of elites, or even—perhaps the most encompassing—a regime is said to exist "in every substantive issue-area in international relations where there is discernibly patterned behavior" (Puchala and Hopkins, 1982: 246–247) or "practices consisting of recognized roles linked together by clusters of rules or conventions governing relations among the occupants of these roles" (Young, 1989: 12–14).

The definitional diversities are not only analogous to those plaguing the integration field over a generation ago, they are in some cases parallel. Even after so much attention to the issue, the character of definitions remains "contested" (Levy et al. 1995: 270), there is continuing reliance on "working definitions" (Hasenclever, 1996: 183), and more generally the amount of "intellectual energy [that] has been spent on preliminary tasks such as concept definition and justification" (Stokke, 1997: 39) suggests perhaps not so much vitality but confusion, making "communication among regime analysts more difficult" (Stokke, 1997: 39), and—more importantly—producing a sense of vague generality. Demonstrating this generality is that regimes can be formal or informal, and they can, but need not be, the result of legislation by international organizations, they may or may not have bureaucratic structures, or they may be simply based on a "consensus of objectives and mutual interest" among the parties: "at the minimum, collaboration entails agreed rules to work together for certain goals and to abstain from certain actions" (Dougherty and Pfaltzgraff, 1990: 168).

Regimes: Presumptions, Specification, and Testing

Regime analysis shares the broader philosophical traditions of liberalism, and thus the underlying presuppositions slowly set the clash with realism, and these unfolded as the battle was joined. As with realism, each observer over the years seems to appropriate specific elements but—perhaps more so than with realism—varying lists of presuppositions establish varying depths around the conceptual enclosures. The earliest establishment in the modern genre (Keohane and Nye, 1977) desired only a basic distinction between interdependence and realism. The former focused on the growing presence of multiple— and not single—channels of negotiation and interaction between governments, and thus the absence of hierarchy among issues—suggesting a potential secondary place for military issues, and the presumed decreasing role of military force in international politics.

An evaluation of the broader emerging liberalism of the time—labeled then merely the "interdependence" school—suggested that four substantially different views about the international system of the 1970s had developed: new actors had emerged, thus presuming units other than states in the system; new issues reflected the newly complex world; that world seemed inexorably moving toward greater interdependence; and because of the first three factors conflict would lessen and war would become outmoded (Sullivan, 1978a; 1982). These were roughly the same categories cited a decade later in positioning liberalism's stance apart from realism (Grieco, 1988: 488–490), with the added specification of liberalism's growing rejection of realism's pessimistic attitude about international institutions.

By the 1990s and the end of the Cold war, liberalism's attraction broadened, and presuppositions extended to more inclusive philosophical bases involving even more basic presumptions: liberalism implies individual human beings are the actors and state interests are both self- and other-directed (Zacher and Matthew, 1995: 118–119), progress is assumed, and the scientific revolution combined with liberalism will result in modernization, development, and even greater human freedom (Zacher and Matthew, 1995: 109–110, 117). Finally, returning to the roots of Keohane and Nye but also narrowing in on the institutional bases of modern liberalism, assumptions about the byproducts and processes of institutions further elucidated liberalism: the impact of "iteration," issue linkage, and increased information and reduced transaction costs were seen as elements of the institutional (regime) approach (Keohane, 1984: 89–95; Mearsheimer, 1994/95: 345).

The growing theoretical tumult of the late 1970s, the fading attraction of realism, and the changing character of international politics all nourished the emergence of these presuppositions, no doubt partly in reaction to the growing behavioral tests of structural realist models. Regimes, introduced mostly as a background, complementary element to "complex interdependence," and later serving as only part of what some see as the broader "neoliberal institutionalism" set out above, produced an early and at least surface convergence on its utility that promptly evolved into a broad umbrella blanketing a wide net. That broad net, however, has become so expansive as to include just about everything; the multiple research products that have resulted vary widely but do invariably consist—with some exceptions (Young and Osherenko, 1993)—of in-depth case studies of various "regimes," which operationally means mostly focusing on historical descriptions of movements toward cooperation within selected, sometimes narrow issue areas, and in the process elaborating either explicitly or implicitly the norms, rules, agreements, and perhaps laws and their encompassing institutions that might be involved. These "data" are sometimes equated with how regimes are established in a given issue area, or it can be implied that the "regimes" that have become "established" are the causal factors bringing about the observed cooperation, raising again the issue of the dependent- or independent-variable character of regimes.

An inventory of such regimes and "tests" concerning them would seem to encompass almost all of contemporary cooperative international behavior, especially of a low politics nature. While an entire catalog is beyond our scope, a sense of "regime analysis" emerges from surveying several, and also demonstrates the behavioral domain encompassed by the concept. Examples of regimes include a "global debt regime," a "Bretton Woods regime," a "Bretton Woods balance of payment" regime, a "trade regime" (Biersteker, 1993: 331; 337); and an "environmental regime" (Breitmeier and Wolf, 1993: 354). Other regimes include civil air transport and telecommunications, the monitoring and controlling of the proliferation of nuclear weapons, international environmental regulations (Keohane, 1993: 778), ballistic missiles regime, and still others (Goldstein 1994: 338–339). At times, "issue specificity" defines regimes; many regimes are characterized by certain commodities, such as tin or coffee. Other commodities, however, apparently cannot be so categorized as regimes: "Textiles or fibres represent a genuine regime, while sardines and shoes do not" and "certain shared environments, such as outer space, are not simply governed by one regime, . . . and other comprehensive regimes, such as the Oceans (UNCLOS III) are likely to disintegrate in a multiplicity of separate regulations with potentially serious externalities" (Kratochwil, 1993: 82).

This sketch, only scratching the surface of which regimes exist, is nonetheless lengthy and impressive, but would seem to confirm what was noted above: almost everything within the broad cooperative behavioral domain becomes either a "regime" or explained by something called "regime theory," although certain areas (sardines and shoes) are excluded. However, such a broad conclusion does not apply from every single regime analysis. International aviation would seem to be one area that "emerges as problematic for regime theory and points to the superior explanatory power of realism" (Nayar, 1995: 168).[9] Certainly, cooperation does occur, but whether levels of cooperation are higher than in previous eras and whether regime "theory" explains this cooperation are more questionable assertions.

But all of this rests ultimately on one's agreeing with the basic anomaly alleged to exist in realist thought, namely, the purported realist postulate that cooperation does not exist when in fact the many regime specificities noted above demonstrate—to use the standard definition—"the existence of many 'sets of implicit or explicit principles, norms, rules, and decision-making procedures around which actor expectations converge,' in a variety of areas of international relations" (Keohane, 1982: 325). Should cooperation—rules, norms, patterned behavior—not be a problem for realism, then elaboration of historical accounts of "cooperation-producing" regimes becomes both less theoretically interesting and substantively salient, unless "regimes" is considered not as a causal agent or explanatory variable but rather as structural characteristics, which themselves result from multiple causes but in turn serve as causal agents *only* when aggregated at a structural level much higher than the specific case studies meant to elucidate "regimes."

To pursue this, it should be noted that case studies of regimes usually focus on low politics economic or economically related issues,[10] which circumscribes their domain. The ultimate impact, however, may be not from structured rules and norms related to the specific economic issue areas of a specific case study, but the spillover of those rules and norms to the extraeconomic realm, and, more broadly, to "regime affect," namely, the perception of "regime" as an issue, whereby the "regime" becomes the agenda. Outside of the economic or environmental arena, the utility of "regime" becomes looser, especially with respect to questions of security; specific operational standards of what is and is not included seem to be somewhat arbitrary. At one end, for instance,

> An arms race . . . is not a regime, even though each actor's decision is contingent on the other actor's immediately previous decision. As long as international state behavior results from unconstrained and independent decision-making, there is no international regime (A. Stein, 1982: 300–301).

On the opposite end, the Concert of Europe is considered "the best example of a security regime" (Jervis, 1982: 362). Yet, just as no regime exists for the global economy, but instead regimes in trade and finance, so also is it in the narrower subareas of security policy where we find cooperative institutions or regimes (Muller, 1993: 360). Four that have been suggested are the strategic nuclear weapons regime, the European military order, the regime for the prevention of nuclear war, and the nuclear nonproliferation regime (Muller, 1993: 361). Others seem to disagree:

> The fact that neither superpower attacks the other is a form of cooperation, but not a regime. The links between the states restrain and their immediate self-interest are too direct and unproblematic to invoke the concept . . . The demand for a security regime is decreased by the apparent stability of the strategic balance (Jervis, 1982: 378, cited in Sullivan, 1990: 186–187).

Nonetheless, regimes have been deemed useful for analyzing the nuclear component of the superpower relationship—despite a lengthy list of caveats (Nye, 1987),[11] including a central one applicable to the entire program: "the concept risks tautology by using the same evidence to establish both the cause and the effect of the regime" (Nye, 1987: 375).[12]

Despite disagreements, security "regimes" have been suggested spanning a broad geographical as well as time domain, from a security regime among the Iroquois League (Crawford, 1994) to an analysis of more contemporary NATO force levels (Duffield, 1992). The latter case study proves instructive, where "regime theory" is called on to account for the "consistency" in NATO conventional force levels, but may in fact illustrate the narrow domain of the "dependent variable" rather than confirming a theory. Beginning with the assumption that NATO capabilities

> determined whether or not a Soviet-led Warsaw Pact conventional attack could be defeated without resort to nuclear weapons and, if not, at what point the alliance would have to cross the nuclear threshold (Duffield, 1992: 821),

the realist contention, it is said, is that balance of power predicts that states "will seek to balance the power of potential adversaries" (Duffield, 1992: 825). If NATO forces remained constant while Warsaw Pact forces changed, then balance of power doesn't work. How might one explain the "high degree of stability that characterized both overall NATO conventional force levels and national contributions in the Central Region?" "Regime theory" would "predict that alliance members would tend to provide forces in accordance with established conventions" and NATO forces "would remain constant as long as the relevant norms and rules did not change" (Duffield, 1992: 839). The case study suggests that force levels did remain constant and thus "regimes" had their effect. What this means, however, is still unclear:

> Rarely . . . will regimes shape behavior in ways that are fundamentally at odds with . . . the distribution of power. Ultimately, . . . incongruities may develop between a regime and the

underlying distribution of power, and when these incongruities become severe enough, the regime will be transformed, replaced, or simply abandoned (Duffield, 1992: 853).

The presumptions underlying regimes manifest a long tradition, and recent specifications have produced multiple case studies, mostly in the nonsecurity arena. Presence of apparent cooperation on security issues plausibly renders the existence of a "regime"— but the implication of causal explanation imposes much broader serviceability than may be warranted.

Regimes: Theory, Hegemony, and Realism

The NATO case study illustrates a key observation, recognized by many: regimes and regime "analysis" often end with some element of "hegemony." That is, of course, most likely because they start with hegemony. Because "regimes" were a reaction to a conceptual world defined in terms of power and realism, they ultimately depend on the notion of hegemony. Two "key questions" apply to the existence and perpetuation of regimes:

> whether international regimes must rely on the support of a single dominant power; and . . . whether the rules of the regimes have significant effects apart from the influence exerted by their supporters (Keohane, 1993: 778).

The perceived decline in U. S. hegemony and the emergence of interdependence may have helped regime "thinking" thrive,[13] but ultimately, since they start with hegemony, regimes must at some point return to it; regimes and power/hegemony are inextricably linked, an idea that has been constant: "The structure of the system (the distribution of power resources among states) profoundly affects the nature of the regime" (Keohane and Nye, 1977: 21).

> To the extent that such [economic and political conflicts] persist, and states continue to comply with regime rules, international regimes matter. When their rules become too inconsistent with the distribution of states' power, however, it is to be expected that the regimes will be bypassed, deprived of substantial funding, or otherwise rendered meaningless (Keohane, 1993: 778).

Even when spelled out in detail the relation between the two domains remains, although not the specifics of the mutual causality:

> Since the use of power can facilitate the construction of regimes, this approach should be seen as complimentary to, rather than in contradiction with, an emphasis on hierarchical authority. Regimes do not enforce rules in a hierarchical sense, but they do change the patterns of transaction costs and provide information to participants, so that uncertainty is reduced (Axelrod and Keohane, 1986: 250).

Thus confirms what has been noted already; the model even within regime analyses themselves appears to look like a model proposed elsewhere (Sullivan, 1990: 194):

> [Hegemony]
> Power >>>>>>>>>>> Regimes >>>>>>>>>>>> Behavior
> [Structure]

If so, then the linkage between the three remains, and the most difficult assignment is to partition out the effects of regimes and structure as causal agents.

That structure-regime relationship has not been spelled out, nor do we know what proportion or exactly what domain might be accounted for by regimes. Reintroducing the concept of power certainly tarnishes the luster of regimes, associated as it is with the Liberal as opposed to the Realist traditions. This problem has certainly been recognized: regimes "could also fit easily with Realist theory. Egoistic self-interest can lead states to create regimes in security as well as economic issues . . ." (Nye, 1987: 374–375). While the liberal component has a long history tracing back to before the Deutschian movement, it fades if one agrees that

> regime theory's most distinctive contribution is to have developed the idea of self-interest and reciprocal benefits and, in general, to have downplayed the traditional emphasis placed on the role of community and a sense of justice . . . states are self-interested actors competing in a world of anarchy, [and] that co-operation need not depend on altruism, that it can develop from the calculations of instrumentally rational actors (Hurrel, 1993: 55–56).[14]

Although the suggestion that regimes and "institutional" analysis are merely "subordinate" to realism (Mearsheimer, 1994/95: 351) would appear to be a bit extreme, the link between realism and regimes has nonetheless been a problematic one (Mearsheimer, 1994/95: 351, n. 77).

These criticisms might be valid, but they could also be the remnants of unimaginative and unreconstructed neorealist thinking. While regime analysts or neoliberal institutionalists can be cast into accepting many realist propositions (Grieco, 1988: 486), to be too insistent on this view would be giving up too easily the ball game of liberal structural analysis. To return to the chameleon, the central question is the type and level of behavior investigated within "regimes," and their geographical as well as issue scope. Large-scale neorealist structural analyses may fail to spell out specific dependent variables, but likewise regime studies tend to focus on small, minute aspects or characteristics of case studies. Regime analysis has not demonstrated that realism is wrong in some ultimate sense but merely limited—perhaps hopelessly narrow and limited for much international behavior. But realism was limited long before the current complexly interdependent world. Thus realism should not be viewed as directly applicable to many of the very specific types of behavior—the case studies of NATO force levels, for instance—that have been the subject of regime analysis, but demonstrating its limitations in such cases could also demonstrate how limiting a regime analysis might be. Two facts are true: "power" is not the ultimate arbiter of all international behavior, and rules and norms are generally in the process of increasing their salience and breadth. Nonetheless, that process might be as slow as that ultimately followed by the European integration movement itself (as well as changes in other large political structures, domestic as well as international, that undergo major transformations), but one that cannot be tracked by the types of point-specific case studies that most regime analyses consist of. In other words, rather than self-contained elaborations of an intact theoretical formulation, each specific case study might merely be seen as a "minor" piece of data itself—or specific elaboration—of a broader change occurring in the system.

This stems partly from the fact that "regimes" analysis emerged to some degree from an inaccurate evaluation of the results of power relations. The declaration of an anomaly in Realist theory—"the existence of many 'sets of implicit or explicit principles, norms, rules, and decision-making procedures around which actor expectations converge'" (Keohane, 1982: 325)—is, as already argued, not an anomaly at all, unless one subscribes to the caricature of Realism. But this assessment is not new. The initial treatise on CI and regimes (Keohane and Nye, 1977) was in fact originally criticized for "attempting to apply old approaches or models to areas for which they were never intended" and therefore "setting up straw men" (K. Holsti, 1978: 525).[15] Going beyond the caricature, it is clear that principles, norms, and rules exist and have always existed: in fact, the empirical data suggest that the majority of international behavior is in fact cooperation, that a minority is conflictual, and that within that minority a very small percentage is warlike—or what one would normally associate with lawless anarchy.[16]

Thus behavioral regularities and cooperation do occur, but "regimes" are not the sole uniform causal factor. Differing structural systems seem to be more or less consonant with the type or strength of cooperative behaviors (or "regimes") [Chapter Six], and other explanations also account for observed cooperative behavior [Chapter Nine]. Rules may, but do not necessarily emerge because a "regime" comes into existence, just as "new" issues do not suddenly emerge on their own and displace previous ones. "Systemic forces play a strong role in the changing issues and therefore in the changing regimes" (Sullivan, 1990: 191).

Part of the reasons, ironically, that "regimes" do not *account for*—that is, explain—the observed cooperative behavior is that regime "theory" is plagued by a central fault characteristic of realism itself:

> Regime analysis, like most other approaches to international politics, lacks a persuasive theory of change, which tends to make it more useful in explaining why and how a particular regime is maintained than in explaining—except in a very general sense—why new regimes emerge or old ones collapse (Rothstein, 1984: 319–320).

But perhaps within that critique is contained unwittingly *why* regimes cannot explain change: they are not meant to. Regimes, in this scheme, is "regime thinking," or what was earlier labeled "regime affect": "despite its conceptual weaknesses, [it] can have a beneficial practical effect by providing a useful, if partial, frame of reference for decision-makers" (Rothstein, 1984: 307). Regimes then become not so much a conceptual apparatus to explain behavior as a "way of thinking" for political actors:

> More awareness of what is implied by a quest for a regime, as distinct from "normal" politics, would not have produced the regime that the Group of 77 desired, but it is at least arguable that it would have produced more than what was achieved (Rothstein, 1984: 325).

The *regime* idea then becomes the issue, just as, regardless of whether democracies actually produce peace or not, at some point that *posited* relationship becomes a driving force and is perceived as the way to believe—perhaps, even, a norm [Chapter Four]. Norms are funny things and can be produced in a variety of ways, as we will see [Chapter Nine]; the regime "idea" might impose upon decision-makers the *belief* that norms of a regime exist, regardless of whether or not they actually do.

These suggestions may appear to wreak havoc, but only on something called regime "theory," not on international institutions either as individual entities or "regime" as more broadly conceptualized as "regime affect." None of this should be too surprising, however, once it is recalled that "regime" began as a background conceptual underpinning, not as a central explanatory concept—let alone a "theory." It has been understandably confused with the more normal definitions of regime as simply a system of management or government, or more generally with a social system or pattern (a diet "regime" of bread and water, for instance). At some point along the passage of its continuous repetition— as so often happens (i.e., realist "theory")—it became transformed into something with connotations never originally meant to apply.

Thus, within the setting of the growing attraction of the "anarchy" metaphor within hegemonic discourse, regimes "fit" nicely as a contesting antithesis because if hegemony "ends" in such an anarchical world, some "thing" is needed to arrive at solutions or problems or cooperation. Curiously, few have bothered to go back to Keohane and Nye's original impetus for CI and question what a "nonregime" is, or what a world that has no regimes would look like, or whether international systems that did not have regimes have ever existed. "Nonregimes" received only one listing in *Power and Interdependence:*

> When there are no agreed norms and procedures or when the exceptions to the rules are more important than the instances of adherence, there is a *nonregime* situation (Keohane and Nye, 1989: 20; emphasis in original).

The cautious admonitions about tautological reasoning noted earlier (Nye, 1987: 375) would certainly be wise advice in assessing such a linkage here between rules and regimes.

Thus, regimes are quite supple; like some forms of earlier notions of "integration," they can include anything and everything: a state of being, an end product, or a process. The story as offered here, however, suggests they started as a state of being—with the major question being "how do regimes change"—and ended up being a "theory"; what exactly the *theory* is remains unclear, and the reason for that is that the theory in regime analysis comes from somewhere else.[17] "Regime" is not a theory but rather a term used to describe a set of enduring questions concerning cooperation among states, which appears to answer those enduring questions because the theory uncovers the cooperation that—it is claimed—realists argue could not occur. But the explanation of that cooperation comes from theories only lumped under the category of "regimes." Respective reviews of the regimes literature over the years demonstrate this: the theories include the structural hegemonic, strategic bargaining, functional and cognitive in one review (Haggard and Simmons, 1987: 500–513), and three equally broadly conceived classifications involving interest-based neoliberalism, power-based realism, and knowledge-based cognitivism (Hasenclever et al., 1996).[18] The specific "theories" such as functional, bargaining,[19] hegemonic stability, and learning theory emerge in a variety of forms in analyzing the multiple component questions that might be asked about regimes, their formation, and their effectiveness (Levy et al. 1995). In addition, implicit in detailed case studies generated by regime analyses but frequently left unexamined are implications about decision-making, or *how* people decide: decision-makers seem to operate with some form of implicit rational-process model, with long-term goals, nonincremental, nonsequential processing of information and negotiating tactics, and arriving at decisions following more or less the "rules" that seem to govern the particular "regime." The case studies intimate—even within institutional settings—"politics as usual," normally with propensities toward implied rational choice.

Therefore if one asks, "What is the *theory* component in 'regimes' similar to or as strong as the component one can find in traditional functionalism or the communication and transaction school of integration," the answer is that the theory resides somewhere else. Norms and rules agreed upon by national actors do exist; when those norms and rules operate, the actors are more likely to cooperate. None of this is meant to suggest that the liberal tradition carried on in the modern era with the integration theories of the 1950s has somehow come to an end. "Regimes" and "neoliberal institutionalism" carry on that tradition certainly in a normative sense; the broader implication of "regime"-type cooperation is that if aggregated at a level higher than specific case studies of specific "regimes," that systemic-level behavior may say something about structural aspects of the international system from the liberal perspective and suggest the existence of larger systems of behavior.

Complexity is a perceived—or perhaps "socially constructed"—phenomenon. In a world perceived as more complex than earlier eras, "simple" explanations become suspect, and "complex" ones attractive. "Realism is replete with global generalizations, lacking qualifications about the conditions under which they may be valid" (Keohane and Martin, 1995: 41). The seeming simplicity of certain versions of realism proved the most attractive draw for competing "complex" analyses, but an equally important attraction throughout was its continuation of the liberal tradition, which many saw as having suffered under Cold War realism. Complex interdependence, regimes, and ultimately neoliberal institutionalism all share in one form or another the "liberal" presumptions and traditions, and all were reactions—as others have been—to simplistic "realist" interpretations, a contrast that seems to have further sharpened with the "end" of the Cold War. The reality in the 1990s is that Europe is—relative to the 1950s—integrated, the concept of "complex interdependence" very much in the backwaters, and "regimes" an intellectual industry of great breadth. "Neoliberal institutionalism" as a label has supplanted and placed an umbrella over many other terms, has an ample following, and combined with the "liberal democracy" formulations found at the domestic level provides an immense attraction in the post Cold War era of neoidealism. While the explanatory value may still very much be contested, the fates of these numerous liberal conceptual approaches stands in marked contrast to the fate of another nonrealist, structural view that potentially possessed several of the qualities of liberal theories but has followed a very different path.

Structural Balance:
The "Ins" and the "Outs"

The "liberal" tradition elects to shy away from power—not completely, but with much less emphasis on it as a *commanding* phenomenon. Early theories of "integration" have sired numerous "liberal" offspring, and some prospered ("Regimes are everywhere!"), while at least one other non-power-oriented approach has not fared as well, perhaps because of its clear association or sole dependence—unlike "liberal" theories—on the structural component, or perhaps because of its transparent neutrality toward power. "Structural balance" theories come in several different variations, and, because of its neutrality on the issue of power, *could* be construed within the liberal tradition, a link, however, that is not clear or necessary, and thus its fate and popularity has been quite different from those—like "regimes"—where the link is direct and popular. A second potential liability is its lack of a complex, sophisticated formulation, having been presented conventionally as the idea that "An enemy of my friend is my enemy; a friend of my friend is my friend." Early classics focused on areas outside of international relations, but the causal linkage is the same: relations *within* a political unit are directly related to that unit's relation with the outside world (Coser, 1956: 88; Simmel, 1955: 92–93; Hopmann, 1967). Conceptualized abstractly, actors A and B have some orientation toward a third actor, X. The relations between the three carry a positive or negative "charge": if both A and B have a "symmetrical" relation to X (both positive or both negative), then the relationship between A and B must be positive for the system to be in "balance." If their respective relationships with X differs, then their relationship with one another should be negative. If the abstract formulation is correct,

> The implications . . . for the study of international cohesion are thus apparent. If cohesion is defined in terms of co-orientation toward salient external objects or events, then symmetry of orientation may be assumed to be a valid indicator of cohesion (Hopmann, 1967: 219–220).

This bears strong similarities to the internal–external conflict hypothesis [Chapter Four]; James Coleman originally proposed this scheme in analyzing community conflicts, noting:

> As controversy develops, associations flourish *within* each group, but *wither* between persons on opposing sides. People break off long-standing relationships, stop speaking to former friends who have been drawn to the opposition, but proliferate their associations with fellow-partisans (Coleman, 1957: 11).

In the international context, conflict with an external enemy should produce internal cohesion; in terms of alliances that nations generate, greater inter-alliance conflict should produce greater intra-alliance cohesion (Sullivan, 1976: 227, 241). It is perhaps ironic to recall that these linkages were first applied to intra-NATO and East-West relations in the early years of the Cold War; it was hypothesized that higher "stress" should produce greater intra-coalition as compared to inter-coalition communication; as the latter decreases, the "distance" between the parties is increasing, and the more this occurs in a conflict situation, the more the system becomes polarized. The Cold War did not spark research on balance and in-group/out-group hypotheses, but certainly added to their attraction through the indirect "liberal" notion of the time, namely, that the tension and hostility between the major powers widely and popularly attributed to basic, nonnegotiable ideological differences could possibly be accounted for by much less ideological and much more structural, sociological—and less ideological—explanations. Such hypotheses could then hypothetically explain much of the unfolding of the Cold War as well as the "end" of that Cold War, without resort to ideological differences. Just as regimes insinuate a certain positive tenor to the nasty world of international politics, so also in its own way is "balance" a "nice" idea; not being necessarily equated with power or ideologies related to power, it describes very basic human tendencies and orientations, and thus possesses a "nice" component—it does not necessarily paint a "grim picture of world politics" (Mearsheimer, 1994/95: 336), nor rely necessarily on any of the extant institutional infrastructures.[20]

Despite its attractiveness and niceness, empirical results have not uniformly proved its utility. Inter-alliance versus intra-alliance communication patterns in the pre–World War I crisis were related to respective stress levels during the crisis and can be interpreted only as indirect, moderate support for balance hypotheses (O. Holsti, 1972: 102). Richardson's early findings can be interpreted as suggesting that while similarity in religion did not necessarily make for peaceful relations, dissimilarity seemed related to war (although similarity in language seemed to have little effect (Richardson, 1960: xi-xii). One analysis expressly directed at "balance" hypotheses focused on the Three Emperor's League of 1873 (Germany, Russia, and Austria aligned against France), with the hypothesis predicting an increase of conflict between the three and the rest of the system, which did occur, but the conflict *among* almost all the signers also increased (Healy and Stein, 1973). However, support was found for shifting structural balance between 1873 and 1878 when Austria improves relations with Russia, and the system became unbalanced: the behavior of Austria and Russia toward Germany was more negative than the reverse. When Germany's positive behavior toward the two others was not reciprocated, something should "give," and it did: between August 1875 and April 1877 all behavior turns positive and the system is again "balanced." From April 1877 to May 1878 the system again became unbalanced, with almost all three major powers positive to one other major power but negative to the second.

> Bismarck cannot be an ally of both Austria and Russia while they are so hostile; likewise, the Tsar cannot trust Bismarck while he is so close to Austria; Austria must also feel tense about Germany's support of Russian moves in the Balkan (Healy and Stein, 1973: 54).

Overall, seven out of nine unbalanced dyads underwent change, while that was true of only nine out of the 20 balanced ones. Based partly on the "liberal" presuppositions already noted, more focus turned on Cold War or Cold War-related phenomena. NATO and communist bloc relations were related in that high inter-bloc tension years of 1950 and 1965 (the Korean War and U.S. bombing in Vietnam) showed much greater agreement within the Eastern bloc than low tension years. The results were confirmed when analyzing intra-NATO "distance" but only when the Soviet Union was the object.[21] For three detente periods,[22] higher inter-coalition conflict was related to intra-coalition unity in terms of Chinese and Soviet perceptions of an external enemy, but data for 1959–1963 between China and Albania, on the one hand, and the rest of the communist bloc on the other, failed to support the hypothesis (Sullivan, 1976: 243). French actions toward the U.S. as a co-member of NATO, and toward the Warsaw Pact nations between 1950 and 1967, were also not in line with the hypothesis.

More systematic analyses of the external threat–bloc cohesion hypothesis were more hesitant. Responding to earlier research (see O. Holsti et al., 1973), which had indicated mixed results but had found "that the level of East-West conflict had played an extremely important role in influencing Western cooperation and attitudinal consensus" (Thompson and Rapkin, 1981: 635), an extension and partial replication found "only changes in external threat (lagged one year) were . . . related . . . with changes in Western within-bloc cooperation," (Thompson and Rapkin, 1981: 635), a finding that, while corroborating the earlier work, was nonetheless somewhat weak statistically. Another replication extending the data to cover the 1950–1988 period produced a significant relationship between U.S. behavior directed at the Soviet Union and the cooperation variable, but no relationship between the same U.S. behavior and the consensus measure. However, "The basic hypothesis . . . tentatively confirmed by Thompson and Rapkin is the only significant relationship found here" (Perez, 1993: 14–15); in terms of Cold War superpower relations, "the dynamic of external threat and bloc cohesion continues" (Perez, 1993: 15).

Analysis of initial "event" data of the early 1970s demonstrated very primitive evidence consistent with "balance" hypotheses when tracking shifts in United States policy toward China—rapprochement—and the unfolding emergence of detente between the United States and the Soviet Union. U. S. moves toward China in 1971 unbalanced the 20-year Cold War structure. Prior to that, the U.S.A.-P.R.C.-U.S.S.R. structure was a roughly "balanced" system (Sullivan, 1976: 246–247). 1970 found a dramatic positive turn in U.S.A.-P.R.C. relations coinciding with the reduction in hostility between P.R.C.-U.S.R. All three dyads shifted in 1971, a year dominated by the American president's announcements of his trips to both China and the Soviet Union, with all three dyads moving even further toward less negative interactions.

A larger project investigated the triangular U.S.A.-P.R.C.-U.S.S.R. relationship removed from the NATO-WTO alliance structure. Only the Soviet and Chinese behaviors toward each other were influenced by the presence of the United States. "By contrast, we found little evidence for triangularity in any of the twelve possible cases bearing on U.S.-Chinese and U.S.-Soviet relations" (Goldstein and Freeman, 1990: 81). However, as expected, United States cooperation toward the Soviet Union increased hostility within the Soviet-Chinese dyad while U.S. hostility toward the Soviets had the opposite effect, drawing the latter two closer together.[23] Interpretation of the multiple results is difficult, but the overall conclusion seems relatively straightforward: "Such inverse triangular responses are consistent with the hypothesis that dyad cohesion is enhanced by an outside threat" (Goldstein and Freeman, 1990: 81).

Ideological overtones might color a European perspective where "triangularity" is renamed in the Cold War context the "imaginary war" (Kaldor, 1990). "Internal pacification was achieved among advanced industrial countries, more successfully in the West than in the East, through the fostering of a bloc identity, which can be termed blocism. This came to augment, if not displace, nationalism" (Kaldor, 1990: 25). Such an "imaginary war" can be distinguished from deterrence:

> The argument that deterrence has kept the peace in Europe is based on the assumption that the only possible conflict was between the blocs. The concept of imaginary war presupposes that the fear of an external enemy is used to deal with conflicts *within* the blocs (Kaldor, 1990: 25).

Structural balance should have been keenly appropriate for analyzing the Cold War, and while for a very brief period the emergence and continuation of that war fostered such tests, as with integration studies little or no attempt was made to continually track patterns throughout the Cold War to assess its "end" or termination point based on the internal-external cohesion hypothesis. Certainly the fact that balance tests were not strongly supported—despite the popularity of the underlying thesis—led to their demise. But with the alleged demise of the Cold War, balance hypotheses should have predicted a decrease of cohesion in the Western bloc:

> It is the Soviet threat that holds NATO together. Take away that offensive threat and the United States is likely to abandon the Continent, whereupon the defensive alliance it headed for forty years may disintegrate (Mearsheimer, 1990: 52).

Certainly data available to the casual observer by the end of the first post–Cold War decade suggests such predictions have not come to pass. But earlier caveats concerning systemic time lags hold: a decade might prove too short to assess such linkages. NATO's role in the Bosnian conflict in the mid-1990s was far from universally popular, and further NATO expansion could provide an external enemy for those left out of NATO (Kennan, 1997), which was already causing tensions into the late 1990s. Balance would suggest that at some macrolevel, the existence of an "Eastern Europe"—with all that symbol implied—was ultimately linked to the continuing unity of Western Europe, and would predict opposite behavior with the demise of that "enemy." Thus, the post–Cold War era could provide an interesting test pitting balance and institutional hypotheses—especially with regard to NATO's role in Europe. That institution has already emerged as an actor that "matters." Its future behavior—institutional success or failure—may help assess balance versus institutional hypotheses. Moreover, expanding the dependent variable to monetary integration in Europe suggests the intriguing possibility that steps toward European monetary integration can be explained by a form of balance theory: U.S. disturbances or shocks to the international monetary system were correlated with advances in European monetary integration (Henning, 1998).

Conclusion

During the heyday of early post–World War II liberal thought, Ernst Haas once noted—concerning regional integration—the lack of agreement on the makeup of the dependent variable. Proponents of what had been called "federalist theory" were thinking in terms of the achievement of a federal union among the units. Communications theorists saw the end product as either a pluralist or amalgamated security community. Neofunctionalists viewed the end product as a political community or union. But as Haas noted at the time,

> one of the more bothersome aspects of these efforts at specifying a dependent variable was the tendency to mix its imputed characteristics with those of independent and intervening variables (E. Haas, 1970: 630).

Haas suggested that "fudge variables" should be discarded—specifically "functional equivalents," "catalysts," "federalizers," "high politics," and "similar mythical animals." Unfortunately, he perpetuated the practice by calling for *multiple* dependent variables, such as "regional state," "regional commune," and "asymmetrical regional overlap" (E. Haas, 1970: 634).

Exactly what exists now in Europe with respect to early theorizing is not quite clear, nor does it appear to be an overwhelming issue for Europeanists, integration theorists, nor for regime analysts. Still, in all the new-found joy of seeing regimes "everywhere," it has been overlooked that Europe has, to a remarkable degree, become integrated. Certainly this is the popular view, and the empirical evidence appears supportive (Smith and Ray, 1993: 26, 219–225; Garrett, 1992).[24]

Nonetheless, one observer notes that

> the economic rules and the political institutions governing the internal market reflect the preferences of the most powerful countries in the EC: France and Germany

and—what any careful observer of the contemporary, especially European, press might sense—namely, that,

> It is reasonable to presume that efforts to bring about further integration of the EC—such as through economic and monetary union, political union, and expansion—*will similarly be affected by power politics* (Garrett, 1992: 560; emphasis added).

Because original integration theories were not emulated into the 1970s–1990s period, it is difficult to assess whether those original theoretical formulations sufficiently incorporated the true explanatory factors that have brought about the integration currently in place; in fact, more recent debates have returned to traditional governmental-level and individual entrepreneurship variables for understanding key EU negotiations and decisions (Moravcsik, 1999; Young, 1999). But just as basic problems haunted the integration literature, closely analogous problems plague its successor, "regime" and institutional studies.[25] Independent and dependent variables are often intermixed, and the primarily case-study methodology produces a behavioral domain that seems to cover just about everything. Yet, despite the extremely low N/V ratio[26]—reflecting their lack of parsimony—case studies of "regimes" not only retain but seem to be increasing their popularity. "Complex interdependence," on the other hand, appearing in the last half of the 1970s, viewed as a breakthrough, a postrealist concept, has been essentially "sent out to pasture, only, of course, to sire multiparous offspring like regime theory, neoliberal institutionalism, and epistemic communities" (DerDerian, 1994: 130).

"Epistemic communities" potentially represent one link between formalized and nonformalized "institutions" as well as embodying an additional leg of the liberal thesis: that sweeping the globe along with the fires of democracy and "cooperation under anarchy" deriving from "regime" activities is yet a new group of "epistemists," trained in their respective fields of inquiry, who will advise and guide national governments from a perch above those governments, representing, in a sense, a novel form of integration. It insinuates a positive aura of effective consensual decision-making (P. Haas, 1992b: 221f.). The promise the epistemic movement holds out is high, its goals are clear, and— if it were able to rise above the political behavior that realists would contend inevitably invades any political endeavor by nature—it does represent a promising, grand, and idealistic goal,[27] perhaps almost considered the "ideal" of regime activity.

But if the regimes stratagem is as profuse as claimed, then they should empirically encompass multiple behavioral dimensions. The abbreviated "regime list" presented earlier suggested the breadth and width of their scope, but given the definition most widely used—sets of "principles, norms, rules and decision-making procedures around which actor expectations converge in a given issue area" (Krasner, 1982b: 185)—then a multitude of Cold War "regimes" could be generated describing a wide variety of "principles, norms, rules, and decision-making procedures" around which "expectations" converged. Rarely, however, do these catch attention from regime "theorists." "No first strike" might have been a regime, as well as the "regime" that developed between antagonists during the Vietnam War about not striking against the enemy "where it hurts" or "at home," namely, in Vietnam directly at Hanoi and Haiphong; both of these imply norms and rules. That norm in the second example terminated, not coincidentally, at about the time the international structure shifted between June 1971 and February 1972 with announcements of presidential visits to Peking and Moscow.

Other regimes could also be cited, none of which are very wide of the mark in terms of regime classification rules, especially since similar types *have* been included in regime studies (Efinger et al., 1993). One involved the conflicts between the U.S. and U.S.S.R. over the status of Austria, and second was the Berlin case. The latter is instructive; one view sees it as representing dramatic, unregulated conflict behavior for the 1948 to mid-1970s period, after which, following the "formation of an international regime based on the Quadripartite Agreement, the parties to the conflict adhered to specific rules concerning access and status matters" (Efinger et al., 1993: 256–257). Such a view restricts regime *narrowly* to the signed agreement and its parameters, ignoring the bargaining and norms worked out prior to the agreement, a limitation many regime theorists might find too narrow (Keohane, 1988: 382–386), and a construction hewing perilously close to resting on the absolute need for a specified, written agreement. But while the latter restriction may be imposed to retain a certain purity for the operational definition, the "regime," as already noted, emerged only in the mid-1970s, once it became very clear major power structural transformations were underway; the two cannot be separated.

Illustrations suggesting systemic constraints bring the model full circle, with several observers noting that at least certain variations of regimes rest directly or indirectly on other structures such as hegemony within a realist framework (Grieco, 1988: 486–487; Sullivan, 1990: 187–194; Duffield, 1992: 853; Hasenclever, 1996: 184–185). Ultimately, as several detailed, nuanced case studies point out, regime processes can recede in importance relative to the conceivably primary prominence of those structural attributes or power distributions, and changes in power distributions, among the nations within the "regimes." Some have even argued that neoliberalism—here equated with "regimes"—is in fact so deficient that it would fail to prevail over realism as an explanatory model in the very area that its proponents see its main strength: international cooperation (Grieco, 1988: 506); others view neoliberalism as merely subordinate to realism, with a deficient causal logic with respect to its alleged focus on absolute vs. relative gains (Mearsheimer, 1994/95: 347–349, 351). Still, regimes analysis took on a life of its own—even referred to as "regime theory" when in fact the theoretical propositions and explanations, as already noted, come from other, already extant theories. One might even ask: can regime case studies be undertaken without utilizing the concept "regime"?[28]

Despite its widespread acceptance, regime analysis has been subject to numerous criticisms. Early broadsides alleged it suffered from "woolliness" and "imprecision" (Strange, 1982).

> There is no agreement in the literature even on such basic issues as boundary conditions: Where does one regime end and another begin? What is the threshold between nonregime and regime? Embedding regimes in "meta-regimes," or "nesting" one within another, typifies the problem; it does not resolve it (Kratochwil and Ruggie, 1986: 763).

These abstract criticisms saw a tension between "its ontological posture and its prevailing epistemological practices" wherein norms were viewed more as "referential functions" as opposed to "communicative": a breach of an obligation within a regime is to be seen as more than an "objective description" of a fact—but an "intersubjective appraisal" of some behavioral misconduct (Kratochwil and Ruggie, 1986: 774). Others have taken on the underlying logic and the empirical record of institutions (Mearsheimer, 1994/95).

Despite criticisms, regime analysis has refocused interest toward cooperation, and one view sees this behavior as emanating from IOs, perhaps reflecting the trust by political scientists in political organizations. However, a long tradition of organizational failures goes beyond the well-known problems of the League of Nations and to a lesser extent the United Nations. Despite the liberal mantra, IOs do produce negative effects because, quite simply, they are organizations and thus subject to the positive as well as negative characteristics of bureaucracies (Barnett and Finnemore, 1999), and negative effects can range from merely failing to understand the operations of complex international systems to actually intensifying international disputes (Gallorotti, 1991: 192–211). Certainly the potential negative roles of the International Monetary Fund and the World Bank have not gone unnoticed in recent years, especially with regard to the former during the economic crises in Asia in 1997 and 1998, predictions that some observers were making a decade earlier: "It is absolutely no use looking to international organizations to wave a magic wand and restore financial order and with it world prosperity . . . international organizations are not free agents. They are created by, and are forever dependent on national governments" (Strange, 1986: 170). Institutions interpreted through the prism of neoliberal institutionalism tend to infer positive outcomes; the same institutions viewed through a hegemonic model do not necessarily produce the same behavior.

This chapter's embarkation point was "hope springs eternal." Root idealism permeates integration, transnationalism, interdependence, regime/institutionalism, and, most recently, "globalization" studies—although the last has also produced a "counter-hegemonic" critical mass. Idealism is a respected and valued tradition, and has taken different substantive forms over the years: the post–World War I idealism of the 1920s, the early Deutsch transactional idealism of the 1950s, regionalism of the 1960s, the growing awareness of pervading interdependence of the 1970s, the sense of growing cooperation through the emergence of more and more "regimes" under the guise of institutionalism in the 1980s, "epistemic communities" in the 1990s, and most recently the widespread belief in growing "globalization." Every wave has carried forward that idealism necessary for bringing out through its underlying positive orientation toward cooperation the realization that such behavior is in fact the norm in international relations—therefore worth investigating.

But like realism, "liberalism" as specifically manifested in "regime" analyses resembles a shapeless covering: attractive and colorful, and capable of blanketing much, not unlike the "muumuu" of times past. "Regime theory" imbues analysis with a theoretical content that is in fact imported; despite the focus on cooperation rather than the tired Cold War elements of confrontation and conflict, it so often seems—because of reliance on realism—to bear strong similarities to "politics as usual." Because actual regimes can entail both international organizations and international law, but loosely possess other components suggesting an "integrative" mode, they represent a nice compromise, a halfway house between anarchy on the one hand and world government on the other. It is a place to achieve that much-needed but almost-impossible-to-get cooperation if some form of anarchy is still assumed, but "world government" still considered hopelessly idealistic. But anarchy is a colorful metaphor, and cooperation is in fact rampant—and always has been. Regimes therefore should be "everywhere." They will ubiquitously materialize again in the realm of strictly economic behavior [Chapter Eight], and, because regimes imply "norms and rules," have been central to bargaining theories for decades [Chapter Nine].[29] Rather than constituting a distinct theoretical enterprise, it is a term used to describe a set of enduring questions concerning cooperation among states. It neither explains nor "uncovers" the cooperation that realists allegedly claim could not occur.

This alleged "anomaly" in realism seen by some as the starting point for regime or institutional studies, therefore, fades once cooperation is taken as a given.[30] However, the focused attention on norms and procedures emphasizes the fact that the bulk of international behavior is cooperative. But from a structural perspective, it should be the occurrence, tracking, and conceptualizing of regimes—or "regime behavior"—over time at an aggregate level that may prove more interesting than elaboration of specific case studies illustrating cooperative behavior. Choosing the structural perspective suggests that "integration" theory might have come almost full circle:

an increasing density of international regimes, all created for different purposes, may initiate a takeoff towards political integration. In this sense, the study of international regimes offers a micro-level approach to understanding the macro-level phenomenon of integration (Levy et al., 1995: 310)

One may see regimes as "procedures for the regulation of conflict" and even—to stretch it a bit—"as contributing to a civilizing process in international politics," but neither of these is necessary to conclude that regimes in the macro might lead to the "conduct of conflict [that] is institutionalized and does not lead to a resort to violence (Levy et al., 1995: 310).[31]

In some ways, therefore, analysis of regimes has proceeded generally through one plateau—the extensive case studies—and has yet to extend to the more clearly structural analysis. Theories of structural balance, on the other hand, never even reached a minimum plateau of acceptance. "Regimes" has provided a normative goal, and a framework under which multiple detailed and nuanced case studies can demonstrate existence of cooperative norm-based behavior in a variety of specific behavioral dimensions. Yet to emerge is the painstaking, moil-like work of tracking the complex pathways by which multiple, microregimes unfold into larger macrolevels of integration. Times have been propitious for the "regime hunt" that has ensued in search of such cooperative behavior.

Without taking away from propitious results of multiple regime case studies, perhaps the single element that devastated structural balance theories more than a failing on the theoretical dimension was a failure to incorporate directly and be as receptive to the normative "liberal" elements widely recognized in regime approaches and so prevalent in the post–Cold War era. Or perhaps its focus was too narrow—not as receptive to the multiple case studies as was regimes. However, the stories of both may not be over yet. The popularity of regimes is due to many factors, but one factor absent is any *parsimonious* ability to systematically explain broad ranges of international behavior. As for well-known balance predictions that the end of the Cold War also means the end of institutions like NATO—the linkages may be parsimonious, but to date, a mere decade after the change in structure, so far incorrect. One other key element, however, where balance might be deficient is in the area of "norms," a realm of growing interest and essential to regimes but only at one level of analysis. The following chapter explores the same issue without the liberal presuppositions.

Chapter Eight ✸

The Invisible Hand That Wasn't

Introduction

In December 1994 Mexico devalued the peso. The United States and other countries responded in rapid-fire fashion with bailout plans. A year earlier, in the fall of 1993, the budding European economic system had been in free fall, prompting the *Economist* to note "something important has changed. The financial markets have discovered, in a way they are unlikely to forget for years, their power to crack the system" (*Economist*, 1993: 25). Both crises were severe, governments worldwide responded, and disaster—or so we are told—was averted. Both episodes received the attention any Cold War crises had, yet not one bullet was fired, troop movement ordered, or casualty incurred. "What," an observer from the 1950s might be moved to ask, "has happened to international politics—has it truly been turned over to the accountants?" These were not aberrant instances. Three years later, the International Monetary Fund stepped in with a special loan to the Philippines to prevent worldwide "market instability." The same occurred shortly after with South Korea, and from there the litany continued.

Two decades earlier, when the American president launched the momentous opening—"rapprochement"—with the People's Republic of China, economic measures the same year also effectively marked the end of the Bretton Woods system. The first event took precedence, and while the second was not buried it did not warrant consideration as earth-shattering because "news and history tend to be written in the context of a Super Story" and the Super Story of the day was the Cold War. Rapprochement and detente assumed the high profile, with the Cold War still considered high politics and economics as low politics—the dominant paradigm. Economics was the "proper occupation of faceless bureaucrats. People write histories about wars, not bookkeeping, and they run for presidents to be warlords, not accountants." Two decades later,

the Super Story may be changing. Regional crises—like Bosnia and Haiti—still grab headlines, but they must now compete with a new Super Story—the one about a world that is becoming more and more economically intertwined. In that world, the President is as much Merchant in Chief as Commander in Chief (Friedman, 1994: 4).

Some claimed a metamorphosis was underway, recognized by few at the time (Cooper, 1968). Explaining the "high politics" thought to describe the Cold War years inevitably confronted that perennially tedious question posed by the 19-year-old non-Marxist undergraduate: "But it *all* comes down to economics, doesn't it?"[1] Still, "high politics" uniformly ruled the day:

> those who are well versed in the modern history of international politics have little difficulty demonstrating that the political impulse is usually stronger than the economic one, and that economic interests are frequently only a rationalization for a nation's will-to-power (Dougherty and Pfaltzgraff, 1990: 235).

While another classic demurred that "Neither state nor market is primary; the causal relationships are interactive and indeed cyclical," nonetheless

> In general, the character of international relations and the questions of peace and war are determined primarily by the larger configurations of power and strategic interest among both the great and small powers in the system (Gilpin, 1987: 9, 58).

Nonetheless, realism is limited, and the growing wisdom suggests that more drives national actors than simple, ugly, basic "lusts" for power or consideration of power distributions. Once behavioral terrain beyond the realist empire is opened up, departures can expand. Beyond integrative or institutional issues is the world of the accountant, and three generally accepted schools of thought describe the major orientations—liberal, Marxist, and realist: positions very familiar by now, although cast here in distinctive terminology.

Liberals fashion a world in which political and economic concerns can and should be separated, in which trade and other economic transactions reside in a relatively politically free environment. *Marxists* view the two as joined, with the capitalist economy characterized as essentially conflictual "given the irreducible antagonism between the capitalist bourgeoisie and the laboring proletariat," where class distinctions constitute the defining dissimilarities, and cutthroat competition between capitalist systems ultimately pits them against each other. Finally, *realists* in this scheme regard nations as the primary actors pursuing power objectives and subordinating economics to politics in that quest. Thus, while

> Liberals believe that trade and economic intercourse are a source of peaceful relations among nations because the mutual benefits of trade and expanding interdependence among national economies will tend to foster cooperative relations (Gilpin, 1987: 31),

nationalists (realists) "ascribe to the primacy of the state, of national security, and of military power in the organization and functioning in the international system." Liberalism might view states as "trading states" interested only in *absolute gains*, "indifferent to the gains achieved by others," while realism sees states as "territorial states" valuing "relative gains" (position) "above all" (B. Cohen, 1990: 274). The two views provide differing prognostications: "liberals see a rosy future" with "shrinking distances" and "opportunities for mutual gain through international interaction," while realism is "pessimistic" with states "focusing more on immediate than long-term benefits" (Krasner, 1996: 119).

The "old" theory of realism after World War II was to be "above all else a 'realistic' depiction of the motives of the actors in international affairs." Focusing on the state as the prime actor, it ignored culture, ideology, and economics. However,

In the 1970s IPE [International Political Economy] developed to view international relations as the affairs of states alone, but it broadened the concept of national interest to include production, trade, and investment. In one rather limiting but popular interpretation, IPE was viewed as the study of trade disputes, economic competition, economic foreign policy and international economic agreements between independent national states (Amin et al., 1994: 5).

Within the larger "liberalist" view of 1970s interdependence, therefore, consequential modifications were bringing out realist underpinnings of apparently liberalist views, for by the 1980s market forces had come to the fore and the international environment had to be seen "as the coming together of two systems of opportunities and constraints—a still realist state system, and the market" (Amin et al., 1994: 6).

But transformations of macrolevel systems are sluggish and prolonged, hard to track accurately—hence the attraction of uncovering abrupt change. "Interdependence" had described one potential shift in the contemporary system, "multiple interdependencies" added a bit, and when imbedded in "liberalism" implications suggest interactions and organizations producing peaceful "regimes." Interdependencies that produce competitive interests along power or hegemonic lines or in a "market" structure might prove to be something quite different. "Markets" are fascinating but also dangerous places, and the manner by which that view of the international system emerged is intricate and complex, involving normative as well as theoretical perspectives over several decades. Moreover, interpretations differ, but the suggestion of one rendition sets the stage for contemporary perspectives in both the academic as well as the policy world.

Another "Paradigm Shift" or the "Invisible" Appears?

One interpretation has already been noted: as one super story faded and the Cold War became routinized and formalized by the mid-1960s, other issues moved onto the agenda; the East-West political system lost its panache, and other issues and depictions of the world emerged, certainly a normal process. Underlying this interpretation, popular in recent years, is that the transformations were not merely surface or quixotic—the usual rearranging of the deck chairs on the Titanic—but reflected basic, fundamental shifts in the way the world was being organized.

Nonetheless, since the unspoken hegemon still ruled, there was not much reason or use in contesting the many economic issues, and therefore "high politics" still ruled. However, even before the alleged growing interdependencies that were to set in and make that hegemonic status potentially irrelevant, economic development and "nation-building" had become key goals of American foreign policy by the early 1960s when it became clear that the "battle" between the two superpowers would not be waged solely through respective military hardware and threats of their use. Factors thought involved in the economic development of the "Third World" emerged as key policy as well as theoretical dimensions. By the late 1960s economic development concerns dominated, even though the relationship to the international political dimension remained bifurcated: development was viewed as part of the Cold War, but also became central for those contending that the condition of less-developed nations was a direct function of their "dependence" upon the developed nations (Frank, 1969; Galtung, 1971). These theoretical formulations, even if motivated partly by normative aims, nonetheless produced relational descriptions of alternative international systems and unconventional views of international political relations compared to the dominant East-West Cold War conception. Beyond normative concerns, the theoretical component promised the potential for explaining both the existence and perpetuation of dependent political and/or economic relations, and by elucidating the noninevitable causes of lower development those normative goals might be achieved: the reversal of economic dependency.

But for theory, one breakthrough was revisualizing the international system, or various relevant subsystems, along systemic economic, not political, lines. The resultant cottage industry of dependency had mostly receded by the 1990s,[2] with some research questioning it entirely, and other products suggesting a more complex analysis.[3] The emergence of the so-called "Four Tigers" of Asia, embarking on effective paths of development and defying propositions contained in dependency theory, "has been a devastating blow to dependency theory" (Krasner, 1994: 15). Given the post-1989 move toward market economies throughout the world, then

> If social scientists in Latin America are more concerned about free trade and market access than exploitation, it will be hard for their colleagues in North America and Europe to sustain any viable research program for dependency theory (Krasner, 1994: 15).

Thus, theories of dependency took an "unabashedly economic view of international politics" (K. Holsti, 1978: 514), boasted a manifest normative undercurrent, but also represented structural views of the international system clearly embodying a non–Cold War perspective. But dependency also fit within a broader theme as "part of a long historical tradition in which subordinate countries seek to manipulate the international economy for national political ends" (Lake, 1987: 233). In sum, dependency reflected only peripherally the growing focus on economic issues, and more importantly burnished a dying Marxist legacy as well as provided alternative structural views of international systems.

Expanding the scope of economic views of contemporary international relations produced the "world system" views, positing an extended historical evolution beginning in the "long" sixteenth century (1450–1640) and proceeding through at least four stages. The existence of a "world capitalist system" suggested the complex operation of core, periphery, and semiperiphery locales united in cc extensive interrelationships based on Marxian notions of capital, labor, and production (Wallerstein, 1979), all in some way fashioned together into a loosely formed "system" at the global level revolving around— regardless of short-term temporal specifics and potential alterations—the posited existence of "capitalist" economics. Nation-states come and go, empires rise and fall, but through all this, a thickly woven system based on underlying economic assumptions and transactions persists.

Dependency provided for radical conceptual restructuring with economic transactions as a basis, and world systems broadened it. In a sense, interdependency furthered the process but also narrowed the time dimension and served as a catalyst for many real—and perhaps some imagined—empirical shifts emerging in the early 1970s. Viewed as "reality" in the post-Vietnam world of "detente," the imprecise concept spawned multiple alternative pictures of the international system and its structure, and represented the first direct assault on the nation-state as the central unmovable unit of analysis, focusing on emerging "transnational" relations, which implied the existence of multiple and overlapping processes and transactions outside the nation-state structure that were so transforming the international system that Cold War realist-oriented theoretical models based on the state-as-unit would become obsolete.

New structures require new frameworks and theories, and a central component was to be the economic—as opposed to "political"—dimension. While vague, unformed visions of emerging interdependence or transnationalism sparked the original shift, the ensuing 20 years saw the development of a variety of less-amorphous and more substantively and empirically grounded concerns. Later specific manifestations of the research agenda focused on point-specific economic relations and issues as opposed to being imbedded within the original broad notions of interdependent transnational relations. "Globalization" may be the last in a long line of voguish concepts, but in this case has begun to carry yet another and somewhat different meaning and impose a much different strain of implications in the 1990s—with its focus on international financial transactions going beyond merely trade or other economic phenomena than had been the case over 20 years earlier.

Central to the interdependency model was the professed growing importance of economics. Traditional realists had not ignored economics so much as they saw it as secondary, although a secondary dimension of importance when cast in the context of a link between imperialism and war (Morgenthau, 1965: 44–71). It was not until the 1980s, following the first contemporary elaboration of the "long cycle" (Modelski, 1978) and the resurrection of the Russian economist Nikolai Kondratieff's notions of links between economic cycles and war (Kondratieff, 1935) that the relationship reemerged as a focus of sustained systematic inquiry, with special emphasis on what was coming to be seen as an underlying reality of international economic and political life—the status of the United States' assumed leadership of the "free world," a view fostered by its sheer economic and military power overlaid on the East-West Cold War division. While "hegemon" was rarely used in the early years of American leadership—too leaden, heavy, and oppressive perhaps, with unpleasant associations of imperialism and unwanted influence *over* other nations—it was also the case more generally that the focus of attention had not necessarily been on the United States as the *economic* leader. Still, the leadership role came with the territory, even though the befogged eyes of the academic realists perhaps failed to see underlying economic constructions.[4]

A shift in empirical reality, therefore, or merely a paradigm departure from 20 years of realism? Some say the Super Story has changed for good, and certainly economic concerns—first the more incendiary trade issues and later international finance and investment more generally—at times sweep traditional issues off the front pages, although beneath many of these seem to be historic concerns with coercion, sanctions, protectionism, and conflict. But "interdependence" undoubtedly altered mental gears in the 1970s; "globalization" is the popular version in the 1990s, but the latter contains the added dimension of "market forces," which seem to even further transcend the confines, dictates, and dimensions of the traditional nation-state.

The shift from Cold War–oriented political to more globally defined issues revolving around economics reflected observable transformations but also the growing intellectual dissatisfaction with the stylized, traditional perception of the "realist" model, a discontent surfacing first in the cognitive school of the 1950s and 1960s and later with the decision-making approaches in the 1960s and 1970s. The further impetus provided by the "interdependentistas" was initially more blunt and marked, an explicit and direct challenge. The cognitive school had questioned realism only implicitly and indirectly, partly because its conscious, specific focus was typically on different, and more limited, dependent variables, but also because of the tenor of the times. It was not coincidental, of course, as the above chronology has suggested, that these shifts in paradigmatic focus by academic scribblers was taking place as the major powers had entered into a tacit agreement that the Cold War was to be accepted and therefore normal, and that certain low politics issues began to surface.

International "Politics," "Economics," or the "Market"

Dominant paradigmatic forces are by definition commanding, and change is infrequent. But certainly by the 1980s observable phenomena suggested that paradigm change was at least feasible, and the debates between the realists and liberals serve as a backdrop for introducing new research domains and questions that seemed to be emerging. At the most basic level, three related problem areas were proposed: the affairs of the state versus affairs of the market; the interaction of the state and the market; and the implications of this interaction for state behavior and interstate relations. Within these broad spectra, more limited questions include the conditions under which a highly interdependent world economy emerges; the relationships between economic change and political change; and the significance of a world market economy for domestic economies (Gilpin, 1987: 12–14). The more specific issues that emerged as the Cold War fatigued revolved around the management of world trade, monetary relations and exchange rates, foreign investment, the role of multinational corporations, international trade "openness" and the distribution of power, national values and international competitiveness, as well as the old standby—national development (Krasner, 1996: 108). While these seem to be the most general substantive issues posed, a "kind of lowest common denominator," and certainly a full academic plate, beyond these "the further extent of the subject" as well as its "rationale" seemed to be unclear (Strange, 1995: 157).

Consistent with the position outlined in Chapter Five—that multiple structural pictures of the international system can be fostered if a limited realism restricted to the Cold War system can be overcome—these problem areas and specific issues open up the opportunity for more accurately representing the contemporary system, and also for understanding behavior that might be anomalous in a traditional, stylized realism. However, to the degree that narrow, specific individual inquiries do not relate back to the paradigmatic level either directly or indirectly, then they would tend to fall more into the genre of specific case studies undertaken for their own sake as opposed to components attempting to shed light on the broader and ultimately more difficult questions of the systemic relationships between the "state" and the "market."

And it is at that juncture, where increasingly the central tension may lie: under *what* circumstances does the market or the state take over the basic influence tasks, and—for the key research questions—are there designs in which that type of general question can be answered? The state retains in many observers' eyes a prominent place; without the state, the price mechanism and market forces would determine the outcome of economic activities, which "would be the pure world of the economist." However, in the absence of the market,

the state or its equivalent . . . allocate economic resources; this would be the pure world of the political scientists. Although neither world can ever exist in a pure form, the relative influence of the state or the market changes over time and in different circumstances (Gilpin, 1987: 8).

It is the "different circumstances" that have by and large remained a mystery, because it is not quite clear how to distinguish "pure power" or "pure market" relations or structures, and whether the two can be or need be considered separately. The introduction of market systems and processes may suggest distinctions between traditional and more contemporary research questions, but mere historical transformations of substantive issues do not necessarily produce different theoretical explanations. The confluence of the "launching" of the end of the Cold War in the early 1970s—an arguable assertion but one consistent with the ongoing contention—with emerging economic issues such as the sudden trade deficit with Japan and heightened by other economic events during the 1971–1973 period, certainly changed the focus to economic issues, but not necessarily so much to the consideration of the role or structure of markets as to other, "low" politics issues merely considered more contemporarily relevant than "Cold War" issues. The slowly declining superpower ideological contest added to the sense that economic considerations not considered in traditional analysis must be weighed, but such transformations in focus do not necessarily lead to consideration of systemic "market" effects. Beyond the specific economic questions already noted, the key theoretical conceptualizations, especially with regard to the structural relations between markets and the state, seem to remain obscure. "Markets" as an issue, however, are of very recent vintage, and it may prove that conceptual tools for the political scientist have yet to be discovered to mesh these newly relevant phenomena with the more traditional. Moreover, markets have not always held the panache of recent vintage, and analysis of more traditional considerations might set the stage for contemporary analysis.

Trade and Conflict, War and Economic Waves, Trade "Policy"

Within the Deutschian "transactional" framework, "trade" had served as the premier indicator of integrating tendencies, while it had never been explicitly part of the realist theoretical lexicon, nor had it garnered one line in Morgenthau's index (1965: xx), and was referred to in the Cold War years with the derogatory term "low politics." It was rarely a power issue, especially for a "hegemon," as long as trade flows were beneficial and hegemonic status maintained. Once trade turns against the hegemon, then the issue for the accountant becomes one for the politician. Despite the United States' hegemonic position for years after World War II, trade ultimately did become such a political issue. If one specific circumstance signaled the evolution of trade from low to high politics, it might be that point where America's bilateral trade picture shifted from surplus to deficit with the nation that was to cause it the most trade difficulties, at least diplomatically if not economically, during the subsequent two decades. The shift occurred in 1971, the same year the American president announced his groundbreaking trips to China and Russia, and the major shift in trade burden occurred with Japan (Sullivan, 1990: 161–165). Other incidents, such as the discontinuation of the Bretton Woods agreement and the first oil embargo two years later, certainly received more public attention, especially since the latter was a crisis in a somewhat traditionally recognized sense. However, from the point when the U.S. trade relationship with Japan went into deficit, trade was no longer of interest only to the economist. It was to obsess U.S.-Japan relations through the boom times in the Japanese economy in the late 1980s, when Japan was held responsible for negatively affecting the American economy, through the domino-like failures of other Asian economics in the mid-1990s—when once again Japan was held culpable, in this instance for failing to stimulate its own flagging economy in order to "save" the rest of Asia.

A major compilation of seminal research on trade (Lake, 1993a) uncovers the major emphases: the greatest attention—63 percent—was devoted to categories involving "protectionism/barriers" and "tariffs," on the one hand, combined with trade wars, conflict, coercion, and sanctions—interests certainly traversing the line between low and high politics. Within the latter, the most consistently analyzed issue has been the time-worn one between trade and conflict, a concern for integration theorists, but one also addressable in a simple, more directed sense outside of that context. While the theoreticians' arguments—and the findings—have certainly been mixed over the years, the thrust, especially in light of recent findings, has exhibited a slightly greater consistency than earlier thought. Traditional formulations viewed the relationship as fused and confusing: while economic intercourse can at times moderate and at other times aggravate relations between nations, "what can be said with some justification is that trade is not a guarantor of peace. On the other hand, the collapse of trade has frequently led to the outbreak of international conflict" (Gilpin, 1987: 58).

Such traditional assertions, satisfying both sides of the dispute with unspecified dependent variables, are legion. And while it is true that trade was often the *source* of conflict between nation-state groups, figuring "significantly" especially between Westphalia and the Treaty of Vienna, the nineteenth century according to one observer "saw the rapid diminution of armed contests over commercial and navigational issues." While these increased during the 1930s and may at times play a crucial role in the contemporary era, when the dependent variable is designated specifically as "problems of a commercial/navigational character" as a source of conflict, these have tended to be regularized or controlled through legal means; on the whole, economic issues as a source of war has declined in percentage terms, according to one set of data, since the 1648–1713 period (K. Holsti, 1991: 316–317).

More point-specific, systematic evidence in the last chapter suggests the positive—and dampening effect—of trade on conflict, supporting interdependence theories. Dyads with greater trade exhibited less conflict, and especially so the more strategic the trade (Polachek, 1980: 67, 71); other findings, while mixed, suggested "that the *noncostly aspects of trade* are associated with a decline in conflict," with, in the end, both schools receiving confirmation: "costly trade produces an increase in conflict while beneficial trade produces a decline in conflict" (Gasiorowski, 1986: 36). Others also found trade related with lower conflict (Sayrs, 1989; Oneal and Russett, 1997: 287; Russett et al., 1998: 457, 462). Reversing the causal arrow, however, also suggests that cooperation tends to promote trade (Pollins, 1989). Certainly one of the largest recent analyses of the potential role of trade suggests a clear pattern: despite differences across several data sets, trade demonstrates a strong negative relationship on the frequency of major power wars, a relationship independent of "any aspect of the distribution of power," but one that is also bidirectional: high incidence of wars involving major powers tends to reduce international commerce (Mansfield, 1994: 126, 233, 240–241).[5]

This specific agenda directed at trade, although most recently associated with the "interdependency" school of the 1970s, has a long history and tradition. The relationship between economies and economic behavior in general, with trade as only a specific component, has an equally long tradition, resurrected periodically, which posits a cyclicality to the growth of economies in general, and a relationship between those cycles and international war. The reason for the periodic "irresistible fascination" (Rosecrance, 1987: 284) with the war-economics cycle is not clear, but the recent short-lived spurt in popularity suggests not so much an underlying strong theoretical and empirical advance as much as evidencing the most recent upswing in "cycles research" itself. Within the context of the dual totality of "cycles" and "global war," a certain deadening finality can emerge, especially in an era of completely destructive weapons. Entertaining propositions that the next upturn (or downturn, depending on the version) will result in major worldwide war can be disheartening, which perhaps explains why cycles theorists have found reason to moderate their views about the finality of cycles (Goldstein, 1988: 369–376; Modelski, 1990; Modelski and Thompson, 1996: 224–229).

Nonetheless, some unmistakable empirical findings have emerged from two related strains, one focusing on the work derived mostly from one article by Kondratieff (1935) and the second from the related "long cycle" model (Modelski, 1978) noted earlier. The theoretical links between "economic long waves" and war are multiple and complex; they include the accelerated pace and economic activity that occurs during economic upswings, the increased struggle for markets, as well as the "wealth to finance wars, technological advances that enhance war-fighting capacities, and increases in international tensions that can boil over into conflict" (Mansfield, 1994: 57). The empirical results are mixed, but with certain general tendencies. One observer finds mostly for a relation between interstate wars and economic upswings in the 1816–1914 period, even though the causal direction is unclear:

> not only the most severe wars but also most of the interstate wars of the 1816–1914 period were initiated during the long wave's upswing. Of thirty five wars, as many as twenty eight (80 percent) began during the upswing. The upswings also encompass twelve of the fourteen most bloody wars. . . . Yet while the degree of association is quite striking, what [we] cannot answer [is] the questions of whether economic long waves help to bring about wars or whether wars contribute to the generation of economic long waves (Thompson, 1988: 171).

Thus, the proffered advice is to "remain[ing] agnostic about the historical existence of Kondratieff's long waves and their hypothesized effects on conflict" (Thompson, 1988: 195).

Other "tentative" and "fragmentary" results are more point- specific, reporting an average annual fatality rate six times higher on upswings than on downswings in the economic cycle and, if the twentieth century is included, 21 times higher during upswings than downswings (Goldstein, 1988: 246): "The hypothesis connecting higher levels of war with the long wave upswing has been strongly corroborated, and the opposite timing rejected" (Goldstein, 1988: 256). Another set of results agrees, finding more wars during upswings than downswings, a pattern occurring mostly for war between smaller states (Mansfield, 1988: 44–45); these results changed slightly in later analyses, resulting in much more confusing—or perhaps refined—conclusions, but with some minimal evidence supporting the positive relationship between upswings and war (Mansfield, 1994: 58–59, 64–65, 139–140). A third analysis concluded that war cycles do not correspond to Kondratieff waves, even though the data do support the hypothesis that wars drive prices up, which in turn may affect casualty rates, but "the process governing the two regimes may result in one causal linkage for the upswing and another for the downswing," but also concludes that the war-price cycle is not a Kondratieff wave (Sayrs, 1993: 230–231).

Associated analyses of innovative activities of global leaders converge more on the traditional political relationships between power transition and global wars [Chapter Six], where global wars are viewed as a function of power concentration and deconcentration, but with a much greater emphasis on geopolitical distinctions as opposed to economic transactions and processes (Rasler and Thompson, 1994: 166–171). Even broader analyses have expanded the notion of Kondratieff waves to encompass more sizable spans of history (Modelski and Thompson, 1996), exemplifying the tension between cycles as constituting long-term causal processes and wars that—to the contrary—tend to be more point-specific (Rosecrance, 1987). As far as comparative tests, none of the competing explanations of the relationship between global economic activity and warlike behavior—long waves, cycles of hegemony, or world leadership cycles—appears superior when the outcome variable is measured as the number of militarized interstate disputes initiated every year between 1816 and 1976, but all perform better than a null, no-relationship model; a "co-evolving" model combining long wave and world leadership components[6] appears to perform somewhat more satisfactorily (Pollins, 1996: 113–114).

The theoretical scope of long wave, long cycle analyses is remote from the concerns spawned directly in the post-1970 era. Linkages between war and economic patterns can tenaciously fascinate, and may relate to contemporary political questions of trade, but ostensibly remain removed from immediate concerns of the contemporary world. In the latter—behavioral domains over which decision-makers appear to exercise some direct, immediate consequence—trade specifically has been the most important generating factor, even though particular views of issues concerning trade have taken on a transformed character. Realpolitik-related concerns of tariffs and protectionism seem to dominate, relating—ultimately—to the concrete policy issues noted earlier: in political parlance, so-called "free" trade versus "fair" trade.

In this domain, tariffs are a key outcome or dependent variable. While overall tariff levels declined throughout the twentieth century, explanations for differing cross-national tariff levels at different times have shifted: international power models seemed robust at the turn of the century whereas more domestic, "rational economic policy" variables better explained tariff levels in the early 1970s (Conybeare, 1983). Domestic and international factors related to business cycles at both levels have been presented as alternative explanations to hegemonic stability itself for varying tariff levels, mostly applied to the ability—or lack thereof—of Great Britain in the nineteenth century to produce an "open" trading system (McKeown, 1983).[7] While debates over tariffs, especially levels and types of U.S. tariffs into the early 1980s, have continued (Lake, 1984: 164–165), the general overall long-term trend in this important outcome variable has been down. Whether that continues is questionable, especially if we turn to more systemic analyses. Trade and protectionism relate in very tangled ways and while in the aggregate appear to move in opposite directions, the general tendency suggests the antecedence of trade on protectionism occurs more frequently than the opposite (Thompson and Reuveny, 1998: 437). However, some rudimentary evidence suggests a relationship between customs revenues—a form of protectionism—and long waves, with downturns in the former associated with upswings in the long waves, with the plausible suggestion that the late 1980s and early 1990s could have been a transition period between growth waves, which would point to potentially higher levels of protectionism in the future (Thompson and Vescera, 1992: 530–532). Two other phenomena potentially concur. One suggests that the hypothesized convergence toward democracy globally creates similar domestic power profiles, thereby empowering similar producers across nations, which, it is argued, ironically might have negative ramifications for continuing open trading systems (Verdier, 1998). The second is the trend toward more preferential trading arrangements (PTAs) (Mansfield, 1998), which could lead in the longer term to greater regionalism and potentially closure.

Perhaps the historic shift toward lower tariff behavior on the whole, as well as growing complexity in tariff relations—producing a more complex and less ideologically based picture than in the past—has thrust other phenomena into the spotlight: overall trade levels themselves as outcome variables as well as trading patterns resembling hypotheses found in realist formulations. "Security externalities" have been used as the basis for investigating trading patterns by relating trade and its benefits to a nation's potential military capability, and for the period 1905–1985, not surprisingly, among the major powers, allies tended to trade more with each other than with adversaries or with non-allies (Gowa, 1994), a finding confirmed elsewhere (Morrow et al., 1998). Those patterns appeared stronger in bipolar than multipolar systems—suggesting that fluidity on the economic dimension, as on the political, is higher in the latter than in the former (Gowa, 1994). This finding was at first contradicted—trade flows seemed to be higher between allies in multipolar systems than between allies in bipolar systems (Morrow et al., 1998: 658–659), but a corrected analysis confirmed Gowa's findings (Morrow et al., 1999: 933). Thus bilateral trade patterns suggest underlying structural causes, and extensions produced other noncounterintuitive findings: for the period 1960–1990, not only do allies conduct more trade with each other than do non-allies, but the very act of alliance formation itself tends to generate increases in trade. Combining these with the additional variable of preferential trading arrangements generates even more commerce between the nations involved than do any of the factors independently, and the impact of alliances and trading arrangements differs for major and minor powers (Mansfield and Bronson, 1997: 105).

Structural trading patterns can imply neorealist analysis, but can enlighten only indirectly when turning to actual trade policy. Trade is patterned, as are trade barriers and policies, even though both may have changed in recent years from historic concern over protection *against* imports to one over *promoting* exports. Protection against imports still plays a role, and all trade postures reflect political components. Even attempts suggesting the reduction of their effect by relying on levels of analysis distinctions—"actor behavior" versus "system management" (B. Cohen, 1990: 264)—and constructing a methodology combining the two in terms of relevant variables (B. Cohen, 1990: 269) does not erase the difficulties of assessing behavior so patently subject to the political realm.

But strategic trade policy and policy questions drain attention from the question of explaining foreign economic policy behavior, let alone building "a formal structure to the interactions between market and politics that appear to be most pivotal in the trade area" (B. Cohen, 1990: 267, 281). Lacking such a structure, actor behavior as opposed to system-level behavior becomes the focus and resurrects the Hobbes-versus-Locke issue of whether greater threats come from binding or loosening ones own and others' hands in the international system, all of which are related to issues of national sovereignty and national identity—and thus logically to national "power" (Moran, 1996: 192–193). Thus despite "regimes" and the potential pacifying effect of economics, the broad spectrum of outcome variables—from actor-specific behaviors at the national level to system-level behaviors—seem ultimately to direct attention back to the insistence, without necessarily spelling out the specifics, of restoring the variable of "power" (B. Cohen, 1990: 281).

Revisiting Hegemony: The Power of Power?

Issues of sovereignty, identity, and power have historically been tangentially related to state/market questions but they currently burden the conceptual background, reflected in theory development in recent years concerning "hegemonic stability" and whether "power" as traditionally conceived is reflected in economic hegemonic theories. Hegemonic stability theory may not be "a theory of peace and war" but rather "attempts to explain the degree of stability in a liberal political economy rather than the incidence or seriousness of military conflict and war" (Levy, 1991: 149); nonetheless, the question alone reflects the conceptual disarray.

The differences become apparent in elaborating the standard depiction of hegemonic stability theory (HST): an open, liberal, interdependent economic system is dependent on a hegemon, and while cooperation is possible without the hegemon,

> what the theory does say is that this scenario is unlikely and that, with the decline of the hegemon, the preservation of a liberal international regime (with emphasis on the term *liberal*) will be much more difficult (Gilpin, 1987: 91).

The theoretical conclusions are straightforward, can be seen as a competitor to multipolar or bipolar "balance of power" explanations for long periods of peace, and add to contentions concerning preponderance having a positive effect on peace (Spezio, 1990: 166, 170).[8]

As tidy as HST seems to be, questions have haunted its development. The most basic question—"When is a state hegemonic?" (McKeown, 1983: 76)—uncovers a variety of weaknesses in the model, including the technical issue of when respective contenders are, or are not, "hegemonic," as well as the more difficult specification of the process of hegemonic governance; the

> failure to discuss precisely what a hegemonic state does in its attempt to regulate international politico-military relations represents a serious omission. . . . it is virtually impossible to adequately account for the failures, or, for that matter, the successes which are presumably related to the exercise of hegemonic governance . . . [the] discussion of the structure of hegemonic governance must be supplemented with analyses that investigate "what . . . hegemonic leaders do when they are being hegemonic" (Spezio, 1990: 179; quotation from James and Lake, 1989: 3).

A second question ponders whether a hegemon's behavior is deliberately and consciously "hegemonic" when they appear to be acting hegemonically, or whether that behavior results for other reasons (James and Lake, 1989: 3–4, 8, 27–28). Finally, the issue of the motivations and capabilities of nonhegemonic states who may or may not possess capabilities relatively close to the hegemonic power and may or may not perceive the desirability of an open trading system, suggest several not-so-peaceful scenarios from such a "hegemonic" system (McKeown, 1983: 76).

Such a system resembles in some ways a unipolar system, and thus while a neorealist Cold War—almost certainly bipolar—system compelled nations to behave in one fashion within one behavioral domain, another system was also operating: a hegemonic economic system. Each system needs tracking, perhaps with different measures, one theory operating largely in the realm of economic behavior and "rules"—but hidden because it was "low politics"—and the other, perhaps a Kaplanesque, set of rules imposed in a political bipolar system. Previous chapters have noted this symbiotic relationship between hegemony and "power" theories, not a new observation (McKeown, 1983: 76–78), and while findings on hegemony were mixed, they did suggest that presence of hegemony tended to exhibit beneficial effects. However, hegemony might also be separated into "leadership" and HST "per se," differentiating the research program contained within the "international security research programs," encompassing hegemony and war, long cycles, and power transition (Lake, 1993b: 461), from a more narrowly defined hegemonic stability theory.[9] By focusing specifically on the dependent variables, at least on the "leadership" side, it delineates relatively discrete phenomena to be explained that relate clearly to the "IPE"—as opposed to "realist"—variation of hegemonic stability theory: what a "leader" is hypothetically supposed to produce in terms of a stable medium of exchange, liquidity, and the basic definition and protection of property rights (Lake, 1993b: 462–463). While these outcome variables seem to be associated only with the "leadership" side of the theoretical divide, in fact they appear also to be in line with an economically oriented HST.

Concern over American hegemony originally generated much of the attention, and discussion of the early development of that American hegemony provides a context. One rendition (Ikenberry, 1992) suggests that the set of Anglo-American agreements on trade and monetary issues resulting in American leadership after World War II issued from a confluence of the specific individuals involved as well as the "ideas" they brought to the postwar negotiations. Utilizing a nonsystemic, nondeterministic "ideas count" explanatory framework portraying the traditional give-and-take among leaders, we find the realist conclusion that "American leaders wanted to promote American interests, and they were willing to use the nation's power capabilities to do so," but within a system that "would have a normative appeal to elites in other nations." Even though outright coercion was eschewed, "This is not to say that the United States refrained from exercising its hegemonic power," but that there were "real limits to the coercive pursuit of the American postwar agenda" and "American officials paid more than insignificant attention to the normative bases of the postwar settlement and why they were willing to make adjustments along the way to give the system a certain legitimacy" (Ikenberry, 1992: 320).

Such an "ideas count" rendition offers high plausibility, a model reliant on individual agency, and yet an equally plausible hypothesis for the emergence of American hegemony could simply be larger, systemic economic factors over which the individuals had little control, but which *placed* the United States at the top of the heap. Conscious decisions certainly eased things along, but were those decisions, elaborated in an agency framework, consequences of an impending hegemony or its causes? The structural outcome of World War II could serve as a causal agent: America came out on top. The same issue is raised with the alleged American "decline" of roughly a generation later. Were there decisions made, or was it brought about by what Nye calls the "vanishing WWII effect" (Nye, 1990: 72–87). One triggering event already cited in terms of public perceptions subsequent to the early 1970s that served as a signal for perceived hegemonic transformation—and carrying implications concerning the "causes" of rise and decline—was the shift in U.S.-Japan dyadic trade, a spark for political contention but also a possible indicator of underlying transformations. We have always thought it naive to assume that nations' actions are simplemindedly based on a "drive" for power (Sullivan, 1976: 157–164); nations do things for many reasons. The U.S.-Japan "problems"—encompassing multiple elements perhaps defining the beginning of the American "decline"—were not generated by Japan alone, or necessarily by Japanese decision-makers, or by any single ingredient. The "Japanese challenge" went beyond trade: Japan, without "aggressing the prevailing order" and through no direct attempt at "proactive" international behavior, may nonetheless wreak great change in the international system:

> one member of the international system may yet provoke long-term change in the structure of the . . . balance of international power simply through sustained superior economic and technological performance (Schmieglow and Schmieglow, 1990: 566).

What produces that "superior economic and technological performance" is itself multifaceted, much of which, however, may bear no relationship to any imposed lust or drive for power. Nonetheless, the end result of such economic performance is system-transformation at the international level.

Debates concerning systemic models "remain unresolved" (Mansfield, 1994: 9), and hegemonic "decline" rests very much within the systemic framework, although formulated within an economic context and in recent years customarily linked more to economic behavior and parameters than to political ones. But the link between economic and political remains, tenuous though it might be, and thus the perceived U.S. "decline" in the 1970s and 1980s yielded ideological and normative as well as theoretical responses. But such terminology—realist to a large degree—carried little cachet until the issue of "decline" became popular. Just as implications of hegemonic status for the rules of the international system were being realized—such as asking the question "After Hegemony"? (Keohane, 1984)—the debate over the empirical reality of U.S. hegemony began (Russett, 1985), and continued in full force (Strange, 1989; Nye, 1990). Reasons for the debate flourished. One suggested that U.S. academics in the 1980s considered the perception of declining U.S. hegemony as an explanation of the mood of the American public in the 1970s,[10] others that hegemonic theory was capable of accounting for—or was consistent with—other empirical realities of the time that would not be consistent with continued American hegemony (Bergeson, 1982: 30–32). Finally, a dense array of normative baggage had already been arraigned against implications some drew from Waltz's attempt to posit beneficial effects of a bipolar as opposed to multipolar world; if extended beyond bipolarity, then it becomes a debate and critique of any system implying hegemony or implied dominance in economic production, finance, and trade, even if these were *not* to be linked necessarily to military capabilities (Gill, 1990).

But what about America's "decline"? Renditions of the emergence of American hegemony have already been highlighted; descriptions of decline abound and revisit the fine line between the economic and political—and therefore of the complicated nature of "hegemonic decline." One "fairly straightforward" description of the general process for "continental and hybrid powers" suggests that nations try to do too much on "limited resource bases," similar to Kennedy's notion of "overstretch": repeated warfare and too many opponents place too much strain on resources: "leading land powers essentially exhaust themselves and are replaced by states that have not yet had a similar opportunity to do so." Other nations that have become preeminent in the global political economy also exhaust themselves and this can—but need not—"precede the wars in which their weaknesses are most clearly displayed." Because nations' rise is predicated "in part on some innovational advantages, their relative decline hinges, to a large degree, on the loss of these advantages." Thus "each innovational era plays itself out." These processes may have applied to the Portuguese, Dutch, and British hegemonies. "Each innovator is succeeded by another state that outperforms the old lead innovator in its specializations and introduces new areas of innovation as well" (Rasler and Thompson, 1991b: 419).

The relevance of this singular description to the issue of American decline is not obviously clear—it is, after all, a "crude theory of relative decline"—because decline can occur either relative to the achievements of other states or compared to historical standards of performance. Of the many elements that describe this process, a key one is simply that other dogs learn new tricks: "Critical technological innovations are diffused throughout the system. Other states catch up" (Rasler and Thompson, 1991b: 420). Diminishing innovation adds to the process of decline, and in this domain at least four internal factors can be at work: the returns on a given innovation diminish with time; leaders become complacent with a lack of competition; institutional rigidities set in that preclude innovative responses to environmental changes; and finally—a process dreadfully familiar to many in the "globalized" world of the 1980s and 1990s—"as the society becomes wealthier, production becomes increasingly more expensive. As a consequence, production tends to move to areas where factor costs are cheaper" (Thompson and Rasler, 1991b: 438). In conclusion, the

> historical pattern seems to be that declining leaders find it difficult to extricate themselves from a descending trajectory. The one exception to date has been 18th century Britain, and that turnaround required what is sometimes referred to as an industrial revolution . . . If the British case is the norm, innovation and decline interact to create a vicious circle, with more decline leading to even less or slower innovation (Rasler and Thompson, 1991b: 438).

So far the crude theory has mostly addressed the economic. The "political" enters when global war—as we saw in Chapter Six—can demarcate the point when a "systemic leader" promotes a new world order. Ultimately, however,

> As the leader's economic position slides down the technological gradient, competitors, allies, and would-be successors alike are encouraged to augment their own military positions. Relative economic decline therefore facilitates relative politico-military decline . . . unless it can reverse its slide down the technological gradient, it will not have the resources to do much more than remain competitive (Thompson, 1988: 165–166).

Theoretical depictions of "decline" are one thing; specification of empirical matches is quite another,[11] especially when dealing with the issue of American decline in the contemporary era. Central questions principally concentrate on who leads, the periods of respective dominance, and then what signifies decline. Thus, a persistent problem is

> identifying the hegemonic power and its period of dominance. Modelski, Goldstein, and others differ greatly on this, and naval power indices (which slight both Louis XIV and Napoleon) are not enough to measure overall military and diplomatic power. Period of leadership is another vexed question . . . (Rosecrance, 1987: 297).

With regard to previous hegemonic periods, no agreement exists on respective hegemons as well as the period of dominance, and the implications can have radical effects on empirical findings (Mansfield, 1992: 758).

The processes enumerated in the "crude theory" continue the disagreements, and raise fascinating questions of a contemporary nature. To be blunt, the question must be addressed; was a book title's assertion at the turn of the decade actually a prescient observation concerning America's position: *Bound to Lead?* [12] Countering the realist bipolar description of the Cold War era, those focusing on economic leadership uniformly list the U.S. as hegemon throughout the period, but by the 1980s the issue of the continuance of American hegemony pitted—in Nye's words—the "declinists" versus the "revivalists." From the economic perspective, evidence suggests a clear decline into the early 1980s. With respect to the U.S.-Japan trade and economic tensions unfolding throughout the 1980s with the onset of the Japanese "miracle," many pictured that process as sure evidence of American decline. Much anecdotal testimony attested to that fact, and empirical evidence suggested support specifically for Japan's emergence (Thompson and Vescera, 1992: 504–506, table 2). Similar data utilized for the United States during that period tracks with at least one previously recognized decline as well as several other transitions of recent vintage (Lake, 1984: 159–167). That is, data for the period 1870–1938 on relative size and productivity indicate a clear linear decline for the United Kingdom beginning in 1880, reducing it from a "hegemonic leader" to a "spoiler."[13] During the same period the United States, although classified as a "supporter,"[14] was clearly on the ascendancy. For the 1950–1977 period it seems clear that the United States' relative position declined (Lake, 1984: 163) to a point in 1977 where the United States and the Federal Republic of Germany, at least as measured by these two measures and relative to each other, had shifted positions. A later assessment of multiple empirical studies suggested four distinct propositions consistent with "hegemony theory": the United States remains a hegemon; it is no longer a hegemon but an "afterglow" maintains international economic openness; it is no longer a hegemon but the system remains open through multilateral cooperation; and, finally, the U.S. is no longer a hegemon (Lake, 1993b: 481).[15]

Nye's influential volume presented not so much a systematic design permitting comparative longitudinal or cross-sectional evaluations, as a picture simply of continuing American dominance. Although he may very well have been right, his conclusion rests on the critical assertions that some declinists had exaggerated American power in the past, and that too much emphasis had been given to the "British analogy." But perhaps Britain was not all that "hegemonic" in its heyday, while the U.S., as a "single, continental-scale economy," was—and we assume remains—"immune to nationalist disintegration since 1865" (Nye, 1990: 65); differences existed in the two countries' "territorial empires" versus "areas of influence"; and, finally, the so-called "contenders" facing both countries were different. Despite Nye's conclusions from data that are strongly suggestive although certainly selective, clear declines do show up by the late 1980s in other sets of his empirical data using military power and share of global economic resources, although Nye dismisses these by asserting first the "vanishing World War II effect," and noting the irony that the empirically observed "decline" was in fact greater during the earlier part of alleged hegemony "and at best very slight in the period of alleged hegemonic decline. Indeed, some measures show no decline at all in the latter period" (Nye, 1990: 87).

Others agree with Nye's overall assessment: one investigation relying explicitly and solely on readily available power data analyzed in a relatively straightforward fashion concluded, "the power of the United States is not declining" (Kugler and Organski, 1989: 126). Others labeled the growing view of America's decline as a "persistent myth," evidenced by the obvious fact that the U.S. defense posture far exceeded any other and the fact that several economic indicators showed continuing American strength through 1980 (and 1985 and 1990 using estimated data) (Strange, 1987: 566–567, tables 1, 2).[16] Nye's analysis also clearly showed superiority in American defense capabilities, even beyond sheer expenditures; and even though it may not rank first place on certain basic resources and military measures in terms of percentage share, it still remained at the top of the rankings on four different economic indicators in the 1980s.[17] Nye's conclusion, "America is rich but acts poor" (Nye, 1990: 259), is not unlike Strange's admonition that collective action against problems is possible "but *only* when the United States takes the lead—when, in short, it still chooses to act as leader" (Strange, 1987: 574). Nau agrees with the "myth" notion[18] but gives a slightly different spin to the perspective of continuing American leadership:

> America leads today, less by sheer size of resources and dominance of international institutions, than by its domestic purposes and procedures, which are widely admired and increasingly emulated around the world. In short, America leads by knowing what it stands for politically and by getting its own house in order economically (Nau, 1990: 371).

Using the Correlates of War (COW) data produces evidence suggesting U.S. decline relative to several other major contenders for the 1950–1980 period (Park and Ward, 1988: 197–198; Sullivan, 1990: 138–145, 159–163), and although the rationale and specific measures differ, the results are strikingly similar—although counterintuitive when looked at from the 1990s.[19] A third analysis presented similar findings on the empirical side but concluded—as did Strange and Nye—that much rests with the decision-makers (Doran, 1991: 72, 225–232).

> The United States is a strong country still near the peak of its power and role in world politics. . . . That nascent relative decline has occurred is a reality. How the United States chooses to deal with this reality is of relevance not only to its own citizens but to the political equilibrium of the international system (Doran, 1991: 232).

A final analysis also suggests decline from 1950 on the economic dimension and 1960 on the military, with the former continuing to decline through 1990 and the military bottoming in 1975 and then increasing in 1990 to a level equivalent to about 1970; an aggregate measure indicates decline from 1955, bottoming in 1975 and remaining relatively stable into 1990 (Volgy and Imwalle, 1995: 824).

No conclusive agreement on the contested empirical question of America's "decline" exists because the data are unclear, and the attachment of significance to any set of data differs from analyst to analyst. Those with a compulsion to *rely more* on available empirical measures seem to veer more toward the "declinist" view, while those *less reliant* on empirical evidence tend to see less evidence of decline. But the network of issues revolving in the last two decades around "hegemonic stability theory" and more specifically American decline are freighted subjects going beyond the empirical, sustaining even familial, religious, and biblical implications (Grunberg, 1990: 456–469), and fraught with ramifications concerning the ever-enduring hypotheses about the rise and fall of peoples and nations, the general role of "hegemony" in society, as well as the place of the United States in the contemporary world. Needless to say for much of the post-detente and post-Vietnam eras, when contending views of Presidents Carter and Reagan and their policies with respect to America's position in the world were strongly debated, "hegemony" nourished a tankerful of ideological connotations. The actual empirical findings for that period do not strongly support either policy position or American decline. Viewed from the early 2000s, subjective and anecdotal data suggest that issues that had flourished about the viability of the U.S. economy and its trading relations mostly faded from the scene, replaced by much talk of a "new" American imperialism especially in terms of business practices and attitudes toward social welfare conditions, but also attitudes toward American behavior in the Persian Gulf War of 1990–1991 and NATO's Kosovo venture in 1999 as potentially indicative of a "new" hegemon.

What all of this might bequeath to the status of "hegemonic stability theory" is unclear, but certainly several considerations might be entertained. First, the "theory" became popularized as a variant of neorealism (hegemony corresponding to unipolarity, as suggested several times already) but with the necessary economic slant to account for changing issues, and its emergence during a period when U.S. hegemony was very much in doubt popularizing talk about America's decline, but within a theoretical framework allowing application to broad sweeps of history. Since talk of America's "decline" was much less frequent at century's end, HST correspondingly seems to be weakening, and—one might conclude—could end up in the piles of "fads," as has been suggested concerning other theories (Krasner 1982: 497). But the second observation is that systematic empirical evaluations of hegemony in general and American hegemony in particular have not proved satisfactory to a wide audience, and it is only such evaluations over longer time periods than have recently been available that could provide answers to those empirical questions—and it is those longer time periods to which the theory was hypothetically applicable to begin with. All of this would of course assume some agreed-upon assessment of the parameters of the international economic system, which is also very much in question.

The International Economic "System"

Equating hegemony with unipolarity is not particularly innovative, and is only a specific illustration of the broader consideration of how close analyses of economic issues come to merely recasting familiar questions with an economic emphasis and variables. Economic analysts readily admit that "power" remains a central concept (B. Cohen, 1990: 281; Strange, 1994: 244), and therefore regardless of how fiercely contested, "hegemony" as power reenters in one fashion or another. The distinctive aspects and questions of power in the economic realm have perhaps not been addressed as consistently as in the purely political, especially when considering the structure of the international economic system.

Structures imply actors and issues; spelling out the actors and the issues immediately subsequent to the dawn of the new interdependence era in the 1970s seemed relatively straightforward, but more recently it may not prove to be as patently obvious. Thus there could be many ways to construct the international "economic" system, some of which may just be emerging, contrary to the international "political system," which at least has traditionally established, well-known structures from which to work [Chapter Six]. For one thing, there should be, hypothetically, differences in terms of what drives states under a structure comprising explicitly economic as opposed to "pure politics" factors and actors. Macro models such as world history, world systems, and Kondrati-eff- or long-wave analyses all contain driving forces other than those associated with *strict* realpolitik. But even within these "large-structure" macro models, identical forces in the form of actors are present, mostly—in the final analysis—nation-states. How-ever, key differences have emerged but they are differences that have gone beyond the conceptual apparatus of the early transnationalists. With very rare exceptions, the work on new economic issues emerging in the early 1970s held few references to "markets" as independent actors as much as they did to other actors deemed important: Inter-governmental Organizations (IGOs), Transnational Corporations (TNCs), Multina-tional Corporations (MNCs), and so on. While those actors have not faded at all from the scene, certainly by the 1990s greater attention has been devoted to "markets" as po-tential "new" actors.

With nations and markets as actors, the debates that surfaced in the 1980s and 1990s—contrary to the 1970s—bear striking resemblances to those of the 1950s and 1960s: competition and issues of winning or losing, now in the international economic realm rather than the political-ideological sphere (Krugman, 1994). A detailed picture of the international economic system in the last part of the twentieth century is beyond our scope, but suggesting the dimensions of primary interest might situate how that sys-tem differs from realist or neorealist pictures already considered, and also the potential changes such a picture itself has undergone. A cardinal dimension would suggest the re-tention of the focus on states as central actors (a contested position, but with some sup-port [Dombrowski, 1998: 24]), although gauged now very differently than in the past: the largest trading nations, partners, and blocs would dominate the hierarchy.

The most obvious parameter of the international trading system has been "open-ness." Subsequent to the abandonment of Bretton Woods, one analysis questioned whether in fact the system had broken down, suffered a reversal, or provoked withdrawal by members, since the opposite seemed to be the case, perhaps because of the absence of a decline in hegemony, the fact that firms had become internationalized, and that "regimes" in trade had developed. More importantly: the "institutionalization of the ide-ology of free trade in the American political system . . . has inhibited protectionism in the most important member of the system" (McKeown, 1991: 152). Thus despite fears by many, the "trading system" had not become a tragedy, the "received wisdom" that the "1930s and 1940s were a period of relative closure and the current era one of greater openness is amply supported," but also that the trading system was as open in the 1920s as before World War I, and that level was not reached again until about the 1970s (McK-eown, 1991: 157). This evidence supporting an open post–World War II era is true only when using trade volumes rather than values, and when the years since 1972 are in-cluded. "For the years 1948–1972 even Stein's (1984) cautious terminology of 'freer' rather than 'free' trade seems inappropriate" (McKeown, 1991: 157–158). In this analy-sis, the post-1973 period is ranked first in "average openness" (McKeown, 1991: 167), although the data also suggests a "more nuanced conception of the differences between eras than hitherto employed" (McKeown, 1991: 169).[20]

"Openness" is relatively straightforward. A broader and more resourceful descrip-tion going beyond the trade openness issue combines relatively uncomplicated mea-sures of economic size (proportion of world trade) and productivity (relative national output per man-hour) into an ingenious picture producing nominal assessments both of states' "roles" in, as well as the structure of, the international economic system, at the same time as providing a dynamic picture of nations' position over time, including the relationship between the output variables of levels of trade, tariffs, and Non-Tariff Barriers (NTBs) with hegemony. The resultant descriptions of the 1870–1938 and 1950–1977 systems are intuitively plausible and demonstrate empirically the changing fortunes "beneath the commerce of nations," which reflect clearly the relative dynamic shifts of the major actors, with the U.K. declining and the U.S. rising in the first system, and the U.S. declining and Japan and Germany rising in the second (Lake, 1984: 159, 163). The underlying rationale, however, utilizing economic measures, remains hegemony.

Thus, structural characteristics of the international economic system—openness and "hegemony"—exist. But going beyond these relatively traditional confines raises a host of both descriptive and analytical questions, relating primarily to the multiplicity—or perhaps confusion—concerning the chameleon-like dependent variable. Recall Strange's admonition concerning the "lowest common denominator" in IPE studies beyond which outcome variables became unclear. Diversity in terms of the dependent variable is not surprising, especially given the persistent linkage between power and economic processes, at least in American IPE:

> Economic processes are conceived as taking place within the political structure. It does not admit of the reverse process—of political processes taking place within the existing economic structure (Strange, 1995: 165).

But certain analyses seem bedeviled by other problems. Convergence of economic policies (such as trade, monetary and fiscal policies, and exchange rates) does not seem accounted for by declining hegemony (Webb, 1991).[21] Increasing coordination or convergence on domestic economies has been linked to increasing interdependence, but does not find support at the national level; distinctive economic policies appear still to be the rule at least in several advanced, developed countries (Garrett and Lange, 1991). Overall, international convergence in the policy or regulatory domains appears more limited than some might expect (Dombrowski, 1998: 8–9, 24), nor does convergence appear to be emerging structurally at the corporate level, at least among the major corporations in Germany, Japan, and the United States; the "globalization template . . . remains quite weak":

> Convergence may be apparent at the level of popular culture and perhaps not coincidentally in the sales reports and marketing campaigns of MNCs, but below the surface, where the roots of leading MNCs remain lodged, our research suggests durable sources of resistance (Pauly and Reich, 1997: 25).

Concerning finance and the movement of capital, the structural contours are also unclear. Certain theoretical speculation concerns the differential effect of unmeasured but assumed growing capital mobility on differential economic sectors within society, changes that then impact the policy preferences of the respective groups and their internal domestic politics, which in turn should hypothetically impact on differential attitudes and perhaps policies toward exchange rate policy externally (Frieden, 1991); the specific results, however, beyond increased intense focus on exchange rates themselves, is not structurally established. Growing international capital mobility itself can become an independent structural variable, an economic equivalent to a neorealist structural analysis of the international system (Andrews, 1994: 203), likewise producing structural incentives for domestic monetary adjustment. The final link in the chain—the ultimate outcome variable in this model—then becomes the individual states' monetary autonomy, which returns us once again to basic power relations affected by changing structural economic factors (Andrews, 1994: 211–214).

A final blend of structural transformations that might be contemplated as definitive of system structure focuses on the emergence of regional trading blocs or Preferential Trading Arrangements (PTAs), which although initially emerging as "public goods" might even be considered as the initial development of another New International Economic Order (NIEO)-type structural view of the international economic system (Mansfield, 1998). Regardless of the fate of hegemony—decline or not—independent trading blocs loom as potential independent actors. The standard scenario suggests challenges from rival trading blocs causing the power distribution to shift not only from an original hegemonic power, but also from the nation as the accepted unit to the bloc as the unit, reducing nation-state autonomy even further and perhaps even introducing outright antagonism between the blocs. Such transformations might produce not only less hegemony, but also fewer unit actors in the system, all taking place with no direct, aggressive, "proactive" behavior on the part of states, economic blocs, or their leaders, and operating outside of any "proactive" dimension of the political, and instead within—at least ostensibly—the "markets." However,

> An important consequence of a market economy for states is due to the fact that economic interdependence establishes a power relationship among groups and societies. A market is not politically neutral; its existence creates economic power which one actor can use against another (Gilpin, 1987: 23).

While "open markets" is as much a political endeavor as an economic one,[22] the formation of blocs or regional alliances is usually associated with the latter rather than the former, and enters into the arena of trade strategy, which can be equally a political act and an economic one; the "challenge" is whether national decision-makers will utilize certain practices "to bolster their economies and polities selectively or will resolutely deny themselves the ability to capture advantage for their own people, neighbors, and allies" (Moran, 1996: 190).

Regional trade pacts seemed to be growing through the mid-1990s, a political policy pressed by the United States, but preliminary contemporary reports suggest potentially negative outcomes (Passell, 1997), and systematic analyses suggest they could lead in the longer term to greater regionalism and potentially closure (Mansfield, 1998). Longer-term analyses play down such potential negative effects and suggest—ironically—that integrating movements may not produce a world of closed trading blocs competing with each other. For Europe, data is consistent with the argument that the very integrating processes undertaken to produce greater internal economic and hopefully political unity have in fact fostered the unintended consequence of making national policy-making, especially in the trade arena, less coherent and forceful, reducing the impact of national decision-making, and thus militating against national protectionist policies (Hanson, 1998).

Trade blocs offer the closest analogue to traditional conceptualizations of system "structure." A more novel and amorphous conception, perhaps already emerging—if conventional wisdom offers any minimal insight—is the growing sense of "markets" and their alleged benign but also propellant nature. Certainly in terms of international finance, the sheer size of international financial transactions, technology, as well as other dimensions, have allegedly marked substantial shifts in significant international processes and interactions (Strange, 1994: 239–243). While it may be true that "fears about governments being left powerless to defend their countries' economic interests have been overdone" (Woodall, 1995: 37), nonetheless the evidence presented in a variety of surveys certainly suggests that those fears are not entirely unfounded (Strange, 1994: 228–249; Woodall, 1995). Hegemony, openness, trading patterns, or new financial transaction processes all suggest the potential for alternative systemic conceptualizations. Specification of the most relevant outcome variables in such differently structured systems has not been well elaborated.

Conclusion

Major transformations can sometimes become momentous only with hindsight. Others—that seem pivotal in the short-term—recede and become merely part of a larger and more interesting contextual picture. Certain events of the 1990s—the three specific incidents that opened this chapter were the European, Mexican, and Asian experiences between 1993 and 1997 with the financial "markets"—would have traditionally been considered, if not irrelevant to fundamental ongoing concerns of international politics, certainly more relevant to the world of the economist or accountant as opposed to the military or political leader. The notion that the international financial "markets" would somehow feel so empowered that they could "crack" the system[23] is certainly a mostly modern phenomenon. Although the appearance of the supreme executive in economically sensitive economic roles is demonstrably not a new phenomenon,[24] the emergence of this role in clear public view after at least a half-century of mostly indifference illustrates with force the growing shift of balance between the state and the market and the relationship between economic change and political change. The specifics may differ only in degree—not in type—from the earlier shifts highlighting initial interest in regional integration, interdependence, transnationalism, the NIEO, and others, but the most recent focus on "markets" and other strictly financial flows and their consequences could represent developments with long-lasting significance for state-market balances, although one extensive review suggests that evidence for such effects has not yet emerged to the degree conventional wisdom asserts (Dombrowski, 1998).

These phenomena, because they bear a very contemporary aura, present several obstacles: one is the risk of being overwhelmed by multiple specific events, the opposite is not capturing macro processes because observational tools are not readily available to adequately track such phenomena empirically, and the third is failure to see in "current" dilemmas the outlines of past puzzles. Thus, hindsight always proves so powerful. As we have seen, scholars, having developed elaborate models and complex measurement schemes to observe, explain, and account for one of the early postwar economic processes—regional integration in the 1950s and 1960s—gave up on it and turned their attention elsewhere when it appeared to them, using those tools, that integrative processes had more or less come to a halt. All along of course integrative process continued, but even into the mid-1990s an adequate picture of the true causal variables producing the integration actually observed in Europe have not been spelled out.

Recently, in an attempt to stay current and not be enervated by outmoded models that investigate the wrong phenomena using antediluvian concepts, reorientation has focused on different central research questions and outcome variables, but questions still remain about how well changes have been captured empirically, and what models are used to describe the new structures. Broad concerns have argued for addressing the balance of power between the state and the market, the relationship between economic and political change, and the very broad links "between international political structures and the international economy" (Lake, 1993b: 459). The schemes, however, have been very diverse, including long wave and Kondratieff analysis, trade and interdependency questions, hegemony, as well as more specifically delineated inquiries having to do with specific economic policies, patterns, or problems. This leads some observers to conclude that "analytical progress . . . is possible" despite the contestations between theoretical orientations (Katzenstein et al., 1998: 683).

An impasse remains, however, relating especially to questions of methodology, perhaps prompting the equally intriguing observation that despite increasing sophistication, "our substantive findings . . . remain meager: counterintuitive, well-documented causal arguments are rare" (Katzenstein et al., 1998: 683). For certain questions, one sometimes wonders, "which comes first, the case study or the theory?" The proliferation of case studies, especially considering political components from the domestic level, shift attention away from the structural and systemic, which, on the one hand, can be beneficial: "one of the greatest strengths" of at least one research program is its "demand that our understanding of changes in global political economy be based on detailed, highly contextualized case studies of local transformation in *all* parts of the world" (Murphy, 1994: 193). At the same time, the limitations can be severe: case study analysis "lack[s] a clear analytical framework," amassing "empirical details that do not appear to 'prove' anything other than that lots of things can happen" (Lohmann, 1995: 261).[25]

Certainly hegemonic stability theory provided a theoretically attractive model, trumpeting assessments and predictions seemingly very relevant to events of the 1980s and 1990s. Much confirmatory testimony from case studies, illustrative, and anecdotal material suggests a theory that through its popularized version has weathered many storms and thus retains that popularity; the hard empirical evidence, both in Chapter Six and presented in earlier sections of this chapter, to date has been lacking: "although it seems supported by . . . 'casual empiricism,' there are many reasons to believe that it is far from accurate"; "Its acceptance far exceeds its credibility in terms of empirical validity or analytic rigor" (Grunberg, 1990: 432, 448). Even the original popularizer for international relations has been viewed as taking an ambivalent attitude toward it, rejecting its overall validity at one point but "seems nonetheless to take it for granted, were it only as an assumption, in [his] book's title"—*After Hegemony* (Grunberg, 1990: 433). Weak points in the theory traced to its "powerful mythology" have been noted,[26] and while appearing bizarre, may nonetheless possess a certain accuracy: HST maintained for a period a popularity not warranted by any substantial systematic empirical support for the underlying propositions: "After two decades of research, the field has every right to be disappointed with the hegemonic stability research program" despite the fact that "it was (and remains) analytically and empirically seductive" (Lake, 1993b: 485, 460).

Such evaluations are devastating until it is appreciated that hegemonic stability theory, not unlike others, involves a relatively modest domain of international behavior, and within that domain may operate sufficiently as an orienting device although systematic empirical evidence may not extensively support hypotheses derived from it. Within the context of other approaches focusing on other behaviors—such as long waves, Krondatieff waves, and the trade/interdependence and war link—it remains a

compellingly different perspective. However, the abiding problem of the potential styl-
ishness of theories remains. We have inferred elsewhere that cycles, "long wave," and
other theoretical schemes have all witnessed their ups and downs, and concomitant with
the alleged decline in popularity of HST may be the increased focus—as suggested at
the end of the previous section—on "markets," representing for some a panacea and lib-
erator, and others the newest scourge. The impact of this focus on theory is unclear.
"Markets" and their "globalization" are not issues that started with the 1980s and 1990s;
they represent only yet another shift in focus on the relevant actors, a phenomenon
noted numerous times. Nations were privileged as actors into the 1960s, MNCs were
seen as the "new actors" of the 1970s, and the "trading state" the emerging actor of the
1980s (Rosecrance, 1987). The 1990s appear to be a battleground between the traditional nation-state, which is fading for some, the "trading" state, a seemingly new wave
of non-state actors, and the "markets." But it might be well to recall an archetypical
characterization of a market economy: it encourages growth; increases the efficient allo-
cation of resources, land, labor, and capital; creates a hierarchical division of labor
among producers; but most importantly "redistribute[s] wealth and economic activities
within and among societies," and "if left to its own devices, has profound effects on the
nature and organization of societies as well as on the political relations among them"
(Gilpin, 1987: 20–21).

The systematic linkages between market processes and the market economy "mentality" on international *political* relations has yet to be explored. Whatever else those
specific incidents faced by Europe, Mexico, and Asia—and more generally the international markets—in the mid-1990s may have represented, they certainly did *not* represent *at the time*, necessarily, the new, beneficial, liberal actors so much explicitly or
implicitly anticipated at least by certain early interdependence theorists over two
decades ago, or those hoping to draft a "new" international economic order. The
panoply of theoretical formulations devoted to international "economic" interactions is
a broad one. Previous sections have made clear that an implicit assumption originally
underlying one recent variety, the modern, non-power-based approaches surrounding
the interdependence issues of the 1970s, was that, revolving as they often did around
economic issues, a regenerated research track would not only reflect more accurately
the "real world," but also move the world away from the problems that traditional conceptualizations had not only failed to solve, but at least in later elaborations were felt
to be the cause of. The long neglected substantive concerns of economics would
broaden the areas of substantive issues beyond the relatively narrow ones defined by
traditional national security, military, and defense parameters, which had been further
magnified by the Cold War and the accompanying theoretical approaches—especially
those implying power, realism, balance of power, hegemony, and hierarchy—all tested
by behavioral hypotheses. In doing so, it would challenge the "realist"-centered theoretical paradigm that—it was claimed—had been dominant in international relations
for too long, with all its assumptions about power and power-related behavior—a goal
that ultimately, which many have forgotten, Keohane and Nye had in mind in their
classic *Power and Interdependence* (Ray, 1989: 416–417).

Such a position derives essentially from an interest in structural analysis, eschewing
for the most part the multitude of specific case studies applied to individual international economic issues[27] in favor of a broader consideration of system structure and—
in the context of developments over the past generation—of system transformation. It
is not unjustified to suggest that structures envisioned in recent years deriving from in-

terdependence have been viewed mostly positively, as better reflecting the unfolding "reality" of the contemporary world, but also incorporating an admittedly low-level but potent normative orientation—the move away from power-dominated models and behaviors involving force, violence, conquest, conflict, and war. The "neoliberal institutionalism" of recent years also flows partly from those early normative yearnings, and in some ways is the strongest element pitted against the realist IPE approach. The trade/interdependency models would be aligned with this school, whereas the long wave, K-wave models, and certain variations of HST would not.[28]

So little time has elapsed since the onset of changes viewed as structurally transformative, that full evaluation might still be some time away; the interminable realist-liberalist debates attest to that fact. But in the context of the central question of the balance of power between the state and the market, warnings of more than a decade ago bear repeating in contrast to some recent post–Cold War, "globalization" formulations[29]:

> in the context of a monetary system, the origins of a key decision may be found both on the side of the market and on the side of political authority. . . . But whatever the origin, whether the change originates with the market or with the authority, the decision will be made by a political authority . . . In this monetary context, therefore, key decisions relate more to the balance of power between market and state (or other political authority) than to the balance of power between state and state (Strange, 1986: 26).

Perhaps many thought that changing the substantive focus, from "power and politics" to "transactions and economics," would bring in more pacifying dimensions contained in the negotiable area of economic interactions, or at least recognize those dimensions and thereby downplay the more contentious political arena. Not discerned in the early international political economy approaches was the possibility of an emerging structure of the international system never before seen or conceptualized, with multiple negative side effects. Attention to trade and other established economic flows might promote various non-power-based systemic perspectives, and increase levels of sophistication as well as specificity more than had previously been the case. But little recognition was given to ingredients potentially as insidious as those supposedly contained in old power-oriented structures. Certainly one characterization—the element long associated with behavioral approaches to power, namely, the inability to measure, to really see, the "power" phenomenon so basic to neorealist models—also seems to be present in the proverbial "invisible hand" of the "markets."

An historical examination of the emergence of newer, economically oriented models has implied that in the 1970s the focus had remained mostly on the state and state interests, while the concept of "national interest" was slowly broadened to include issues such as production, trade, and investment. By the 1980s and the emergence of the "markets" it was beginning to become clear that in fact there might be in existence two systems: "the realist state system and the market" (Amin et al., 1994: 6). But the account becomes a bit more complex, for such a view sees the story unfolding in fragments: since the early 1980s a "new" IPE had surfaced and within this new breed, we are told, there is the convergence of three elements, all of which have emerged—interestingly enough—in earlier chapters in diverse ways: a view of the social sciences as admittedly subjective (the postmodern characteristic), the encouragement of a variety of different explanatory modes (the theoretical diversity characteristic encompassed in a certain genre of "case study"), and more importantly for our purposes:

the old categories of Marxism and liberalism are transcended; IPE is seen in its own historical specificity: *contemporary globalization.* In short, the route to understanding globalization of IPE out of IR has led to basic epistemological questioning of our activities as researchers. The new "IPE" is not alone in reaching this position (Amin et al., 1994: 6–7; emphasis added).

But this raises the question of whether "contemporary globalization" is merely a 1990s restatement of interdependence and transnationalism of the 1970s, perhaps with novel normative imperatives, or an assertion of some ill-defined broader "globalizing" tendencies than that which characterizes the earlier era, carrying potentially both positive but also negative consequences. One parallel is the hypothesized transcending of the nation-state, a familiar theme. Whereas in international diplomatic relations "states decide to make war or to make peace . . . The action is between foreign ministers and diplomats," for monetary systems things are different. Although perhaps not in the "fairyland of economic theory," certainly in the real world "a monetary system must have both political authority and a market." Moreover,

> a monetary system cannot work efficiently unless there is political authority to say what money must be used or may be used; to enforce the execution of agreed monetary transactions; and to license, and if necessary support, major operators in the system (Strange, 1986: 25–26).

Despite globalization rhetoric, not much systematic evidence has been forthcoming delineating respective influence levels of the "markets" or in what way that very phenomenon is the basis of growing state-market conflict. However, the very same large-scale pressures viewed as moving the world toward more globalization—increased trade, financial transactions, communication—are in fact the very forces that may be at work reinforcing the existence and strength of the phenomenon of the nation-state, because it might be the growing *threat* of the "markets" that revivifies the state. A compelling but very complex historical argument involving the competitiveness of the state and its recognition and imitation by others suggests that the sovereign territorial state as an entity first subdued rival institutional forms, which sheds light on "why the sovereign territorial state continues to exist given the apparent tension between spatially defined authority and the increasingly nonspatial nature of the international economy," and therefore "despite the much-lamented existence of sovereign territoriality, it is in fact a method of structuring international relations that makes interactions more predictable and regularized" (Spruyt, 1994: 555–556).

The picture painted here is neither optimistic nor pessimistic. With "markets," no diplomacy exists in the traditional sense—bargaining certainly, but no diplomacy. Political diplomacy in the traditional sense is necessitated where there is an absence of the very element that underpins the existence of a market—an agreed-upon medium of exchange. The aura of the "post–Cold War world" implies many positive things, one being the emergence of "markets" worldwide but especially in areas that would have been unheard of even at the end of the 1980s: the former Soviet Union and its satellites, China, and even Cuba to a slight degree. But rosy early pictures have a way of changing. The Czech Republic in the early 1990s was a particularly heralded bright positive spot in post–Cold War Eastern Europe, exemplified by the popularity of its new prime minister, Vaclav Havel, his promise to end Czech arms exports, and the invitation to it to join NATO in

1997. The euphoria was short-lived, for, as one official noted, while "President Havel is a man of high moral principles . . . the world is not moral. . . . Armaments are a commodity and Czech weapons have a good reputation worldwide" (Perlez, 1993: 7).

The positive post–Cold War immediacy has not left time yet for truly root questions concerning the appropriate models for investigating state and market relationships. Elements and approaches of only very recent popularity have already faded: one might ask of Marxism, dependency, and the NIEO: "where are they now?" Marxism for many possessed a well-developed and historically rooted theoretical substructure. Its offspring, dependency, produced research questions somewhat more narrowly defined but theoretically challenging and also freighted with normative associations. The NIEO was an operational extension of both, with a clear normative and policy orientation to assist Third World, developing nations, but one based on an attractive theoretical substructure, partly deriving from the "prevailing orthodoxy" of world system and dependency schools (Lake, 1987: 217). But NIEO-I—the system was structured to the disadvantage of the developing economies—gave way for a time to NIEO-II sometime in the 1980s and 1990s, a system allegedly structured to the disadvantage of workers in the developed economies. The truth probably lies somewhere in between (Krugman and Venables, 1995: 858–859, 876). Now NIEO-III may have superseded both—with the real possibility of a flourishing regional trade structure, but combined with a growing nation-state-oriented analysis based on *national* competitiveness, all subsumed under the globalization umbrella.

It is appropriate at this point therefore that we turn in the next chapter to the issues of bargaining mostly analyzed within the setting of nation-state interactions over traditional and predominantly political questions, but close here noting that the fortunes of social theories at times seem not to differ much from the travails of "political" ideas. Although the latter, even though couched within theoretical terminology, often have much more direct impact on real-world decisions—operating as they do in the "policy" world[30]—the relationship between current theory and currently popular policy may reflect the well-known curve in the progress of ideas moving from innovation to acceptance and then passing to "peak, popularization, vulgarization and overextension, and then descending into caricature and collapse." The "clutch of ideas that produced the monetarism-free-market-deregulation theory . . . known best as Reaganism-Thatcherism" may be one such "clutch of ideas," but "the great lack in market theory is its lack of social consciousness . . . It leaves justice to the indifferent workings of the market place" (Pfaff, 1993: 15). Popular narratives tell us that "markets" are on their way to becoming the "new" politics and therefore the "new" power (Woodall, 1995). Perhaps the invisible hand is emerging. If so, the concerns of the international theorist at the turn of the century differ from those modeling the international system during mid-century at the peak of the Cold War, differences that might include the appropriate political variables but more importantly the appropriate empirical data and theoretical variables describing the economic system. "Markets" as an abstraction with real-world consequences would appear to be dominating not only national-level economic processes but also other international phenomena in the contemporary era not unlike the fashion in which integrating processes slowly began overrunning political processes more than a generation ago.

Chapter Nine ✹

Games, Rules, and Norms
in International Politics

Only the Name Changes

Over three decades ago Charles McClelland employed an American Colonel's account of his interaction with a Russian counterpart on the road to Berlin in 1948, when the Russian halted the American convoy to inquire how many vehicles, officers, and men were headed towards the divided city. When informed of the numbers, the Russian indicated they violated the agreement. "What agreement?" asked the American. "The Berlin agreement," he was told. The American responded, "Perhaps you are confusing some offhand estimate made by one of our officers as to what we would need with an actual agreement"—to which the Russian replied abruptly, "There is an actual agreement." Wrote the American colonel later: "At that, I felt the hairs rising on the back of my neck."[1]

The access road to Berlin served as the centerpiece for over 40 years for what many thought was the essence of the Cold War: incessant crises and confrontations. There had been episodes before, and many after. President Kennedy and Premier Khrushchev played a similar "game" at a different level in the early 1960s, each "seeking to convince the other that it had the willingness to fight, with nuclear weapons if need be, if pressed too far . . . Both were caught in a vicious cycle" (Carleton, 1963: 287); one bargaining exchange stands out:

> Kennedy returned home [from the Vienna summit of 1961], called up reserves and exhorted the nation to build bomb shelters. [The East Germans] built a wall of concrete and barbed wire between East and West Berlin . . . The Americans increased their counterforce capacity . . . The Russians broke the truce on nuclear-weapons testing . . . The Americans resumed underground testing. The Russian tests continued . . . Then the Russians began another round of tests, which were followed by more American tests, which were followed by still more Russian tests . . . (Carleton, 1963: 288).

Now at the turn of the century, such actions seem to be a world apart, irrelevant after the Cold War. Yet, in the spring of 1996, the United States and China engaged in sparring behavior that paralleled their interactions four decades earlier, serious enough to lead to Chinese shelling and the dispatch of American warships to the area around Taiwan. Not to be limited to the "security" arena, on May 9, 1996 (10:38am EDT), Reuters news service broadcast a story on the growing U.S.-Chinese trade dispute over pirated goods, and reported that Zhang Yuejiao of the Chinese Ministry of Foreign Trade and Economic Co-operation had remarked: "If the U.S. announces any sanctions targeting China, we will immediately release a tit-for-tat package with even greater value involved."

The "brushfire" wars of the early Cold War years—engaging an enemy in a distant part of the world in proxy engagements—were also part of the game, but, as Charles McClelland also noted once during the height of the Vietnam War, brushfire wars sometimes turned out to be "not so brushy." The widely acknowledged arms race between the two superpowers possessed characteristics similar to the interactions specifically in Berlin and in brushfire interactions elsewhere; years later, the American Strategic Defense Initiative (SDI) escalated the dangerous game just as the Cold War was winding down in the 1980s. Even though the name and parameters have changed, the analogy and model of a "game" remains. With the growing interest in the "competitive edge" of nations, burgeoning trade disputes constitute expansions to a potentially different arena.

Thus, the Cold War and the Vietnam debacle are not historical oddities: the stand-off between China and the United States over the island of Formosa in early 1996 and again in mid-1999, or any of the recurrent crises in recent years—Somalia, Haiti, Bosnia, Kosovo, East Timor, Chechnya—bring forth once again the foreign policy "experts" inside and outside government with the well-known patois. Specific terminology has changed, but the timbre remains: "sending the right message," putting troops "in harms way," calling for "clear policies" for intervention, asserting the "national interest." This imagery of nations sparring with adversaries, and the resultant terminology, is not a time-bound phenomenon that ended in 1989—or 1991. It is a constant of international interaction, and opens up conceptual avenues in fact obscured by remaining locked into the realist-liberal debate. Ironically, it has not drawn noteworthy attention from critics of realism, even though several variations of this orientation can be considered to fall outside of realism and in fact share in basic ways the key components of norms and rules allegedly at the basis of regimes. In fact, its avowed origin, the Cold War "system" and certain elements essential to it utilized in more contemporary game theoretic jargon—"iteration" and the "shadow of the future" come to mind (Axelrod, 1984)—obscures its long tradition. Clausewitz was talking much the same talk: his celebrated phrase, "War is a mere continuation of policy by other means," is only the most famous using "game" terminology; others include iteration ("War Is Never an Isolated Act," "War Does Not Consist of a Single Blow,") and the "shadow of the future" ("The Result in War Is Never Absolute") (Clausewitz, 1996: 316–317). While deterrence theory may conjure up pictures of contemporary nuclear relations, in fact

> many of the concepts of contemporary deterrence theory . . . were implicitly part of the diplomatic practice of the balance-of-power system, without being articulated in this kind of terminology (George and Smoke, 1974: 14).

Clausewitz symbolized military concepts; the Cold War invoked images of arms races and superpower deterrence. But the bargaining extends much beyond these narrow confines. Our old friend "regimes" happens onto the scene once again, for regimes involve rules and norms, which can imply legal properties, but recently refer to much looser strictures under which nations operate. But norms in fact underlay the interactions that have always taken place between nations—the bargaining over what issues should be on the table, *how* agreements should be arrived at and *then,* the "more agreement" one gets, or the "closer" one gets to an agreement, or the "easier" it is to achieve agreement, the "more," "higher," or "significant" is the *regime*. "Regimes" may possess a modern cachet, but similarities exist with Clausewitz and Cold War bargaining concepts.

The contemporary rhetorical questions—"how do nations cooperate 'without' or 'after' hegemony," "under anarchy," or "without institutions or 'regimes'"—become less novel when recognizing that nations have always cooperated, that cooperation can result from what has been called the "characteristic instabilities of the dynamic process" (Rapoport and Chammah, 1965: 199), and that the hunt for institutions or "regimes" or the search for the secret to cooperation "under anarchy" or "after hegemony" may be mis-directed questions. We already know that explanations for international behavior do not derive exclusively from understanding the policy substance supposedly driving decision-makers' behavior. The latter is often driven by popular or conventional wisdom, which is often not only simplistic, but frequently wrong. The "domino theory" of the 1950s comes to mind. Justifying U.S. policy time and again, it turned out in some very important re-spects to be fallacious; it governed thinking about U.S. foreign policy for over two decades, justifying actions, such as Vietnam, that became spectacular mistakes.

"Brinkmanship"—"the deliberate creation of a recognizable risk of war, a risk that one does not completely control . . . the tactic of deliberately letting the situation get somewhat out of hand" (Schelling, 1963: 200)—was popularized during the steward-ship of John Foster Dulles and the rise to prominence of military strategists, and is an-other bit of conventional wisdom. The vulgar—or conventional wisdom—version of the "theory" dictated that a threat backed with a "strong will" was sufficient to deter or coerce an opponent, a view still widely held even into the 1990s. Seldom specified were what *kinds* of threats or what *kinds* of action might work. Commitments were impor-tant, and "credible" commitments were the only kind, but the enigmatic question was how a nation could "commit [itself] in advance to an act that [it] would in fact prefer not to carry out . . . in order that [its] commitment may deter the other party?" (Schelling, 1963: 36). The truly perplexing answers of what *subsequent* actions would be appropriate *should* the unthinkable happen—if the adversary did not "blink" in a cri-sis—were absent.[2] What did happen, of course, was Vietnam and other adventures, pro-ducing a more cautious U.S. policy into the 1990s, in effect certifying certain policies of the 1950s and 1960s as failed, despite the certitude at that earlier time—the conven-tional wisdom—about how to "play the game."

The important point is that those certitudes derived from substantive policies related to how to "play the game," and despite high conflict levels and lack of perceived "regimes" at the time, much cooperation was achieved. Yet the complexities—regardless of the spe-cific issue—besetting "bargaining" between and among nations while *negotiating* their environment remain. And the policies driving that bargaining behavior are driven by the-ories. At times policy implications drawn from systematic analysis of theoretical proposi-tions runs very much counter to the "policy advice" of conventional wisdom. When the two clash, the latter frequently wins. Before investigating those clashes and components of more systematic analyses, a further examination of the transformation of this field over the years and its potential role in the contemporary world provides an interesting story.

Bargaining, Influence, Diplomacy, and System = Norms

Discontent with conceptualizing power as national capabilities has always turned scholars for succor to "psychological power" or "influence" as a fallback; "power means influence," and the classic formulation is now standard as well as tedious: country A has power over country B if it can influence B to do something B would not normally do (Dahl, 1957).[3] Operationalizing such a formulation in international relations has proved elusive. A second mysterious component of bargaining is its traditional association with the romantic world of the diplomat, the person traditionally thought to possess attributes of truthfulness ("scrupulous care to avoid the suggestion of the false or the suppression of the true"); precision ("the negotiator should be accurate both in mind and soul"); and calmness ("avoid . . . irritation when confronted by . . . stupidity, dishonesty, brutality or conceit" (Nicolson, 1963: 110–116). In the days of instant communication, such depictions have faded from the scene, but diplomacy still entails "construction, representation, negotiation, and manipulation of necessarily ambiguous identities" and even where "basic terms of what is going on may be contested, people behave diplomatically, at least as long as they wish to continue conducting relations with one another" (Sharp, 1999: 33–34).

What actually happens in diplomacy and bargaining, however, may be little more than simplistic assumptions of human behavior applied by basically abnormal individuals (namely, those who have risen to the top of the diplomatic hierarchy, by whatever means) to the relations between states; cynics might conclude that diplomacy affords certain individuals the opportunity to satisfy deeply rooted psychological needs or tendencies through the medium of interstate diplomacy (Steinberg, 1996). Nonetheless, whether substantive focus is on traditional military-security issues or more contemporary international economic issues, behavioral regularities of interstate or intergroup bargaining can be the subject of fruitful inquiry.

That is, regardless of substantive issue, the persistent, repetitive *interactions* between states constitute an action system: actions produce calculated counteractions, and even though the calculations are sometimes dead wrong, "each player's strategy will depend on his expectation about the other player's strategies" (Harsanyi, 1965: 450).[4] Nations can become "locked in" through these sequential interactions, and then the discriminating element of this conceptualization is that behavior can become independent of any original goals, motivations, or substantive policy maneuvers that may have originally been the driving force, and once the behavior constitutes a "system," it then may operate independent of any hegemony, balance of power, anarchy or other conceptual apparati constructed by the analyst and often linked to *realpolitik*. It is this *repetitive sequence of actions, reactions, or interactions* that then constitutes the "system," which becomes the object of inquiry.

Thus, despite the complexity, high stakes, and ideological intensity in superpower relations of the Cold War era, cooperation occurred, solutions were found, and "rules of the game" prevailed. Cooperation "after hegemony" or "under anarchy" might seem to be of recent vintage (Fearon, 1998: 269–270), but it was long ago suggested that somehow the complex interplay works out regardless of dominating structures, and the classic quote from Schelling, written so long ago it has now been forgotten, tells it all:

> The . . . outcome must be a point from which neither expects the other to retreat; yet the main ingredient of this expectation is what one thinks the other expects the first to expect and so on. . . . out of this fluid . . . situation that seemingly provides no logical reason for anyone to expect anything except what he expects to be expected to expect, a decision is reached. These infinitely reflexive expectations must somehow converge on a single point, at which each expects the other not to expect to be expected to retreat (Schelling, 1963: 70).

To reiterate, then, cooperation is achieved—or conflicts end—not necessarily because one party loses or resolves to end the conflict, or because of "hegemony" or regimes or any other construct. Conflicts end for all kinds of reasons: it may be the power structure, the "tactics employed" (Schelling, 1963: 70), or it may be routinization: one or both parties tire of it. Specific elements of Cold War-derived bargaining beliefs appear irrelevant to the contemporary world, in which crises and deterrence seem to be replaced by longer-term trade and arms control negotiations, leading in turn to iteration issues ultimately related to enforcement (Fearon, 1998). Yet regardless of substance, the principal is that conflicts are not necessarily deviant nor motivated by evil people, nor will they end in some future millennium once reason prevails or the right persons occupy important policy-making positions, or when "History Ends" (Fukuyama, 1992). Conflict is normal, and therefore bargaining is a normal, dynamic part of international relations concerned with the *process* of interaction, with what types of action-reaction patterns exist most often in international politics. It is not by accident that such a view flourished in the Cold War era, distinguished by the succession of major superpower confrontations labeled "acute" international crises (McClelland, 1961). The Berlin Blockade of 1948 spawned the interest in why certain crises begin and then abate while others lead to war, the original interest propelling an entire research agenda devoted to the "tracking" of nations' events.

To suggest—especially at the height of the Cold War—that acute superpower crises might *not* result from a clash of *ideologies* or conflicting *power* interests, both reflecting a *realpolitik* view, but merely that, when a "succession of extraordinary inputs begetting new outputs begetting new inputs, etc., passes some point in volume and intensity, the whole phenomenon begins to be called an international crisis" (McClelland, 1961: 199), surely countered conventional wisdom of the time. Actions, however, do not always result from realpolitik grand strategies, "troublemakers," the bipolar or multipolar structure of the international system, declining hegemony, or any such exogenous set of variables. Rather, mistakes and misperceptions occur, behavior can be misinterpreted, and each move contributes to a continuing series of moves that becomes—whatever else it might be in terms of ideology or power—simply each side's attempt to elicit information from the other. At least two empirical questions arise: (1) do such crises exhibit similar traits? and (2) do the very interactions making up the crisis suggest the direction it will take? The fact that especially the latter question was never explicitly answered in no way diminishes their intrinsic importance nor the effect their asking had on steering a subsequent research agenda.

Although crisis bargaining may appear a bit antiquated in a "neoliberal" institutionalist era,[5] the model should remain attractive because it does not rely on power-driven "realist" assumptions,[6] neorealist structures, hegemony-based models, or neoidealist institutions. Antirealism did not serve as the explicated rationale for the development of the approach, but that in no way takes away from its potency as a challenge to such models. While implications concerning "rules" and "norms" that embody regimes are contained within the bargaining framework, one need not buy into any other components of the regime approach to think of international relations in terms of bargaining.

Theoretical Considerations:
A Quick History

"Bargaining theory" in international relations has covered a broad spectrum: lengthy, tortuous case studies of conflicts or crises, listings of hypothetical bargaining scenarios or plausible explanations of conflict outcomes cast in a "bargaining" framework, as well as complex and lengthy categorizations of various types of strategies (Sullivan, 1976: 259ff). Early pretheoretical work achieved much popular acclaim and clear orientation toward policy-makers enmeshed in repetitive Cold War crises by suggesting definitions, categories, and "types" of bargaining accompanied by suggested bargaining "positions" (Kahn, 1962).[7] Little attention was devoted to systematic strategies that could be used in specific situations, what patterns of bargaining moves were usually made prior to the use of these specific tactics, or how to counter their use by an opponent. *Recognizing* or labeling a bargaining tactic in a static sense differs from predicting its effect, determining what response is appropriate, the pattern of actions likely to surround such tactics, or assessing under what specific situations they are to be most successful. The singular most important missing element was the dynamic consideration.

Despite this drawback, bargaining models and scenarios captured the imagination of theorists and policy-makers faced with what appeared to be an unending series of "acute" international crises. Rarely asked was whether they could be answered through *any* research strategies, and hypotheses were at times merely descriptions or superficial predictions:

> conditions of crisis raise incentives both to demonstrate resolve clearly and to react in a prudent fashion to the dangers of destructive outcomes. The resultant cross-pressures tend to produce bargaining patterns among the principals which are unpredictable and subject to erratic oscillations (Young, 1968: 177).

Others were almost true by definition:

> deterrence is more likely to be successful when the initiator believes the defender has adequate capabilities, high motivation, and is free from internal constraints, and by "the defender's supplementing deterrence with appropriate inducement policies vis-a-vis the potential initiator" (George and Smoke, 1974: 530–531).

Crises for some were "almost completely intractable" entities, each possessing "innumerable 'contingencies'"; bargaining theory was criticized as often asserting that "international relations *is* bargaining behavior" in which "'anything' might happen" (Sullivan, 1976: 261–262).

These brush-clearing operations were undertaken during and associated with the Cold War tensions, crises, and "brinkmanship" of the 1950s and 1960s, when theories of deterrence were all the rage. Nuclear weapons added a new catalyst. When the Soviet Union first attained nuclear capabilities, strategic thinking changed, and under the provisions of MAD (Mutually Assured Destruction), the thinking became more complex. As the nuclear stalemate wore on, we can now with hindsight suggest that even though deterrence theorizing continued (G. Snyder, 1961; George et al., 1971; George and Smoke, 1974), nuclear weapons had at some point become anachronistic: a "line" had been reached, or perhaps crossed, beyond which policy decisions relating to nuclear weaponry became marginal. This "line theory," not dissimilar to MAD, states that a point is reached where such weapons become so numerous and destructive that increasing, decreasing, or maintaining a given level are all equally plausible policy options, and each carries, respectively, little more than minor technical implications. Debates over further nuclear acquisitions either from a theoretical deterrent or actual hardware perspective become essentially meaningless. The final policy actualization of this only came years later with the INF Treaty in 1987, a treaty possessing at least two remarkable characteristics: it occurred when theories at the individual and decision-making levels suggested a contrary policy outcome, and it came and went with relatively little fanfare, suggesting that by that time the underlying issues were very much secondary. More importantly, perhaps, all the previous bargaining had "routinized" the Cold War—and the signing of INF became one more routine behavior.

With the early work as background, years were spent grappling with deterrence issues (Lebow, 1981; Lebow and Stein, 1990; Huth, 1988a; Harvey, 1998), resulting in findings far from unanimous in deciding where, under what circumstances, and how deterrence actually worked. In the end, serious questions were raised about the monumental amounts of money spent on the military hardware supposedly backing such diplomatic policies.[8] Even though it is still not known exactly what specifics produce successful and unsuccessful deterrence, certain evidence seems to be emerging to help in that direction (J. Stein, 1991: 57).

Deterrence: Hype, Advice, or Fad?

The bulk of the deterrence research began with the classic rational "calculus" of decision-making (G. Snyder, 1961; George and Smoke, 1974: 503f.), which has a broad range of theoretical applicability but a narrow operational capability, involving assessment of objectives, costs of the probability of each response by an opponent (including no response), the probability of attaining objectives with each response the opponent might make, and so on. Not addressed was whether the adversary was working off the same calculus, the implications of that, and whether the calculus in reality applied to *either* side. The calculus was "not unlike the rational process models":

> each side . . . is a unitary, purposive actor; the payoffs and choices of the actors can be deduced by assuming an overall "rationality" . . . the answer to the question, When is deterrence utilized?, rests heavily on the validity of that assumption. The most obvious and superficial answer is that deterrence will be used when one side calculates that his objectives can be achieved or that there is a high probability of achieving them (Sullivan, 1976: 263–264).

But a stated "policy" of deterrence does not necessarily mean deterrence is actually carried out.

While development over the years not only specified the theory but also placed it within that broader context—"theories of deterrence are a subset of theories of rational choice"—it is also true that "they include far more . . . than the assumption of rational calculation" and that they are "oversimplified as a theory of motivation" (J. Stein, 1991: 9, 11). Over time deterrence theories did move beyond the simple, unitary actor of traditional models, with only one group consisting of that classical model of unitary actors with well-defined interests. A second rejected the unitary actor model and the rationality assumption and called on bureaucratic or domestic political interests, organizational theory and social psychology to understand why deterrence doesn't work. The third body of literature—labeled the "quantitative empirical"—differed not on conceptual grounds necessarily but methodological, although the latter will often produce results that clearly challenge the traditional rationality assumption and model of deterrence (Levy, 1988b).

Within the classical model, however, much of the history of this field was relatively consistent in proposing essential factors involved in deterrence; key theoretical variables reemerged in later formulations and case studies. Proposed ingredients involved in "coercive diplomacy," for instance, a perceptual and motivational approach, were factors such as "asymmetry of motivation" to demonstrate cognitive variables affecting the process and outcome of deterrence (George, Hall, and Simons, 1971; George and Simons, 1994). Not unlike Morgenthau's near-microscopic dissection of the measurement of power, asymmetry of motivation demonstrated equal complexity; a defending power must

> calculate the strength of the opponent's motivation to resist . . . The coercing power's own motivation is also an important factor that must enter into the calculus of a coercive strategy . . . The chances that coercive diplomacy will be successful will be appreciably greater if the objective selected—and the demand made—by the coercing power reflects only the most important of its interests that are at stake, for this is more likely to create an asymmetry of motivation favoring the coercing power (George, Hall, and Simon, 1971: 26).

Thus, a "classic case" in international bargaining would be one wherein "intensity of feeling or strength of resolve" is substituted for "deficiencies in numerical strength or physical capabilities" (Young, 1968: 33): the party "that can effectively demonstrate that the underlying issues at stake in a crisis are of more fundamental and far-reaching importance to itself than to its opponent" (Young, 1968: 216) will have the advantage. Credibility of a threat increases

> by implicating additional values beyond the bare value of the territorial objective, values which would be lost if the threat were not carried out (G. Snyder, 1961: 23).

As Schelling had noted, commitments are essential (Schelling, 1963: 36), and the calculus here has not changed much over the years, usually involving four factors: the communication of unacceptable behavior and commitment to respond, along with capability and resolve to act (Lebow, 1981: 82–92; Harvey, 1998: 676–678).

While a specific era may have produced such hypotheses, and Vietnam exemplified their application, it would be too facile to "blame" the Vietnam involvement on the literature produced during this period. Not unlike the broader domino theory, much of "deterrence theory" turned out to be conventional wisdom gone awry. It could even be suggested that policies of deterrence and compellance may have been as much provocative as they were restraining, perhaps even prolonging the Cold War and eliciting behavior that deterrence theory suggested they should prevent. Still, the continuing series of "acute" international crises in the context of the intense bipolar struggle not surprisingly directed scholars into key research agendas. Operational success continued to elude most of these endeavors. Even a shift to the potential role of "reassurance" strategies as opposed to deterrence, which produced nuanced illustrations of five different strategies of reassurance, was compelled to conclude that the "evidence that is available is fragmentary, often episodic, frequently open to multiple interpretation, and difficult to evaluate" (Stein, 1991: 57). The one unquestioned conclusion has been the recognition of the diversity and complexity of what many in the policy community utilizing conventional wisdom had thought to be quite simple.

Deterrence: Broader Visions

Thus, a symbiotic relationship grew between the policy and research communities, but crossing that boundary remains difficult. Distinctions between "influence" attempts, whether something be deterrence or reassurance, have not produced agreement; even with the elaboration of strategies of "reassurance," the distinction between the two is still muddled (Stein, 1991: 32–35). Because of this continuing diversity and disagreement concerning categories of influence attempts, but recognizing that some categorization is beneficial, a scheme put forth many years ago (Patchen, 1970) remains serviceable. The distinction was made between *cognitive, learning,* and *reaction* process—or stimulus-response—models; these categories remain valid because they provide a conceptual umbrella for not only specifying notions of bargaining but also broader ideas involving interactions in general. They also provide a benchmark for assessing views of "influence attempts" as they have changed in the intervening years and assessing which ones seem to have survived the test of time better than others.

Cognitive models rely on decision theories and view a nation's actions as dependent upon both its perception of the results of its own actions, and on the estimate of the other country's future reactions. Research on what *situations* would give rise to successful deterrence are examples. Russett's classic study (1963) was the harbinger of the later Extended Immediate Deterrence (EID) literature, with the central research question and design representing in microcosm the Cold War model of deterrence: an aggressor likely to undertake action against a small, pawn country with a third country as potential defender.[9] Strong and visible preexistent ties (military, political, and economic) between the defender and the pawn were found to be more likely to result in successful deterrence.

Learning models, the second category, have always held a fascination, boast numerous mutations, and are once again fashionable with the renewed interests in "agency" and "ideas" [Chapter Two]. Illustrations of this second category are numerous. One to be considered at length below is the "tit-for-tat" strategy; a second involves the specific hypothesis that long-term "learning" might occur in recurrent "acute" international crises (McClelland, 1961)—a suggestion with implications for understanding the "end" of the Cold War; a third proposes a loose and intuitive version of superpower nuclear relations (Nye, 1987) and hypotheses concerning Gorbachev's role in "ending" the Cold War (J. Stein, 1994).[10]

The basic generic learning model has not radically changed over the years; a country's actions are dependent upon the previous results of its interaction with another actor, the focus being on the interaction patterns themselves, in which both parties' range of bargaining points are unknown. Interaction involves mutual adjustments in which each side tests out the other through bids and counterbids. Rejection of bids—and perhaps the speed or intensity of rejection—constitutes information, indicating where the true settlement point might be: "in sequence lies information" (Dixon, 1987: 77). Straight offers as well as bluffing or "sham" bids are legitimate inputs, and become information for the bargainers; the classic conclusion frequently is that

> much of the variance [in behavior] is accounted for not by inherent propensities of the players to cooperate or not cooperate, but rather by the characteristic instabilities of the dynamic process which governs the interactions in Prisoner's Dilemma (Rapoport and Chammah, 1965: 199).

Colorful labels describe respective strategies. Thus a strategy of initial cooperation followed by unconditional cooperation and then conditional cooperation was labeled the "reformed sinner"; the "lapsed saint" involved a strategy of initial cooperation followed by conditional cooperation (Harford and Solomon, 1967: 108). Years later a program labeled "Tester" was "designed to look for softies, but is prepared to back off if the other player shows it won't be exploited" (Axelrod, 1984: 44).

While structural restraints, or the *conditions* of successful deterrence, do not necessarily imply "learning," similarities between the two remain, and an extensive agenda devoted to (EID) (Huth, 1988a; 1988b; 1990; Huth and Russett, 1984; 1988; 1993) has expanded on Russett's early small-n (17) study. Most findings suggest a combination of power relations and bargaining behavior or strategy are necessary for successful deterrence, but the factors associated with successful deterrence, as opposed to whether a defender will fight, are not necessarily the same: the only variable important for both outcomes was the existence of a military alliance between defender and pawn. The balance of forces seems important, and nuclear weapons not particularly important (Huth and Russett, 1988; Geller, 1990), but as noted in one review (Levy, 1988b), unlike previous findings, political/military ties in this case were not important. For respective behavioral repertoires, reciprocal firm-but-fair strategies were more successful in deterrence behavior, while conciliatory or "bullying" were not. Tit-for-Tat (TFT) was successful whereas excessively firm or cautious policies were not.[11] The complexity of the multiple studies as well as the criticisms of research design decisions (to be noted below [Lebow and Stein, 1990]) suggest that above everything else the sophistication of the "model" necessary to understand the process and outcome of deterrence emerges as most important, as well as the fact that multiple variables are necessary in almost all cases. The low success rate for "traditional" variables of a *realpolitik* sort—"military might" and a clear verbalized "threat" to the potential attacker—also looms as a major finding.[12]

With the advent of empirical investigations of successful and unsuccessful deterrence, critiques have been persistent, some focusing on limited specifics and others engaging broader theoretical concerns. One important specific, however, pertains to case selection (Levy, 1988b: 507–510; Lebow and J. Stein, 1990; J. Stein, 1991: 13–17); while basic agreement exists on the definition of deterrence ("when an attacker contemplates military action against another country and a third party commits itself to the defense of the country threatened with an attack" [Lebow and Stein, 1990: 342]), disagreement arises about many coding rules, including which cases are truly deterrence attempts, and assessment of success or failure (Harvey, 1998: 696–699). Illustrative is the problem of assessing the threat to attack when reliance is

> heavily on a threat to attack as an indicator of intention to attack. But threats do not always equate to intention: leaders may bluff and threaten war in circumstances in which they are not prepared to use force (Lebow and Stein 1990: 343).

A second specific dispute returns to the distinction between, for instance, deterrence and compellance; cases listed as "deterrence," which are actually instances of "compellance," obviously refer to potentially different outcome variables, and relating both types of behavior to the same structural situations should skew results.

Rising above these and other specific disputes,[13] however, and focusing only on the broad outcome variables, the original distinctions in deterrence literature between categories such as deterrence and compellance—for all the merit they might have had at the time—with hindsight turn out to be not so helpful in the ultimate scheme of the research agenda when that "scheme" is defined as comparing those two types of behaviors, for instance, to all the other behaviors nations exhibit toward one another. Within that larger context, drawing fine distinctions between compellance and deterrence becomes less meaningful, especially if both are considered under the broader umbrella of "learning." Moreover, in such large-*n* investigations, dispute is naturally going to arise over design decisions concerning inclusion or exclusion of specific cases, but given the number of observations relative to the normal size in many deterrence case studies, where *n*=1,[14] some leeway might be allowed in assessing the findings—and confidence in them because of the large number of observations. Although quantitative analyses of causes of deterrence success or failures have been few (J. Stein, 1991: 13), perhaps the more interesting to note are those, as observed earlier, which are counterintuitive: "one of the themes . . . is that the possession of military superiority by the defender is no guarantee that deterrence will work" (Levy, 1988: 507).

> Nor is successful deterrence and war avoidance merely a matter of behaving in a tough, unyielding manner. To the contrary, attempted bullying against a more or less equal adversary is likely to be no more productive than excessive conciliation (Huth and Russett, 1988: 43).

Nonetheless, reanalyses of three different data-sets suggests that of four factors, the specifics of a "commitment" to deter is less important than the communication of unacceptable behavior, capability, and resolve (Harvey, 1998: 686–702).

General, as opposed to immediate deterrence, focuses on conditions under which crises might arise as opposed to what happens once a crisis begins—and here the line between learning and "cognitive" becomes a bit blurred. Evidence from 278 cases since 1945 suggests five of seven "deterrence model" variables are related to "dispute initiation," with the most important apparently being the "recent conflict behavior" of the target, defined as whether the target was involved in another dispute, was stalemated, or suffered a defeat in the previous year; if that were the case, the challenger would more likely initiate a military dispute (Huth and Russett, 1993: 64–65; 68–69). Four of eight "deterrence theory" variables tested in 97 cases of great power deterrence encounters from a longer period—1816–1984—were found significantly related to success or failure of deterrence whereas variables based on structural realism received little or no support (Huth et al., 1993).

While specific critiques and counterintuitive findings support or contradict deterrence hypotheses and may impact on policy-making, we return here to the essential background assertion that deterrence theories are a subset of rational choice (J. Stein, 1991: 9), for this indirectly relates to broader realist-liberal debates. Early deterrence theory derived directly from tenets of realpolitik and "realism," a way of handling the complexities of the Cold War–nuclear world through rational manipulation, but imbedded within a realist view of the clashing power dimensions that were themselves imbedded in the "laws" of the Morgenthauian world. "Consistent with the realist framework, rational deterrence theory also argues that the challenger weighs the costs and benefits of escalating [a] dispute" (Huth et al., 1993: 612). The irony, then, is that while it seems fairly clear that several tenets of basic deterrence theory have not been confirmed by empirical studies over the years—while others have—nonetheless when combining both rational deterrence theory as well as implications derived from structural realism—the apparent stepchild of realism and cousin of neorealism—together in one design, those from structural realism are contested by "rational deterrence theory": "[Our] results are that the hypotheses derived from deterrence theory receive considerable support, whereas none of the hypotheses derived from structural realism are supported" (Huth et al., 1993: 609).

Despite the complexity and breadth of the design and data analysis, two considerations stand out. First, only four of the eight "rational deterrence" hypotheses are strictly deterrence in a bargaining sense, with the others resembling structural variables.[15] Second, the dependent variable is limited to the escalation of deterrence encounters among the great powers, 1816–1984, and even though a variety of causal variables are used as predictors, including structural, risk propensity, and behavior in previous disputes, and even with fairly straightforward conclusions, the scope of the implications—interesting though they may be—must remain a bit limited given the exact specifics of the operational measures.[16] The findings—deterrence theory supported while structural realism was not—are perhaps more interesting for the fashion in which they contrast the two theoretical streams of realism and rational deterrence theory, both of which contain strong similarities: one seems more related to the *escalation* of great power disputes and the other definitely related to *onset* of great power disputes. This differentiation of outcome variables has been one important byproduct of the deterrence field—although one not often noted let alone heralded, especially since by the 1990s many decided that the Cold War context had produced too myopic a focus on outcome variables isolated to the deterrence sphere.

The distinction between cognitive, learning, and reaction process models suggests disparate theoretical orientations toward bargaining "systems." Traditional deterrence literature saw fruition in the cognitive and learning approaches, expanded on in both immediate and general deterrence studies, but the broader implications of the extensive theoretical and less-replicable quantitative research of earlier years is unclear in the 1990s. Certainly the contingent nature of many nonquantitative findings (J. Stein, 1991) could possibly find their way into the domain of more contemporary case study-oriented analyses of international economic negotiations. However, despite much research, deterrence and compellance remain enigmatic, with some contending that motivational factors, beliefs, and images might ultimately be the key variables, with a high degree of uncertainty affecting success or failure (Rosati, 1995: 144), and others questioning whether evaluation of success or failure of strategies of compellence and deterrence are even wise (C. Hermann, 1996: 313). Such critiques take on special weight when recognizing that despite continuing endeavors to operationalize deterrence militarily and theoretical endeavors to explain its fine points, the entire issue of the "undeterrability" of certain leaders has never been completely explored (Jentleson, 1994: 203–206; J. Stein, 1992).

Justice cannot be done to the entire literature on deterrence that played such a formative and influential role for so long but now seems to have receded, but at this point the third part of the triad noted above—reaction process or simple stimulus response—should be reconsidered. Not only has this blossomed in a somewhat different formulation, but it raises further questions about the utility of very complex deterrence theories by introducing, ironically, empirical referents to the "norm"-based assumptions of constructivist and regime analyses.

Action-Reaction and Stimulus-Response Become "Norm of Reciprocity"

Once considered too simplistic for significant analysis of complex international relations, "stimulus response," with its origination in psychology and the most famous dog in the history of social science, was not considered seriously by theoreticians as a viable explanation of international behavior. Yet analyses undertaken over the years have transformed and elaborated this model from an overly simplistic view of the world to a "norm."

Action-reaction, stimulus-response is simple: an actor responds in kind to another's previous action. Lewis Richardson's early investigation of arms races (Richardson, 1960) asked: what would prompt a nation to increase arms when common sense suggests such behavior is costly and may be provocative. He pondered: only if individuals did not "think" about the ultimate result of their behavior—in today's terminology, consideration of the "shadow of the future." The unsophisticated preliminary findings are well-known: increases in a nation's armaments should result from the change in armaments levels of another party (within a model including variables such as the opponent's level of strength, the incentive to accumulate arms because of opponent's strength, fatigue and cost, and the level of grievance against the opponent). Going beyond the narrow confines of armaments, action begets reaction, hostility begets hostility, and one might logically argue—although few did—cooperation begets cooperation; states should react in accordance with what they receive.

The transformation of this simple model has been as remarkable as the emergence of "regimes," to which, not surprisingly, it is related. Acceptance of action-reaction as a viable description of reality is difficult for those wishing to impose the complexity and nuanced interpretations of deterrence, for the more the simple reciprocity model can account for behavior, the less relevant are the complex formulations. Moreover, the original inspiration—arms races—has itself seen many changes over the years, from analyses suggesting clear action-reaction patterns in superpowers' arms expenditures to others suggesting no patterns whatsoever.

But stimulus-response went much beyond arms races. The earliest popularized "policy"-oriented version, Graduated Reduction in Tension (GRIT), appeared radical when proposed in the 1960s: where two sides are locked into a mutual interaction process of increasing hostility, one side should unilaterally reduce tension with a single cooperative move as a signal to the other side (Osgood, 1962), with criteria for monitoring each side for signs of reciprocation. A long-forgotten case study of the breaking of East-West tensions in the early 1960s illustrated the approach (Etzioni, 1967), suggesting that the superpower thaw beginning in 1963–1964 originated as a series of relatively simple cooperative actions on each side. In June 1963 the U.S. president outlined his "Strategy for Peace" at American University, and took the unilateral initiative of stopping atmospheric nuclear tests. The Soviets allowed the speech to be published in the Soviet Union, followed with a halt on the production of strategic bombers. Both sides made conciliatory moves at the United Nations. The Test Ban Treaty was signed in early August 1963, the Soviets called for a nonaggression agreement between the Warsaw Pact and NATO, and Americans called for cooperative ventures in space.

Systematic evidence gathered over the years supports the transformation from a simplistic, naive, mechanistic notion of human behavior to a "norm" of international politics, thus coupling it inadvertently with "regimes." Data on arms races interpreted as stimulus response are considered below. One of the first sets of systematic Cold War data demonstrated action-reaction patterns in aggregated diplomatic events for the 1946–1963 period (Gamson and Modigliani, 1971): years of high conflict by one bloc were years of high conflict by the other, and the same occurred for cooperation. Data from studies on World War I, the Cuban Missile Crisis, and Soviet-Chinese relations also showed moderate but consistent correlations between the original stimulus a nation received and its subsequent response (Sullivan, 1976: 287–289). Even though specific types of actions may have been correlated differently across different countries, and while a country's domestic conflict sometimes entered into the equation, nonetheless the "general stimulus-response model was not only strong, but stronger than other explanations" (Sullivan, 1976: 291; see also Philips, 1973; Feierabend and Feierabend, 1969). Thus, an assortment of systematic analyses supported the general finding that international behavior can be a function of the behavior of other actors.

A multiplicity of diverse analyses over the next two decades continued to demonstrate reciprocity of behavior. Five different crisis situations spanning almost 100 years, from Schleswig-Holstein (1863–1864) to the Cuban Missile Crisis in 1962, showed "a strong degree of reciprocity in conflict behavior in all five cases" (Leng and Goodsell, 1974: 217), with no evidence of differences across the historical eras. In 20 dyadic disputes, while a "reciprocating strategy is the most effective means of avoiding a diplomatic defeat without going to war, especially when it is employed against a bullying opponent" (Leng and Wheeler, 1979: 655), and while nations might not consciously employ "reciprocating strategies," nonetheless a norm of reciprocity received "an *implicit* recognition on the part of the participating states" (Leng and Wheeler, 1979: 681). "Reactivity" emerged in very simple "behavior-begets-behavior" models, and nations tended toward reactivity with no evidence of long- or short-term memory mechanisms operating (Ward, 1982: 123).

The continuing findings consistently confirmed earlier results covering a broad empirical domain, and one arena wherein reciprocity became encompassed was the context of Axelrod's popular computer tournament and resultant findings on the TFT strategy (Axelrod, 1984).[17] "Reciprocity serves as the primary norm for interaction in systems of self-help ranging from primitive communities to the interstate system" (Leng, 1993b: 3). However, reciprocity differs from TFT; first, it follows the same strategy "but it relaxes the requirement that there be a single unilateral initiative on the opening move, to allow one or two cooperative initiatives to be initiated later in the crisis" (Leng, 1993b: 11). Second, TFT works within a Prisoner's Dilemma (PD) environment in which there is no communication, whereas reciprocity requires open communication.

Regardless of the differences, however, or the simplicity of certain PD games compared to more complex ones,[18] or the simplicity of the data, the conclusions from Axelrod's tournament are too intriguing to ignore, for the four ostensible characteristics of TFT suggest striking implications when compared to complex deterrence theorizing. That is, TFT is nice, firm, forgiving, and clear (Axelrod, 1984: 33–39), and when comparing results of reciprocating to TFT strategies within the four categories using real-world data, attributes of the former—reciprocation—are highlighted that are most significant in promoting peaceful outcomes in interstate crises: the side engaging in reciprocation demonstrated its resolve first, coupling offers to cooperate with threats or warnings, thus *niceness* tended to be backed up by "prudent demonstration of resolve" (Leng, 1993b: 37). *Firmness* was most usually used with flexibility. For *forgiveness,* "The states employing reciprocating strategies generally followed the TFT criterion of responding in kind to cooperative initiatives, even if they had been preceded by negative inducements" (Leng, 1993b: 37). Finally, *clarity* seemed to have an effect on success:

> All seven of the [25] cases in which there was none, or just one, of the categories of noise present ended in diplomatic victories or compromises for the side employing a predominantly Reciprocating strategy; whereas only half (nine of eighteen) of the other cases achieved successful outcomes (Leng, 1993a: 177).

Although differences in the two strategies are subtle, strong support appears for recip-rocation and even some suggestion that such a strategy offers a way of communicating a firm-but-flexible strategy better than TFT.

More important than conceptual divergences and possible differential success rates between TFT and reciprocation was the convergence of experimental and real-world studies. Such is not uniformly the case; one review of experimental studies, computer simulations, and real-world bargaining studies concluded:

> A policy of unconditional cooperation tends to bring exploitation by an adversary whereas a policy of consistent coerciveness tends to lead to a fight. However, a strategy that begins with firmness—including the threat or use of coercion—in the early stages of a dispute and then switches to conciliation appears generally to be effective in securing cooperation from an opponent (Patchen, 1987: 182).

A follow-up review confined to U.S.-Soviet relations concluded that simple reciprocity did not necessarily describe the many complexities in that dyad, but was nonetheless a consistent presence. The central conclusion led to "overall support for the proposition that Soviet-American interactions have tended to be governed by the principle of reci-procity," more so for cooperative than for conflict behavior. Conflict behavior was more likely to be reciprocated when the potential reciprocator was strong relative to the rival, and when "initial coercive behavior was not so vigorous as to be intimidating" (Patchen, 1991: 139–140). Minor provocations tended to be "over-matched," and major provo-cations "under-matched." "Each side appears to react, at least in part, to deviations in the behavior of its rival from past levels rather than to the absolute level of cooperative or conflictual behavior" and "reciprocity may occur on a long-term rather than a short-term basis" (Patchen, 1991: 140).

In contrasting reciprocity with two other models—routine and rational expecta-tions (Goldstein and Freeman, 1991: 20)—"considerable evidence" exists for both al-ternatives, but at the same time, "there is also compelling evidence . . . that great powers respond to the behaviors of other great powers," even though the results "chal-lenge the idea that great powers actually play simple tit-for-tat strategies." In fact, there seems to be

> pervasive reciprocity among the U.S., Soviet Union, and China, providing heartening news for those who view reciprocity as a key norm underlying the possibility of international co-operation. But we have also shown that reciprocity operates in a more complex environ-ment than most theorists realize . . . with considerable bureaucratic routine as well as asymmetrical triangularity (Goldstein and Freeman, 1991: 30–31).

Moreover, as proposed in Chapter Seven, the norms that result merely from ongoing reciprocity can also constitute regimes: "longstanding norms of reciprocity can lead to a great power security regime" (Goldstein and Freeman, 1991: 31).[19]

Superpower reciprocity, however, could be time-dependent; "the most consistent U.S. reciprocity occurred some decades ago, and the most consistent Soviet reciprocity occurred more recently," which leads to the suggestion that

> superpower cooperation has blossomed in recent years . . . Despite the uneven pace of progress over forty years, the presence of reciprocity and the absence of inverse response

have undoubtedly helped to establish norms and mutual understandings in the superpower relationship (Goldstein, 1991b: 207).[20]

Correlating individual-level variables to the "norms" that may have transpired and been "learned" through the interaction processes of 40 years of the Cold War, it is posited that "during this decade (the 1980s) the norms of U.S.-Soviet relations were altered, specifically by Gorbachev's rise to power and the policies instituted by perestroika and glasnost" (Ward and Rajmaira, 1992: 346). Thus even within the context of empirically observed reciprocity, "agency" operates in that change in norms was "driven largely by Soviet initiatives" (Ward and Rajmaira, 1992: 343), suggesting that the Soviet Union responded to received cooperation

> with further increases in the level of cooperation, whereas the U.S. tended to reduce cooperative behavior under such circumstances. . . . Soviet cooperative initiatives altered the norms of behavior, but these changes tended to be viewed warily by U.S. decision makers (Ward and Rajmaira, 1992: 365).

While disagreement remains about reciprocity into the 1980s for the superpowers, nonetheless a pattern persisted, despite the intensity in the relationship. Likewise, even within the context of a continuing, deep, enduring, long-term bilateral relation of hostility between India and Pakistan, an 11-year analysis demonstrated clear, reciprocal interactions on the conflict-cooperation dimension (Rajmaira, 1997: 551–552, 558, figures 1–3). In a much shorter temporal framework, that of the Balkan conflicts emanating from post–Cold War breakdowns, reciprocity has been unearthed, although not pervasive and at times minimal in the aggregate—a not unexpected result when dealing with such short time periods (Goldstein and Pevehouse, 1997; Pevehouse and Goldstein, 1999).[21]

It has become abundantly clear that an unsophisticated clone from psychology has become an accepted determinant of international behavior. The extensive data suggests a finding that can potentially play an important role in understanding a broad array of diverse international behavior.[22] Within the broader assertions that nations have always cooperated, that cooperation does not constitute extraordinary behavior, and that the hostility-surrounded and overly nuanced view implicit in earlier conceptualizations of bargaining (Young, 1968) might be less accurately descriptive than originally thought, cooperation through bargaining processes appears to coincide with what we would expect to be the case if a simple stimulus-response model were accurate. The next section turns to reciprocity in the defense area, but several concluding comments seem merited. First, our conclusions derive from diverse investigations in multiple behavioral domains. Second, not all the evidence unquestionably supports the unadulterated, simple S-R model; for instance, in U.S.-Soviet interactions, the Americans and Soviets clearly responded to each other during different periods in different ways (Ward and Rajmaira, 1992: 343, 365), and in test ban negotiations, despite clear evidence for reciprocity, a certain bullying did seem to occur, and relations were more significant in the test ban negotiations than in Strategic Arms Limitation Treaty (SALT) (Jensen, 1984: 546).

Third, Axelrod's tournament and varied experimental and real-world findings suggest an appealing clarity and simplicity, but the experimental results are only consistent and effective technically within the simple and limited PD structure. However, since within that world TFT according to Axelrod is the "best" strategy, and substantial evidence abounds that S-R *does* operate in international behavior, not reliant on "regimes" or "theories of cooperation"—in other words, a true behavioral "norm"— then what nations *do* produces norms. These conclusions remain despite the assertion that "a closer look raises doubts about whether the evidence from trade negotiations supports the proposition that specific reciprocity facilitates international cooperation" (Keohane, 1986b: 13). Point-specific domains are always fraught with problems both for the analyst and the policy-maker. The real-world evidence in support of this "norm" occurs best when aggregated at certain levels—by year, for instance—or "diffuse" reciprocity (Keohane, 1986b: 19–24). Nonetheless, the patterns say something about real-world behavioral regularities that actually do exist, a point that cannot be too strongly stressed.

Ironically, such findings stand in stark contrast to the accepted conventional wisdom of the Cold War period, which produced policy actions consistent with that wisdom—that pressing an adversary, hostility, should produce docility in the other party, while docility by itself would produce further aggressiveness on the part of the adversary (Leng, 1984). The evidence here suggests that across a wide domain of behavior the opposite seems to be the case. Reciprocity does, in fact, work, with evidence appearing while the Cold war was very much a hot item; thus, while regimes and neoliberal institutionalism might claim its ownership (Goldstein and Pevehouse, 1997: 515, 528), its existence, conceptualization, and much analysis was put to the empirical test long before either became so fashionable. By the time much of the empirical research had been underway, Keohane, citing authorities such as Blau, Homans, and Gouldner, noted:

> This school emphasizes that reciprocal obligations hold societies together. Participants typically view diffuse reciprocity as an ongoing series of sequential actions which may continue indefinitely, never balancing but continuing to entail mutual concessions within the context of shared commitments and values. In personal life, bargaining over the price of a house reflects specific reciprocity; groups of close friends practice diffuse reciprocity (Keohane, 1986b: 4).

The distinction between specific and diffuse reciprocity is readily transparent, merely appreciating the separate levels of aggregation of behavior noted above. One would *want* specific reciprocity, such as occurs in the bargaining over the price of a house, but in the interactions between nations the amount of "noise" overwhelms, and specific reciprocity is rarely the case. This applies slightly less so in low politics trade negotiations, at least at one level of aggregation. But reciprocity, mostly diffuse, does occur, and can be recognized and tracked—in ways that, while more systematic, are certainly less interesting than case studies of specific reciprocity. Most important, however, is that this reciprocation occurs outside of any institutional or "regime"-oriented conceptual or empirical umbrella. While institutions are helpful and important for reciprocity in certain domains (Keohane, 1986b: 24–26), they may be less central in the constant ebb and flow of diplomatic exchange. Here, the "dynamics" of the situation may take over and begin to constitute their own "system," one characteristic being reciprocity; whether that be called a "regime" or not is ultimately a semantic issue.

The "Meaning" of Defense Expenditures:
Arms Races and Other Odd Phenomena

A persistently "hot" item throughout the 40-year Cold War system was superpower military expenditures, and a profusion of empirical endeavors for more than 30 years devoted attention to that policy domain, beginning with the posthumous publication of L.F. Richardson's pioneering work (Richardson, 1960) and continuing at a much lesser level of intensity in more recent years. No better time exists, perhaps, than during the calm after the Cold War storm to assess the hot ticket items such as defense buildups, "arms races," and the role of the Soviet "threat," all in the context of exploring the "meaning" of defense expenditures.

An alternative title for this section might have been "Defense Expenditures: The Paramount Test for 'Public Policy' Studies," for ultimately the issue is what defense expenditures actually "mean" in terms of questions of national security, the making of "rational" public policy, or—in the context of so much theorizing discussed here—deterrence. Do expenditures result from policy actually directed to real-world security, to "rational choice" and—ultimately—to deterrence? Or are they driven by essentially "nonrational" factors, one of which could simply be the Cold War bargaining "system" that took on a life of its own unrelated to rational concerns about security and deterrence of adversaries? And how do defense expenditures fit into the observable reciprocities that we have found to exist outside of the defense arena?

For defense issues traditionally, simple external threat or domestic pressure models were the norm, but following from Richardson, early systematic research seemed to gravitate toward an automatic assumption that patterns in defense expenditures should fit an action-reaction model—perhaps because it seemed so obvious, but also because it offered a non-realist, more cognitive-oriented explanation that could theoretically be linked to warlike behavior. A wide assortment of investigators have over the years migrated into and out of the diverse defense expenditure–arms race literature, driven by multiple preoccupations. Capturing the nuances of such a diverse agenda is impossible, and the following four models only serve as tentative organizing devices: *first,* defense expenditures could fit a strict arms race model in which expenditures simply beget expenditures; *second,* a stimulus response model might apply in which arms expenditures might be seen as one component in a stimulus-response model with the other part occupied by diplomatic or verbal conflict; a *third* model is one where defense expenditures do not fit into any action-reaction model but rather serve as the independent variable related to some other dependent variable such as escalation of ongoing conflict or the outbreak of war; and, *fourth,* a residual, nonreactivity model would be one in which defense expenditures themselves are "explained" by other variables, in which the "meaning" of defense expenditures rests for instance at the domestic political level or within a simple model of incremental decision-making.

A chronological assessment conveys the flavor of shifting conclusions. Support for the *fourth* model—the residual one—emerged when compared to either an action-reaction or tension-related explanation of defense expenditures in Europe from 1950 to 1974. While reactivity was discernible, "bureaucratic momentum" was the "single most important determinant" of defense spending in European states and WTO nations (Rattinger, 1975: 593). Lack of support was also uncovered for the *first,* simple action-reaction model as well as the organizational politics model, the *fourth* category; compared to a "naive, no-change model," "it is not possible to differentiate between the performance of the two . . . to a degree that would justify either model being identified as more accurate." Both the reactivity and organizational politics model forecasts were less accurate than the "naive" model, and, in attempting to forecast "ex post" for the years 1970–1973, neither model was accepted as an adequate forecasting tool (Ostrom, 1977: 258–259). However, limited support for an organizational model for British, U.S., and Japanese naval expenditures between the wars was unearthed: "the excellent fit of the organizational process model even when its parameter's value changes, provides prima facie evidence that the model is most appropriate empirically" (Lucier, 1979: 36). Early reviews of the literature also concluded that bureaucratic factors seemed to be carrying the day over action-reaction models (Moll and Luebbert, 1980). For the 1949–1978 period, the *fourth* model also received confirmation:

> Regardless of the country studied or the data series employed . . . the model that has done extremely well in explaining US expenditures is based on domestic political and economic considerations [especially the] political and economic cycles the US goes through and in which the economy is manipulated and support is sought from the populace (Cusack and Ward, 1981: 459–460).[23]

However, support did emerge for the *first* model—action-reaction—for the 1948–1970 period at least for the U.S. having reacted more to *changes* in Soviet arms than to *levels* of Soviet arms; for the Soviets, the process was the reverse, reacting more to levels than changes, "though neither reaction seems particularly strong" (Hollist, 1977: 523). Little support for a narrow action-reaction interpretation was found in 12 separate dyads conventionally viewed as having had some form of arms race during the 1948–1975 period; in seven of the 12 cases armaments of each side were found to be basically independent of the adversaries' arms, while in the five remaining cases, "some form of interdependence between the military expenditures of the dyads was discovered" (Majeski and Jones, 1981: 282).

The evidence at first therefore seemed to be favoring the overriding influence of the internal or bureaucratic factors as opposed to the external arms "races" variables. However, the use of relative stocks of military capabilities of the superpowers rather than defense expenditures produces support for portions of a reactivity model:

> The United States and the USSR do appear to be reactive to one another, yet not through budgets alone. Rather they each try to achieve or maintain a lead over the other in terms of the stocks of weapons, both strategic and conventional, for which the budget is spent . . . Moreover, whereas the United States decreases its expenditures in relation to a friendlier diplomatic climate with the USSR, the reaction of the USSR is in the opposite direction: increased investment in the face of a more cooperative international political climate (Ward, 1984: 309).

Recall that the *third* model views "reactivity" itself as an independent variable, and support for this model does occur, primarily from findings concerning arms races and war—called "unusually strong" in an early analysis (Wallace, 1979: 14); even though later questioned, a reanalysis produced results that "even under assumptions extremely tilted against [the original] propositions" continued to support the link between arms races and war (Weede, 1980: 286; Wallace, 1980). No support emerged for certain relationships between arms expenditures and war, but "great power wars are more likely to be preceded by increasing military expenditures and rates of change as opposed to declining military spending rates of change" (Thompson, Duval, and Dia, 1979: 647). Such a relationship has been found elsewhere (Smith, 1980: 260), and further refinements showed that, in specifying different types of arms races, "wars follow races showing upward concavity, and peace follows wars showing downward concavity, granted the caveat of small sample size" (Smith, 1988: 220). Arms races ending in wars were characterized by "initially generally slow rates of increase which grow rapidly," and those that end in peace "may show rapid initial growth which levels off over time" (Smith, 1988: 223). Even controlling for confounding variables—issues, history of the dispute, and relative power balance—mutual military arms buildups were highly related to disputes' escalating to war between 1816–1993—an outcome more than twice as likely than disputes not preceded by mutual arms buildups (Sample, 1998: 169–170). Others may be much more sanguine but only with respect to a nuclear arms race and the outbreak of war in a bipolar world containing two nuclear powers, such evidence of course implying much less historical reliability than most other data-based studies (Intriligator and Brito, 1984).

A "rivalry" model applied to the superpower system between 1949–1978 includes a combination of dyadic hostility as well as arms expenditures, and finds "a stable system of interactions . . . very robust to exogenous shocks," which suggests "rational expectations" about others' behavior despite "myriad sources of bias and inefficiency that seemingly plague U.S.-Soviet relations," all of which can apparently be taken as confirmation of some manner of reactivity model at work relating to multiple behavioral components, not just expenditures (McGinnis and Williams, 1989: 1118). However, while clear evidence of "rivalry" emerges, and "the behavior of these two states is closely related," the *fourth* model enters in when "the continued separation of domestic and international factors is no longer an appropriate research strategy for the analysis of foreign policy" (Williams and McGinnis, 1992: 113).

Although no single summary statement unearths the "meaning" of defense expenditures, certainly several tentative conclusions can be suggested. First, overwhelming support had *not* been forthcoming for the distinct existence of lawlike patterns of "arms races" that many had expected, especially given conventional wisdom as well as efforts of policy-makers to suggest such a race. Moreover, certain studies arriving at those conclusions suffered from overly simple correlational techniques, and other methodological problems, as well as data reliability—especially concerning the possibility that portions of Soviet data were merely extrapolations from previous trends (Anderton, 1989: 351).[24] Third, critiques written quite some time before revelations in the mid-1990s of extensive mole and counterespionage activities between the superpowers' intelligence agencies unearth a potentially key dilemma related to the research-policy nexus especially in this domain:

> The variables in arms race models are *perceived* variables. If policy-makers in the United States use CIA estimates of Soviet military expenditures when formulating their policy, then CIA data are the best measure of US policy-makers' perceptions of Soviet military expenditures. In this *perceptual sense* IISS or SIPRI data would be inferior to CIA estimates of Soviet military spending. Ironically, up-dated (more accurate) estimates of Soviet military spending *for previous years* are inferior measures (relative to the old, inaccurate data) of US policy-makers' perceptions of Soviet military expenditures *in those years* (Anderton, 1989: 351, emphasis in original).

Ironically, inaccurate data might almost be irrelevant, for decision-makers react—or so the models suggest—to perceptions, and not to what may or may not be the reality: "Arms race modelers studying the behavior of policymakers must identify the data that the policymakers used, not the data they (the arms race modelers) think is the most accurate" (Anderton, 1989: 352). Other problems in inference concerned the use of military expenditures vs. actual military hardware: two nations could hypothetically be competing on specific hardware issues, which might not necessarily show up in the overall aggregates of spending. The tenuous relationship between actual military expenditures and actual weapons stocks also clouds the picture: stocks could hypothetically be rising while actual expenditure dollars are falling (Anderton, 1989: 352).

Clearly arms races and the underlying military expenditures that would support them are much more complex phenomena than was at least originally conceived by the inheritors of Richardson's legacy, perhaps accounting for the confusion concerning the findings as well as the critiques (McGinnes, 1991: 444, 453, 463–466). Thus, the simple question—what *did* defense expenditures "mean"—is not easily answered, either in terms of the manifestly important policy arena of superpower substantive relations, or in terms of any bargaining structures that those relations might define. With respect to one narrow policy question, the two biggest U.S. military adventures of the Cold War—Korea and Vietnam—ended either in stalemate or defeat, depending on one's coding rules, and yet both involved massive military expenditures. With regard to the "Reagan defense buildup"—in reality, the "Carter-Reagan buildup" if one respects the time series of those data[25]—a mighty stretch is required to argue that those increased expenditures were necessary for the military involvements in Grenada in 1983, Panama in 1989, or even the defeat of Iraq in 1991. But certainly the conventional wisdom tells us that the "buildup" was instrumental in the collapse of the Soviet Union, forcing Soviet leaders to pour expenditures into the military in reaction to the United States until they reached a point of exhaustion. This popular interpretation is hard to square with several facts. First, despite widespread reciprocity in internation relations generally, this section suggests nations tend *not* to behave in conformance with such an S-R model with expenditures. Second, most observers by at least the 1985–1987 period recognized that the United States itself would be economically unable to continue such massive military expenditures, and in fact time series data on expenditures show a leveling off—in some cases as early as 1986–1987—at least two to four years before the generally accepted date for the "end" of the Cold War. Third, subsequent intelligence disclosures concerning the large Soviet double-agent operation—in which KGB disinformation may have led U.S. policy-makers to overestimate the Soviet threat—certainly must raise questions about which tail might have been wagging which dog.[26]

What to make, then, of the U.S.-U.S.S.R. "arms race" and the Soviet "defeat"? Certainly the conventional explanation is plausible, convenient, and simple, but necessitates reliance on a model not overwhelmingly supported here. An alternative possibility is that a set of synchronous decisions were almost inadvertently made by both sides, ones that had been in the wings for some time and perhaps only tangentially related to "defense buildups" and ultimate reversals of each side. That is, defense expenditures involve both bargaining—arms racing—as well as domestic, political, and bureaucratic components. But, in addition, it might be suggested that expending on defense needs a "decision rule," that decision rules change, and those changes occur for many reasons. Is "security" less an issue in the 1990s because of the "collapse" of the Soviet Union and therefore lower defense expenditures can occur without public outcry, or has the decision simply been made that one can psychologically live with less "defense"? We have maintained at several points that the Cold War was in fact "ending" for quite some time, perhaps a decade and a half before the symbolic destruction of the Berlin Wall in 1989, and therefore that symbolic "end" very likely does not totally account for the reduced defense expenditures. A major restructuring of the superpower system had occurred in the 1971–1973 period, as well as the last major East-West crisis, and U.S. defense expenditures had peaked in the 1985–1987 period, a fact well-recognized at the time (Korb, 1987) and several years before hammers were taken to the wall. Perhaps the "decision rule" on the need for defense expenditures had simply been changed.

Such analyses can generate rather jaundiced views of the entire defense expenditure enterprise, whether from a theoretical, empirical, or a policy standpoint. The "arms race" literature descended from early Richardson-based mathematical models, which in some ways were really attempts to merely elucidate what was "obviously" there but needed formal mathematical or statistical expression and confirmation. As the research continued, it became rather apparent that simple reactivity models did not reflect what seemed to be the actual reality.[27] Second, with that recognition came the dawning realization that domestic determinants might hold greater sway than anticipated, although it should be noted that such a conclusion cannot necessarily be read as in opposition to any systemic, structural, or "realist" argument. Stimulus-response might *not* apply to armaments, not only because of all the multiple domestic political considerations, but without a clear, sudden international crisis, arms expenditures, because of those many constraints, constituencies, and driving forces, are very hard to "move." On the one hand, built-in bureaucratic and incremental forces are at work, and on the other, political forces—witness the early difficulty in *reducing* the massive U.S. defense budgets meaningfully after the Cold War had purportedly ended. While diplomacy can sometimes shift on the proverbial dime, arms expenditures are more akin to supertankers.

The "paramount" test for public policy studies would be developing the linkage from policy concerns to public policy actions. Broader policy issues are of course always present to justify how defense expenditures evolve, and the simple S-R bargaining model would appear not to apply to these behaviors. We also know that deterrence attempts often fail, and little evidence exists linking defense "buildups" to deterrence. One wonders, therefore, where the overarching policy directives exist that would put "meaning" into a major component of international behavior over the last half century—the arms expenditures of the major powers. Substantive policy concerns and intense ideological debates were certainly present, and apparently important for so much of the Cold War, but could be basically irrelevant—or constitute sideshows—as far as operative variables in defense expenditures. The "meaning" of defense expenditures becomes to that extent somewhat more mysterious.

Conclusion

International actors maneuver through their environment in ways not dissimilar to how individuals "maneuver" through their own bounded daily environments, negotiating in a variety of ways with that environment and the actors that occupy it. Nations are "interdependent" with other nations not just through power-structural relations or economic interactions; interdependence emerges also through the interminable daily, weekly, and yearly interactions that go to define much of "international relations." Power theorists focus on power relations, and interdependence theorists on the potential upside of the possible positive effects of economic interdependence. But there is a downside, too. The prisoners in PD are interdependent, but also realists: "As a general theory, game theory brings the contending 'interdependence' and 'Realist' positions together in a common framework" (Snidal, 1986: 56).

A theme in this chapter has been the interplay of "systems" and diplomacy, of structures defined in a very distinctive fashion, and "agency." Historical case studies have always provided the "agency," and in some ways, the case study approach detailed as so popular in the last chapter on economic issues could be seen as bringing diplomacy "back in," that "art" traditionally considered open only to the understanding of "the few," an arena where gifted individuals worked their skills, successfully coaxing other actors into agreement, convincing adversaries that continued actions would bring forceful responses. Despite the professed change in international issues and the rise of economics, agency exists, diplomacy still operates, and even the phrase "sending the right message"—the diplomatic mantra of the 1980s and 1990s—is reminiscent of other similar messages of earlier eras: the "domino theory" and brinksmanship come to mind. In fact, whether justified under the rubric of the latter two "theories" or more recently under the broad umbrella of a "new world order," the truth is that the *wrong* messages are often sent as frequently as right messages, from those sent by America especially to North Korea and China in 1950, to North Vietnam in the 1960s, and finally to Iraq throughout the 1980s (Jentleson, 1994: 31–138). But the point is that "sending the right message" is what "bargaining" is all about.

But "sending the right message"—like deterrence—turns out to be more difficult than common sense suggests. Verbal propositions litter the foreign policy literature, often encased in detailed case studies that infer agency. For many years these were little more than suggestive illustrations, with little systematic research. The inherent problems were set out a quarter of a century ago: "The would-be influencer benefits from . . . theory in knowing that he should mix two streams of deprivation and indulgence and that he should use both verbal and physical acts in explicit sequences." Unfortunately, the problem

> is in knowing how to arrange the combinations. The theory tends to be silent on the details of managing the mixes and the sequences. In fact, traditional writings usually consign these details to the realm of art. The effective diplomat or statesman is said simply to "know" when and how to initiate which moves according to the requirements of the situation (McClelland, 1970: 5–6).

That remained the case into the early 1970s even though a relatively sophisticated "influence model" was already widely known (Singer, 1963: 427).[28] Two decades later, things in some ways seem not to have changed much:

> Strategies of reassurance, like deterrence, are difficult to implement. They . . . must overcome strategic, political, and psychological obstacles . . . Other obstacles are specific to strategies of reassurance and derive from the political and psychological constraints leaders face.
>
> Designing strategies of conflict management that combine components of deterrence and reassurance in appropriate mixtures and sequences is no easy task (J. Stein, 1991: 34, 59).

However, all is not lost. Recent elaborations of five strategies of "reassurance" as a counterpoint to deterrence theory demonstrate the illustrative method of case study applications (J. Stein, 1991: 35–56) (although distinctions between deterrence and re-assurance remain somewhat hazy). Such case study analyses are nuanced and specific, but even at the more aggregate level, we do know some things that we weren't quite so sure of a quarter century ago. Stimulus-response or reciprocity "works" in that it has received widespread empirical support, and TFT seems to be a sensible bargaining strategy—with full recognition that the evidence as noted is not unvarying. The *specific* moves are still clouded in mystery but perhaps the most significant suggestion might be that the specific moves may be less important than the overall behavioral repertoire, which of course implies inferences about specific vs. diffuse reciprocity (Keohane, 1986b). Specific daily behaviors may represent noise and get "lost" in the commotion of the daily activity, but in fact may not be that important. TFT is about the simplest repertoire imaginable. Combined with the "norm" of reciprocity and the empirical finding that *when aggregated at a certain level* stimulus-response does in fact operate, broad general advice can be useful.[29] Specific empirical findings on bargaining strategies (Leng, 1993a) combined with the larger structural variables associated with, for instance, successful deterrence (Huth, 1988; Huth and Russett, 1984; 1988) presents a picture quite different from conventional assumptions. The "norm" of reciprocity suggests that S-R works—in the "large" although not in the "small"—and should affect any decision-maker considering influence attempts, regardless of the issue, but also regardless of the temptation to focus on the "small"—the immediate—as opposed to the "large."

According to Axelrod's "evolution" of cooperation, the latter can "get started even in a world of unconditional defection," work even when "many different kinds of strategies are being tried," and finally, "once [cooperation is] established on the basis of reciprocity, can protect itself from invasion by less cooperative strategies. Thus, the gear wheels of social evolution have a ratchet" (Axelrod, 1984: 21). Many specific derivations have spun off those suggestions, such as one, in reusing data from the second tournament, that:

> the success of strategies adhering to the reciprocity norm is extremely robust . . . The interpretation of TFT's success has long been that its reciprocal play encourages opponents to cooperate. Our findings emphasize an additional and complementary interpretation, at least for interactions in a world of more than two players. That is, cooperative strategies will do well in adverse environments if the majority of others adhere to the norm of reciprocity. *Our twist on this argument is that the general population need not even reciprocate cooperation, but rather only defection.* If states act in this manner, a strategy of long-term defection will prove counterproductive (Busch and Reinhardt, 1993: 443).[30]

Stimulus-response has been presented as simple and possessing a "nice" quality; the one single property that distinguished high- from low-scoring entries on Axelrod's tournament was also "niceness," "which is to say never being the first to defect" (Axelrod: 1984: 33). The empirical evidence suggests that simple stimulus-response works, and in terms of policy, the "forgiveness" characteristic could be the most telling:

> Even expert strategists from political science, sociology, economics, psychology, and mathematics made the systematic errors of being too competitive for their own good, not being forgiving enough, and being too pessimistic about the responsiveness of the other side (Axelrod, 1984: 40).

Similarities with Schelling's admonition noted earlier about what is involved in bargaining is enlightening; being clever runs the risk of leaving out the "reverberating process," where "the other player is adapting to you, you are adapting to the other, and then the other is adapting to your adaptation and so on" (Axelrod, 1984: 121). Moreover, the "interdependence" integral to the bargaining model does not get slighted:

> As long as the interaction is not iterated, cooperation is very difficult. That is why an important way to promote cooperation is to arrange that the same two individuals will meet each other again, be able to recognize each other from the past, and to recall how the other has behaved until now (Axelrod, 1984: 125),

called "enlarging the shadow of the future" (Axelrod, 1984: 129).

Much of this is of course traditional diplomacy and bargaining fashioned in fancy words. In recent years, however, it has been absorbed within the underlying tenets of regime-based neoinstitutionalism (Axelrod and Keohane, 1986; Keohane, 1986; 1988), where its major attraction is that the vagaries present in daily diplomacy can often be overridden within the context of institutions. But within bargaining and deterrence situations, all of this nonetheless suffers from the restrictive parameters of PD nonexistent in the real world. That fact alone makes certain findings even more interesting, and conclusions from real-world crises coincide with Rapoport's analyses of his tournament:

> If there is another lesson to be learned from the relative effectiveness of Reciprocating influence strategies, it lies in the benefits that come from not attempting to be too clever . . . There is much to be said, in diplomacy as in other human affairs, for behaving in a straightforward and reasonable manner, for the choice of clarity over subtlety (Leng, 1993a: 206).

Nonetheless, PD games are different than the components found in early Cold War crises, nuclear gamesmanship, recent crises in south-central Europe or over the continuing status of Formosa—as well as the many "new" international economic crises noted in the previous chapter. Or at least one would think so. They may not, however, be completely irrelevant to such contemporary concerns. If "political-economic and military-security issues can be analyzed with the same analytical framework" even though "economic issues usually seem to exhibit less conflictual payoff structures than do those of military security" (Axelrod and Keohane, 1986: 231), then findings from the areas of concern during the Cold War might have applicability to the present era. Rather than threats, reassurances, and compellance behavior, discussion focuses on transaction costs and rent-seeking as factors impacting trade relations (Conybeare, 1986: 156f.), debt negotiations (Aggarwal, 1996), economic coercion, sanctions, or retaliation (Morgan and Schwebach, 1997; Gawande and Hansen, 1999). While at times only indirect, game parameters are compatible with economic interactions, in which reciprocity, retaliation, and iteration play central roles within a GATT or WTO structure, and even the "shadow of the future" if consideration to spillover of trade disputes or future negotiations is considered.

But for the more irresolute military-security area, conclusions from both experimental[31] and real world data on crises might caution a leader against engaging in diplomacy—threats, escalatory maneuvers—that violates admonitions derived from this research, as difficult as such counsel might be, given the disarray and numerous countervailing variables, the constant "noise" impacting on daily diplomacy, and counterintuitive underpinnings of such advice. Still, the theoretical and empirical evidence does not support employing such behavior. At the same time, the findings also prompt doubts about the complex theorizing that went into deterrence inquiries during the Cold War years. Just as recent analyses have suggested that much of the technological effort—and massive amounts of money—that went into nuclear weapons development might have been in fact "wasted" (Passell, 1995), it is also conceivable that much of the intellectual effort that went into deterrence theorizing overcomplicated what ultimately could be fairly simple processes—albeit easier to understand at higher rather than lower levels of aggregation. It is not coincidental that just as technology and interest in defense expenditures—compared to the 1950s and 1960s—have slipped to a second-tier interest, so also the interest in deterrence theory has declined. Perhaps the genre that included the complex, in-depth case studies upon which portions of the deterrence literature were based served the purpose of explicating the multiple possible ways of conceptualizing that behavior, but in the final analysis such complexities are too difficult to model for any input into the daily environment of international politics. Notwithstanding the exciting and intriguing results emanating from more structurally oriented—e.g., EID—designs, ultimately everything is very complex; deterrence theorists were, and "chaos" theorists are, correct. Yet underlying that complexity perhaps resides a simplicity at least marginally suggested by the analysis of findings in this chapter.

What was traditionally thought to be "known" by the artist—the diplomat—has become something quite a bit less of a mystery, if only insofar as the individuals sequentially playing the role of the artist have so consistently miscalculated the other "artists," and thus so consistently gotten so many nations into so much trouble. Policy advice given to decision-makers is often of the most rudimentary sort, yet cast in either sophisticated academic or diplomatic jargon on the one hand, or infantile street talk on the other. The street talk does not take into account the complexities, while the sophisticated academic or diplomatic jargon fails to recognize the simple realities. The contemporary phrases are well-known: "Responding forcefully to aggression," "teaching a lesson," "sending the right message," "line in the sand"—all are meant to imply that stated policy is to insure that "future aggressors will be deterred." Unrecognized is that the aggression allegedly being currently deterred in any given specific crisis was obviously not originally stopped or deterred by decisions previously to respond to aggression so it "does not happen in the future."

But our focus here has been somewhat narrowly on aggressive behavior, which nation-states in fact infrequently exercise—popular perceptions to the contrary. Nor does this assertion apply merely to the very contemporary post–Cold War era; it was also the case during the Cold War. In fact, the empirical point stressed numerous times is that cooperation between nations is much more the norm than is conflict, which is why the focus on "regimes" and cooperation is in some ways misplaced. But all standard definitions of "regimes" involve rules and norms, and a central norm now recognized as such is reciprocity—a simple one, but a norm nonetheless. "Regimes" therefore constitute a form of "bargaining" between nations, which involves the interactions that have always taken place: over what issues should be on the table, *how* agreements should be arrived at, and then, the "closer" one gets to an agreement, or the "more agreement" one gets, the "more," "stronger," or "significant" is the "regime." To the extent that attention rests on the formal rules and/or organizations involved in the regimes, the less is the focus on the process leading to the regime.[32]

Elements of international politics once thought central from a policy and a theory perspective seem recently to have become something of historical oddities: brinksmanship and the domino "theory" come to mind. Now we have regime "theory," and one can only speculate when and under what conditions in the future it also may become an oddity. But even in the era of regime popularity, certain elixirs seem time-independent in the policy realm: "send the right message" has been noted several times as a contestant for longevity, for it continues—contrary to many of the findings analyzed here—to imply that the "right" message can be sent and that the *same* message will be received and will have the effect desired by the sender. This harks back to the complex theorizing that occurred in the deterrence literature, much of which has become mostly dormant. Many will say that it has been the "end of the Cold War" that has produced that dormancy, but in the real world of international relations—as well as the simplified confines of PD games—much more simple formulations might be operative in terms of what really "works." The policy advice continues nonetheless:

> The prospects for peace in post–Cold War Europe, and other areas of the globe where great-power interests may conflict, may depend more importantly on the maintenance of credible deterrent policies (Huth et al., 1993: 619).[33]

The story has yet to be written, however, on whether the threats and other bargaining behavior that were part of the Cold War deterrence arsenal ever worked—whether in Berlin, off Formosa in the 1950s or later in the mid-1990s, or whether they achieved the desired effect in south-central Europe in the late 1990s or potentially again over Formosa in 2000. It would be unfortunate if the continuing operative word remained "credibility," still left unoperational in the post–Cold War world, when in fact the underlying bargaining processes turn out to be more uncomplicated and unpretentious than all the theories suggest.

Chapter Ten ❀

Anarchy or Contention?

The Territoriality of Theorists

In a world of arguably interminable and momentous transformations, "truisms" and received knowledge of the past at times seem no longer true and no longer viewed as part of the "accepted wisdom." "National interest" as the driving factor sufficient to conceptually describe state preferences seems certainly passé as a serious scholarly explanation,[1] although essential to realism. But realism itself has for many become a dilapidated conceptual apparatus, and replacements seem in vogue, this despite the fact that realism and the writings of Hans Morgenthau for years appeared to constitute much of the accepted wisdom. In fact, the caricatures of realism so often critiqued were not nearly as prevalent nor was its hold as potent as many of the critiques insisted.[2]

The "truisms" defining the discipline for many years were in subtle ways changing long before the neoidealism of the 1980s and 1990s. Each half generation seems compelled to produce a "new truth," which then takes on—in a bizarre replay of certain very contemporary views of international relations—a certain hegemonic character. These might be theoretical, methodological, substantive, ideological, or more likely a combination of several. Neoidealism and liberal institutionalism are a product of their times, as are the calls for postmodern or feminist interpretations of international relations. Weaving through the "new" idealism, "triumphant liberalism" (Gaddis, 1992: 179–186), the "concert-based collective security system" (Kegley and Raymond, 1994), and the "democratic peace" movement (Russett, 1993; Maoz and Russett, 1993; Schweller, 1993) is a view of the world quite distant on the surface from the views of just a generation ago, and even though possessing a life of less than a decade, this accumulation of beliefs has emerged as a serious contender in the last decade of the twentieth century.

In the face of apparent fast-paced change, no one wants to be left standing at the station, and a host of issues—and research questions—appear to have become antiquated. The acute international crises, from Berlin in 1948 to Iran in 1980, seem to some to be ancient memories in a "global" world; arms control and disarmament seem less immediate in the "postrealist"—and partly disarmed—era; nuclear war and the agonizing worries over potential spread of nuclear weapons seem rather outmoded in a "neoidealist" era.[3] European integration, central to policy and theoretical concerns for two decades, continues in fact to plod along but with reduced theoretical attention—an "accepted" fact of the "modern" world. Burning issues of international pollution and depletion of natural resources continue, and even though the attention seems muted compared to the 1970s, the nucleus of theoretical endeavors shifts in response to events in the world:

> The focus is on arms control when technological advances in weapon systems appear likely to escalate the arms race, on the environment when there are severe famines or dying rivers and lakes, on the international monetary system when currency fluctuations grow intolerable, on capital flows when debtor countries are on the verge of bankruptcy, and so on (Ferguson and Mansbach, 1988: 217).

And thus in the 1990s, "markets," their operations, and emerging economies—or powers, if one wishes—have become a central concern, as have issues of transnational decision-making. Investment, development, and capital flows are the surface foci, but traditional debates about power and hegemony suggest that the names of the games that players play have changed, but familiar issues and contests have reemerged. The "Nye initiative" on U.S.-Japanese security issues comes to mind; ironically with the Cold War over, security relationships may be more important than ever.[4] Internationalist concerns for the environment continue, hopes for multilateralism have gained speed, and many "new internationalisms" such as epistemic communities have emerged. Perhaps with the end of the Cold War, Fukuyama is correct: one history has ended, or another has just begun.

The "ostensibly interminable transformations" noted above refer obviously to the real-world changes that have become part of conventional "reality," but also relate directly to the disputes over conceptual, theoretical, and paradigmatic premises. Routine lamentations denigrating the status of theory—the "quest for theory in international relations . . . [is] probably leading nowhere"—are especially suspect when compared to alleged "advances" in other areas: "genuine empirical theory as convincing and useful, say, as that which students of American politics have in the field of voting behavior seems entirely beyond our grasp" (Ferguson and Mansbach, 1988: 212, 185). The confined scope of outcomes such as voting behavior cannot compare in any fashion to the scope of international outcome variables: crises, wars, fluctuating hegemonies, internation and interbloc trade disputes, and contentious state-market relations, to name just a few.

While true that "debates among international relations theorists" often consist of "the same (often stale) arguments and emphases . . . despite superficial changes in concepts and language" (Ferguson and Mansbach, 1988: 218), it is not true that "The scientific revolution, which never really got under way despite the best efforts of its advocates, has now been all but abandoned as a goal" (Ferguson and Mansbach, 1988: 221). Substantive work, "scientific" and otherwise, continues even while the debates endure—and very often in spite of them: whether behavior is externally or internally generated, or whether the state does—or does not—matter, whether it should be either "in" or "out" (Zurn, 1993); the largely futile "agent-structure" dialectic—nothing more, really, than a new form of the old levels of analysis issue[5] or, going back even further, the free will versus determinism dialectic—although carried along on a newly sophisticated "metatheoretical" level.[6] In some cases the same research program has moved from "out" to "in": system-level field theories of the mid-1960s changed to a mediated externally generated model (Rummel, 1969a) and later to a model almost completely dependent on a single internal characteristic (although most fruitfully conceptualized in dyadic terms) (Rummel, 1983; 1995).

The most feverish and growing controversies, however, have pitted realism and neorealism against liberalism, neoliberalism, and liberal institutionalism, debates consuming an enormous amount of energy, but with a questionable heat-to-light ratio (Sullivan, 2000). Realism has been called a theory, a paradigm, and a research program—and been criticized for being labeled all three[7]—but it may be nothing more than a conglomerate of personal prejudices. Realist thought

> is not a coherent, integrated theory of state behavior; it is a collection of descriptive and prescriptive observations and hypotheses loosely tied together by logic. It is a first-class "shape-shifter": as such, it can continue to resist definitive tests almost indefinitely (Bremer, 1995: 540).

Territorial boundaries are pervasive, and while certainly related to the ongoing real-world research, at times a sense of schizophrenia emerges in which the territorial disputes seem distant and only indirectly descend into the arena where the work goes on. This has been for some time most strongly reflected in issues of whether one is considered on the inside or the outside of "realism," or, more recently, lamenting whether anyone still represents the true "realist" tradition (Legro and Moravcsik, 1999). But realism seems to weather the attacks over the years, and the serious work of research in those vast trenches continues—much of it almost regardless of the hijacked metatheoretical debates.

A Walk Through the Trenches

Nonetheless, what goes on in those trenches has certainly changed, and while no short section can do justice to it all, general observations at this point might be merited. For all the fervor about the agent-structure debate, "agency" was always displayed in case studies, biographies, and diplomatic histories, a research strategy recently reemerging and labeled "contextualization." For many reasons, including the dissatisfaction with the overdetermined nature of case studies, by the 1950s and 1960s systematic studies began investigating particularly where and in what ways "agency" might systematically impact behavior, focusing on usually more narrow and detailed explanatory and outcome variables. Data difficulties at this level have been perennial, partly serving to reenergize overdeterministic models and resurrected in the "Ideas Matter" school. No one ever doubted, of course, that ideas "matter," but why they count so much in some circumstances rather than others is the key question. The same ideas have different effects under different circumstances. For the "end of the Cold War," as an illustration, the "ideas" that had "emanated from a transnational liberal internationalist community comprising the U.S. arms control community, Western European scholars and center-left policymakers, as well as Soviet institutchiks" (Risse-Kappen, 1994: 212–213) were certainly relevant to the outcome, and possibly even "causally consequential for the end of the cold war," but the same ideas had been bobbing around in one form or another for some time, and a very thin and tenuous line separates plausibility from *mere* plausibility, and both are often separated by a wide chasm from causality. More distinctive, perhaps, is the fact that the first wave of systematically oriented research focusing on "agency" in the 1950s and 1960s tended to view individual perceptions and beliefs as a potentially troubling element, namely, that *misperceptions* were as likely causes of decisions as were accurate perceptions, and rigidly held beliefs to be as likely as rationally-cultivated "ideas" in explaining behavior. Recently, "ideas" seem to emerge and ripen untrammeled by the many odd human idiosyncrasies that other areas in the social sciences suggest can be very disabling. Using the individual for explanatory purposes traditionally exhibited high plausibility, an easy criterion to satisfy. Such used to be the case also with decision-making analysis, relatively simple because "interest defined in terms of power"—pure realism, rational choice—was the explanation for why nations do what they do. And "national interest" always seemed to make plausible sense; the data "fit." By the early 1970s it was clear, however, that such a model could no longer be glibly employed. Though not much excessive contention about "realism" flourished in those days—that came along later—myriad decision-making analyses were making it clear that a more "realistic" account of decision-making involved questioning and eliminating many components that had been *thought* to be part of classical realism. Once that genie was out of the bottle, assorted approaches assailed the "realist" perspective, most singularly popularized by Models II and III in Allison's reporting on the case study of the Cuban Missile Crisis, as well as many other social-psychological or cognitive models of decision-making. But as so often is the case, these in turn were also recontested—if not specifically, at least generically—by a slow return to a focus on rational process, now labeled "rational choice" or "expected utility." Within a relatively short period of time, therefore, theoretical avenues almost diametrically opposed to each other emerged, a phenomenon more comprehensible if one recognizes the effect of the chameleon: the dependent outcome variables in these many instances were also diametrically different.

This phenomenon of diverse outcome variables is also exemplified in the "behavior begins within" school. While always present in geopolitics and nationalism, the empirical "within" school flourished once outcome variables became more clearly specified with data generated from traditional theoretical linkages; in some ways the more the data became systematic and sophisticated, the more it outran the theory. In time it resurged with the "putting the state back in" movement, the most startling development occurring within one relatively small corner of that entire undertaking, wherein the notion discredited during the Vietnam era—the hypothesized positive impact of democratic systems—became an old theory that very quickly, within less than a decade, was enshrined by many into a "law." The jump from the actual empirical findings—many of which, while excellent in their own right, were nonetheless narrow in scope—to a law, suggests that the findings might have been stretched beyond their explicit confines without careful enough attention to either theoretical anomalies (Spiro, 1994) or certain historical complexities (Thompson, 1996).

Nonetheless, multiple theoretical nuances have been elaborated within the "democratic peace" classification, but more striking than the theoretical aspect has been the development, extension, and refinements mostly in the area of design, measurement, and statistical analysis—which is of course one avenue followed by "normal science." Moreover, the increasingly complex and extensive findings taken as a whole have seemed to support for the most part the basic underlying tenets of the numerous theoretical developments—notwithstanding the many critiques leveled at one or more specific undertaking—and have overshadowed other areas of "state level" analysis, especially the growing resurgence in geopolitics in the form of "borders" and the renewed interest in diversionary theories. All of which suggests that in certain behavioral domains in the real world as well as the world of theoretical constructs, the nation-state endures.

Controversy has swirled around all manner of constructs, state level as well as larger structural conditions, which itself has a long history. In the contemporary era, the basic evolution has been from formalized, excessively abstract "general" system formulations into elaboration of more stylized but specific and time-bound *types* of systems, followed in turn in more recent years once again by the development of grand world systems, world history, and even "coevolving" political/economic systems spanning multiple centuries but grounded in specific historical realities. Structural analysis in the contemporary era spans integrative and power systems in the 1950s (Deutsch and Kaplan) followed by bargaining systems for the 1960s (McClelland) to further refinements of neorealist systems by Rosecrance, Singer, and Waltz, and finally the development of the grand world systems and long cycles of Wallerstein, Modelski, Goldstein, and Thompson. It is paradoxical that the most sizable promotion for a clearly systems—and "scientific"—approach was later seen to have come from Kenneth Waltz's 1979 work, *Theory of International Politics,* which, while controversial, was confined to the theoretical level, and basically continued and refined lines of thought that had been in existence for some time (Keohane, 1986a: 15). Much of the structural debate had already occurred within the quantitative, "scientific" subculture for two decades.

While many findings at the structural level confirm one another, disagreement still persists over specific findings as well as more broadly over whether the evidence for which these data provide answers has been the focus of the most relevant research questions at the structural level, an argument taking several different forms. First, the leap to apply findings to the contemporary era remains in question, with a reluctance to forecast for one's own current world the pessimistic predictions derived from structural models. The tendency seems to be that *even if* empirical findings appeared relevant, the current world is a changed one: "it's different this time."[8] Second, a widespread intractable disagreement persists over the description of the contemporary world: whether "hegemony" still operates in this world and is therefore a meaningful concept; the correct number of "major" powers or even whether the concept of "major powers" itself remains significant; the role and importance of traditional non-state actors; and—most importantly—whether the existence of other international or "global" processes especially in the economic dimension have begun to take precedence over the power relations embodied in state-to-state relations. "Globalization" serves as the most recent code word for this panoply of potential changes describing the contemporary international system.

A final daunting methodological and theoretical problem facing all structural analysis is the appropriate time lag. Humans very much enmesh themselves in the daily flow of events, and the time lags between occurrence and recognition of large-scale structural changes is not always apparent and can involve long periods, especially between recognition and ultimate impact. *Which* time lags are the most appropriate remains contentious both in the short term (Dixon, 1987; Goldstein, 1991) and in the more cosmic, long term (Ruggie, 1993). Therefore, for instance, not only is the debate over American hegemony far from settled, but even those taking the view that such an exalted status has passed do not agree about when and in what ways its effect will or has taken hold. Dealing with intermediate- and long-term social processes plagues the theoretician applying high-level structural variables to ongoing processes that some observers—the consumers referred to in Chapter One—think they can see for themselves.

Structural theories have not been limited to realist-based formulations; nonrealist structural concepts originally focused on the hopes for integration and were meant to apply primarily to the post–World War II European context but have burgeoned to encompass a broad set of research agenda ostensibly more aligned with the contemporary era. Ironically, the very structural phenomena that should have been amenable to long-term tracking with relatively reliable data—European integration—were sleighted in favor of these many other processes thought to be taking precedence over limited European or regional integration. In fact, the latter has now been imbedded at times within broader structural formulations in which at least two mechanisms have taken hold. The first was the emergence of "complex interdependence" and "regimes," two concepts propelling integrative thoughts along much different pursuits and which themselves each followed quite distinct paths in subsequent years, one fading and the other flowering—according to some—into a full-blown "theory." This latter occurred despite continuing confusion about the looseness and vagueness of central definitions, and the fact that regimes have *always* been present in international politics in one form or another. None of this has stymied the enthusiasm of their pursuit, almost as if "regimes" satisfies some felt need for a concept or an agreed-upon "explanation" that accounts for something that either should not exist, such as "cooperation under anarchy," or accounts for what appears to be happening in the contemporary post–Cold War and post-realist world, namely, cooperation. The second was a shift from sociological to economic models, which carried numerous implications for understanding processes in Europe but also more broadly, especially if one endorsed the emerging notion by the 1980s that while international politics involves certain material interests, it may also pertain to the "reproduction and transformation" of "identities and interests":

> Integration theorists appreciated this suggestion long ago, but their nascent *sociology* of international *community* has been lost in the *economics* of international *cooperation* developed by realists and rationalists (Wendt, 1994b: 394).

Regimes, while elusive, nonetheless elicited agreement: institutions now "matter," and regimes both describe and—for many—"explain." Another, quite distinct theoretical framework traveled a much different route. "Balance theory" has been essentially ignored despite its clear inclusion within the "realpolitik" family, and its clear nonreliance on "power" notions as traditionally conceptualized. One view sees it as nothing more than traditional power politics ("vintage realpolitik it was supposed to be" [Jentleson, 1994: 16]) in which nations rationally line up based on their relations with other, third parties. Such a rationalistic basis need not necessarily be imposed, however; very normal human psychological processes might be driving the same behavioral tendencies. Perhaps its very simplicity and lack of nuanced theoretical sophistication produces little interest and the resultant scarcity of systematic attention.

Perhaps the greatest transformation for both substantive and theoretical reasons has been the general boundary problem potentially encompassing relations between the market and the state, a relationship yet to be modeled, but which has served as an underlying orienting tension within which the "economics of international cooperation" (Wendt, 1994b: 394) has been investigated, and which has come to occupy a broad panoply of historical, contemporary-empirical, and theoretical focus. No distinctive characteristic of theory or explanation has emerged from this domain, but the substantive economic issues present multiple differential outcome variables encompassing an enticingly wide and ever-popular domain, and, for many, supplanting particular traditional concerns. Under the surface of certain specifics, however, traditional theories having to do especially with hegemony and based frequently on underlying realist premises continue to play a dominant role. The multiple nuances that differing behavioral outcomes represent do require, however, conceptualizations that go beyond simplified realism, many of which have come to be associated with organizational and institutional imperatives, but "international organization" here defined as thriving much beyond the restraints and limits of traditional organizations. The relatively new and emerging "market mentality" of the 1990s, hypothetically set within the broader state-market tension, has not yet established a central theoretical impact.

The popularization of "anarchy" as a dominant metaconceptual description of the international system especially during the later Cold War years served to move theoretical development toward metaconcerns, and as the Cold War wound down and faded, the commonsense notion of the pervasiveness of "rules" emerged as a counter to anarchy. But the discovery of "rules" is nothing new: the Cold War "system" itself is replete with observed rules. Imbedding them within a concept like "regimes" provides a convenient agreed-upon tent, but is not necessary to envision how "rules" might emerge and influence behavior in a variety of different contexts even going beyond the recent interest in economic or environmental issues to which they have been applied:

all social action depends on the preexistence of rules, implying that even under anarchy, rules are an essential prerequisite for action. It asserts the impossibility and inconceivability of social behavior without rules; the issue of whether a centralized authority exists or not is beside the point. Rules . . . are both logically and praxiologically necessary for social action (Dessler, 1989: 458–459).

It was the very same insight many years before that spawned the generation of research into bargaining and interstate interaction, and that flourished in the apparently conflict-ridden world of the Cold War. That specific spatio-temporal genesis moved the research agenda toward policy-related issues of deterrence, and if one dominant theme emerged from the empirical research into those questions, however, it was that much of the conventional wisdom about correlates and causes of deterrence that had great influence on policy was flawed. It could very well be that in addition to defects on the theoretical level, the sense of faulty policy implications has resulted, with the end of the Cold War, in a less directed focus on deterrence questions.

The Cold War has not had that consequence for the more simply designed stimulus-response model, which provides at least conceptual unity—if not explanatory capability—across a broad spectrum of behavior, a finding ultimately accepted although relabeled as the "norm of reciprocity." This unadorned explanatory linkage possesses attributes beyond simplicity: it conforms with the recent focus on norms—especially reciprocity—and relates to the more philosophical interest in elaboration of "rules," for it contains, especially as manifested in the simplest of PD games, the most uncomplicated of behavioral admonitions, and it produces cooperation. As such, it transcends the specific issues of the Cold War and may very well prove quite serviceable in understanding the substantive economic processes that seem to have supplanted the Cold War political issues.

Such may not be the fate for one hotly contested specific issue of the Cold War years, however, since the "meaning" of that issue—defense expenditures—seems much more ambiguous in light of the empirical research than was the case two decades ago. "Arms race" and "deterrence" explanations of that behavior have not fared well. It would appear, in fact, that defense expenditures considered as an outcome variable, especially for the major powers, results from a much more complex combination of factors, especially domestic, that bear only minimal or tangential relationship to the broader issues of sparring with the enemy in a deterrence paradigm or providing in some "policy" realm for the national defense. Even though the Cold War is conventionally accepted as over, not much outcry exists even though American defense expenditures are more than five times the next highest spender (which, ironically, by the end of the 1990s, happened to be Japan).[9] Deterrence posturing and bargaining may have existed in a realm very much removed from the actual decisions affecting amounts proposed and legislated for defense spending among the major powers, and at least the possibility must be entertained that much of the extensive deterrence theorizing in this substantive domain may have been misdirected.

<h2 style="text-align:center">The Elusive Quest[10]:
A Theory of International Relations?</h2>

What occurs in the trenches seems at times to bear little relationship to meta-debates and dialectics that operate at highly charged abstract levels, with generalized controversies establishing broad domains and territories operating very much in relative disregard for the former. Will there ever be "a" theory of international relations from all this, combining the disparate dimensions of both? Despite Waltz's implication,[11] and despite much heat on this issue, the answer remains "No." Is it possible to produce complex multivariate models or explanations of international behavior? The answer here is most likely in the positive, even though systematic multivariate explanations often give way to more narrowly construed endeavors, which in turn may seem narrow, but consist of multivariate models in reality. The popular "agent-structure" debate, if it were to go operationally beyond the traditional free will vs. determinism issue,[12] certainly insinuates the possibility of multivariate explanations as a "sub-text,"[13] for it argues that, while "agency counts," that alone is not a particularly insightful observation. Much more difficult is establishing exactly *where* and in *what* ways all those things casually lumped under agency actually do "count," and in what situations structural factors take precedence.

While some attempts at multiple levels of analysis with respect to the end of the Cold War have been made (Lebow and Risse-Kappen, 1995), a very primitive attempt to tabulate where distinct theoretical approaches appeared to have the most effect (Sullivan, 1976: 301–325) suggested that the bulk of multivariate models extant at that time focused at the system level. Likewise, it has mostly been forgotten that over the years various versions of "field theory" have been floated, a comprehensive and—at times—parsimonious multivariate perspective first introduced by Quincy Wright, wherein the "field" was partitioned into geographical and analytical components:

> each international organization, national government, association, individual or other "system of action," or "decision-maker," may be located in a multidimensional field. Such a field may be defined by co-ordinates, each of which measures a political, economic, psychological, sociological, ethical, or other continuum influencing choices, decisions, and actions important for international relations (Wright, 1969: 445).

Agency and structure were very much a part of Wright's field, although terminology appears outmoded: nations objectively vulnerable to attack should become more hostile if they are "in psychic relations of opposition"; if structure—geographic and technological conditions—make nations invulnerable to attack, then psychic relations of opposition—agency—"are not likely to lead to conflict" (Wright, 1969: 453). Similarly, if psychic distances "are diminishing more rapidly than strategic distances, peace becomes increasingly probable. But if strategic distances are diminishing more rapidly than psychic distances, war is probable" (Wright, 1969: 453). While Rummel's later version first specified "distances" on designated attributes that posited a *general* field with relations covering *all* units as a function of general distances, later more particular specifications saw relations mediated by nation characteristics, at times by *unspecified* characteristics of the nation: "differences in attributes are general forces all right, but their impact on the behavior of each nation is modified by forces within each nation" (Rummel, 1969a: 30). While those "forces" were not specified, yet another irony, as we have seen, is that the singular "within" force that has recently received the most attention is the one denigrated a generation ago, namely, form of government.

"Field" theory possessed a "unifying" characteristic, and many early attempts to get at complexity and cross-level analysis involved field notions, but were not limited to that specific conceptual umbrella. Cross-level multivariate undertakings suffered partly from a lack of sophistication, but also because the bulk of these were carried out at the system level (Sullivan, 1976: 307–313) with few cross-level analyses—which would address an assessment of the questions raised by the agent-structure debate. At the individual and decision-making levels, ad hoc analyses combined numerous approaches in an attempt at multivariate analysis, but few systematic attempts were made to assess the relative influence of various individual-level factors (Sullivan, 1976: 302–303). At the state level, multiple attributes did not necessarily produce more interesting findings than single variables, but in comparing attributes and system-level distance factors, evidence suggested rather clearly that the latter was a better explanation of certain behaviors than the former (Sullivan, 1976: 315–317).

More recently, a "turn" toward seductive case studies demonstrates ad hoc theorizing and establishes the impact of multivariate, cross-level possibilities. The methodology has been rightly castigated for its inability to add to general theory building, but certainly one distinct advantage is that dependent variables can be broadly defined, and therefore an "explanation" of earth-shattering events or phenomena can be produced, such as the "end of the Cold War" (Lebow and Risse-Kappen, 1995). In contrast to case studies, *systematic* data-based analyses, while illustrating empirical sophistication without the same methodological drawbacks, at the same time place into stark contrast the very different—and limited—categories of dependent variables that such studies tend of necessity to generate.

Two such studies exemplify these latter observations. The first clearly specified variables at the system, dyadic, and unit levels (Huth et al., 1992). System-level variables included number of states, number of clusters, concentration (CON) of military capabilities, and cross-cutting ties; dyadic variables were balance of capabilities, trends in industrial-military power, arms races, power transition, and the rival's past behavior; unit-level variables were domestic political conditions, current conflict behavior, and the possession of nuclear weapons.[14] The system variables operationally reduce to a concept termed "system uncertainty" (Huth et al., 1992: 485), and the dyadic and unit-level variables reduce to "risk propensity," the "expected payoff of military confrontation," and the "expected payoff of status quo."[15] All of the factors combine to effect the "net utility evaluation," which then should be related to the dependent variable, the "decision whether to challenge the status quo by force" (Huth et al., 1992: 485). Tested on great power rivalries from 1816–1975, system-level variables emerged as "consistently statistically significant" even when controlling for dyadic- and unit-level variables, though these have "comparable substantive effects"

(Huth et al., 1992: 513–514). Contending that increases in system uncertainty "have a negative effect on conflict initiation independent of risk attitude," the findings support the Deutsch and Singer (1964) argument that multipolar systems are more stable than bipolar ones, and thus contest the "Waltzian argument that uncertainty in the international system leads to more conflict" (Huth et al., 1992: 513). However, that crucial element—the limited scope of the dependent variable—ultimately takes its toll:

> Our findings do not support the arguments of scholars such as John Mearsheimer (1990) and John Lewis Gaddis (1986), who have emphasized the importance of low levels of system uncertainty in preserving the postwar "long peace" in Europe—*at least as far as that peace is measured by dispute initiation* (Huth et al., 1992: 514; emphasis added).

The implications appear theoretically sweeping, but the dependent variable definitely does not correspond to that sweep.[16] Impressive as the design, execution, and findings are— especially with respect to its cross-level effort—a dependent variable measured as a "dyad-year" differs substantially from "stability," "conflict," or the "long peace."[17] Nonetheless, even within the confines of a limited dependent variable, such findings tease out the possible differential relevance of contending independent variables, each of which might be operating across very divergent levels of analysis—an undertaking with systematic data that has been noted as presenting complex problems in the past (Sullivan and Siverson, 1981: 15–18).

The second multilevel attempt focused on the *onset of war in pairs of states* as the outcome variable. Combining seven independent variables produced the conditions characterizing a "dangerous dyad": in declining importance, these were contiguity, absence of alliance, advanced economy, democratic polity, overwhelming preponderance, and the presence of a major power (Bremer, 1992: 309). The difference in the dependent variable highlights a seemingly innocuous but fundamental detail: "war-prone dyad" differs from the "dispute-initiation dyad-year" even though both are related to conflict behavior as conceptualized at some systemic level. Those differences might take on more or less significance depending on the analyst's concern, but more importantly, both differ quite radically from anything as broadly and loosely conceived as peace, stability, the "long peace," the Cold War or—a more contemporary interest—the "end" of the Cold War. Any implications must therefore be recognized as applying *only* within these confined behavioral parameters. Still, several levels emerged as important. At the nation level, geographical contiguity led in terms of importance, democracy remained important even after other effects had been removed, and overwhelming preponderance—a system-level variable—remains a "pacifying condition" (Bremer, 1992: 337). Nonetheless, not unlike the example just noted, very broad implications are drawn: the four most important variables—contiguity, alliance, economy, and polity—are

> twice as important as each of the last two. If the order of this list were compared to that of the implicit research priorities that have guided war and peace research, the correlation would not be positive. This leads to the rather sobering conclusion that our priorities may be seriously distorted.
>
> Taken together these results give a stronger endorsement to the idealist prescription for peace than to the realist one. The results . . . do not constitute a head-to-head test of idealism versus realism . . . but they do suggest that a deeper examination of the idealist position

might bring us closer to understanding the conditions that foster peace. We now have neo-realism; perhaps it's time to seriously entertain neoidealism (Bremer, 1992: 338).

While the multilevel effort must be recognized, and "onset of war" in pairs of states may or may not equate with "peace," certainly it is a leap to "confirmation" of "Wilsonian" over "realist" models given the limited outcome variable under consideration.

It is the very aspiration to address broad theories and conclude in favor of one general theory over another—usually realism pitted against liberalism or idealism in recent de-bates—that loosens the inhibitions against jumping from limited outcome variables to general assessment of the idealist-realist divide. Resolution of that divide will never be reached, partly because methodological issues intrude, both with respect to the implica-tions of findings focused on limited-domain dependent variables—which are dictated by the need for a large *n* and a correspondingly low number of explanatory variables—as well as addressing multivariate, cross-level designs capable of assessing respective potency. In the latter case, small-*n* studies—the "end of the Cold War,"[18] for instance—by defining out-come variables more broadly and allowing multiple streams of competing as well as com-plementary explanatory variables from individual, unit, and system levels to operate, seem to combine multiple-level designs in a convincing fashion; still, assessment of respective potency remains elusive. Thus, serious issues plague both large- and small-*n* studies, which in turn leads to questionable assessments of competing theories.

In addition, a single, overarching theory of international politics may be an illusion simply because of the variety of behaviors encompassed in international relations; any claims to do so are—at minimum—suspect. An interminable theme reiterated many times is that contending "theories" claim victory because each are addressing different parts of the animal we call international relations. Although multivariate approaches and designs can assist in assessing *which* theoretical approaches—and which levels—are best at accounting for very specific types of international behavior, the consumer must keep in mind the not particularly novel distinction just noted between those studies seem-ingly able to "explain" expansive dependent variables ("the end of the Cold War"), but which consist of a low *n* accounted for by an excessively large number of variables, con-trasted with those more parsimonious tests with exceptionally high numbers of obser-vations coupled with a small number of explanatory variables—but able to account for a much more limited-in-scope dependent variable.[19]

The Major Powers:
Their Fate in a "Nonrealist" World

A more fitting title for this section might have been, "End of the Cold War = Death of Realism; Again." The bliss with which the world heralded the "end of the Cold War" is matched by corresponding emotions of those desirous of seeing the "old" world of international relations theory fall. A repeated new truism has been that a new world order has descended with the end of the bipolar system and the rise of economic over political issues that only a few had anticipated almost a quarter century ago (Bergsten, Keohane, and Nye, 1975; Keohane and Nye, 1973). In this nonrealist world, the en-tire structure of relations changes. Despite the dearth of actual empirical studies sup-porting these transformations, the important point is that they have been accepted as fact. And, it is hoped, nations and actors in world politics will react to these presumed

facts, and fit their behavior into the conceptual categories derived from the models describing this "new world order."

While there is much on the horizon supporting this view—albeit mostly idiosyncratic, anecdotal, and ironically somewhat lacking a very long historical perspective—
still the process may remain very much a murky picture. For one thing, traditional views
in some ways captured these very changes. Gilpin, for instance, reads Morgenthau to be
saying that

> if the nation-state is to disappear, as in the case of earlier forms of the state (empires, city-
> states, and absolute monarchies), it will do so through age-old political processes and not
> as idealists would wish through a transcendence of politics itself (Gilpin, 1984: 299).

As for Morgenthau himself, his own words of many years ago might startle many whose
exposure to him has been through others' renditions of his ideas:

> international peace through the transformation of the present society of sovereign nations
> into a world state is unattainable under the moral, social, and political conditions prevail-
> ing in the world in our time. If the world state is unattainable in our world, *yet indispens-*
> *able for the survival of that world,* it is necessary to *create the conditions* under which it will
> *not be impossible* from the outset to establish a world state (Morgenthau, 1965: 539; em-
> phasis added).

Despite writing from the depths of the bipolar Cold War, Morgenthau nonetheless
viewed change as a very real option for decision-makers and for future transformations
in world politics.[20]

The specifics of those transformations are very much in debate. The role of hegemony spelled out in various theories, never clear to many in the past, is perhaps even
more nebulous in the 1990s, especially given the rapid ascent in the theory's original
popularity and then, apparently, its prompt decline, as well as questions about its empirical role. Despite the decline-of-the-U.S. mania of the 1980s (Kennedy, 1987: 514ff.;
Ray, 1998: 240ff.) and empirical evidence lending support to that view [analyzed in
Chapter Eight], there were dissenters (Russett, 1985; Strange, 1987), and the United
States was seen by many to have regained its hegemonic status in the 1990s and then
some. To support this, any number of specific anecdotal pieces of information could be
cited: its crucial role in leading the UN coalition against Iraq in 1990; its intervention
in Bosnia in 1996, considered vital for the success of that "internationalist" peacekeeping operation; U.S. leadership after the Mexican, Asian, and Russian economic fiascoes
from 1994 through 1998, averting a potential world economic crisis; and its crucial
leadership role in NATO's action against Serbian forces in Kosovo in the spring of 1999.
Augmenting these specifics was the unquestioned supremacy of the U.S. economy
through the European travails of low employment and weak economies of the early
1990s and the Asian problems with currency stability and bank failures a half decade
later. The modern world may mark a benchmark of change from previous eras on the
traditional dimension of territoriality (Ruggie, 1993), and events such as those just
noted from one sense can confirm such views because they can be interpreted by use of
a transnational, transborder, extraterritorial model. But interpretation, and the proverbial forest-versus-the-trees problem, remain: how many specific indicators and of what
type are enough to suggest a movement in which direction, and what impact do the ob-

servers' values play in assessing movement away from traditional structures?[21] Does changing the terminology (from "trees" and "forests " to "sediments" and "particles") expedite assessing movement toward the alleged internationalization of authority (Wendt, 1994b: 392)? While a transnational model can fit certain enumerated events, others might see the same or other events more consistent with a hegemonic one, and here again assessing hegemonic positions or transformations proves more difficult in the empirical dimension than positing either from the lofty heights of casual observation and metatheoretical contrivances.

And at the same time, *other* trees and *other* sediments might suggest further support for hegemonic strivings: for one thing, the rather clear evidence that China was undoubtedly emerging as a new center of the Pacific Rim. For the first time in 40 years, since the intense offshore island crises of the mid-1950s during the first full decade of the Cold War, the United States and China engaged in a traditional standoff in the spring of 1996—the issue revolving around the persistent question of the status of the island of Taiwan—and again three years later when Taiwan made a startling announcement inferring its existence as an independent country, almost as if to say, "Territory lives!" Concern was also growing that arms races could break out among and between several nations in the region. Even broader potential tension-points became popular in one controversial analysis that—for all the criticism of its underlying assumptions—certainly rose above the stale Cold War structural analysis (Huntington, 1994).

Few in the current debates admit that the picture of the contemporary "world" is truly up for grabs; the extensive empirical studies that might allow some detached evaluation concerning these assessments have not been done. However, a central bedeviling problem with contentions concerning the "death of realism" and power politics is that much of it is posited on the perceived "emergence" of cooperation in the contemporary system. While that conventional perception might seem accurate based on casual observation, the empirical studies have not been produced confirming that belief. In fact, the few comparative systematic analyses that do exist suggest that cooperation has always been a component of the international system, and a major one. Latter-day breakthroughs suggesting the "emergence" of cooperation are not unearthing anything especially new; it is more likely the case that agreement now exists that the cooperative component of international behavior as opposed to the conflictual is as deserving of attention. This may reflect nothing more than a shift in focus as opposed to a change in the underlying objective reality.

But perhaps that is part of what happens in "placid" times.[22] Territoriality, viewed as a divisive component in international politics, is called into question as an enduring entity. Sediments become the particles in the move toward the internationalization of authority. "Because the great powers of the future will be nonunitary actors focusing primarily on maximizing their wealth," then "the major powers will gravitate toward one set of shared norms—namely, economic liberalism and political democracy," which will then result in the avoidance of military means to settle disputes, and while conflicts among the great powers will still be common, "they will be played out in boardrooms and courtrooms, not on battlefields or in command and control centers." In this world, rather than balancing, "core states are seeking to bandwagon, not around a power pole but around a shared set of liberal beliefs, institutions, and practices" (Goldgeier and McFaul, 1992: 468–469, 480).

The fate of the alleged enduring major powers in a nonrealist world can be worked out very well in speculative ventures; the conclusions derived from these speculations, however, depend on either a nonhegemonic or newly fashioned hegemonic world without the traditional implications of hegemony. Such altered states, however, could very well be resting on relatively short-term and selected observations of system change.

The Lust for Paradigm Shifts

Pictures drawn recently are indeed ones of relatively "placid" times. Contemporary attitudes reflect a variety of factors, not the least of which would appear to be a generational rotation represented by the "neoidealist" belief. That is, to steal a not particularly innovative page from the postmodernist's playbook, attitudes toward and evaluation of contending paradigms cannot be considered apart from the context in which those attitudes have developed. "Liberal beliefs, institutions, and practices" are the order of the day, we are told. "A war between great powers simply would be impossible to wage today" (Goldgeier and McFaul, 1992: 482). Much of what the "consumer" views in contemporary international behavior appears to support these contentions. Paradigm shifts can be a funny business, though. Unfortunately, they sometimes lack "historical perspective." In the late 1960s, a conference debated the question, "Is the Business Cycle Obsolete?"; the unbroken expansion of the 1960s had convinced many that the answer was "Yes." By the time the conference proceedings were published in 1969, the United States was already moving into a mild recession, a prelude to a larger one in 1974.

> A myopic view of the past had convinced many that the economic system had changed. The mistakes of those economists should be heeded by political analysts when trying to analyze the meaning of the contemporary structure of the international system (Sullivan, 1978a: 98).

Whether those words have relevance to contemporary economic and political systems 20 years later is of course the center of much dispute. Certainly the contention of the irrelevance of business cycles has itself been recycled (Weber, 1997), and one need only recall the growing mantra that had developed in the 1980s and early 1990s concerning the "Asian miracle"—the seemingly endless upward thrust of key Asian economies. Applied first mostly to Japan in the 1960s and 1970s, as time went on the perception of Asian "powerhouses" spread to include Thailand, South Korea, Formosa, Indonesia, and even Malaysia. The crash of the Japanese stock market and then economy beginning just after 1990 modified those views, but they held steady through at least mid-1997 for the remainder of the Asian economies. At that point the financial crises noted in Chapter Eight began to loom, and by early 1998, with the succession of financial meltdowns careening throughout Asia, the optimistic and widely held views of only six months earlier had been dashed.[23] It might be noted also that the long bull stock market in the United States, which had begun—depending on how one counts these things—either in 1974 or 1982, had, as with the business observers of the 1960s, begun to effect perceptions of the entire system. Talk of a "new paradigm" emerged that was to explain the continuously expanding American economy and the concomitant burgeoning American stock market; old ideas and paradigms didn't seem to work anymore (Norris, 1995). It was to be a concept—"new paradigm"—cited many times over the next several years.[24]

For international politics, the same issue applies: is this truly a "new era"? Is it really "different" this time, demanding "new paradigms?" What exactly would "different"

mean in this context? Much casual evidence from the international political arena supports that supposition, although to date there is a dearth of well-defined systematic evidence—and the "cooperation" that seems to be present in current "regime-think" does
not quite seem sufficient for proof. Nonetheless, paradigm shifts are popular, in the political as well as in the fields of investment and economics. Attitude changes at the domestic level coincident with both attitude and possibly structural changes at the
international level do occur and are enticing; whether at the microlevel or macrolevel the
sediments indicative of that "neoidealistic moment" are enduring is of course the central question.

Still a consistent theme has been the shift to a new neoidealism or neoliberal institutionalism. Another has been from structure back to agency, and within that context we
find the coupling of some very strange bedfellows. The call for "agency" takes implicitly
as a departure the contention that focusing on structure diminishes "agency"; critiques
of traditional realism focus on the *blind* "lusts for power," just as critiques of structural
realism focus on the billiard ball assumptions of neorealist models: both reduce the role
of individualized agency. And yet:

> [one] interpretation of classical realism acknowledges that meaning is contingent and so-
> cially constructed, and further, acknowledges historical variability. While, of course, no
> mention is made within Morgenthau's work of gender, such an account creates a space for
> the analysis of gender and IR . . . [It] . . . suggests . . . how those meanings are constructed
> depends upon the activities and struggles of individuals and collectivities acting within par-
> ticular historical conjunctures . . . In other words . . . Morgenthau's realism recognizes
> agency . . . (Whitworth, 1994: 44).

Likewise, while agency implies purpose and meaning, "long cycles" would seem to
populate the opposite end of that spectrum. Yet, an intriguing twist to the question of
power and hegemony rests on the concept of leadership, in this case "global leadership,"
but which ultimately implies agency:

> "Global leadership" is a fairly new concept in the literature of world politics . . . where, for
> the past generation, "power" in its various forms has held centre stage. We do not ignore
> "power" (and seapower in particular) but we do believe that a more rounded view of poli-
> tics must also consider "purpose" and "meaning." Definitions, explanations and justifica-
> tions of goals, motives and objectives, all general statements of policy, belong equally with
> "power" in the study of world politics. The analysis of leadership accomplishes this func-
> tion nicely, allowing us to translate past experience into lessons for the future (Modelski
> and Modelski, 1988: 2).

The picture does indeed become confusing. This chapter began with notions of old
and new "truisms," all of which require their own paradigms or paradigm-sets. Some
new truisms revolve around the multiple requiems for realism:

> International relations among the developed democracies has taken on many of the char-
> acteristics of the relationships in domestic societies. An increasing number of states has
> begun to acknowledge the necessity of regulating their political and economic intercourse
> through rules, norms, and agreements. As in domestic relations, this high degree of com-
> pliance is motivated by enlightened self-interest (Lebow, 1994: 277).

And yet the empirical realities may not be completely clear:

It may be that the community of developed nations will become more peaceful and generate structures that encourage peaceful behavior. It is also possible that unforeseen developments could bring about a return to a self-help system and the kind of behavior identified
with realism. *Only time will tell* (Lebow, 1994: 277; emphasis added).

"Only time will tell" suggests that prognostications concerning behavior-shifts based on
presumed paradigm-shifts are about as reliable as the evening newscast, from whence the
admonition comes. Predictions are difficult to make because the factors involved belong
to the disputed paradigms, and the isolation and assessment of how many states and actors are actually engaging in these allegedly new behaviors, to what extent they are doing
so, or what the "unforeseen developments" might be which would sidetrack the predictions produced by the new truisms has not been carried out. More disturbing, however,
are those suggestions that the intractability lies not with the objective problems most
people view in the world, but rather with those constructing models of international
politics at variance with the newly recognized "truths." Truths require believers, which
then implies nonbelievers, and the nonbelievers become the problem:

> Contemporary realists remain committed to the goal of peace but find it difficult to accept
> that the postwar behavior of the great powers has belied their unduly pessimistic assump-
> tions about the consequences of anarchy. Ironically, their theories and some of the policy
> recommendations based on them may now stand in the way of the better world we all seek
> (Lebow, 1994: 277).[25]

These calls are not new. A quarter century ago, a modern "global" textbook (Sterling, 1974) called for many changes and proposed prescriptions for the international
system; one such proposal was for general economic "redistribution," with the underlying hypothesis being: "Without such a redistribution there can be no hope for a viable (a reasonably peaceful) world society" (Sterling, 1974: 15). But, it was later
noted, "redistribution may *not* create a more stable world than the present one," primarily because the empirical reality of that assertion was still untested (Sullivan, 1990:
14–15). A contemporary review of the text made the same point more broadly: the
author "describe[s] the problems that he thinks must be solved and then assign[s] to
nations the duty of adopting the perspective and values that would lead some of them
to act for the sake of humanity" (Waltz, 1976: 297).

All of this might constitute little more than yet another historical footnote, except
that a quarter century later a similar theme emerges:

> many would argue that, rather than continuity, the mounting problems facing the world
> call for global solutions requiring extensive global cooperation, a significant break with past
> practices (Barkdull, 1995: 669).

The players assigned the task of solving these problems are once again the nation-states,
for such problems facing the world "might require fundamental political reorganization—
perhaps even the formation of a world government" (Barkdull, 1995: 669), and those
standing in the way with certain views—such as neorealism or anarchy—are singled out
because within these views

> any political response that requires institutional transformation or close cooperation
> among competing states is unlikely and probably impossible to achieve. Rather, the anar-

chic structure of international politics promises to perpetuate the self-regarding pursuit of power by sovereign nation-states (Barkdull, 1995: 669).

In a traditional sense, so far so good: competing models including one assuming an "anarchic structure" involving the "pursuit of power," and a second that calls for global solutions, possibly a world government. But the disturbing conclusion is to suggest that the issue is not one of assessing whether one model is wrong, but to assert that

> If ideas affect political action, then the view that Waltz forwards is distinctly disempowering to those who urge institutional change to deal with worsening global problems. (Barkdull, 1995: 669).

Thus "Waltz's views have policy implications that cause displeasure and even distress in a variety of intellectual constituencies most directly concerned with those policy issues" (Barkdull, 1995: 669, citing Ruggie, 1986: 141).

Disempowerment does not come from an academic scribbler, and it is not at all clear *what* the solutions might be to contemporary problems. As the arguments unfold in this way, however, they recycle to the "if only" assertions of many years ago (Sullivan, 1976: 329). It might be well to recall that "research guided by a paradigm resembles puzzle solving" and that "puzzles must have assured solutions, but the solutions need not be intrinsically important" (Lijphart, 1974: 55) To cite Thomas Kuhn of almost four decades ago,

> On the contrary, the really pressing problems, e.g., a cure for cancer or the design of a lasting peace, are often not puzzles at all, largely because they may not have any solution (Kuhn, 1962: 36–37).

Traditional realism, balance of power, collective security, and   more recently—neoliberal institutionalism or regimes may have been seen as solutions to problems that in fact did not have "solutions," perhaps one of the forgotten reasons why young scholars by the 1960s had instituted behavioral and quantitative research: to move away from analysis of unanswerable questions toward "problem solving," an approach denigrated in more recent years (Cox, 1996: 127–128) for a variety of well-intentioned but often inaccurate reasons.

To return to the "if only" syndrome, "theories" such as collective security were predicated on the assumption that "peace" was something attainable, an end, with only the details needing to be worked out, the specific "methods" or "techniques" isolated or the "right" people convinced of the "right" ideas: in other words, "if only":

> Each one of these schemes . . . contains a series of "if only" propositions: "if only" states would act in a certain way; "if only" the great powers would band together; "if only" those allied would abide by their agreement; "if only" large powers would not sell arms to small powers (Sullivan, 1976: 329).

Truisms in recent proposals suffer the same malady but are not always recognized because of the self-label of "new" paradigm; the theoretical components and interrelationships that should shed light on the conditions that make certain "ifs" more or less likely than other "ifs" are often absent or poorly delineated. To the extent that difficult task remains unaccomplished, then any proposed new paradigms still rely on the "if onlys":

Our argument rests heavily on the belief that the trend among the great powers is toward economic liberalism and political democracy and that these two factors are the key to a change in great power politics. *If* any of the current or potential great powers reverts from democracy to authoritarianism or *if* a nondemocratic nation becomes a great power, our argument will be considerably weakened (Goldgeier and McFaul, 1992: 488; emphases added).

As we noted already, assertions about the community of "developed nations" producing structures that will generate peaceful outcomes rest on the assumption that "unforeseen developments" will not occur, for if the latter were to happen it might presage a "return to a self-help system and the kind of behavior identified with realism" (Lebow, 1994: 277). Just as real-world decision-making rarely corresponds to the dictates of the mythical rational process model, so also schemes for peace tend not to work, and "it is not the scholar's role to lament that fact but to find out why, which means solving 'puzzles'" (Sullivan, 1976: 329). But solving puzzles—that is, problem-solving—has come to be associated with structural endeavors, and both have taken a flogging; few have attacked neorealists' motives, which are normally those of most analysts ("committed to the goal of peace"), but their theories and models have been viewed as the problems (Lebow, 1994: 277; Wendt, 1995: 80). It appears now that "if only" the realists would relent, recant, or quit, the world could move on. Critical theorists see this occurring through "alternative orders which are feasible transformations of the existing world" (Cox, 1996: 128), which would consist of a "coalition of opposition . . . built at local and national levels among groups that are aware of their day-to-day coexistence and are prepared to work to overcome what keeps them apart"; moreover, these "organic intellectuals of the countertendency" will construct their alternative order that "goes beyond the strictly economic to include the political foundations of world order" (Cox, 1997: 170)—in short, toward the goal of peace, justice, and ultimately a better world.

Such views might be prosaic but are also commanding; "solving puzzles" might fit the first description but probably not the second, and yet that does not necessarily imply that solving puzzles is in any way inconsistent with a desire for a "better world." But knowing what the appropriate "puzzles"—or questions—might be involves to some degree the zone of contention, namely, the politics. Critical theorists—and other utopians—see a "bad" world as the problem and a "better" world as the solution. But a "bad," "unequal," or "unjust" world is in effect a "dependent variable," and just as we have noted that confusion reigns over the appropriate outcome variables in specific problem-solving venues, so also much confusion exists in broader normative or utopian settings.[26] One exercise some time ago that related the variety and range of behavioral categories to competing extant theories in the "problem-solving" domain endeavored to ascertain which theoretical approaches had been more successfully applied to specific puzzles, using the "outcome" or dependent variable as the criterion (Sullivan, 1976: 333). The underlying assumption—so simple that it was not felt necessary to dwell on it—is rather basic: no one theoretical approach, or level, or set of interrelated or even roughly similar hypotheses are going to be able to explain a broad range—let alone all—of international behavior. But this simple idea tends to be the forgotten element; the growing debates pitting neorealism against the democratic peace, for instance, imply that the two sides are talking about the same phenomenon, when in fact most structural, neorealist analyses are usually considered to be relevant only to the broadest "outcome" variables, whereas the preponderance of empirically

oriented "democratic peace" analyses exemplify the opposite extreme: very well-speci-
fied but usually narrowly construed dependent variables. Implications drawn from the
latter are often taken well beyond the actual empirical domain accounted for. While the
unabashedly three-image Waltzian construction (Sullivan, 1976) certainly can be criticized for having slighted certain phenomena or behavior (Caporaso, 1997: 565–566),
the important point remains valid, namely, that "international relations" consists of a
broad range of behavior occurring at a variety of levels such that no one of the three
traditional images in a gross sense could be expected to explain all of international behavior. But this central point receives further confirmation if one admits that these
three are not necessarily the only metatheoretical perspectives fruitfully utilized. Per-
sisting in loosely defining, characterizing, and measuring the outcome variable—as is
true of gross structural analyses as well as critical theory—has one definite upside: in
the end everyone can be "right," and "the chameleon lives!"

But international relations is not *one* thing (i.e., *one* hegemonic world), and multiple
manifestations are quite obviously accountable only by a variety of theoretical approaches at very different levels of analysis. The ever-popular fashion of trashing an entire paradigm—realism and neorealism have been the targets of choice in recent
years—because an independent variable contained in what is momentarily cast as a competing paradigm can explain, for instance, the level of warlike behavior during a specified, perhaps short, period of time[27] is not only elementary, but can be misleading
and—because it is relatively easy to do—perpetuates the phenomenon of "paradigm-
bashing." In a sense, even imposing the three-level Waltzian paradigm (Sullivan, 1976:
333–336) was an operational bid to put some specification into the later, and loosely defined, "agent-structure" debate, to go beyond the vague generalities to specify *exactly
where* in the behavioral realm "agency"—as opposed to "structure"—appeared to have
been more successfully applied. In some ways, despite sophisticated advances in terminology and conceptualization, certain elements of continuing debates have not moved
far from somewhat similar ground that had been staked out more than two decades ago.
But talk of paradigm "shifts" is inherently attractive, and perhaps resorted to out of frustration with the continuing intractability of world problems.

"Relevance," Policy, and Critical Theory

During the waning years of the Vietnam War, a vexing concern for many was the perceived lack of "policy relevance" of international relations research. While a considerable
portion of the criticism at the time was directed at the growing reliance on quantitative
analysis, it was suggested that these critiques could be easily broadened to other, more
traditional pursuits and methodologies (Sullivan, 1973). Nonetheless, the accumulated
genre comprised in some ways a more particular although less theoretically interesting
harbinger to the later "critical theory" movement. Both derived from the same underpinning—a desire for a better world. But everyone wants a better world, and those who
responded to those early critiques certainly had that in mind.[28] Recent criticisms of
"problem solving"—criticisms implying ready acceptance of the abiding system and
therefore manifesting a conservative orientation—has allowed critical theorists to seize
the moral high ground. But to propose meaningful policy it helps to know how things
work, and that is what "problem solving" is all about. The puzzles may not be solved
very well, nor may policy recommendations flow easily from such problem-solving
work, but that does not mean that the puzzles or problems are unimportant or that one

could avoid solving them by engaging in utopian thinking, regardless of how well-"constrained" such thinking may be "by its comprehension of historical processes" (Cox, 1996: 128).

Once one attempts advice on how to change the system, however, the real world intrudes. Bipolar systems appear to be less conflictual and more stable, but that is advice many people do not want to hear. Outside the stability domain, worldwide environmental degradation received considerable attention long before the "greenhouse" issue became so prominent. Concrete issues could include which actors pollute most, which actors abide antipollution treaties more frequently, or whether their observance is higher at certain times rather than at other times, or whether pollution system-wide is likely to be higher at certain times than at others. (Sullivan, 1976: 339). Large, developed states are logically going to be the biggest polluters, and perhaps low concentration system-wide (equal power distribution) might result in more active development, which would result in greater worldwide pollution. Stable, highly concentrated systems may be less likely to produce uncertainty, and states might be less likely to move so vigorously into the different pollution-producing phases of development (Sullivan, 1976: 339).

In a contemporary era that some view as multipolar and nonhegemonic, and others as characterized by a growing U.S. hegemony, is there any sense that behavior now is different on this policy issue? Is it accurate to suggest that environmental concerns no longer serve as the moral anchor they once did? The Rio and Kyoto Conferences of 1992 and 1996 garnered much attention, interest has continued, and evidence suggests that the longer-term rise in an environmental "regime" continues unabated but not in a uniform linear fashion (Meyer et al., 1997).[29] Yet by December 1996 agreement was not reached in Kyoto nor four years later in the Hague, Netherlands, primarily because of the United States' restrictive position. Perhaps high uncertainty—for example, a shift either to multipolarity or return to hegemony from bipolarity—equates to less agreement with and adherence to antipollution statutes. If in fact it is more accurate to depict the United States as an emerging hegemon, then certainly a very rudimentary realist proposition would be consistent with the United States' "hegemonic" behavior both at Kyoto and at the Hague. Yet others have even suggested the inapplicability of general theory in this domain:

> despite a long history of international environmental regimes and increasing concern for the environment, theory in this issue area remains ill formed and has been of little help to policymakers . . . the unique character of international environmental issues demands theory developed specifically for this issue area rather than theory adapted from international relations metatheory (Harrison, 1996: 145).

Whether focused on realist concerns for stability or the more restricted domain of environmental policy, the relationship between knowledge, power, and policy is much more complex than merely "wanting a better world"; the assertions could be made about the entire panoply of developmental or "equality" issues that paralleled the development of dependency and world system analysis—as well as the more traditional war-and-peace sphere. But it is imperative to remember that policy "often needs to be formed in advance of evidence, [and] there is uncertainty about causes and effects and about distributional outcomes" (Harrison, 1996: 148)—which is to say that one can make policy on inadequate theory and expect negative outcomes. But if one insists on going beyond the theory-policy link—

> The logic of the global commons and the problems of equity and justice that undergird most analyses of sustainable development . . . demand a reexamination of the moral foundations of international policy (Harrison, 1996: 148)

—then we cannot expect necessarily much assistance concerning the operations of the political processes revolving around development, equity, environment, or pollution, let alone traditional stability issues. Truly solving such issues requires an operational format.

A policy-related conceptual domain with less immediate history than others because of its fluctuating fortunes is the issue of implications flowing from the "democratic peace" sphere; its status at late-century is far different from the evaluation conferred upon it during the latter part of the Vietnam War years—the period of most heightened interest in "relevance" in international relations research. But within the context of the complex relationship between knowledge, power, and policy, it is instructive to keep that Vietnam experience in mind in surveying the present situation, for the "democratic peace" has become a central tenet of the "new" liberalism, or whatever catchword describes the current mainstream thinking. Few seem to question the worthiness of pursuing the "democratic peace," cast by some as so tenuous in existence that it must be "grasped" (Russett, 1993) lest time run out, implying a sense of urgency that during the last decade of the twentieth century a window of opportunity had opened up for those interested in the normative outcomes to be accrued from a central hypothesis subjected to ridicule a generation earlier.

Policy advice, relevance, and critical theory can take odd turns, however. It would be wise to remember that it was this very slogan—"democracy"—that, packaged with others, constituted part of the rallying cry for which the United States entered the Vietnam debacle in the 1960s in the first place, an involvement that continued for a long 12 years. Untold scores of statements to that effect reside in the presidential documents on Vietnam, especially during the crucial years of the mid-1960s. Try as latter-day liberals might to dispel the notion that symbols—including "democracy"—did not play a role, that it was not believed, or that it can be either forgotten as an odd historical fact, explained away as mere political "rhetoric," or viewed as a legacy of the pre-"new liberal" days of the present, the point is that it represented—with a bundle of analogous symbols—a key rhetorical pretense and basis *for* the continuing American involvement. More to the point with respect to recent theoretical orientations, it served as a key "construction" or "idea" at the time for policy-makers, despite the fact that ironically it was grist for so much ridicule among the liberal cognoscenti. Those who recall that era can be forgiven a bit of uneasiness when the link is drawn today between actual policy actions such as foreign aid, and especially military aid, to those countries showing advances in "democracy." That proverbial slippery slope, which numerous decision-makers found so attractive in the 1950s and 1960s, has not been banished from real-world decision-making despite the many rational calculi that academics imbue decisions with, and human processes operate just as habitually as in the past.

Current popular policy nostrums—the "democratic peace" is only one—do have parallels in issues that involved America in foreign nations, such as Vietnam, almost a half century ago. Then it was called "nation-building" as well as "freedom and democracy," but the idea was the same. Many failed policies were proposed to achieve those ends—and they were believed as intensely then as are beliefs now in current ideas. More evidence may exist now favoring certain policies, although much remains contested, and one would be legitimately concerned if the rush to "grasp" the democratic peace resulted in unwise interventions; certainly evidence reviewed in Chapter Four suggests clearly that democratic countries are not the least bit averse to engaging in interventionist activities. And it would not ease matters if we were to hear that such interventions in the contemporary era—unlike the "bad" interventions of the Cold War era—rather represent "good" interventions of the new, post–Cold War neoliberal world. Contemporary crusades and interventions always appear much more attractive than previous ones, which have undergone the harsh scrutiny of history and been undertaken—with the hindsight of that historical analysis—under what appears to be the guise of outmoded slogans.

Other linchpins of very current policy-making, with linkages to theory that have not yet been fully grounded, revolve not around "beginnings" but rather the "endings" of two pivotal phenomena that opened this book—Cold Wars and hegemonies. For the former, the pervading sense of the Cold War having ended implies that most everything associated with it can now be discarded, appearing almost passé, and that it is time to get on with the obvious profusion of cooperation to be expected in the post–Cold War world. Such a major jettisoning project would also encompass any theoretical or policy formulations either seemingly inextricably linked to the Cold War or that, with hindsight, were unable to "predict" its demise. More significant meaningful questions about exactly what it was that "ended" between 1989 and 1991 or whether that "ending" had not in fact been in the process of unfolding for some time have been almost completely ignored. It is not at all clear, however, that the complex of international political behavior cloaked in phenomena associated with the Cold War can so easily be discarded with its seemingly sudden and abrupt "end," a hopelessly simplistic appraisal of extremely complex processes. It would therefore also be judicious to temporize any policy implications drawn from ending processes that may not be well understood.

But implications so instantaneously drawn from end-of-the-Cold-War analyses are analogous in many ways to end-of-the-state contentions; both are theoretically tethered as well as linked with respect to policy implications. In addition to its seductive attraction, the end-of-the-state proposition displays an orderliness to it that is as unlikely in the real world as the presumed orderliness of the "beginnings" of the state and associated sovereignty, "Westphalia and All That": the widely accepted popular and conventional view of both phenomena doesn't really match the historical complexities and irregular development and change that actually went on concerning a very complex idea and process. Contrary to the notion that once upon a time sovereignty emerged and immediately rearranged politics into a new system, in reality the development and emergence was a long-term, complex process not marked indelibly as having occurred at any one point in time:

> Westphalia was not a beginning or an end. Sovereign practices had existed hundreds of years before 1648 and medieval practices continued for hundreds of years after. The actual content of sovereignty and the principle of exclusive control have been, and continue to be, challenged (Krasner, 1993: 264).

Likewise in the contemporary era, the end of the Cold War and the emergence of the new world order and globalization will certainly not turn out with hindsight as being nearly the clearly established turning points confined to the very short three-year period of 1989–1991 as has become accepted orthodoxy; implications drawn from what may well turn out to be such an unreliable benchmark are certainly to be defective, and any rush to develop "new" theory based on these alleged transformations may prove presumptuous. We await a future revisionist's analysis entitled, "The New World Order and All That." The story has not ended, the actual historical reality is much more complex than conventional wisdom suggests, and detached theoretical analyses have yet to be constructed: "policy implications" drawn from observations possessing such defects should be suspect.

Corresponding assertions need to be noted concerning the other major transformation beloved by those wishing to draw policy implications from observations of contemporary events: the fate of the concept, meaning, and reality of "hegemony," all three greatly contested elements. The definitive works signifying either whether American hegemony, apparently along with the Cold War, has ended, or whether that hegemony has reemerged, have yet to be done. It is ironic, however, that just as one can often unearth components of realism in works arguing for "newer" approaches to international relations, so also do considerations questioning the continued existence of "hegemonies" in the contemporary international system often seem to evoke the very concepts contested. The opposite of hegemony might be an international "society," exemplified in one analysis by the Gulf War, in which the structural position of this society could be described using a series of concentric circles wherein "In the center circle stood the United States, which was willing to lead only if followed and to fight only if given a wide support and assistance." In the other circles are the other nations in respective positions, with the sixth circle being those prepared to oppose the action (Buzan, 1993: 349–350). From this it is hypothesized that

> If international society is understood in these terms, it is clearly more than a regime. It might be seen as a regime of regimes, adding a useful element of holism to the excessively atomized world of regime theory (Buzan, 1993: 350).

Such a meta-regime—a "regime of regimes"—does not replicate but does seem dreadfully akin to what traditionally has been called a unipolar system or hegemony rather than an entirely new breed. More importantly, however, the implications for such alleged changes are drawn from events occurring during only a very short-term time frame.[30]

Findings on the effects of system structure on cooperation and conflict are in some instances—as we have seen in earlier chapters—on adequately solid empirical grounds, but those concerning hegemony were not nearly as supportive of general theoretical trends as other structural views. Thus implications drawn from any claimed "end" of hegemony would be very much disputed. Widespread empirical evidence concerning what happens after specific types of transformations in the international system occur does not exist and, as alluded to at several points, bringing in the effect of time lags complicates these relationships. Simply put, the empirical parameters of system transformation is a "problem" not yet resolved.

Conclusion

The new "truisms" that drive much recent thinking are multiple, but can be encapsulated in several major components. More cooperation is now said to exist in international politics in the "post"–Cold War era; relations among democracies are taking on many of the characteristics of relationships in domestic societies, with more rules, norms, and agreements—cooperation—than in the past; this increased cooperation spills over and combines with "markets" to produce "globalization"; and all of this blends with changes in and views toward hegemony.

As gratifying as such a picture might be, the unanswered question is whether systematic evidence can be brought to bear on these conclusions. It is this area where the drudgery has only begun, establishing the types of questions to be answered in a problem-solving mode, and producing the evidence that could confirm or deny these trends. Anecdotal evidence exists in certain dimensions, but differs across respective domains. One thinks, for instance, of the multiple case studies on "regime" behavior and the continuing outpouring of basic research on issues of the "democratic peace." Common to both, in contrast to more traditional views and designs, is the focus on the *cooperative* rather than the *conflictual* component, and almost regardless of the underlying empirical veracity, the pervasiveness of cooperation in a sense becomes one of the new myths. It is well to remember in this regard that democracies exhibited just as little conflictual behavior toward each other compared to other types of political systems in previous decades as they do in the 1980s and 1990s—as several studies indicated at the time—but the difference is that it is now *recognized* as such; it was not a truth ripe for an earlier era.

For all the territoriality, paradigm shifts, "quests" for general theories, as well as emerging mountains of replicable evidence, in the real world the myths or organizing devices we use to look at the world change, and they do so for sometimes strange and unfathomable reasons. "Regimes"—to use only one widespread example—has now become part of an agreed-upon organizing device. In some ways the "Cold War" can also be considered as having been a convenient organizing "construct." Not that something that can be described as the Cold War didn't occur, but debate still revolves around its beginnings as well as the processes and stages describing its history. But the myth—or perhaps accepted "construct"—about its "ending," surprisingly, has been readily accepted, and in some ways once again the empirical accuracy of that assertion is beside the point, for it has now been agreed upon, conveniently at a time when certain paradigms—realism is usually the target—can be castigated for not having predicted it and when cooperation seems to have flowered.

The minefield of IR theory remains perilous and tenacious (M. Elman, 1999: 102–103), although "beginnings and endings" seem to provide for some a clear criterion for success or failure—"hits and misses." One clear predicament, however, in gauging successful or unsuccessful theoretical formulations is the very real chameleon factor—the bedeviling ambiguity and transforming character of the dependent variable from one analysis to another. The behaviors of interest in recent times have certainly changed the image or picture of international relations. The analysis of the beginnings and endings of cold wars and hegemonies, and the roles of democracies, markets, and market processes all attest to such changed perceptions of the behavior to be studied. Certainly all four substantive areas would seem to be the pivotal areas around which much theoretical work and empirical investigation will be revolving into the next several decades.

Notes

Chapter One

1. See *International Organization* 48 (spring 1994), later expanded in Lebow and Risse-Kappen (1995).
2. Roger Masters has written: "Few periods in world history have seemed to encompass such extensive and rapid change as the twentieth century. The pace of events has been staggering." Masters penned those words over a generation ago, at the very height of the Cold War (Masters, 1967: 253).
3. See Sullivan (1976: 301–325). Two decades later the same conclusion holds: "Realism is compelling for the right reason—power is *a* crucial determinant of political behavior; but it is also false because power is not the *only* determinant" (Fozouni, 1995: 507).
4. See Sullivan (1976: 327–342) for a primitive attempt. The symposium referred to in note no.1 recognized this from the explanatory side of the equation, yet failed to establish explicitly the *various, multiple* dependent variables that all could represent the "end of the Cold War."
5. Bueno de Mesquita claims that the outcome of the Cold War as an "emergent property" had antecedents as early as 1948, and in that narrow sense was "predictable" at a relatively early stage (Bueno de Mesquita, 1998: 153–154).
6. The five general conditions suggested as possibilities for anticipation of the Cold War's end (Gaddis, 1992/93: 18) are all only rough approximations of an "outcome" variable, or what would have satisfied "predicting" an outcome. Much dispute could be generated concerning what empirical values would be given to these five conditions a decade after the "end" of the Cold War—which would then question whether any predictor variable might have produced a false positive prediction.
7. Peters (1992: 3B); the book was Tom Peters, *In Search of Excellence* (1982).
8. See note no. 6.
9. Exceptions are widespread and one good example of carefully delineated dependent variables and linkages is contained in Frieden (1994).
10. Feminist theorists propose an interesting reorientation of the dependent variable of security, but one that may not necessarily require augmentation of the key independent variables, despite the attractiveness of the new definition for its social significance (Tickner, 1997: 624–626).
11. A tortuous logic arrives at the same conclusion concerning realist theory, which, it is argued, "'explains' a comparatively small number of the behavioral patterns in international politics" (Fozouni, 1995: 505).
12. When Wendt (1992) concluded in his famous phrase, "Anarchy is what states make of it," he obviously was thinking along the lines of this entire argument, in which states could hypothetically come to the conclusion that anarchy need not exist *even in a supposed "state of anarchy."*
13. See Rosenau (1967) for elaboration on this very issue more than a generation ago.

14. Others arrive at the same conclusion ("the notion of anarchy has little if any substantive significance distinctively related to international politics") by more formal means (Powell, 1993: 115).

15. This turns out to be good advice in many realms; former United States Attorney General John Mitchell, in justifying governmental practices during the Nixon administration, once said: "Watch what we do and not what we say." In that case, as many wags later pointed out, they were watched and ultimately received the boot.

16. This analysis has not gone unchallenged; see Hall and Kratochwil's critique (1993) and Fischer's response (1993).

17. To illustrate, see Mansbach and Vasquez (1981: 68–83) and Reus-Smit (1997: 563f.)

18. We have not belabored the multiple definitions of theory. The issue is contentious (see note no. 19) and means different things to different people, an assertion repeatedly demonstrated in the following pages. One definition—"an intellectual construct that helps one to select facts and interpret them in such a way as to facilitate explanation and prediction concerning regularities and recurrences or repetitions of observed phenomena" (Viotti and Kauppi, 1999: 3)—is as workable as most.

19. Some perhaps take it too far, exemplified by the title of one conference paper: "Forget IR Theory" (ISA *Newsletter* [December 1995] 52).

20. Against the backdrop of a failed Vietnam policy by the late 1960s, "it was not coincidental that theorizing about foreign-policy decision-making . . . moved increasingly away from reliance upon the rational model" (Ferguson and Mansbach, 1988: 149).

21. The phrase is adapted from a subheading in Chapter Three, which in turn is taken from Trudeau (1973).

Chapter Two

1. Specific titles demonstrate the underlying approach: Lasswell's *World Politics and Personal Insecurity,* Strachey's *Unconscious Motives of War,* and Kelman's *International Behavior: A Social-Psychological Analysis,* are examples.

2. Parts of the following draw on Sullivan (1976: 34–40).

3. And, it is to be noted, this is as far—"consistent with"—that certain personality-oriented analyses are willing to take their own evidence (Walker, 1995: 715).

4. Even an extensive analysis of Gorbachev as "uncommitted thinker" in the transformations of the 1980s veers away from attribution of specific personality characteristics, with only fleeting reference to the perceptual attribute discussed here—integrative complexity (J. Stein, 1994: 168–169, 173–175, 182).

5. These are labeled respectively cognitive consistency, schema theory, and attribution theory (Hybel, 1993: 5–6), but these are not mutually exclusive, and the labels and descriptions of them can be confused with labels used by others; see, for instance, Young and Shafer (1998).

6. For further critiques of White's images, see Levy (1983a: 78–80). Research on American perceptions during the Vietnam involvement reported elsewhere in this chapter failed to produce enough inter-coder reliability in using White's six categories to produce reliable data on those images.

7. Questions include "What is the essential nature of political life?" "How much control or mastery can one have?" "How are risks of political action calculated?" (Walker, 1977: 131; H. Starr, 1984: 44–73)

8. See Shimko (1991: 106 [table 7.2], 113).

9. "a simplistic, Manichean view of . . . the challenge of communism" and "a liberal faith in the value of education, reason, and communication as the means to overcome conflicts" (Shimko, 1991: 240–241).

10. Thus ultimately, "when old practices are discredited, ideas acquire greater importance" (Blum, 1993: 389).

11. The issue of meaningful change in belief systems has never been extensively developed, and original formulations hinted that changes that did occur—especially in Soviet "operational codes"—were more likely surface ones (George, 1969: 216–220).

12. With respect to the increase in I/C of Soviet leaders from late 1984 through late 1986 (the end-point of these data), "One possibility is that the current Soviet leadership is indeed genuinely interested in reversing the deterioration of American-Soviet relationships of the early 1980s, in placing limits on superpower competition, and in reaching mutually beneficial compromises on divisive issues" (Tetlock, 1988: 117).

13. This led to speculation that "this unpredicted and atypical finding reflects President Bush's growing confidence in the overwhelming military superiority of coalition forces and his certainty of victory when they went into action" (Wallace et al., 1993: 103).

14. See Sullivan (1976: 55) for a reanalysis that suggests some contradictions in the original analysis.

15. One detailed case study of decision-making in 1914, cast within a game theoretical formulation, concludes also that "misperceptions were the taproot of the war; any realistic program for peace would have required their elimination" (Van Evera, 1986: 116).

16. "Ideas" certainly counted in post–World War II reconstruction efforts, but the more important point is which individuals' ideas counted; it was in fact the British and Americans, for the latter "wanted to promote American interests, and they were willing to use the nation's power capabilities to do so" even though admittedly desiring to "promulgate a post-war system that would have a normative appeal to elites in other nations" (Ikenberry, 1993: 84).

17. "For every idea that appears to play a major role in politics, tens of thousands play no role at all . . . too often an argument about the role of ideas amounts to an assertion that an idea mattered without a persuasive explanation for why or how it had influence" (Garrett and Weingast, 1993: 203).

18. See Walker (1994: 168–169); Wendt (1994a: 1040).

19. Confusion about what behavior perceptions can explain is understandable with systemic dependent variables. Accounting for war by looking at perceptions illustrates these problems. The following conclusions are all proffered: "The analysis . . . supports the hypothesized effects of perceptions"; "variations in beliefs had a significant effect . . . across . . . periods of differing polarity"; and "differences in perceptions increase the likelihood that the situation will involve warfare" (Kim and Bueno de Mesquita, 1995: 62–63), despite the fact that no *concrete* measures of perceptions apparently exist in data constructed from systemic-level sources: "we have identified a formulation that allows *ex ante* predictions of how decision makers will behave in crisis situations based on their *apparent* perceptions of the circumstances they find themselves in" (Kim and Bueno de Mesquita, 1995: 63; emphasis added).

20. These I/C data end in the fourth quarter of 1986, and therefore any conclusions cannot be projected beyond that point.

21. We noted earlier (note no. 11) that the question of meaningful change in belief systems has never been extensively developed; see George (1969: 216–220).

Chapter Three

1. Charles Mohr, "McNamara on Record, Reluctantly, on Vietnam," *New York Times*, May 16, 1984, p. 10.

2. "For problems involving the risk of war, we assume that issues collapse to a single policy dimension having to do with the overall contribution of the putative policy to the welfare of the leadership's backers and opponents. This is broadly consistent with the realist notion that treats the state as a unitary actor" (Bueno de Mesquita and Siverson, 1995: 843). The authors claim to depart from the realist approach in that, despite the *process* allegedly involved, the decisions are *driven* by variables endogenous to the political system,

in contrast to a realist position, which sees systemic variables exogenous to the system as the operative ones.

3. The one major application, the U.S. response to North Korea's invasion of South Korea in 1950, illustrates the point: 68 percent of the 366-page manuscript focused on the historical conditions as well as a day-by-day account of specific decisions (Paige, 1968).

4. These include: illusion of invulnerability, inherent morality of the group, collective rationalization, stereotype of outgroups, self-censorship, illusion of unanimity, pressure on dissenters, and self-appointed mindguards (Janis, 1982: 244).

5. Not all findings overwhelmingly supported every component of groupthink; see Tetlock et al., 1992: 418.

6. The specific characteristics were: surveying alternatives and objectives, assessing costs and risks, information search, bias in processing information, rejecting original alternatives, and follow-up plans on the actual decisions made (Herek, Janis, and Huth, 1987: 204–205).

7. A half decade before the first introduction of similarity in military alliance commitments as a measure of "expected utilities," the same measure was employed for purposes of a structural analysis *without* inferences concerning "expected utilities" (Bueno de Mesquita, 1975).

8. See note no. 19, Chapter Two, and note no. 9 in this chapter for further elaboration.

9. Ultimately this is admitted: "High-quality data do not yet exist for the variables of greatest importance to a theory such as ours" (Bueno de Mesquita and Lalman, 1992: 270). For "utility," no measurement procedure simultaneously satisfied several criteria: "(1) ensures no dependence on hindsight; (2) requires no case by case, ad hoc judgments by researchers; (3) is fully replicable by any researcher; and (4) *is truly a measure of utility.*" The current measures of utilities "satisfy (1) through (3) and . . . *provide information we believe is highly correlated with (4)*" (Bueno de Mesquita and Lalman, 1992: 287; emphasis added). At the same time, ironically, "alliance formation may itself be part of an elaborate signaling game," and then "Alliance policies may not be an accurate reflection of preferences precisely because strategic actors realize that alliances may be seen as revelations of true preferences." Further qualifications concerning alliance similarities as indicators of interests, and their inability to indicate any leader's utility for a specific outcome are clearly spelled out (Bueno de Mesquita and Lalman, 1992: 221, 289, 294ff.). Others have focused on similar problems with such measures (Huth et al., 1993: 615). Further discussion of the problems, with elaboration and extension of the basic measure, is contained in Signorino and Ritter (1999: 140–141).

10. The title of this section is taken from Trudeau (1973).

11. Thirty years after America's first military moves in Vietnam, a 1991 movie *(JFK)* and 1992 book (Newman, 1992) rekindled the debates, the emotional issue of youthful opposition to the war in the 1960s reemerged in the presidential campaign of 1992, and in 1995—as noted earlier—the publication of Robert McNamara's memoirs of the Vietnam War years opened the wounds on early involvement once again.

12. Insisting on adherence to historical fact takes issue with recent "counterfactual" thinking (Tetlock and Belkin, 1996). Despite the sophistication of the developing methodology (Sylvan and Majeski, 1998), such provocative analysis also introduces troubling tendencies. Counterfactual scenarios can easily become equated with actual historical scenarios, and causal relations posited in the counterfactuals too easily attain equal status to those found in actual historical accounts based on factual history. It is ironic that in accounting for the American involvement in Vietnam, one could interpret hypothetical explorations actually undertaken by top American decision-makers as perfectly exemplifying counterfactual theorizing, theorizing that drove them in the early 1960s toward further escalatory operations in Vietnam as opposed to following different alternatives (Khong, 1996: 96–97, 116).

13. Portions of the following analysis draw from Sullivan (1976: 74–81; 1985: 51–85).

14. The respective positions are spelled out in Bostdorff and Goldzwig (1994: 530, n. 62), and much of the debate rests on what Kennedy "said" and what he actually "meant." The authors note that "public words can take on a life of their own and make policy reversals extremely difficult to undertake."

15. In this context, the assertion that counterfactual analysis suggests that "a harder-line policy could have been a winning one in November, 1961" (Sylvan and Majeski, 1998: 104) is hard to interpret because during the ensuing two years of the Kennedy presidency escalatory behavior did occur—although perhaps not to the extent that certain extreme hardliners would have liked.

16. Ironically, an "expected utility" analysis of the Persian Gulf crisis of 1990 predicted that the crisis could be resolved without conflict because the "analyst overstated peace despite clear model indications that war was probable" (Kugler et al., 1994: 113). In what is certainly the most blunt admission of subjective bias in modern social science, this resulted because "our judgment was clouded by a personal desire to see a peaceful resolution of the Gulf crisis . . . the main errors in this paper are ones of interpretation driven by the authors' desire for peace" (Kugler et al., 1994: 142).

17. Since the concern here is with the apparent disutility of the bureaucratic politics model, the alternative is not developed; for elaboration, see Rhodes (1994: 31–39).

18. All of which makes the strong reaction through the 1980s and 1990s, 20 years later, to Waltz's "neorealism"—with its apparent assumption of unitary actors—all the more amazing (Sullivan, 2000).

19. The authors do leave room for "arational" factors in perceptions to occur. "War can be stumbled into when one nation judges the intentions of a rival too optimistically. War can begin even with full information if it is motivated by a fear of ceding any advantage, however small, that is attached to the first use of force" (Bueno de Mesquita and Lalman, 1992: 250). But, to reiterate, none of the data utilized in expected utility approaches consist of tangible perceptions. While *mis*perceptions might enter into the decision-making equation in this caveat, they can in no way enter *the* equations of "expected utility" because these do not deal directly with the perceptual data referred to when talking about "expectations," the "judging intentions," perceptions or—by implication—misperceptions.

20. See Sullivan (1985: 13–25). Any historical work focused on a specific historical incident gives the impression that decision-makers were obsessed with that one policy issue; works focused exclusively on Vietnam (Newman, 1992) certainly demonstrate that. Since decision-makers have many items on their plate, concluding from such evidence that the same issue was "vitally important" to the decision-makers could be misleading.

21. Extensive critical comment has been levied against Newman's analysis earlier in this chapter, and Chomsky also utilizes it (1993) in a critical vein; this critical view of Newman is not universal (Sylvan and Majeski, 1998: 104).

22. David Halberstam, remembered for his effective reporting from Vietnam in the early 1960s, has come to represent those who critically analyzed American decisions in Vietnam. Halberstam himself, however, reflecting a "historical imperative," actually supported continuing activities in Vietnam in the mid-1960s (Sullivan, 1985: 185–186).

23. Although political scientists may have a professional *stake* in seeing rational processes in political decisions, economists have been more strongly associated with "rational choice," and it was in that field that a new decision-making trend for the hiring of young academic economists emerged in the early 1990s. Top economics departments vied for the three or four "top" new economics Ph.D.s and, if unsuccessful, were reportedly unwilling to go below that top tier, refraining from hiring until the next annual hiring cycle. The practice of focusing on one or two "hot shot" candidates was not necessarily well-received throughout the profession, prompting one economist to label such a market for new candidates "irrational" (Nasar, 1995: C4).

24. The words omitted in this quote are: "in the critical interval on the power cycle" (Doran, 1991: 197); we return to Doran's and others' views of the "power cycle" in Chapter Six.

Chapter Four

1. A view captured by Thomson: "This book's message for international relations specialists is that they would do well to abandon the notion that the state is the state is the state" (1994: 149).
2. "[T]he less people are inclined to venerate the state and rely on unqualified patriotism as solutions to their problems, the more will they favor bargaining and accommodation over shrill and nonnegotiable demands as ways of handling conflicts" (Rosenau, 1990: 434).
3. *Economist,* May 29, 1993, p. 13.
4. "Long ago and far away in graduate school, the first author of this piece remembers a graduate student actually laughing in ridicule at the . . . [democratic peace] argument when it was presented by another student" (Ward and Cohen, 1995: n. 6).
5. The two were the various editions of *World Handbook of Political and Social Indicators* edited by Bruce Russett and Charles Taylor, and R.J. Rummel, *Dimensions of Nations* (1972).
6. Russett found economic development, communism, intensive agriculture, size, and "Catholic Culture"; Rummel isolated economic development, size, Catholic culture, density, foreign conflict, and domestic conflict (Sullivan, 1976: 106).
7. Certain dimensions were not used either because they did not make clear theoretical sense (i.e., Catholic culture) or because the variables indexing those dimensions loaded highly on other dimensions.
8. A lengthy variety of further elaborations on this link can be drawn out; see Russett (1993: 40).
9. See Russett (1993: 35–36) for further enumeration of the elements of the "cultural" model.
10. We follow conventional practice in focusing on the highly quantified genre of empirical studies, slighting earlier research that confounded then-conventional wisdom. Specifically, Quincy Wright's investigation of traditional Leninist theories of imperialism found that capitalist countries tended to be *more* peaceful than socialist countries (Wright, 1964: 302, 305). Other designs investigated the nonconforming alliance behavior of France and China during the Cold War; France's more open system should possess constraints against sudden policy changes, while China's closed system should exhibit spillover because elites cross issue areas (Holsti and Sullivan, 1969). China's behavior was nonconforming across multiple issue areas; France's nonconforming behavior occurred only in the security area (Sullivan, 1976: 120).
11. Most of the reported statistical relationships, including the *capability ratio*—measuring a systemic variable—appear to be significant (Maoz and Russett, 1993: 632–633), with standard errors in many cases for the capability ratio smaller relative to unstandardized estimates than they are for democracy. Z-scores (table 5) show significance only with the domestic conflict variable. Data reported elsewhere show standard errors for democracy are consistently higher relative to parameter estimates than those for most other variables (Russett, 1993: 85, tables 4.2 to 4.4 especially), perhaps suggesting all the variables are *significant,* including democracy.
12. Dixon (1994) reports similar results. As noted with earlier findings, so also here: control variables appear to have an impact (Dixon, 1993: 62; 1994: 29).
13. This may be a general pattern: "Although the incidence of war among democracies has been much lower than can be expected by chance alone, autocratic dyads also have had fewer wars or disputes than one would expect from their frequency distribution . . . In other words, mixed dyads have been more war-prone than dyads with similar regime characteristics" (Chan, 1997: 82–83).

14. While the democracy variables are consistently significant, the realist variable of "balance of forces" appears to be as strong, or stronger, than the individual democracy variables (Rousseau et al. 1996: 521, 524, 527 [tables 1,3, and 5]).

15. Utilizing an event count model as opposed to standard Ordinary Least Square (OLS) regressions.

16. It is also true, however, that the "diplomatic record still includes a number of instances in which democracies have used overt military intervention, below the threshold of full-scale war, to influence the outcome of conflicts within other states that were free or partly free" (Kegley and Hermann, 1995: 10–11, table 4). The data also suggest over time a slight percent *increase* in interventions by "free" and "part free" nations and a decrease by "non-free" (Kegley and Hermann, 1995: 7, table 2). One single nation—the United States—accounted for 13 percent—29 out of 230 interventions—during the period (Kegley and Hermann, 1995: 8 [table 3]).

17. "Keep in mind the unusual nature of this proposition: It is not a statement of correlation, association, or relationship. It is an absolute (or 'point') assertion: There will be *no* violence between libertarian states. *One* clear case of violence or war unqualified by very unusual or mitigating circumstances *falsifies* the proposition" (Rummel, 1983: 29; emphasis in original). This has led to continuing scuffles over what the "democratic peace" hypothesis is asserting (see Farber and Gowa, 1997: 455; Thompson and Tucker, 1997b: 465).

18. "Thus, we think, the Farber and Gowa (1995) intercentury finding revolves more precisely around turn-of-the-century principal rivalry dealignments than around pre-1914 versus post-1945 patterns in common interests" (Thompson and Tucker, 1997a: 439). Not highlighted here however is the perhaps equally important apparent finding that contiguity and power status appear to play as important a role in pre–World War I militarized disputes as joint democracy (Thompson and Tucker, 1997a: 438, table 3, cols. 3,4, and 5).

19. "States undergoing regime change engage in more wars than do stable polities" (Thompson and Tucker, 1997: 444). Such contradictory conclusions impact on fundamental theoretical propositions but derive from very specific issues concerning the contested operationalization of regime types, appropriate time lags, the advisability of treating emergence from colonial status as regime change, and the difficulty of meshing assorted data-sets (Thompson and Tucker, 1997a: 446–450; Mansfield and Snyder, 1997; Thompson and Tucker, 1997b: 466–476). Chan (1997: 65–74) presents a review of many of these issues in a broader comparative perspective.

20. This has already been noted. Such alternative explanations have included political stability (Maoz and Russett, 1992: 261–263), and "prior management" of disputes as well as "power balance" (Dixon, 1993: 62).

21. The question of whether "0" is a meaningful figure within the "demo-demo" portion of a larger data distribution seems almost trivial, and even demonstrating that does not demolish the entire edifice.

22. Whatever else might be involved in these debates, a central focus has been the pitting of realists against "others" (Russett, 1993; Maoz and Russett, 1993; Gowa, 1995; Mansfield and Snyder, 1995; 1997).

23. See Russett (1990a: 119–124), Siverson and Emmons (1991), Gowa (1995), Farber and Gowa (1995).

24. While Sorokin's data are difficult to work with and at times both support and contradict the hypothesis, nonetheless overall the data tended to support it. See Sullivan (1976: 121–132).

25. "Severity" is a measure of the seriousness of ongoing events, including number of crisis actors, great power involvement, geostrategic salience, heterogeneity among the participants, range of issues and level of violence (James and Oneal, 1991: 318–320).

26. These results must be taken with some caution; large, ambitious designs produce ambitious measures—see Huth (1998: 758).

27. Issues of "ethnic/religious unification/irredenta" constitute individually both a relatively small percentage of the total issues (ranging between 2 percent and 6 percent) as well as

frequency as a percent of wars (between 7 percent and 17 percent) in any given time period (K. Holsti, 1991: 307–308). Expanding this to sympathizing "with those whom [one] consider[s] their ethnic, religious, and ideological kin" shows a composite index declining from 32 percent as a source of war in the 1815–1914 period to 21 percent in 1945–1989, and from 10 percent as a percent of all issues in 1815–1914 to 7 percent in 1945–1989 (K. Holsti, 1991: 317–318).

28. Cultural and religious similarity emerge as important, but both variables have strong competition from the simple variable of geographical contiguity, and the former variables' importance differs depending on which time periods are analyzed and whether specific large-scale wars are included or not (Henderson, 1997: 663–664, tables 1 and 2).

29. Employing the dyad-year as the unit of analysis is widely regarded as a potentially serious problem of lack of interdependence of observations (Ray, 1995a: 34), and it plagues many studies (i.e., Maos and Russett, 1993), relating both to measurements of democracy as well as conflict data (Ray, 1995a: 45). It may also apply to situations where given wars persist, and to sequential years of peace as well as to instances where several nations join together in war, such as World War II (Chan, 1997: 73–74).

30. "There is . . . no denying that the study of world politics is inherently faddish by nature. Nor are analysts of world politics immune to changes in their environment" (Thompson, 1988: 21). See also Krasner (1982: 497).

31. If National Support for World Order (NSWO) constitutes a meaningful outcome variable, then a related analysis also suggested that nations should endeavor to "foster world-wide development and open countries" (Sullivan, 1978b: 116).

32. Implications of these findings are extended in Morgan and Schwebach (1992: 309). See also Morgan and Campbell (1991: 190).

33. One becomes dubious about policy implications resting on design decisions assuming rapid change in democratic ranking or status of a country over relatively short periods of time; for examples of how such instances of changed democratic status can occur, see Ward and Gleditsch (1998: 56).

34. One wonders, given the ease with which the United States has utilized force in international politics, exactly what time, space, and geographic domain is the reference point when it is noted that "a previously unappreciated benefit of being considered democratic in the current international system is the expectation conveyed to other states that one values negotiation, mediation, compromise, and consensus over the use of force" (Hermann and Kegley, 1996: 454).

35. Perhaps a concentrated focus on state-level attributes could have provided earlier indicators of the momentous changes to occur between 1989 and 1991. Data on life expectancy and infant mortality were showing even by 1980 that the Soviet Union, for instance, was potentially in serious trouble: "If demography is destiny, this was a society growing ill. Or, if you like, breaking down" (Moynihan, 1993: 40).

36. On the Kyoto Conference: "The United States, by virtue of its economic weight, international influence and huge emissions of greenhouse gases, is the 900 pound gorilla of international climate politics" (Stevens, 1997: B7). On the Test Ban Treaty, Shaukat Umer, Pakistan's ambassador to the talks, noted: "If the largest power is out of this, it's all over—this treaty is dead" (McNeil, 1999: A11).

Chapter Five

1. "Students of international relations have for the last decade or so been fascinated by the idea of utilizing systemic conceptions in their efforts to understand the workings of the international policy. So far, however, the employment of this approach has failed to yield impressive results" (Young, 1978: 241). "Scholars have a remarkable capacity for rediscovering the wheel, and so it was that in the 1950s students of political science in general

and international relations in particular were smitten with the concept of 'system'" (Ferguson and Mansbach, 1988: 194).

2. The official title is *General Systems: The Yearbook of the Society for the Advancement of General Systems Theory.*

3. Even in testing complex sophisticated combinations of diverse systemic approaches, the importance of such idiosyncratic factors—although disregarded completely in the analysis—is reiterated: "I believe that no complete theory of international conflict can rely solely on the systemic level of analysis, because systems do not choose to go to war, national leaders do" (Pollins, 1996: 104).

4. While the underlying philosophical orientation taken here was manifested in the first of the events/data systems, developed mostly in Charles McClelland's World Event Interaction Survey (WEIS), the offspring have been multiple. Early ones included the Conflict and Peace Data Bank (COPDAB) system developed by Edward Azar (1980), and Charles Hermann's Comparative Research on the Events of Nations (CREON) (C. Hermann et al., 1973). Later attempts to improve, expand, and contextualize such collections include the Global Event Data System (GEDS) (Davies and McDaniel, 1994) and KEDS (Schrodt et al., 1994). Each project possesses slightly different philosophical assumptions, but similar underlying assumptions concerning the use of "events." See Schrodt (1994) for further elaboration of theoretical underpinnings related to statistical characteristics; Duffy (1994) for a "poststructuralist" critique; and Merritt (1994) for an historical overview of the major data-sets.

5. Declaring such "acute" international crises a thing of the past may be premature. Beginning in 1990 in the Middle East, and continuing through the decade in the broad south-central European area, familiar international crises buffeted the system. Even more clearly producing *deja vu* were the tensions between China and Taiwan beginning in March 1996—40 years after the last confrontation—and repeating several times in subsequent years.

6. The "long cycle" has been most popularized in Paul Kennedy's *The Rise and Fall of the Great Powers* (1987). The theme is familiarly simple: nations rise and fall because of multiple economic, political, and military factors that constantly change. Kennedy's account is saturated with discrete historical facts woven into a picture of rise and decline, and predictions, as always, are hazardous. In 1987, Kennedy wrote: "Moscow has a congenital dislike of withdrawing from *anywhere,* and also worries deeply about the political consequences of a reunited Germany . . . Even more fundamental a point: how could Russia withdraw from East Germany without provoking the question of a similar withdrawal from Czechoslovakia, Hungary, and Poland—leaving as the USSR's western frontier the dubious Polish/Ukrainian borderline, which is temptingly close for the fifty million Ukrainians?" (1987: 477).

7. The archetype of such debates is found in the exchange between Rosecrance and Waltz (Rosecrance, 1981: 707, 712–713; Waltz, 1982: 681; Rosecrance, 1982: 685).

8. "It is therefore possible for more than one international or 'world' society to coexist or for one part of the system to have an international society while other parts do not" (Buzan, 1993: 337). "Coevolving systems" combine changes in both global economic activity with changes in global political order to produce combined models (Pollins, 1996; Modelski and Thompson, 1996).

9. Bull presents the picture one way (1977: 41–46), Schelling another (1978: 21–22).

Chapter Six

1. Few serious observers consider the "unitary actor" assumption to be reflective of what goes on inside nations with respect to foreign policy, yet it continues to represent a target for critiques of structural approaches. Ironically, one of realism's defenders also presents what can only be considered a caricatured picture of a realist world (Mearsheimer, 1994/1995: 338–339).

2. The picture here mostly approximates Morgenthau's "six principles of political realism" (Morgenthau, 1965: 4–12). Variations over the years have not strayed far, but each observer has a specific assortment of rules and principles consistent with their realism; see, for example, Wayman and Diehl (1994: 8–13); Mearsheimer (1995: 337–339; 1999: 2–4); Elman and Elman (1997: 924); Schweller (1997: 927); and Walt (1997: 932).

3. Portions of the following draw on Sullivan (1990: 82f.).

4. Three factors are said to distinguish "empires" from the "Modern Pattern": the triumph of the nation-state as the major actor, the "advent of sustained economic growth based on modern science and technology," and the emergence of a world market economy (Gilpin, 1981: 116).

5. Levy (1991) elaborates several transition theories specifically with respect to the "long peace."

6. The similarities in the sequential specification of the respective cycles is very clear (Toynbee, 1954: 255, reprinted in Goldstein, 1988: 116; Modelski, 1987: 6).

7. The latter have been labeled "'interpretative' accounts of hegemony and international economic leadership," which exhibit "difficulties of specifying concrete causal statements" (Lake, 1993b: 461).

8. Goldstein claims this occurred from the case of World War II following immediately on World War I (Goldstein, 1988: 244).

9. See Chapter Five, pp. 102–103.

10. The list of problems would appear troubling, including dating of cycles, periods involved, naming of the hegemonies, and whether the unit of analysis is the international political system, the capitalist world system, or a combined, linked system (Boswell and Sweat, 1991: 130).

11. One symposium announcing again the recent death of realism used subtitles such as "What Distribution? What Capabilities?" (Lebow, 1994: 255ff.), and cited familiar complexities noted earlier from Morgenthau as well as Waltz's concern with the complexity of power.

12. The literature demonstrating the adequacy of many measures of nation- and system-level power concepts is voluminous, and merely demonstrated, for instance, in de Soysa et al. (1997); Doran and Parsons (1980); Geller (1992; 1993) Houweling and Siccima (1988; 1991); Kugler and Arbetman (1989); Mansfield (1993; 1994); Modelski and Thompson (1996); Nye (1990); Rasler and Thompson (1994); and Sullivan (1990).

13. It is also true that balance of power "theory" rests truly in the eye of the beholder. See the exchange in *American Political Science Review* 91 (December 1997) 899–935.

14. "We continue to find encouraging results in the individual-level perspective, but have discovered no evidence that decision makers act as if they were significantly constrained by variations in the structural attributes we examined" (Bueno de Mesquita and Lalman, 1988: 20). Earlier chapters have pointed out that the individual-level variables appear to be measured by systemic-level indicators.

15. Analysis of Hopf's data do in fact appear to support this last assertion, although minimally, with respect to frequency, magnitude, and average severity (casualties per year) (Hopf, 1991: 486, table 4).

16. Certain empirical findings utilizing both bipolar and hegemonic variables are difficult to interpret because the variable of bipolarity appears to have been constructed without regard to measurements of multipolarity (Volgy and Imwalle, 1995: 831).

17. Using trade as the outcome variable, an initial analysis questioned neorealism explicitly by showing trade flows higher between allies under multipolarity compared to bipolarity (Morrow et al., 1998: 659); a corrected analysis concluded by implication that realism was supported: trade was reduced within alliances under multipolarity and increased under bipolarity (Morrow et al., 1999: 933).

18. Comparisons are drawn between these data and Gilpin's formulations (1981), although closer similarities are suggested with Doran (1991) and especially with Goldstein (1988) (see Rasler and Thompson, 1994: 165–167).

19. Within this array of findings (Mansfield, 1988: tables 3, 5, and 7) a simple frequency count of the number of observations showing all wars "begun" during hegemonic vs. non-hegemonic years shows a clear tendency for more wars generally in hegemonic compared to nonhegemonic years, whereas for major power wars the number of wars begun is divided almost evenly between hegemonic and nonhegemonic years.

20. This conclusion comes mostly from analysis of Mansfield (1994: 50, table 2.3) and calculating the frequency of hegemonic versus nonhegemonic periods with "more," "equal," or "less" wars.

21. The exceptional methodological sophistication here notwithstanding, several measures, while possibly the only ones available, nonetheless raise questions: "risk propensity" utilizes the aforementioned "expected utility," transposing structural-level indicators into individual-level variables, and the key variable of bipolarity and multipolarity rests solely on Waltz's nominal assessment (Huth et al. 1993: 615–616).

22. Deterrence encounters and dispute initiation may constitute very different outcome variables. Broad conclusions referring to the "Waltzian argument" that uncertainty in the international system leads to more conflict may be unrelated to either of these specific outcomes. To conclude that "an increase in system uncertainty should not generally lead to an increased incidence of dispute initiation" (Huth et al., 1993: 619) may have little impact on Waltz's much broader hypothesis.

23. In a summary presentation (Huth, 1996: 65, table 2), all "international context" variables predict what a realist model would, the "domestic context" variables do *not* predict what a conventional realist model would, and the "issue" variables are mixed. On balance, the findings appear to support as many of the realist hypotheses as they support the "modified realist" model. See Huth (1996: 72 [table 3]; 115 [table 10]; 145 [table 13]; 156 [table 15]).

24. The widespread controversy elicited by *Theory of International Politics* (Waltz, 1979) is in some ways difficult to understand, since as suggested, the claims of an anarchic system involving more or less functionally equivalent units whose capacity varies and shifts over time were basic structural notions current in the discipline for many years, at least implicitly, as were the underlying philosophical assumptions of the scientific enterprise. Perhaps the timing of the publication—just as Keohane and Nye's antirealist complex interdependence model (Keohane and Nye, 1977) was beginning to hit its stride—placed Waltz's rigidified and overly simplistic picture of a realist international system in stark contrast. Perhaps it was "[Waltz's] own criticisms of contrary positions [which] assume such a tone of *hauteur* and reflect such a sense of certitude" (Ruggie, 1983: 272) that invited the intense reaction, and outright and continuing rejection. Or perhaps its implicit adherence to the positive benefits of the then current bipolar superpower world aided in its elevation to a central role in the debates.

25. Thus the widespread attention to Waltz's *Theory of International Politics* is doubly mysterious given its limited domain: it "has one major dependent variable, the war-proneness of international systems, that is explained by one independent variable, the polarity of the system" (Lebow, 1994: 253).

26. The unfolding continues with elaborations comparing "deep structure" with distributional structure; see Ruggie (1986); Buzan et al. (1993: 37–47; 51–65; 86–90; 165–168); Kaufman (1997: 184–186).

27. Thus, while realism might "fail[s] . . . to show why particular ideas were selected over others that were equally possible but that would have led to different foreign policies," nonetheless "sophisticated realism" might be able to account for "how structural conditions and Western policies created a *window of opportunity* and thus a demand for new ideas in foreign policy" (Risse-Kappen, 1994: 190; emphasis added).

28. No originality is claimed in pointing out that respective variations of realism "explain" everything, and that it is capable of reformulating itself in light of criticism; see note no. 27. While one of realism's notable attractions, it has also been labeled a "proliferation of emendations," creating what is claimed to be a "degenerating paradigm" (Vasquez, 1997: 899). Such recent exchanges duplicate similar debates of over a generation ago, and continue to demonstrate realism's chameleonlike character and thus the criticisms; see especially Elman and Elman (1995) and Schroeder (1995), and the exchange in *American Political Science Review* 91 (December 1997) 899–935.

29. Claude certainly seemed to be implying the basic elements of the "agent-structure" debate. Despite much talk about the "co-constitution" between agent and structure (Onuf, 1997: 7), the fundamental idea is the same.

30. "The balance of power is the very heart of Realist strategy in world politics" (Doyle, 1997: 161).

31. Critical theorists make much of the assertion that neorealists especially are more interested in "problem solving" within an already existing, and therefore "accepted" system, than in changing that system. Proposing to "change the system," however, involves broaching the issue of policy advice and the "relevance" of social science research, an intense topic a generation ago (Sullivan, 1973). In fact, portions of several chapters in the precursor to this volume were devoted to policy advice that might be derived from systematic research (Sullivan, 1976), and thus directed at issues—perhaps indirectly—of changing the system.

32. The "requirements" as well as the "factors and trends conditioning the advent of" a potentially new, Great Power Security Regime have been set out (Kegley and Raymond, 1994: 232–233, tables 10.1 and 10.2) especially focusing on the variable of "norms," but the assessments are necessarily subjective.

33. "[T]here is no possibility of returning to the past, continuing to live as in the past, or avoiding a transformation of the world system. But the nature of this transformation is not yet determined; it depends on the choices we make . . . how that transition occurs, and where it leads, is up to us to choose" (Goldstein, 1988: 376).

34. Somewhere along the line it was decided that Waltz's "model" implied strict structural determinism, and as with so many such debates few bothered to investigate the original source. That misinterpretation continued and unfortunately and incorrectly became a central element; some have taken pains to correct that misinterpretation (Buzan et al., 1993: 23).

35. In fairness, Gilpin did note that certain developments have historically been shown to "destabilize bipolar systems and trigger hegemonic conflict," but lists a wide variety of situations under which the bipolar system might become transformed and/or hegemonic conflict might break out. To be bluntly honest, however, these situations cover just about every broad eventuality imaginable (Gilpin, 1981: 235–238).

Chapter Seven

1. Headline from *The New York Times,* July 1, 1993; quote from the *Economist,* "A Survey of the European Community," July 3, 1993, p. 5.

2. See Zacher and Matthew (1995), from which our categories have been drawn; a somewhat narrower view is in Doyle (1997).

3. The *Economist,* April 10, 1993, p. 72.

4. Certain findings (Harf et al., 1974) may have been a design artifact as opposed to evidence for discounting the pacifying effect of IGOs (Sullivan, 1976: 331–332).

5. Other interpretations are less sanguine: "integration research flourished . . . at a time American leaders were enthusiastic about the prospect of a united Europe as a buttress against the Soviet Union . . . Its decline occurred as frictions grew between the United

States and Western Europe and interest in U.S.-Soviet detente increased" (Ferguson and Mansbach, 1988: 202).

6. "The average trade openness of the group of twelve economies now in the EC, expressed as a ratio of exports and imports to gross domestic product, rose from less than 40 percent in 1960 to over 60 percent by the early 1980s . . . Moreover, intragroup trade as a portion of the total trade of group members also grew in the same period from around 40 percent to almost 55 percent" (Garrett, 1992: 538, n. 15).

7. An early 1970s issue of *International Organization* expressed pessimism about integration theory and the process of integration in Europe because of the "flagging fate of the European Economic Community after the Gaullist challenge in 1965," and the "internal agricultural and related institutional crisis," all of which "appeared to sap the spirit and call into question the very purpose of European integration." That special issue was "essentially completed just as the European Community seemed to acquire new life" (Nau, 1979: 121).

8. Studies of European integration had not ended. While focus on trade integration continued to a limited degree (Harrop, 1989: 169), others viewed the decision to complete the "internal market" as a function of the bargaining that ultimately reflected the respective power of the key states, especially Germany and France (Garrett, 1992).

9. The reasons justifying this conclusion are instructive. The role of the organizations involved has been "limited to the technical sphere, outside of economic benefits" and the "structure of power inside both institutions mirrors the structure of power in the world. The two organizations have been state-dependent" (Nayar, 1995: 169).

10. Regimes have been equated with "liberal institutionalism" (Mearsheimer, 1994/95: 335), both largely ignoring security issues and focusing on economic and, to a lesser extent, environmental issues (Mearsheimer, 1994/95: 342).

11. This case study of the superpower nuclear relationship documents a mesmerizing era that has not yet received the attention it deserves, but conclusions imputing underlying "psychological processes" do not particularly strengthen our understanding of the causal mechanisms that operated during that period, and several linkages between regimes and "learning" are not particularly significant (Nye, 1987: 398–401).

12. A caveat recognized by proponents: "institutionalist theory conceptualizes institutions both as independent and dependent variables" (Keohane and Martin, 1995: 46).

13. The link between American scholars' perceived decline of American hegemony and the emergence of regime "thinking" was spelled out at length by Susan Strange (1982; 1987).

14. Not only does regime analysis set itself apart from its predecessor, integration theory, by offering "a far more pronounced articulation of agency and intentional pursuance of self-interest," but distances itself also by assuming "a cautious attitude toward agency-distant and apparently unidirectional phenomena such as incrementalism, spillover, and sense of community" (Stokke, 1997: 36).

15. In one extensive review of *Power and Interdependence,* little mention is made of "regimes" other than implicitly as a background, assumed phenomenon to be explained, as in how "regimes change"—an observation that would apply also to the original work. In the single table in the review delineating the differences and similarities between dependence and interdependence, the term "regime" does not appear (K. Holsti, 1978: 528–529).

16. One of the earliest studies indicated that for an admittedly narrow slice of time, 1966, only 31.5 percent of event interactions among nations was conflictual, and only 7.5 percent of the total was actual "conflict actions" (as opposed to offensive or defensive "verbal" conflict) (McClelland and Hoggard, 1969: 716).

17. Two other renditions of the migration from integration through international organizations and to regimes can be found in Kratochwil and Ruggie (1986) and Rochester (1986).

18. Those listed in Haggard and Simmons (1987) have been covered respectively in Chapters Six, Nine, Seven, and Two. Those in Hasenclever et al. (1996) have been covered in Chapter Seven, Six, and Two.

19. One critical analysis of the "institutional" approach has highlighted the bargaining hypotheses inherent in assumptions about the operations of institutions, and proposes a set of "flaws" in the causal logic linking institutions with cooperation, focusing almost exclusively on the "relative-absolute" gains debate, which likewise pertains to how nations bargain with other nations (Mearsheimer, 1994/95: 346–351).

20. "Niceness" is an underappreciated component in international theory (Axelrod, 1984: 33; Leng, 1993a: 202; Leng, 1993b: 12), a fascinating ingredient noted further in a later chapter within the context of "bargaining." "Niceness" in the present setting might imply that anyone whom I have befriended *has* to be nice—for the obvious reasons—and others "should" be able to see that. Ultimately, the system should gravitate toward balance based on "my" perceptions. Whether such characteristics exist in a "realist's" world is an interesting question.

21. For further analysis and some disconfirmation of these findings, see Sullivan (1976: 241–242).

22. Nikita Khrushchev's U.S. visit in 1959, the "bargaining period" during the Cuban Missile Crisis in 1962, and the Test Ban Treaty of 1963.

23. This was true in only two data-sets, COPDAB and ASHLEY, and not true in WEIS, where "Sino-Soviet relations get a boost from U.S. cooperation toward the Soviets." However, given the specific "response curve(s)," these latter data are "consequently . . . hard to interpret" (Goldstein and Freeman, 1990: 81).

24. For legal integration, the role of certain institutions is still in process; evidence and arguments on institution-state relations with respect to the ICJ appears in Alter (1998); Garrett et al. (1998); and Mattli and Slaughter (1998).

25. We have followed Mearsheimer and others here and treated both as synonymous (Mearsheimer, 1994/95: 335). Even within the "institutional" literature, "institutions" are treated both as real-world organizational entities, on the one hand, and as much looser norm-setting bodies (Keohane and Martin, 1995).

26. Karl Deutsch's admonition to produce *high* N/V ratios—large numbers of cases with small numbers of variables—is breached especially in case studies.

27. In one case, however, the "capturing " of the U.S. was essential to achieving the end (P. Haas, 1992b), suggesting high-politics processes. Moreover, the expertise and competence essential to an epistemic community's effect have not always been recognized, their claims to policy-relevant knowledge have been disputed, and their ideas often attacked from political and military groups (Evangelista, 1995: 36). In less highly charged areas—such as stratospheric ozone issues—political actors at times use expert knowledge to enhance their power (Harrison, 1996: 146).

28. The same observation was noted with respect to one of the first empirical applications of regime analysis (Young, 1979) to compliance with international agreements: "this conceptual apparatus seems to be virtually divorced from the case studies: no reference to either case can be found outside of their respective chapters" (Sullivan, 1981: 282).

29. "Specifically on the matter of *cooperation,* liberals do not think that the existence of a hegemonic power is necessary for cooperation; rather, *mutual interests can sustain* international regimes" (Zacher and Matthew, 1995: 119; emphasis in original). We will see in Chapter Nine that mutual interests can result from iterations in long-term bargaining, and theories embodying these processes constitute equally plausible models for cooperation; the presence or absence of a "liberal" ideological or normative conviction could be completely irrelevant.

30. Analogies from other fields are always suspect, but one from the medical field might be appropriate here: just as the latter field looks at "deviant" behavior—illness—despite the fact that most humans most of the time occupy in one form or another a status of "health," so also international relations scholars have traditionally investigated deviant behavior—war and conflict—despite the fact that the "state" of the international system

most of the time and the relations between most international actors most of the time is peaceful and cooperative.

31. The sentence following the above quotations is a bit confusing: "Interestingly, both integration theory and Elias's (1976) theory of civilization highlight the existence of a 'core area' or a 'hegemon' as a prerequisite for such processes" (Levy et al., 1995: 310).

Chapter Eight

1. Ironically, those investigating the economic side of the ledger deliver the opposite refrain; describing the dissonance between the economists' theories of international trade with the "real world, where forces of mercantilism and protection always seem rampant," one has noted: "try as we might to find logical reasons for all this in the tenets of our own discipline, ultimately we are tempted simply to throw up our hands and proclaim: 'It's all politics!'" (B. Cohen, 1990: 261–262).

2. Scholarly affection for terminology can exhibit a short half-life. One review of Keohane and Nye's *Power and Interdependence* (K. Holsti, 1978) focused especially on its potential relationship to "dependency," a term very much in vogue in the 1970s. Not a single reference in an entire review was made to "regimes," central to an entire theoretical approach ten years later, while "dependency" itself retains little cachet in the 1990s.

3. In comparative tests of hypotheses derived from Amin, Frank, and Galtung, several elements belonging to the "hardcore" of dependency were not supported, other elements received "mixed results," and others received clear support. The key appears to be whether the outcome variable of interest is the integration of the developing countries into the international trade system or exploitation. "Dependence has a positive influence on the level of exploitation, while exploitation positively influences development"— which is "clearly irreconcilable with" dependency theory's main thesis (Hout, 1993: 165–167).

4. Susan Strange's epigram from Gore Vidal perhaps sums it up: "The American Empire is one of the most successful inventions in history, and all the more remarkable because no one knows its there" (Strange, 1989: 161).

5. These effects are the same whether considered simultaneously or lagged (Mansfield, 1994: 186–190).

6. Described by the author as "crude simplicity," it is a straightforward combination of the predicted effects of only two of the four respective models analyzed separately (Goldstein, Wallerstein, Modelski/Thompson, and Gilpin), namely, the long wave of Goldstein and the world leadership cycle of Modelski and Thompson (Pollins, 1996: 116, 111).

7. Others contend that it was France, not Britain, that instigated free trade during that period (Verdier, 1998: 9).

8. Extensive empirical analysis of this was discussed in Chapter Six.

9. Excluded were the "'interpretative' accounts of hegemony and international economic leadership" of Wallerstein (1974), Gill (1990), and Cox (1986) because they "lack a clear deductive foundation" as well as the "ongoing difficulties of specifying concrete causal statements" (Lake, 1993b: 461).

10. "This is not, however, the first time that social scientists have behaved like generals who, overtaken by events, make elaborate preparations to fight the last war" (Strange, 1989: 169).

11. Descriptions of broad historical decline have themselves a long contemporary history; Toynbee (1954), Modelski (1978), Gilpin (1981), and Kennedy (1987) are only a few of many major works that could be cited. Explicit tests of "decline" hypotheses are less numerous and with a shorter life span (Rasler, 1990; Spezio, 1990; Rasler and Thompson, 1991a; 1991b).

12. Nye (1990).

13. "Spoilers" possess relatively low productivity and are of middle size, which "affect . . . the strength of the regime through their protectionist behavior"; such nations may even "undermine the international economy by their protectionism" (Lake, 1984: 151).

14. A "supporter" possesses only moderate influence in the international economy, has the ability to "free ride," and "during periods of declining hegemony [supporters] become critical in determining the continued openness or closure of the international economy" (Lake, 1984: 152).

15. This equivocal evaluation leads to the critique that calls the entire HST program into question as "poorly articulated" with propositions resting on "tenuous logic," variables left "undefined," and with empirical tests that are rare and "prone to either underspecification or over-extension" (Lake, 1993b: 485).

16. It was also the United States that was defeated in the Vietnam War during what surely was its most militarily hegemonic period. And despite its continuing economic hegemonic status, of eight distinct measures presented here, two are roughly level for the 1970–1990 period, one doubled and one increased slightly; four declined. The picture for "structural" power even with these data, therefore, would have to be considered mixed (Strange, 1987: 567).

17. See Nye (1990: 88–89, table 3.5; 109, table 3.12).

18. Nau's argument resembles Nye's more than Strange's. Even within a relatively rosy picture, however, the actual evidence can be interpreted more cautiously in terms of supporting a clear picture of America's continuing hegemony (Nau, 1990: 63–64, tables 2–2, 2–3, 2–4).

19. Both analyses, especially Sullivan (1990), constructed indexes of several different measures and relative—in the latter case—to 17 other nations rather than investigating discrete indicators for the U.S. on any given measure. While these may provide a broader and contextually rich comparison, and do possess certain advantages, these findings certainly appear contradicted by more contemporary perceptions of the U.S. in the late 1990s.

20. Different conclusions are derived from other analyses with quite distinct purposes for investigating the specific data (Mansfield, 1992: 757).

21. Partly because the entire enterprise is called into question by asserting both the uncertainty of how to measure hegemonic decline as well as the imprecision of measurements of international coordination (Webb, 1991: 340–341).

22. As for the United States' push for open trade, the persistent issue has been whether it promotes words or actions; in terms of "anti-dumping" actions—sometimes seen as a "politically neat method of protecting a particular industry"—the United States far outranks all other nations in the mid-1990s (The *Economist*, November 8, 1997, p. 85–86).

23. The *Economist*, October 23, 1993, p. 25.

24. The role of the executive in the "internationalization" of the tariff in the 1890s and the move toward protectionism in the 1909–1913 period compares favorably to other explanations based on interest group or legislative powers (Lake, 1988).

25. The issue of case study methodology and its relationship to theory building has not been adequately addressed. For a brief analysis of the tendency to favor extensive case studies perhaps to the detriment of following through on earlier original theoretical endeavors toward establishing "generalizable theory" in the field of international financial transactions, see Andrews (1996).

26. These refer to the familial, religious, and even biblical implications (Grunberg, 1990: 456–469), containing roots even in "cosmological observations" wherein hegemonies may decline while providing for the rest of the world, where self-sacrifice may be crucial and "may be derived from Christian thought, from earlier fears about the death of the sun" (Grunberg, 1990: 476–477).

27. Examples include James and Lake (1989), and analyses focusing mostly on domestic policy, decision-making, and political processes (*International Organization*, Winter 1988), and to a lesser degree, studies such as FDI (Goodman et al., 1996).

28. This conclusion rests on evidence cited earlier from numerous cycle studies suggesting that upswings in the international economy tend to be associated with more conflict in the international system.

29. The following quote from Strange (1986) stands in some contrast to more recent arguments in Strange (1996: 66–87).

30. It may be true that most social science theories "are rarely good enough to provide concrete guidance for policy makers" (Krasner, 1996: 124), but that does not presuppose that the theories operating within the political world are any more reliable—merely that they are more often used as referents by policy-makers and therefore as justifications for policy.

Chapter Nine

1. This exchange in McClelland (1968: 173) was taken from the original (Howley, 1950: 30).

2. Reference here is to the alleged remark by one top American decision-maker at the height of the Cuban Missile Crisis, when it first appeared the Soviets might acquiesce to American requests: "I think the other side just blinked."

3. Baldwin (1989) compiles recent problems associated with power as "influence."

4. Constructivists view the same phenomenon and arrive at broader portrayals: "The process of signalling, interpreting, and responding completes a 'social act' and begins the process of creating intersubjective meanings" (Wendt, 1992: 405).

5. For two exceptions, see Keohane (1986) and Axelrod and Keohane (1986).

6. This general assertion is not contradicted by the fact that in certain specific formulations deterrence rests clearly on a "realist" model of world politics (Huth et al., 1993).

7. Examples included, "It is in your interest"; "Somebody has to be reasonable"; "My partner won't let me"; "This is my last demand"; "Put yourself in my place" (Kahn, 1962: 178ff.).

8. "A close look at the quarter of all defense outlays that has gone into nuclear weapons suggests that a good portion was wasted" (Passell, 1995).

9. Three instances cited by John Foster Dulles as having established the viability in his mind of brinkmanship all fit this general description: the negotiations on Korea and Vietnam, and the crises over the offshore islands contested by the People's Republic of China and Taiwan.

10. Levy (1994) presents multiple perspectives and pitfalls of attempting to apply "learning" concepts across a broad spectrum of international modelling situations.

11. Since the bargaining strategies, as opposed to military capabilities, are relevant here, analysis of Huth's manipulation of these data can be found in summary form in Huth and Russett (1988: 36–37) and in extended form in Huth (1988a: chapter 4).

12. Wu (1990) tests "utility" and "probability" definitions without the strategic "bargaining" feature, in essence testing "mere capabilities" (Huth/Russett) against "capabilities as a measure of utilities" (Wu). While technically pitting the structural against "expected utility," a key difference is that deterrence has a policy orientation and, within the confines of cognitive models, strives to decipher which constraints or situations *amenable to the policy-maker* are most related to successful deterrence. If the variables contained in an EID model fall into that category more so than expected utilities, the former would be more successful in the policy-orientation dimension. And, to repeat a point made in Chapter Three, despite the labels "utilities" and "preferences," Wu's evaluation of EID contains no *direct* data on either.

13. Including the nature of the evidence, the alleged paucity of cases of EID, as well as the broader question concerning the use of quantitative aggregate data to test theories of deterrence (Lebow and J. Stein, 1990: 346–349).

14. In Lebow (1981), n=13; Huth and Russett (1988), n=58; in Wu (1990), n=30.

15. Nonetheless, these other variables—although structural—were still recognized as part of the "cognitive" bargaining model noted earlier, which highlights further the problems of assessing realism. Because realism is so all-encompassing, attempting to test and contrast deterrence hypotheses "against" any formulations derived from realist "theories" faces serious problems: the broad expanse of the latter is such that hypotheses generated ostensibly to test deterrence can very easily be included within realism, in which case "tests" are inconclusive. This is not limited to but can be illustrated in the extensive elaborations of the more ambitious of the empirical studies (see specifically Huth et al., 1993: 614–617; Gelpi, 1997a: 340–346).

16. Both "escalation of deterrent encounters" as well as "initiation of great-power disputes" (Huth et al., 1993: 619) could be considered limited in terms of behavioral domain.

17. GRIT is viewed by some as one of two variants of generalized reciprocal strategies, the other being TFT (tit-for-tat) (J. Stein, 1991: 53f.).

18. See Snyder and Diesing (1977) for extensive elaborations, Aggarwal (1996) for applications outside of the security area, and Brams (1999) for elaboration to dynamic PD games.

19. Further, these findings support the "'spiral model' of reciprocal response rather than the 'deterrence model' of inverse response for the Cold War" (Goldstein and Freeman, 1991: 31)

20. The findings noted earlier are reiterated: "The absence of inverse response by either country underlines the fallacy of hard-line approaches: neither country is generally induced to cooperate by the other's hostility" (Goldstein, 1991b: 207).

21. In some instances disaggregated periods are as small as eight months. In Goldstein and Pevehouse (1997) support for bilateral reciprocity occurs mostly in these disaggregations, with one of the time periods encompassing only a very small portion of the entire data (Goldstein and Pevehouse, 1997: 527, table 4 and n. 34).

22. Some contend that studies of reciprocity are limited to "a few cases of great-power relations . . . and [are] contentious" (Goldstein and Pevehouse, 1997: 515, n. 1). While partly true, still numerous areas beyond that realm have been investigated, such as patterns in South African foreign relations (Van Wyk and Radloff, 1993), Rhodesian policy (Moore, 1995), and arms control negotiations (Jensen, 1984).

23. Cusack and Ward were not the least bit sanguine about the use of then-Soviet and Chinese military expenditure data (Cusack and Ward, 1981: 459–460).

24. When analyzed statistically, such data would by definition tend to support a bureaucratic, incremental model.

25. Specifically, realizing the two-year time lag operating in defense budgets, most series show the first decisions for military increases occurring in the Carter years—approximately 1979 and 1980—and continuing into about the mid- to late-1980s.

26. Overestimates of Soviet strength may have come from such disinformation, but also from understandable Pentagon/CIA overestimates, as well as from "blowback," whereby one element of an agency disseminates disinformation, only to be picked up unwittingly by another governmental unit, which then uses it in all seriousness as "intelligence."

27. Perhaps a sense of progression was portrayed by increased sophistication, but the results of statistical tests were interpreted too literally. Even with ever more sophisticated statistical techniques to test models, "interpretations of these tests revolve around a few recurring themes," one of which is the comparison of relative magnitudes and/or levels of statistical significance of coefficients, "evidence that was generally taken to demonstrate that there was virtually *no* reaction *in seemingly obvious cases of arms races,* thus raising

doubts about the validity of the very concept of an arms race" (McGinnis, 1991: 452–453, first emphasis in original, second emphasis added).

28. Figure 3 in Singer's ambitious and prescient "Inter-Nation Influence: A Formal Model" spelled out the "hypothesized" relevance of various influence techniques broken down between "persuasion" and "dissuasion" situations, with suggestions about which actions might be most appropriate given desired outcomes (Singer, 1963: 427).

29. Results on TFT and reciprocity are not universally supported: certain "tentative" findings are "not encouraging for those who are sanguine about the evolution of cooperation through reciprocity"; see Bueno de Mesquita and Lalman, 1992: 141–142.

30. A more formal analysis suggests similar conclusions: that pure defection strategies are in some ways inefficient and therefore less stable, whereas reciprocal cooperative strategies reach an equilibrium that is easiest to reach and retain (Bendor and Swistak, 1997).

31. For an incisive critique of the utility of extrapolating from Axelrod's and others' PD experiments, see J. Stein (1991: 53–56).

32. Fearon's model suggests that the two phases of bargaining about issues and then enforcement of agreements are interrelated, such that harder bargaining may occur during the former stage, fostering costly standoffs and despite the shadow of the future, and potentially impeding cooperation. In this scheme, regimes then are viewed more as "forums for bargaining" as opposed to institutions (Fearon, 1998: 298).

33. It bears repeating again: the findings from which these implications are drawn are limited only to the "prospects for peace" when the latter is defined as "incidence of dispute initiation"; as far as any other "peace" or "non-peace" behaviors—or outcomes—all bets are off.

Chapter Ten

1. One recent view sees national interests as the ultimate in idiosyncratic configuration, not a response to "systemic incentives or imperatives" nor as an attempt to "maximize" anything: "no model with a tractable set of independent variables would predict either the nature or intensity of the [specific] interest." The specific national interest in question, Japan's claim to the "Northern Territories," is a "path-dependent result of historical and political accidents—chaotic interactions of transient domestic, diplomatic, and strategic imperatives—at work in a thickly textured cultural and psychological context." Original considerations that had shaped it had become "ossified" such that the original interest outlived its usefulness (Kimura and Welch, 1998: 232).

2. One thinks here especially of Ashley's virulent critique (1984). Even proponents of realism present a picture that must in some respects be considered caricatures of a "realist" interstate system (Mearsheimer, 1994/95: 338–339).

3. Not everyone shares this view, of course. After Pakistan's and India's detonation of nuclear weapons in the spring of 1998, one senior Indian advisor on foreign affairs noted that the United States seemed to have misread the end of the Cold War as the end of threats to national security everywhere: "The United States of America . . . proposed a new thesis, that the principal dynamic or relations would be trade and commerce. The United States assumed everyone thought the same" (The *New York Times*, June 15, 1998, p. A6).

4. The "Nye Initiative" reflects the "intensified" dialogue on security issues with Japan suggested by Joseph Nye, assistant secretary for international security in the Department of Defense in the early 1990s, and coauthor (with Robert Keohane) of *Power and Interdependence* (1977; 1989). See "Is Japan Normal?" The *Economist* June 24, 1995, pp. 25–26.

5. Lest this be considered a glib reference, Dessler (1989: 471) suggests this comparison in so many words.

6. Once again, Dessler for all intents and purposes has cast the debate in this fashion (Dessler, 1989: 443); see also Onuf (1997: 9).

7. One recent extensive critique has branded realism a "degenerating" research program (Vasquez, 1997), spawning five different responses in the *American Political Science Review* 91 (December 1997).

8. Thus, while "the general principle based on past experience remains: As hegemony declines, eventually hegemonic war occurs," yet, "The current generation sits atop a great divide between the past ten thousand years, in which war has played a central role in human civilization, and a 'postwar' era of the future, marked by at least minimal global political stability" (Goldstein, 1988: 364). While "rising nationalisms" should be linked to "major power confrontations and animosities" (although admitting the predictions are "open-ended") (Modelski, 1978: 235), Modelski concludes 12 years later: "via the long cycle, evolutionary learning also defines the direction of change for these institutional orders: the global leadership assuming greater complexity, the community moving toward democracy, and macrodecision making moving toward alternatives to global war" (Modelski, 1990: 24).

9. The *Economist,* June 20, 1998: p. 120.

10. We have taken the liberty of using a portion of the title of Ferguson and Mansbach (1988).

11. Waltz, *Theory of International Politics* (1979).

12. See Onuf (1997: 9–10) for elaboration of the agent structure debate as related to the free will-determinism dichotomy.

13. Dessler (1989: 469–471) certainly suggests this to be the case.

14. Clearly missing is the unit-level dimension of individual "agency"—an obvious drawback in such large-*n* studies.

15. These three respectively are (1) the dyadic trend in relative power and domestic political conditions; (2) a combination of five dyadic and unit-level variables; and (3) a combination of three variables at the dyadic level.

16. Dispute initiation is an important dependent variable, but the operational definition demonstrates its limited nature; it occurs only "if the designated challenger(s) is the first state in a dispute to threaten or resort to the use of force against its rival (and protege[s] where relevant . . .) in a given year" and it will be considered absent if otherwise (Huth et al., 1992: 495). The unit of analysis therefore is the "dyad-year," with those dyad-years excluded "in which the challenger is involved in an ongoing dispute or war with the rival that was initiated in a previous year and continued for more than half of the current year" (Huth et al., 1992: 495).

17. While a "dyad-year" measurement might serve as a proxy for "stability," the fact that ongoing years and disputes are excluded might mitigate that argument. When such an initiation is limited to occurring only *in one year,* and is excluded when related to any ongoing wars or conflicts between the disputants, its limitations as a proxy are clear. The findings apply therefore only to "dispute initiation" as narrowly defined.

18. For reference to the "end of the Cold War" viewed as "a mere data point," see Lebow and Risse-Kappen (1995: ix).

19. Low N/V ratios—small number of cases relative to the number of variables—tend to be associated with expansive dependent variables, and high N/V ratios with more limited dependent variables.

20. Early critics of realism "misrepresent and distort the realist viewpoint. Even a hasty reading of *Politics Among Nations* would have revealed not a hierarchical preference for military conflict but rather a desire for its prevention" (K. Thompson, 1996: 123).

21. One scholarly panel, entitled "Globalization: Is Seeing Believing or Believing Seeing?" captures the quandary (ISA *Newsletter,* December 1995: 48).

22. "[I]n placid times, and even in times that are not so placid, the belief that power politics is ending tends to break out" (Waltz, 1995: 76).

23. The economic turmoil spilled over into the political realm, spelling the end of the Indonesian strongman, President Suharto's, 30-year reign.
24. It has been said that the four most dangerous words on Wall Street are: "It's different this time." Certainly with the dawn of the new year, 2001, such words had begun to haunt many investors in the new paradigm, "new economy" technology and internet stocks.
25. Analogous charges have been made and responded to elsewhere (Wendt, 1995: 80; Mearsheimer, 1995: 92).
26. By implication, even the dichotomy between critical theory and problem solving is of course a false one (Keohane, 1998: 194).
27. Examples of this pattern are spelled out in Sullivan (2000).
28. Portions of seven different chapters in the predecessor to this volume were devoted to the "policy" relevance of various theoretical analyses (Sullivan, 1976).
29. The "hazard rate" (rate of formation) of four separate indicators of environmental regimes all increase through the early 1970s, then decline into the early and mid-1980s, followed again by an increase into 1990. The only exception to this pattern was formal intergovernmental environmental treaties, which showed a continuing decline in hazard rate to 1990 (Meyer et al., 1997: 626, figure 2).
30. Moreover, the relevant behavior—the Persian Gulf War of 1990–1991—is cast as a result of "a fundamental challenge to the existence of one of its accepted members" (i.e., Kuwait) (Buzan, 1993: 349), an explanation itself seriously contested.

References

Aggarwal, Vinod. *Debt Games: Strategic Interaction in International Debt Restructuring*. Cambridge: Cambridge University Press, 1996.

Alker, Hayward R. and Donald Puchala. "Trends in Economic Partnership: The North Atlantic Area, 1928–1963," in J. David Singer (ed.), *Quantitative International Politics: Insights and Evidence*. New York: Free Press, 1968. Pp. 287–316.

Allison, Graham. *The Essence of Decision: Explaining the Cuban Missile Crisis*. Boston: Little, Brown, 1971.

Allison, Graham, and Morton Halperin. "Bureacratic Politics: A Paradigm and Some Policy Implications," *World Politics* 24 (supplement spring 1972) 40–79.

Allison, Graham and Philip Zelikow. *Essence of Decision: Explaining the Cuban Missile Crisis*. 2d ed. New York: Longman, 1999.

Alter, Karen J. "Who Are the 'Masters of the Treaty'?: European Governments and the European Court of Justice," *International Organization* 52 (winter 1998) 121–148.

Amin, Ash, Barry Gills, Ronen Palen, and Peter Taylor. "Editorial: Forum for Heterodox International Political Economy," *Review of International Political Economy* 1 (spring 1994) 1–12.

Anderton, Charles H. "Arms Race Modeling: Problems and Prospects," *Journal of Conflict Resolution* 33 (June 1989) 346–367.

Andrews, David M. "Capital Mobility and State Autonomy: Toward a Structural Theory of International Monetary Relations," *International Studies Quarterly* 38 (June 1994) 193–218.

Andrews, David M. "Money Matters: Currency Relations and Power Politics," *Mershon International Studies Review* 40 (October 1996) 308–310.

Ashley, Richard K. "The Poverty of Neorealism," *International Organization* 38 (spring 1984) 225–286.

Attina, Fulvio. "Organization, Competition, and Change of the International System," *International Organization* 16 (No. 4, 1991) 317–334.

Axelrod, Robert. *The Evolution of Cooperation*. New York: Basic Books, 1984.

Axelrod, Robert and Robert O. Keohane. "Achieving Cooperation under Anarchy: Strategies and Institutions," in Kenneth A. Oye (ed.), *Cooperation under Anarchy*. Princeton: Princeton University Press, 1986. Pp. 226–254.

Azar, Edward E. "The Conflict and Peace Data Bank (COPDAB) Project," *Journal of Conflict Resolution* 24 (March 1980) 143–152.

Babst, Dean. "Electoral Governments—A Force for Peace," *The Wisconsin Sociologist* 1 (1964) 9–14.

Babst, Dean. "A Force for Peace," *Industrial Research* (April 1972) 55–58.

Baldwin, David. *Paradoxes of Power*. New York: Basil Blackwell, 1989.

Barkdull, John. "Waltz, Durkheim, and International Relations," *American Political Science Review* 89 (September 1995) 669–680.

Barkin, J. Samuel and Bruce Cronin. "The State and the Nation: Changing Norms and the Rules of Sovereignty in International Relations," *International Organization* 48 (winter 1994) 107–130.

Barnett, Michael N. and Martha Finnemore. "The Politics, Power, and Pathologies of International Organizations," *International Organization* 53 (autumn 1999) 699–732.

Barrett, David M. *Uncertain Warriors: Lyndon Johnson and His Vietnam Advisers.* Lawrence, Kansas: University Press of Kansas, 1993.

Bates, Robert H., Philip Brock, and Jill Tiefenthaler. "Risk and Trade Regimes," *International Organization* 45 (winter 1991) 1–18.

Beck, Nathaniel. "The Illusion of Cycles in International Relations," *International Studies Quarterly* 35 (December 1991) 455–476.

Beer, Francis A. and Robert Hariman. *Post-realism: The Rhetorical Turn in International Relations.* East Lansing: Michigan State University, 1996.

Bendor, Jonathan and Thomas H. Hammond, "Re-thinking Allison's Models," *American Political Science Review* 86 (June 1992) 301–322.

Bendor, Jonathan and Piotr Swistak. "The Evolutionary Stability of Cooperation," *American Political Science Review* 91 (June 1997) 290–307.

Bennett, D. Scott. "Security, Bargaining, and the End of Interstate Rivalry," *International Studies Quarterly* 40 (June 1996) 157–184.

Bennett, D. Scott and Allan C. Stam, III. "The Declining Advantages of Democracy," *Journal of Conflict Resolution* 42 (June 1998) 344–366.

Benoit, Kenneth. "Democracies Really Are More Pacific (in General)," *Journal of Conflict Resolution* 40 (December 1996) 636–657.

Bergeson, Albert. "The Emerging Science of the World System," *International Social Science Journal* 34 (#1, 1982) 23–36.

Bergsten, C. Fred, Robert E. Keohane, and Joseph S. Nye. "International Economics and International Politics," *International Organization* 29 (1975) 1–36.

Biersteker, Thomas J. "Constructing Historical Counterfactuals to Assess the Consequences of International Regimes: The Global Debt Regime and the Course of the Debt Crisis of the 1980s," in Volker Rittberger (ed.), *Regime Theory and International Relations.* Oxford: Clarendon Press, 1993. Pp. 312–338.

Blum, Douglas W. "The Soviet Foreign Policy Belief System," *International Studies Quarterly* 37 (December 1993) 373–394.

Bostdorff, Denise M. and Steven R. Goldzwig. "Idealism and Pragmatism in American Foreign Policy Rhetoric: The Case of John F. Kennedy and Vietnam," *Presidential Studies Quarterly* 24 (Summer 1994) 515–530.

Boswell, Terry and Mike Sweat. "Hegemony, Long Waves, and Major Wars: A Time Series Analysis of Systemic Dynamics, 1596–1967," *International Studies Quarterly* 35 (June 1991) 123–150.

Boulding, Kenneth. "National Images and International Systems," in James N. Rosenau (ed.), *International Politics and Foreign Policy.* New York: Free Press, 1969. Pp. 422–431.

Brams, Steven J. "To Mobilize or Not to Mobilize: Catch–22s in International Crisis," *International Studies Quarterly* 43 (December 1999) 621–640.

Brecher, Michael. *Crises in World Politics: Theory and Reality.* Oxford: Pergamon Press, 1993.

Brecher, Michael. "International Studies in the Twentieth Century and Beyond," *International Studies Quarterly* 43 (June 1999) 213–264.

Brecher, Michael. "Reflections on a Life in Academe," *International Studies Notes* 20 (fall 1995) 1–8.

Brecher, Michael and Jonathan Wilkenfeld. *A Study of Crisis.* Ann Arbor: University of Michigan Press, 1997.

Brecher, Michael and Jonathan Wilkenfeld, "International Crises and Global Instability: The Myth of the 'Long Peace'," in Charles Kegley, Jr., *The Long Postwar Peace: Contending Explanations and Projections.* New York: Harper Collins, 1991. Pp. 85–104.

Brecher, Michael, Patrick James, and Jonathan Wilkenfeld. "Polarity and Stability: New Concepts, Indicators, and Evidence," *International Interactions* 16 (No. 1, 1990) 49–80.

Breitmeier, Helmut and Klaus Dieter Wolf. "Analyzing Regime Consequences," in Volker Rittberger (ed.), *Regime Theory and International Relations.* Oxford: Clarendon Press, 1993. Pp. 339–360.

Bremer, Stuart A. "Dangerous Dyads: Conditions Affecting the Likelihood of Interstate War, 1816–1965," *Journal of Conflict Resolution* 36 (June 1992) 309–341.

Bremer, Stuart A. "Democracy and Militarized Interstate Conflict, 1816–1965," *International Interactions* 18 (No. 3, 1993) 231–250.

Bremer, Stuart A. "Review of *Reconstructing Realpolitik*," *American Political Science Review* 89 (June 1995) 539–540.

Bremer, Stuart A., J.David Singer, and Urs Laterbacher, "The Population Density and War Proneness of Nations, 1816–1965," *Comparative Political Studies* 6 (October 1973) 329–348.

Buchanan, James M., and Richard E. Wagner, *Democracy in Deficit: The Political Legacy of Lord Keynes.* New York: Academic Press, 1977.

Bueno de Mesquita, Bruce. "An Expected Utility Theory of International Conflict," *American Political Science Review* 74 (December 1980) 917–931.

Bueno de Mesquita, Bruce. "Big Wars, Little Wars: Avoiding Selection Bias," *International Interactions* 16 (No. 3, 1990) 159–170.

Bueno de Mesquita, Bruce. "The End of the Cold War: Predicting an Emergent Property," *Journal of Conflict Resolution* 42 (April 1998) 131–155.

Bueno de Mesquita, Bruce. "Measuring Systemic Polarity," *Journal of Conflict Resolution* 19 (June 1975) 187–216.

Bueno de Mesquita, Bruce. *The War Trap.* New Haven: Yale University Press, 1981.

Bueno de Mesquita, Bruce. "Systemic Polarization and the Occurrence and Duration of War," *Journal of Conflict Resolution* 22 (June 1978) 241–268.

Bueno de Mesquita, Bruce and David Lalman, "Empirical Support for Systemic and Dyadic Explanations of International Conflict," *World Politics* 41 (October 1988) 1–20.

Bueno de Mesquita, Bruce and David Lalman. *War and Reason.* New Haven: Yale University Press, 1992.

Bueno de Mesquita, Bruce, David Newman, and Alvin Rabushka. *Forecasting Political Events: The Future of Hong Kong.* New Haven: Yale University Press, 1985.

Bueno de Mesquita, Bruce and Frans N. Stokman. *European Community Decision-Making: Models, Applications, and Comparisons.* New Haven: Yale University Press, 1994.

Bueno de Mesquita, Bruce and Randolph M. Siverson. "War and the Survival of Political Leaders," *American Political Science Review* 89 (December 1995) 841–855.

Bull, Hedley. *The Anarchical Society.* New York: Columbia University Press, 1977.

Burke, John P. and Fred I. Greenstein, *How Presidents Test Reality: Decisions on Vietnam, 1954 and 1965.* New York: Russell Sage Foundation, 1989.

Burrowes, Robert and Bertram Spector, "The Strength and Direction of Relationships between Domestic and External Conflict and Cooperation, Syria: 1961–1967," in Jonathan Wilkenfeld, ed., *Conflict Behavior and Linkage Politics.* New York: David McKay, 1973. Pp. 294–321.

Busch, Marc L. and Eric R. Reinhardt. "Nice Strategies in a World of Relative Gains," *Journal of Conflict Resolution* 37 (September 1993) 427–445.

Buzan, Barry. "From International System to International Society: Structural Realism and Regime Theory Meet the English School," *International Organization* 47 (summer 1993) 327–352.

Buzan, Barry, Charles Jones, and Richard Little. *The Logic of Anarchy: Neorealism to Structural Realism.* New York: Columbia University Press, 1993.

Caporaso, James A. "Across the Great Divide: Integrating Comparative and International Politics," *International Studies Quarterly* 41 (December 1997) 563–592.

Caporaso, James A. and Alan L. Pelowski, "Economic and Political Integration in Europe," *American Political Science Review* 65 (June 1971) 418–433.

Carleton, William G. *The Revolution in American Foreign Policy.* New York: Random House, 1963.

Carment, David and Patrick James. "Internal Constraints and Interstate Ethnic Conflict," *Journal of Conflict Resolution* 39 (March 1995) 82–109.

Cederman, Lars-Erik. "Emergent Polarity: Analyzing State-Formation and Power Politics," *International Studies Quarterly* 38 (December 1994) 501–534.

Cederman, Lars-Erik. *Emergent Actors in World Politics: How States and Nations Develop and Dissolve*. Princeton: Princeton University Press, 1997.

Chan, Steve. "In Search of Democratic Peace," *Mershon International Studies Review* 41 (Supplement No. 1, May 1997) 59–91.

Chan, Steve. "Mirror, Mirror on the Wall . . . Are the Freer Countries More Pacific?" *Journal of Conflict Resolution* 28 (December 1984) 617–648.

Chan, Steve and Melanie Mason, "Foreign Direct Investment and Host Country Condition," *International Interactions* 17 (No. 3, 1992) 215–232.

Chase-Dunn, Christopher. "Interstate System and Capitalist World-Economy: One Logic or Two?" *International Studies Quarterly* 25 (March 1981) 19–42.

Checkel, Jeffrey. "The Constructivist Turn in International Relations Theory," *World Politics* 50 (January 1998) 324–348.

Cheon, Seong, Andrew F. Cooper, and Niall Fraser. "Partial Security Regimes and Verification of Compliance," *International Interactions* 16 (No. 1, 1990) 117–136.

Chomsky, Noam. *Rethinking Camelot: JFK, the Vietnam War, and U.S. Political Culture*. Boston: South End Press, 1993.

Claude, Inis. Jr. *Power and International Relations*. New York: Random House, 1962.

Clausewitz, Karl von. "On the Nature of War," in John A. Vasquez (ed.), *Classics of International Relations*. 3d ed. Englewood Cliffs, NJ: Prentice-Hall, 1996. Pp. 314–318.

Clinton, W. David. *The Two Faces of National Interest*. Baton Rouge: Louisiana State University, 1994.

Cobb, Roger W. and Charles Elder. *International Community*. New York: Holt, Rinehart, and Winston, 1970.

Cohen, Benjamin J. "The Political Economy of International Trade," *International Organization* 44 (spring 1990) 261–281.

Cohen, Saul B. "A New Map of Global Geopolitical Equilibrium," *Political Geography Quarterly* 1 (1982) 223–241.

Cohen, Saul B. *Geography and Politics in a World Divided*. New York: Random House, 1963.

Coleman, James. *Community Conflict*. New York: Free Press, 1957.

Collins, John. "Foreign Confict Behavior and Domestic Disorder in Africa," in Jonathan Wilkenfeld (ed.), *Conflict Behavior and Linkage Politics*. New York: David McKay, 1973. Pp. 251–293.

Conybeare, John. "Tariff Protection in Developed and Developing Countries," *International Organization* 37 (summer 1983) 441–468.

Conybeare, John. "Trade Wars: A Comparative Study of Anglo-Hanse, Franco-Italian, and Hawley-Smoot Conflicts," in Kenneth A. Oye (ed.), *Cooperation under Anarchy*. Princeton: Princeton University Press, 1986. Pp. 147–172.

Cooper, Richard. *The Economics of Interdependence*. New York: McGraw-Hill, 1968.

Coser, Lewis. *The Functions of Social Conflict*. New York: Free Press, 1956.

Cox, Robert W. "Global *Perestroika*," in George T. Crance and Abla Awami (eds.), *The Theoretical Evolution of International Political Economy*. 2d ed. New York: Oxford University Press, 1997. Pp. 158–172.

Cox, Robert W. "Social Forces, States, and World Orders," in John A. Vasquez (ed.), *Classics of International Relations*. 3d ed. Englewood Cliffs, NJ: Prentice-Hall, 1996. Pp. 126–134.

Crawford, Neta C. "A Security Regime Among Democracies: Cooperation Among Iroquois Nations," *International Organization* 48 (summer 1994) 345–386.

Cusack, Thomas R. and Michael Don Ward. "Military Spending in the U.S., U.S.S.R., and China," *Journal of Conflict Resolution* 25 (September 1981) 429–470.

Dahl, Robert A. "The Concept of Power," *Behavioral Science* 2 (July 1957), 201–215.

Davies, John L. and Chad K. McDaniel. "A New Generation of International Event-Data," *International Interactions* 20 (Nos. 1–2, 1994) 55–78.

Dennis, Michael. "The Policy Basis of General Purpose Forces," *Journal of Conflict Resolution* 18 (March 1974) 1–32.

DerDerian, James. "Radical Interdependence without Apology [Review]," *Mershon International Studies Review* Supplement No. 1, Vol. 38 (April 1994), 130.

deRivera, Joseph H. *The Psychological Dimension of Foreign Policy.* Columbus: Charles E. Merrill, 1968.

DeRouen, Karl L. Jr. "The Indirect Link: Politics, the Economy, and the Use of Force," *Journal of Confict Resolution* 39 (December 1995) 671–695.

de Soysa, Indra, John R. Oneal, and Yong-Hee Park. "Testing Power-Transition Theory Using Alternative Measures of National Capabilities," *Journal of Conflict Resolution* 41 (August 1997) 509–528.

Dessler, David. "Beyond Correlation: Toward a Causal Theory of War," *International Studies Quarterly* 35 (September 1991) 337–355.

Dessler, David. "What's At Stake in the Agent-Structure Debate?" *International Organization* 43 (summer 1989) 441–474.

Deutsch, Karl W. "Communication Theory and Political Integration," in Philip E. Jacob and James V. Toscano (eds.), *The Integration of Political Communities.* Philadelphia: Lippincott, 1964.

Deutsch, Karl W. "Integration and Arms Control in the European Political Environment: A Summary Report," *American Political Science Review* 60 (June 1966) 354–365.

Deutsch, Karl W. "On the Concepts of Politics and Power," in James N. Rosenau (ed.), *International Politics and Foreign Policy.* New York: Free Press, 1969.

Deutsch, Karl W. and J. David Singer. "Multipolar Power Systems and International Stability," in James N. Rosenau (ed.), *International Politics and Foreign Policy.* New York: Free Press, 1969. Pp. 315–324. [Reprinted from *World Politics* 16 (1964) 390–406.]

Deutsch, Karl. W. et al. *Political Community and the North Atlantic Area.* Princeton, NJ: Princeton University Press, 1957.

Deutsch, Karl W. et al. "Political Community and the North Atlantic Area," in *International Political Communities: An Anthology.* Garden City, N.Y.: Doubleday 1966. Pp. 1–92.

Diehl, Paul F. "Geography and War: A Review and Assessment of the Empirical Literature," *International Interactions* 17 (No. 1, 1991) 11–28.

Diehl, Paul and Gary Goertz. "Territorial Changes and Militarized Conflict," *Journal of Conflict Resolution* 32 (March 1988) 103–122.

Dixon, William J. "A Lag Sequential Approach to the Analysis of Foreign Policy Behavior," in Charles F. Hermann, Charles W. Kegley, Jr., and James N. Rosenau (eds.) *New Directions in the Study of Foreign Policy.* Boston: Allen and Unwin, 1987. Pp. 77–95.

Dixon, William J. "Democracy and the Management of Inernational Conflict," *Journal of Conflict Resolution* 37 (March 1993) 42–68.

Dixon, William J. "Democracy and the Peaceful Settlement of International Conflict," *American Political Science Review* 88 (March 1994) 14–32.

Dixon, William J. "Interdependence and Cooperation in Foreign Policy Behavior: A Comment on Vincent," *International Interactions* 16 (No. 2, 1990) 109–114.

Dixon, William J. and Stephen M. Gaarder, "Presidential Succession and the Cold War: An Analysis of Soviet-American Relations, 1948–1988," *Journal of Politics* 54 (February 1992) 156–175.

Dombrowksi, Peter. "Haute Finance and High Theory: Recent Scholarship on Global Financial Relations," *Mershon International Studies Review* 42 (May 1998) 1–28.

Doran, Charles F. *The Politics of Assimilation: Hegemony and Its Aftermath.* Baltimore: Johns Hopkins University Press, 1971.

Doran, Charles F. *Systems in Crisis: New Imperatives of High Politics at Century's End.* Cambridge: Cambridge University Press, 1991.

Doran, Charles F. "The 'Discontinuity Dilemma' of Changing Systems Structure." Paper delivered at the International Studies Association annual meeting, Chicago, March 26, 1995.

Doran, Charles; and Wes Parsons. "War and the Cycle of Relative Power," *American Political Science Review* 74 (December 1980) 947–965.

Dougherty, James E. and Robert L. Pfaltzgraff, Jr. *Contending Theories of International Relations.* New York: Harper and Row, 1990.

Downs, George W., David M. Rocke, and Peter N. Barsoom. "Managing the Evolution of Multilateralism," *International Organization* 52 (spring 1998) 397–419.

Doyle, Michael. "Kant, Liberal Legacies, and Foreign Affairs, Parts I and II," *Philosophy and Public Affairs* 12 (No. 3/4, 1983) 205–235 and 332–353.

Doyle, Michael. "Liberalism and World Politics," *American Political Science Review* 80 (December 1986) 1151–1169.

Doyle, Michael. *Ways of War and Peace: Realism, Liberalism, and Socialism.* New York: W.W. Norton, 1997.

Druckman, Daniel. *Human Factors in International Negotiations: Social-Psychological Aspects of International Conflict.* Beverly Hills: Sage Publications, 1973.

Duffield, John S. "International Regimes and Alliance Behavior: Explaining NATO Conventional Force Levels," *International Organization* 46 (autumn 1992) 819–856.

Duffy, Gavin. "Events and Versions: Reconstructing Event Data Analysis," *International Interactions* 20 (No. 1/2, 1994) 147–167.

Efinger, Manfred, Peter Mayer, and Gudrun Schwarzer. "Integrating and Contextualizing Hypotheses: Alternative Paths to Better Explanations of Regime Formations?" in Volker Rittberger (Ed.). *Regime Theory and International Relations.* Oxford: Clarendon Press, 1993. Pp. 252–282.

Ellsberg, Daniel. *Papers on the War.* New York: Simon and Schuster, 1972.

Elman, Colin and Miriam Fendius Elman. "Correspondence; History vs. Neo-realism: A Second Look," *International Security* 20 (summer 1995) 182–193.

Elman, Colin and Meriam Fendius Elman. "Lakatos and Neorealism: A Reply to Vasquez," *American Political Science Review* 91 (December 1997) 923–926.

Elman, Meriam Fendius. "The Never-Ending Story: Democracy and Peace," *International Studies Review* 1 (Fall 1999) 87–103.

Enterline, Andrew J. "Regime Changes and Interstate Conflict, 1816–1992," *Political Research Quarterly* 51 (June 1998a) 385–410.

Enterline, Andrew J. "Regime Changes, Neighborhoods, and Interstate Conflict, 1816–1992," *Journal of Conflict Resolution* 42 (December 1998b) 804–829.

Etheredge, L.S. "Personality Effects on American Foreign Policy, 1898–1968: A Test of Interpersonal Generalization Theory," *American Political Science Review* 72 (June 1978) 434–451.

Etzioni, Amitai. "The Epigenesis of Political Communities at the International Level," in James N. Rosenau (ed.), *International Politics and Foreign Policy.* New York: Free Press, 1969. Pp. 346–358.

Etzioni, Amitai. "The Kennedy Experiment," *Western Political Quarterly* 20 (June 1967) 361–380.

Evangelista, Matthew. "The Paradox of State Strength: Transnational Relations, Domestic Structures, and Security Policy in Russia and the Soviet Union," *International Organization* 49 (winter 1995) 1–38.

Eyerman, Joe and Robert A. Hart, Jr. "An Empirical Test of the Audience Cost Proposition: Democracy Speaks Louder than Words," *Journal of Conflict Resolution* 40 (December 1996) 597–616.

Farber, Henry S. and Joanne Gowa. "Polities and Peace," *International Security* 20 (fall 1995) 123–146.

Farber, Henry S.; and Joanne Gowa. "Building Bridges Abroad" [Response], *Journal of Conflict Resolution* 41 (June 1997) 455–456.

Farnham, Barbara. "Roosevelt and the Munich Crisis: Insights from Prospect Theory," *Political Psychology* 13 (June, 1992) 205–235.

Fearon, James D. "Bargaining, Enforcement, and International Cooperation," *International Organization* 52 (spring 1998) 269–306.

Feierabend, Ivo; and Rosalind Feierabend. "Level of Development and International Behavior," in R. Butwell (ed.). *Foreign Policy and the Developing Nation.* Lexington: University of Kentucky Press, 1969.

Ferguson, Yale H. and Richard W. Mansbach, *The Elusive Quest: Theory and International Politics.* Columbia: University of South Carolina Press, 1988.

Ferris, Wayne. *The Power Capabilities of Nation-States.* Lexington, MA: Lexington Books, 1973.

Finnemore, Martha. *National Interests in International Society.* Ithaca: Cornell University Press, 1996.

Fischer, Markus. "Feudal Europe, 800–1300: Communal Discourse and Conflictual Practices," *International Organization* 46 (spring 1992) 426–466.

Fischer, Markus. "On Context, Facts, and Norms: Reply to Hall and Kratochwil," *International Organization* 47 (summer 1993) 493–500.

Fischhoff, B. and T. Beyth-Marom. "Failure Had Many Fathers," *Policy Sciences* 7 (1978) 388–393.

Fisher, W. E. "An Analysis of the Deutsch SocioCausal Paradigm of Political Integration," *International Organization* 23 (spring 1969) 254–290.

Flynn, Gregory and Henry Farrell. "Piecing Together the Democratic Peace: The CSCE and the 'Construction' of Security in Post–Cold War Europe," *International Organization* 53 (summer 1999) 505–536.

Fordham, Benjamin. "Partisanship, Macroeconomic Policy, and the U.S. Uses of Force, 1949–1994," *Journal of Conflict Resolution* 42 (Autumn 1998a) 418–439.

Fordham, Benjamin. "The Politics of Threat Perception and the Use of Force: A Political Economy Model of the U.S. Use of Force, 1949–1994," *International Studies Quarterly* 42 (September 1998b) 567–590.

Fozouni, Bahman. "Confutation of Political Realism," *International Studies Quarterly* 39 (December 1995) 479–510.

Frank, Andre Gunder. *Latin America: Underdevelopment or Revolution.* New York: Monthly Review Press, 1969.

Frieden, Jeffry A. "International Investment and Colonial Control," *International Organization* 48 (autumn 1994) 559–594.

Frieden, Jeffry A. "Invested Interests: The Politics of National Economic Policies in a World of Global Finance," *International Organization* 45 (autumn 1991) 425–452.

Friedman, Thomas L. "A Nixon Legacy Devalued by a Cold War Standard," *New York Times,* May 1, 1994, section 4, p. 4.

Fukuyama, Francis. *The End of History and the Last Man.* New York: Free Press, 1992.

Gaddis, John Lewis. "International Relations Theory and the End of the Cold War," *International Security* 17 (winter 1992/93) 5–58.

Gaddis, John Lewis. *The United States and the End of the Cold War.* New York: Oxford University Press, 1992.

Gallorotti, G. "The Limits of International Organization: Systematic Failure in the Management of International Relations," *International Organization* 45 (spring 1991) 183–220.

Galtung, Johan. "East-West Interaction Patterns," *Journal of Peace Research* 3 (No. 2, 1966) 146–177.

Galtung, Johan. "A Structural Theory of Imperialism," *Journal of Peace Research* 8 (No. 2, 1971) 81–117.

Gamson, William and Andre Modigliani. *Untangling the Cold War: A Strategy for Testing Rival Theories.* Boston: Little, Brown, 1971.

Garnham, David. "Power Parity and Lethal International Violence, 1969–1973, *Journal of Conflict Resolution* 20 (September 1976) 379–394.

Garrett, Geoffrey. "International Cooperation and Institutional Choice: The European Community's Internal Market," *International Organization* 46 (spring 1992) 533–560.

Garrett, Geoffrey, R. Daniel Kelemen, and Heiner Schulz. "The European Court of Justice, National Governments, and Legal Integration in the European Union," *International Organization* 52 (winter 1998) 149–176.

Garrett, Geoffrey and Peter Lange, "Political Responses to Interdependence: What's "Left" for the Left?" *International Organization* 45 (autumn 1991) 539–564.

Garrett, Geoffrey and Barry Weingast. "Ideas, Interests, and Institutions: Constructing the European Community's Internal Market," in Judith Goldstein and Robert O. Keohane, (eds.), *Ideas and Foreign Policy: Beliefs, Institutions, and Political Change*. Ithaca, NY: Cornell University Press, 1993. Pp. 173–206.

Gasiorowski, Mark J. "Economic Interdependence and International Conflict," *International Studies Quarterly* 30 (March 1986) 23–38.

Gaubatz, Kurt T. "Democratic States and Commitment in International Relations," *International Organization* 50 (winter 1996) 109–140.

Gawande, Kishore and Wendy L. Hansen. "Retaliation, Bargaining, and the Pursuit of 'Free and Fair' Trade," *International Organization* 53 (winter 1999) 117–159.

Gelb, Leslie. "Vietnam: Some Hypotheses About How and Why," Paper delivered at the 66th American Political Science Association, Los Angeles, September 8–12, 1970.

Geller, Daniel S. "Capability Concentration, Power Transition, and War," *International Interactions* 17 (No. 3, 1992) 269–284.

Geller, Daniel S. "Nuclear Weapons, Deterrence, and Crisis Escalation," *Journal of Conflict Resolution* 34 (June 1990) 291–310.

Geller, Daniel S. "Power Differentials and War in Rival Dyads," *International Studies Quarterly* 37 (June 1993) 173–194.

Gelpi, Christopher. "Crime and Punishment: The Role of Norms in Crisis Bargaining," *American Political Science Review* 91 (June 1997a) 339–360.

Gelpi, Christopher. "Democratic Diversions: Governmental Structure and the Externalization of Domestic Conflict," *Journal of Conflict Resolution* 41 (April 1997b) 255–282.

George, Alexander A. "The 'Operational Code': A Neglected Approach to the Study of Political Leaders and Decision-Making," *International Studies Quarterly* 13 (June 1969) 190–222.

George, Alexander L. "Assessing Presidential Character," *World Politics* 26 (January 1974) 234–282.

George, Alexander L. and Margaret George, *Woodrow Wilson and Colonel House: A Personality Study.* (New York: Dover Publications, 1964).

George, Alexander L., David K. Hall, and William E. Simons. *The Limits of Coercive Diplomacy: Laos, Cuba, and Vietnam.* Boston: Little, Brown, 1971.

George, Alexander L. and William E. Simons. *Limits of Coercive Diplomacy.* 2d ed. Boulder, CO: Westview, 1994.

George, Alexander and Richard Smoke, *Deterrence in American Foreign Policy: Theory and Practice.* New York: Columbia University Press, 1974.

Gibbons, William Conrad. "The 1965 Decision to Send U.S. Ground Forces to Vietnam." Paper prepared for the annual meeting of the International Studies Association, Washington, DC, April 16, 1987.

Gill, Stephen. *American Hegemony and the Trilateral Commission.* Cambridge: Cambridge University Press, 1990.

Gilpin, Robert G. "The Richness of the Tradition of Political Realism," *International Organization* 38 (spring 1984) 287–304.

Gilpin, Robert G. *The Political Economy of International Relations.* Princeton: Princeton University Press, 1987.

Gilpin, Robert G. *War and Change in World Politics.* Cambridge: Cambridge University Press, 1981.

Gleditsch, Nils Petter and Havard Hegre. "Peace and Democracy: Three Levels of Analysis," *Journal of Conflict Resolution* 41 (April 1997) 283–310.

Gochman, Charles and Aaron Hoffman. "Peace in the Balance? A Matter of Design," *International Studies Notes* 21 (spring 1996) 20–25.

Goldgeier, James M. and Michael McFaul. "A Tale of Two Worlds: Core and Periphery in the Post–Cold War Era," *International Organization* 46 (spring 1992) 467–492.

Goldstein, Joshua S. *International Relations.* New York: Harper Collins, 1994.

Goldstein, Joshua S. *Long Cycles: Prosperity and War in the Modern Age.* New Haven: Yale University Press, 1988.

Goldstein, Joshua S. "The Possibility of Cycles in International Relations," *International Studies Quarterly* 35 (December 1991a) 477–480.

Goldstein, Joshua S. "Reciprocity in Superpower Relations," *International Studies Quarterly* 35 (June 1991b) 195–210.

Goldstein, Joshua S. and John R. Freeman. *Three-Way Street: Strategic Reciprocity in World Politics.* Chicago: University of Chicago Press, 1990.

Goldstein, Joshua S. and John R. Freeman, "U.S.–Soviet-Chinese Relations: Routine, Reciprocity, or Rational Expectations?" *American Political Science Review* 85 (March 1991) 17–35.

Goldstein, Joshua S.; and Jon C. Pevehouse. "Reciprocity, Bullying, and International Cooperation: Time Series Analysis of the Bosnia Conflict," *American Political Science Review* 91 (September 1997) 515–530.

Goldstein, Judith and Robert O. Keohane. eds., *Ideas and Foreign Policy: Beliefs, Institutions, and Political Change.* Ithaca, NY: Cornell University Press, 1993.

Goodman, John B., Debora Spar, and David B. Yoffie. "Foreign Direct Investment and the Demand for Protection in the United States," *International Organization* 50 (autumn 1996) 565–592.

Gowa, Joanne. *Allies, Adversaries and International Trade.* Princeton: Princeton University Press, 1994.

Gowa, Joanne. "Democratic States and International Disputes," *International Organization* 49 (summer 1995) 511–522.

Gowa, Joanne. "Politics at the Water's Edge: Parties, Voters, and the Use of Force Abroad," *International Organization* 52 (spring 1998) 307–324.

Grieco, Joseph M. "Anarchy and the Limits of Cooperation: A Realist Critique of the Newest Liberal Institutionalism," *International Organization* 42 (summer 1988) 485–508.

Grunberg, Isabelle. "Exploring the 'Myth' of Hegemonic Stability," *International Organization* 44 (autumn 1990) 431–478.

Gurr, Ted Robert. "Peoples against States: Ethnopolitical Conflict and the Changing World System," *International Studies Quarterly* 38 (September 1994) 347–378.

Guttieri, Karen, Michael D. Wallace, and Peter Suedfeld. "The Integrative Complexity of American Decision Makers in the Cuban Missile Crisis," *Journal of Conflict Resolution* 39 (December 1995) 595–621.

Haas, Ernst B. "The Balance of Power: Prescription, Concept, or Propaganda," in James N. Rosenau (ed.), *International Politics and Foreign Policy.* New York: Free Press, 1961.

Haas, Ernst B. "On Systems and International Regimes," *World Politics* 27 (No. 2, 1975) 147–174.

Haas, Ernst B. "The Study of Regional Integration: Reflections on the Joy and Anguish of Pretheorizing," *International Organization* 24 (autumn 1970) 607–648.

Haas, Michael. "Social Change and National Aggressiveness, 1900–1960," in J. David Singer (ed.), *Quantitative International Politics: Insights and Evidence.* New York: Free Press, 1968. Pp. 215–245.

Haas, Michael. "International Subsystems: Stability and Polarity," *American Political Science Review* 64 (March 1970) 98–123.

Haas, Michael. "When Democracies Fight One Another, Just What Is the Punishment for Disobeying the Law?" Paper prepared for the annual convention of the American Political Science Association, Chicago, September 1, 1995.

Haas, Peter M. "Introduction: Epistemic Communities and International Policy Coordination," *International Organization* 46 (winter 1992a) 1–36.

Haas, Peter M. "Banning Chlorofluorocarbons: Epistemic Community Efforts to Protect Stratospheric Zone," *International Organization* 46 (winter 1992b) 187–224.

Haggard, Stephan and Beth A. Simmons. "Theories of International Regimes," *International Organization* 41 (summer 1987) 491–517.

Halberstam, David. *The Unfinished Odyssey of Robert Kennedy.* New York: Random House, 1968.

Hall, Rodney Bruce and Friedrich V. Kratochwil. "Medieval Tales: Neorealist 'Science' and the Abuse of History," *International Organization* 47 (summer 1993) 479–492.

Hallin, Daniel C. *The "Uncensored War": The Media and Vietnam.* New York: Oxford Unversity Press, 1986.

Haney, Patrick J. "The Nixon Administration and Middle East Crises," *Political Research Quarterly* 47 (December 1994) 939–960.

Hanson, Brian T. "What Happened to Fortress Europe?: External Trade Policy Liberalization in the European Union," *International Organization* 52 (winter 1998) 55–86.

Harf, James E. et al. "Systemic and External Attributes in Foreign Policy Analysis," in James N. Rosenau (ed.), *Comparing Foreign Policies: Theories, Findings, and Methods.* New York: John Wiley, 1974. Pp. 235–250.

Harford, Thomas and Leonard Solomon. "'Reformed Sinner' and 'Lapsed Saint' Strategies in the Prisoner's Dilemma Game," *Journal of Conflict Resolution* 11 (March 1967) 104–109.

Harrison, Neil. "In Search of Theory in International Environmental Politics [Review]," *Mershon International Studies Review* 40 (Supplement No. 1, April, 1996) 145–149.

Harrop, Jeffrey. *The Politial Economy of Integration in the European Community.* Aldershot, UK: Gower, 1989.

Harsanyi, J. "Bargaining and Conflict Situations in the Light of a New Approach to Game Theory," *American Economic Review* 75 (May 1965) 447–457.

Hart, Jeffrey. "Symmetry and Polarization in the European International System, 1870–1879," *Journal of Peace Research* 11 (No. 3, 1974) 229–244.

Harvey, Frank P. "Rigor Mortis or Rigor? More Tests: Necessity, Sufficiency, and Deterrence Logic," *International Studies Quarterly* 42 (December 1998) 675–708.

Hasenclever, Andreas, Peter Mayer and Volker Rittberger. "Interests, Power, Knowledge: The Study of International Regimes," *Mershon International Studies Review* 40 (October 1996) 177–228.

Healy, Brian and Arthur Stein. "The Balance of Power in International History," *Journal of Conflict Resolution* 17 (March 1973) 33–62.

Henderson, Errol A. "Culture or Contiguity: Ethnic Conflict, the Similarity of States, and the Onset of War, 1820–1989," *Journal of Conflict Resolution* 41 (October 1997) 649–668.

Henderson, Errol A. "The Democratic Peace Through the Lens of Culture, 1820–1989," *International Studies Quarterly* 42 (September 1998) 461–484.

Henning, C. Randall. "Systemic Conflict and Regional Monetary Integration: The Case of Europe," *International Organization* 52 (summer 1998) 537–574.

Herek, Gregory M., Irving L. Janis, and Paul Huth. "Decision Making during International Crises: Is Quality of Process Related to Outcome?" *Journal of Conflict Resolution* 31 (June 1987) 203–226.

Herek, Gregory M., Irving L. Janis, and Paul Huth. "Quality of U.S. Decision Making during the Cuban Missile Crisis," *Journal of Conflict Resolution* 33 (September 1989) 446–459.

Hermann, Charles F. "Some Issues in the Study of International Crisis," in Charles F. Hermann (ed.), *International Crises: Insights from Behavioral Research.* New York: Free Press, 1972. Pp. 3–17.

Hermann, Charles F. "Sorting Out Crisis Outcomes," *Mershon International Studies Review* 40 (October 1996) 311–313.

Hermann, Charles F., Maurice A. East, Margaret G. Hermann, Barbara G. Salmore, and Stephen A. Salmore. *CREON: A Foreign Events Data Set.* Beverly Hills: Sage, 1973.

Hermann, Margaret. "Leader Personality and Foreign Policy Behavior," in James N. Rosenau (ed.), *Comparing Foreign Policies: Theories, Findings, and Methods.* New York: John Wiley, 1974.

Hermann, Margaret. "Explaining Foreign Policy Behavior Using Personal Characteristics of Political Leaders," *International Studies Quarterly* 24 (March 1980) 7–46.

Hermann, Margaret G. "Personality and Foreign Policy Decision-Making: A Study of 53 Heads of Government," in Donald A. Sylvan and Steve Chan (eds.), *Foreign Policy Decision-Making: Perceptions, Cognition, and Artificial Intelligence.* New York: Praeger, 1984. Pp. 53–80.

Hermann, Margaret G. and Charles W. Kegley, Jr. "Ballots, a Barrier against the Use of Bullets and Bombs: Democratization and Military Intervention," *Journal of Conflict Resolution* 40 (September 1996) 436–459.

Hermann, Margaret S. and Charles W. Kegley, Jr. "Re-thinking Democracy and International Peace: Perspectives from Political Psychology," *International Studies Quarterly* 39 (December 1995) 511–534.

Herrmann, Richard K. "Analyzing Soviet Images of the United States," *Journal of Conflict Resolution* 29 (December 1985) 665–698.

Herrmann, Richard K. and Michael P. Fischerkeller. "Beyond the Enemy Image and Spiral Model: Cognitive-Strategic Research after the Cold War," *International Organization* 49 (summer 1995) 415–450.

Hilsman, Roger. *To Move a Nation.* New York: Delta, 1968.

Hollist, W. Ladd. "An Analysis of Arms Processes in the United States and the Soviet Union," *International Studies Quarterly* 21 (September 1977) 503–528.

Holsti, Kalevi J. "National Role Conceptions in the Study of Foreign Policy," *International Studies Quarterly* 14 (September 1970) 233–309.

Holsti, Kalevi J. "A New International Politics?" *International Organization* 32 (spring 1978) 513–530.

Holsti, Kalevi J. *Peace and War: Armed Conflicts and International Order, 1648–1989.* Cambridge: Cambridge University Press, 1991.

Holsti, Ole R. "The Belief System and National Images," in James N. Rosenau (ed.), *International Politics and Foreign Policy.* New York: Free Press, 1969. Pp. 543–550.

Holsti, Ole R. *Crisis, Escalation and War.* Montreal: McGill-Queens University Press, 1972.

Holsti, Ole R. "Individual Differences in 'Definition of the Situation,'" *Journal of Conflict Resolution* 14 (September 1970) 290–307.

Holsti, Ole R. "The 1914 Crisis," *American Political Science Review* 59 (June 1965) 365–378.

Holsti, Ole R. "The Search for the Elusive Essence of Decision," in Joseph Kruzel and James N. Rosenau (eds.), *Journeys through World Politics: Autobiographical Reflections of Thirty-Four Academic Travelers.* Lexington, MA: D.C. Heath, 1989.

Holsti, Ole R., Richard A. Brody, and Robert C. North. "Measuring Affect and Action in International Reaction Models," in James N. Rosenau (ed.), *International Politics and Foreign Policy.* New York: Free Press, 1969. Pp. 679–696.

Holsti, Ole R. and John D. Sullivan. "National-International Linkages: France and China as Nonconforming Alliance Members," in James N. Rosenau (ed.), *Linkage Politics.* New York: Free Press, 1969.

Hopf, Ted. "Polarity, the Offense-Defense Balance, and War," *American Political Science Review* 85 (June 1991) 475–493.

Hopmann, P. Terrence. "International Conflict and Cohesion in the Communist System," *International Studies Quarterly* 11 (September 1967) 212–236.

Hout, Gil. *Capitalism and the Third World.* Brookfield, VT: Edward Elgar Publishing, 1993.

Houweling, Henk W. and Jan G. Siccama. "Power Transitions as a Cause of War," *Journal of Conflict Resolution* 32 (March 1988) 87–102.

Houweling, Henk W. and Jan G. Siccama. "Power Transitions and Critical Points as Predictors of Great Power War," *Journal of Conflict Resolution* 35 (December 1991) 642–658.

Howley, Frank. *Berlin Command.* New York: Putnam's, 1950.

Huntington, Samuel P. "American Ideals versus American Institutions," *Political Science Quarterly* 97 (spring 1982) 1–38.

Huntington, Samuel P. "The Clash of Civilizations?" in *Foreign Affairs: Agenda, 1994: Critical Issues in Foreign Policy.* New York: Council on Foreign Relations, 1994.

Hurrel, Andrew. "International Society and the Study of Regimes," in Volker Rittberger (ed.), *Regime Theory and International Relations.* Oxford: Clarendon Press, 1993. Pp. 49–72.

Huth, Paul. *Deterrence and War.* New Haven: Yale University Press, 1988a.

Huth, Paul. "Extended Deterrence and the Outbreak of War," *American Political Science Review* 82 (June 1988b) 423–442.

Huth, Paul. "The Extended Deterrent Value of Nuclear Weapons," *Journal of Conflict Resolution* 34 (June 1990) 270–290.

Huth, Paul. "Major Power Intervention in International Crises, 1918–1988," *Journal of Conflict Resolution* 42 (December 1998) 744–770.

Huth, Paul. *Standing Your Ground: Territorial Disputes and International Conflict.* Ann Arbor: University of Michigan Press, 1996.

Huth, Paul, D. Scott Bennett, and Christopher Gelpi. "System Uncertainty, Risk Propensity, and International Conflict among the Great Powers," *Journal of Conflict Resolution* 36 (September 1992) 478–517.

Huth, Paul, Christopher Gelpi, and D. Scott Bennett. "The Escalation of Great Power Militarized Disputes: Testing Rational Deterrence Theory and Structural Realism," *American Political Science Review* 87 (September 1993) 609–623.

Huth, Paul and Bruce Russett. "Deterrence Failure and Crisis Escalation," *International Studies Quarterly* 32 (March 1988) 29–45.

Huth, Paul and Bruce Russett. "General Deterrence between Enduring Rivals: Testing Three Competing Models," *American Political Science Review* 87 (March 1993) 61–73.

Huth, Paul and Bruce Russett. "What Makes Deterrence Work? Cases from 1900 to 1980," *World Politics* 36 (1984) 496–526.

Hybel, Alex Roberto. *Power over Rationality: The Bush Administration and the Gulf Crisis.* Albany, NY: State University of New York Press, 1993.

Ikenberry, G. John. "The Irony of State Strength: Comparative Responses to the Oil Shocks in the 1970s," *International Organization* 40 (winter 1986) 105–138.

Ikenberry, G. John. "A World Economy Restored: Expert Consensus and the Ango-American Postwar Settlement," *International Organization* 46 (winter 1992) 289–322.

Ikenberry, G. John. "Creating Yesterday's New World Order: Keynsian 'New Thinking' and the Anglo-American Postwar Settlement," in Judith Goldstein and Robert O. Keohane (eds.), *Ideas and Foreign Policy.* Ithaca: Cornell University Press, 1993. Pp. 57–86.

Intriligator, Michael D. and Dagobert L. Brito. "Can Arms Races Lead to the Outbreak of War?" *Journal of Conflict Resolution* 28 (March 1984) 63–84.

ISA *Newsletter,* Vol. 22, No. 10 (December 1995), 48.

James, Patrick. "Structural Realism and the Causes of War," *Mershon International Studies Review* 39 (Supplement No. 2: October 1995) 181–208.

James, Patrick and John R. Oneal. "Influences on the President's Use of Force," *Journal of Conflict Resolution* 35 (June 1991) 307–332.

James, Scott C. and David A. Lake. "The Second Face of Hegemony: Britain's Repeal of the Corn Laws and the American Walker Tariff of 1846," *International Organization* 43 (winter 1989) 1–30.

Janis, Irving L. *Groupthink: Psychological Studies of Policy Decisions and Fiascoes.* Boston: Houghton Mifflin, 1982.

Janis, Irving L. *Victims of Groupthink: A Psychological Study of Foreign-Policy Decisions and Fiascoes.* Boston: Houghton Mifflin 1972.

Jensen, Lloyd. "Negotiating Strategic Arms Control, 1969–1979," *Journal of Conflict Resolution* 28 (September 1984) 535–559.

Jentleson, Bruce W. *With Friends Like These: Reagan, Bush, and Saddam, 1982–1990.* New York: W.W Norton, 1994.

Jervis, Robert. "From Balance to Concert: A Study of International Security Cooperation," in Kenneth A. Oye (ed.), *Cooperation under Anarchy.* Princeton: Princeton University Press, 1986. Pp. 88–79.

Jervis, Robert. "Political Decision-Making: Recent Contributions," *Political Psychology* 2 (1980) 86–101.

Jervis, Robert. "Security Regimes," *International Organization* 36 (spring 1982) 357–378.

Jervis, Robert. "Systems and Interaction Effects," in Jack Snyder and Robert Jervis (eds.), *Coping with Complexity in the International System.* San Francisco: Westview Press, 1993. Pp. 25–46.

Kacowicz, Arie M. "The Problem of Peaceful Territorial Change," *International Studies Quarterly* 38 (June 1994) 219–254.

Kahn, Herman. *Thinking about the Unthinkable.* New York: Horizon Press, 1962.

Kaldor, Mary. *The Imaginary War: Understanding the East-West Conflict.* Oxford: Basil Blackwell, 1990.

Kaplan, Morton. *System and Process in International Politics.* New York: John Wiley, 1957.

Kaplan, Morton. "Variants on Six Models of the International System," in James N. Rosenau (ed.), *International Politics and Foreign Policy.* New York: Free Press, 1969. Pp. 291–303.

Kapstein, Ethan B. "Is Realism Dead? The Domestic Sources of International Politics." *International Organization* 49 (autumn 1995) 751–774.

Katzenstein, Peter J., Robert O. Keohane, and Stephen D. Krasner. "*International Organization* and the Study of World Politics," *International Organization* 52 (autumn 1998) 645–686.

Kaufman, Stuart J. "The Fragmentation and Consolidation of International Systems," *International Organization* 51 (spring 1997) 173–208.

Kaufmann, Chaim D. "Out of the Lab and into the Archives: A Method for Testing Psychological Explanations of Political Decision-Making," *International Studies Quarterly* 38 (December 1994) 557–586.

Kegley, Charles W., Jr. "The Neoidealist Moment in International Relations Studies?" *International Studies Quarterly* 37 (June 1993) 131–146.

Kegley, Charles W., Jr. and Gregory Raymond. *A Multipolar Peace? Great-Power Politics in the Twenty-First Century.* New York: St. Martin's Press, 1994.

Kegley, Charles W. Jr. and Margaret G. Hermann. "Military Intervention and the Democratic Peace," *International Interactions* 21 (No. 1, 1995) 1–21.

Kelly, Philip. "Escalation of Regional Conflict: Testing the Shatterbelt Concept," *Political Geography Quarterly* 5 (1986) 161–180.

Kennan, George. "A Fateful Error," *New York Times* February 5, 1997, A19 [California edition].

Kennedy, Paul. *The Rise and Fall of the Great Powers.* New York: Random House, 1987.

Keohane, Robert O. *After Hegemony.* Princeton: Princeton University Press, 1984.

Keohane, Robert O. "Beyond Dichotomy: Conversations between International Relations and Feminist Theory," *International Studies Quarterly* 42 (March 1998) 193–198.

Keohane, Robert O. "The Demand for International Regimes," *International Organization* 36 (spring 1982) 325–356.

Keohane, Robert O. "International Institutions: Two Approaches," *International Studies Quarterly* 32 (December 1988) 379–396.

Keohane, Robert. "Realism, Neorealism, and the Study of Politics," in Robert O. Keohane (ed.), *Neorealism and Its Critics.* New York: Columbia University Press, 1986. Pp. 1–26.

Keohane, Robert O. "Reciprocity in International Relations," *International Organization* 40 (winter 1986) 1–28.

Keohane, Robert O. "Regime," in Joel Krieger (ed.), *Oxford Companion to Politics of the World.* New York: Oxford University Press, 1993. P. 778.

Keohane, Robert O. and Lisa L. Martin. "The Promise of Institutionalist Theory," *International Security* 20 (summer 1995) 39–51.

Keohane, Robert O. and Joseph S. Nye. *Power and Interdependence.* Boston: Little, Brown, 1977.

Keohane, Robert O. and Joseph S. Nye. *Power and Interdependence.* 2d. ed. Glenview IL: Scott Foresman, 1989.

Keohane, Robert O. and Joseph S. Nye. *"Power and Interdependence* Revisited," *International Organization* 41 (autumn 1987) 725–753.

Keohane, Robert O. and Joseph S. Nye. "World Politics and the International Economic System," in C. Fred Bergesten (ed.), *The Future of the International Economic Order: An Agenda for Research.* Lexington, MA: Lexington Publishing, 1973.

Khong, Yuen Foong. "Confronting Hitler and Its Consequences," in Philip E. Tetlock and Aaron Belkin (eds.), *Counterfactual Thought Experiments in World Politics.* Princeton: Princeton Univeristy Press, 1996. Pp. 95–118.

Kim, Woosang. "Power Transitions and Great Power War from Westphalia to Waterloo," *World Politics* 45 (October 1992) 153–172.

Kim, Woosang and Bruce Bueno de Mesquita. "How Perceptions Influence the Risk of War," *International Studies Quarterly* 39 (March 1995) 51–66.

Kim, Woosang and James D. Morrow. "When Do Power Shifts Lead to War?" *American Journal of Political Science* 36 (November 1992) 896–922.

Kimura, Masato and David A. Welch. "Specifying 'Interests': Japan's Claims to the Northern Territories and Its Implications for International Relations Theory," *International Studies Quarterly* 42 (June 1998) 213–244.

Kirby, Andrew M. and Michael D. Ward. "The Spatial Analysis of Peace and War," *Comparative Political Studies* 20 (October 1987) 293–313.

Klotz, Audie. "Norms Reconstituting Interests: Global Racial Equality and U.S. Sanctions against South Africa," *International Organization* 49 (summer 1995) 451–478.

Kondratieff, Nicholas D. "The Long Waves in Economic Life," *Review of Economic Statistics* 17 (No. 6, 1935) 105–115.

Korb, Lawrence J. "Spending without Strategy: The Fiscal Year 1986 Annual Department of Defense Report," *International Security* 13 (spring 1987) 166–178.

Koslowski, Rey and Friedrich V. Kratochwil. "Understanding Change in International Politics: The Soviet Empire's Demise and the International System," *International Organization* 48 (spring 1994) 215–248.

Kowert, Paul A. and Margaret G. Hermann. "Who Takes Risks? Daring and Caution in Foreign Policy Making," *Journal of Conflict Resolution* 41 (October 1997) 611–637.

Krasner, Stephen D. "The Accomplishments of International Political Economy," in Steve Smith, Ken Booth, and Marysia Zalewski (eds.), *International Theory: Positivism and Beyond.* Cambridge: Cambridge University Press, 1996. Pp. 108–127.

Krasner, Stephen D. "International Political Economy: Abiding Discord," *Review of International Political Economy* 1 (spring 1994) 13–19.

Krasner, Stephen D. "Regimes and the Limits of Realism," *International Organization* 36 (spring 1982a) 497–510.

Krasner, Stephen D. *Sovereignty: Organized Hypocrisy.* Princeton: Princeton University Press, 1999.

Krasner, Stephen D. "Structural Causes and Regime Consequences: Regimes as Intervening Variables," *International Organization* 36 (spring 1982b) 185–206.

Krasner, Stephen D. "Westphalia and All That," in Judith Goldstein and Robert O. Keohane (eds.), *Ideas and Foreign Policy: Beliefs, Institutions, and Political Change.* Ithaca, NY: Cornell University Press, 1993. Pp. 235–264.

Kratochwil, Friedrich. "Contracts and Regimes: Do Issue Specificity and Variations of Formality Matter?" in Volker Rittberger (ed.), *Regime Theory and International Relations.* Oxford: Clarendon Press, 1993. Pp. 73–93.

Kratochwil, Friedrich. "Preface," in Friedrich Kratochwil and Edward D. Mansfield (eds.), *International Organization: A Reader.* New York: Harper Collins, 1994.

Kratochwil, Friedrich and John G. Ruggie. "International Organization: A State of the Art or an Art of the State," *International Organization* 40 (autumn 1986) 753–775.

Krugman, Paul. "Competitiveness: A Dangerous Obsession," *Foreign Affairs* 73 (March/April 1994) 28–45.

Krugman, Paul and Anthony J. Venables. "Globalization and the Inequality of Nations," *Quarterly Journal of Economics* 110 (November 1995) 857–879.

Kugler, Jacek. "The Politics of Foreign Debt in Latin America," *International Interactions* 13 (No. 2, 1987) 115–144.

Kugler, Jacek and Marina Arbetman. "Choosing among Measures of Power: A Review of the Empirical Record," in Richard J. Stoll and Michael D. Ward (eds.), *Power in World Politics.* Boulder: Lynne Rienner, 1989. Pp. 49–78.

Kugler, Jacek and A.F.K. Organski, "The End of Hegemony?" *International Interactions* 15 (No. 2, 1989) 113–128.

Kugler, Jacek, Lewis W. Snider and William Longwell. "From Desert Shield to Desert Storm: Success, Strife, or Quagmire?" *Conflict Management and Peace Science* 13 (No. 2, 1994) 113–148.

Kuhn, Thomas S. *The Structure of Scientific Revolutions.* (Chicago: University of Chicago Press, 1962).

Lake, David A. "Beneath the Commerce of Nations: A Theory of International Economic Structures," *International Studies Quarterly* 28 (June 1984) 143–170.

Lake, David A., ed., *The International Political Economy of Trade.* Brookfield, VT: Edward Elgar Publishing, 1993a.

Lake, David A. "Leadership, Hegemony, and the International Economy: Naked Emperor or Tattered Monarch with Potential?" *International Studies Quarterly* 37 (December 1993b) 459–489.

Lake, David A. "Power and the Third World: Toward a Realist Political Economy of North-South Relations," *International Studies Quarterly* 31 (June 1987) 217–234.

Lake, David A. "Powerful Pacifists: Democratic States and War," *American Political Science Review* 86 (March 1992) 24–37.

Lake, David A. "The State and American Trade Strategy in the Pre-Hegemonic Era," *International Organization* 42 (winter 1988) 33–58.

Lampton, David M. "The U.S. Image of Peking in Three International Crises," *Western Political Quarterly* 26 (March 1973) 28–50.

Larson, Deborah Welch. *Origins of Containment: A Psychological Explanation.* Princeton: Princeton University Press, 1985.

Lebow, Richard Ned. *Between Peace and War: The Nature of International Crisis.* Baltimore: Johns Hopkins University Press, 1981.

Lebow, Richard Ned. "The Long Peace, the End of the Cold War, and the Failure of Realism," *International Organization* 48 (spring 1994) 249–277.

Lebow, Richard Ned and Thomas Risse-Kappen, eds. *International Relations Theory and the End of the Cold War.* New York: Columbia University Press, 1995.

Lebow, Richard Ned and Janice Gross Stein. "Deterrence: The Elusive Dependent Variable," *World Politics* 42 (April 1990) 336–369.

Leeds, Brett Ashley and David R. Davis. "Domestic Political Vulnerability and International Disputes," *Journal of Conflict Resolution* 41 (December 1997) 814–834.

Legro, Jeffrey W. and Andrew Moravcsik. "Is Anybody Still a Realist?" *International Security* 24 (fall 1999) 5–55.

Lemke, Douglas and Suzanne Werner. "Power Parity, Commitment to Change, and War," *International Studies Quarterly* 40 (June 1996) 235–260.

Leng, Russell. "Influence Techniques in Militarized Crises: Realpolitik vs. Reciprocity," in Frank W. Wayman and Paul F. Diehl (eds.), *Reconstructing Realpolitik.* Ann Arbor: University of Michigan Press, 1994. Pp. 125–160.

Leng, Russell. *Interstate Crisis Behavior, 1816–1980: Realism Versus Reciprocity.* Cambridge: Cambridge University Press, 1993a.

Leng, Russell. "Reagan and the Russians: Crisis Bargaining Beliefs and the Historical Record," *American Political Science Review* 78 (June 1984), 338–355.

Leng, Russell. "Reciprocating Influence Strategies in Interstate Crisis Bargaining," *Journal of Conflict Resolution* 37 (March 1993b) 3–41.

Leng, Russell and Robert A. Goodsell. "Behavioral Indicators of War Proneness in Bilateral Conflicts," in Pat McGowan (ed.), *Sage International Yearbook of Foreign Policy Studies, II.* Beverly Hills: Sage, 1974. Pp. 191–226.

Leng, Russell and H. Wheeler. "Influence Strategies, Success, and War," *Journal of Conflict Resolution* 23 (December 1979) 655–684.

Levi, Ariel S. and Glen Whyte. "A Cross-Cultural Exploration of the Reference Dependence of Crucial Group Decisions under Risk: Japan's 1941 Decision for War," *Journal of Conflict Resolution* 41 (December 1997) 792–813.

Levy, Jack S. "Alliance Formation and War Behavior, 1495–1975," *Journal of Conflict Resolution* 25 (December 1981) 581–614.

Levy, Jack S. "The Diversionary Theory of War: A Critique," in Manus I. Midlarsky (ed.), *Handbook of War Studies.* Boston: Unwin Hyman, 1989. Pp. 259–288.

Levy, Jack S. "Domestic Politics and War," *Journal of Interdisciplinary History* 18 (spring 1988a) 653–673.

Levy, Jack S. "Learning and Foreign Policy: Sweeping a Conceptual Minefield," *International Organization* 48 (spring 1994) 279–312.

Levy, Jack S. "Long Cycles, Hegemonic Transitions, and the Long Peace," in Charles W. Kegley, Jr. (ed.), *The Long Peace: Contending Explanations and Projections.* New York: Harper Collins, 1991. Pp. 147–176.

Levy, Jack S. "Misperception and the Causes of War: Theoretical Linkages and Analytical Problems," *World Politics* 36 (October 1983a) 76–99.

Levy, Jack S. "The Polarity of the System and International Stability: An Empirical Analysis," in Alan Ned Sabrosky, ed., *Polarity and War: The Changing Structure of International Conflict.* Boulder: Westview Press, 1985. Pp. 41–66.

Levy, Jack S. "Prospect Theory, Rational Choice, and International Relations," *International Studies Quarterly* 41 (March 1997) 87–112.

Levy, Jack S. "Review Article: When Do Deterrent Threats Work?" *British Journal of Political Science* 18 (1988b) 485–512.

Levy, Jack S. *War in the Modern Great Power System: 1495–1975.* Lexington: University of Kentucky Press, 1983b.

Levy, Marc A., Oran R. Young, and Michael Zurn. "The Study of International Regimes," *European Journal of International Relations* 1 (No. 3, 1995) 267–330.

Lijphart, Arend. "The Structure of the Theoretical Revolution in International Relations," *International Studies Quarterly* 18 (March 1974).

Lindblom, Charles E. "The Science of Muddling Through," *Public Adminstration Review* 19 (spring 1959) 79–88.

Lohmann, Susanne. "Review," *American Political Science Review* 89 (March 1995) 259–261.

Lucier, Charles E. "Changes in the Values of Arms Race Parameters," *Journal of Conflict Resolution* 23 (March 1979) 17–40.

McClelland, Charles A. "Acute International Crises," *World Politics* 14 (October 1961) 182–204.

McClelland, Charles A. "Field Theory and System Theory in International Politics." Los Angeles: University of Southern California, June, 1968, mimeo.

McClelland, Charles A. *Theory and the International System.* (New York: MacMillan, 1966).

McClelland, Charles A. "Verbal and Physical Conflict in the Contemporary International System," (Los Angeles: University of Southern California, 1970), mimeo.

McClelland, Charles A. and Gary D. Hoggard. "Conflict Patterns in the Interactions among Nations," in James N. Rosenau (ed.), *International Politics and Foreign Policy.* New York: Free Press, 1969. Pp. 711–724.

McDermott, R. "The Failed Rescue Mission in Iran: An Application of Prospect Theory," *Political Psychology* 13 (June 1992) 237–264.

McGinnis, Michael D. "Richardson, Rationality, and Restrictive Models of Arms Races," *Journal of Conflict Resolution* 35 (September 1991) 443–473.

McGinnis, Michael D. and John T. Williams. "Change and Stabilty in Superpower Rivalry," *American Political Science Review* 83 (December 1989) 1101–1123.

McInerney, A. "Prospect Theory and Soviet Policy towards Syria, 1966–1967," *Political Psychology* 13 (June 1992) 265–282.

McKeown, Timothy J. "A Liberal Trade Order? The Long-Run Pattern of Imports to the Advanced Capitalist States," *International Studies Quarterly* 35 (June 1991) 151–172.

McKeown, Timothy J. "Hegemonic Stability Theory and 19th Century Tariff Levels in Europe," *International Organization* 37 (winter 1983) 73–92.

McNeil, Donald G. "Weight of U.S. Treaty Vote Emerges at Vienna Panel," *New York Times,* October 8, 1999: A11 [AZ Edition].

Majeski, Steven J. and David L. Jones. "Arms Race Modeling," *Journal of Conflict Resolution* 25 (June 1981) 259–288.

Majeski, Steven J. and David J. Sylvan. "Simple Choices and Complex Calculations: A Critique of *The War Trap,*" *Journal of Conflict Resolution* 28 (June 1984) 316–340.

Mandel, Robert. "Roots of the Modern Interstate Border Dispute," *Journal of Conflict Resolution* 24 (September 1980) 427–454.

Mandelbaum, Michael. "Is Major War Obsolete?" *Survival* 40 (Winter, 1998/1999) 20–38.

Mansbach, Richard W. and John A. Vasquez. *In Search of Theory: A New Paradigm for Global Politics.* New York: Columbia University Press, 1981.

Mansfield, Edward. "Capabilities and International Trade," *International Organization* 46 (summer 1992) 731–764.

Mansfield, Edward. "The Distribution of Wars over Time," *World Politics* 41 (October 1988) 21–51.

Mansfield, Edward. *Power, Trade, and War.* Princeton: Princeton University Press, 1994.

Mansfield, Edward D. "The Proliferation of Preferential Trading Arrangements," *Journal of Conflict Resolution* 42 (October 1998) 523–543.

Mansfield, Edward D. and Rachel Bronson. "Alliances, Preferential Trading Arrangements, and International Trade," *American Political Science Review* 91 (March 1997) 94–107.

Mansfield, Edward and Marc L. Busch. "The Political Economy of Nontariff Barriers," *International Organization* 49 (autumn 1995) 723–749.

Mansfield, Edward D. and Jack Snyder. "Democratization and the Danger of War," *International Security* 20 (summer 1995) 5–38.

Mansfield, Edward D. and Jack Snyder. "A Reply to Thompson and Tucker," *Journal of Conflict Resolution* 41 (June 1997) 457–461.

Maoz, Zeev and Nasrin Abdolali. "Regime Types and International Conflict, 1816–1976," *Journal of Conflict Resolution* 33 (March 1989) 3–35.

Maoz, Zeev and Allison Astorino. "The Cognitive Structure of Peacemaking: Egypt and Israel, 1970–1978," *Political Psychology* 13 (No. 4, 1992) 647–662.

Maoz, Zeev and Bruce M. Russett. "Alliance, Contiguity, Wealth, and Political Stability: Is the Lack of Conflict among Democracies a Statistical Artifact?" *International Interactions* 17 (No. 3, 1992) 245–268.

Maoz, Zeev and Bruce M. Russett. "Normative and Structural Causes of Democratic Peace, 1946–1986," *American Political Science Review* 87 (September 1993) 624–638.

Masters, Roger D. "The Lockean Tradition in American Foreign Policy," *Journal of International Affairs* 21 (No. 2, 1967) 253–277.

Mattli, Walter and Anne-Marie Slaughter. "Revisiting the European Court of Justice," *International Organization* 52 (winter 1998) 177–210.

Mearsheimer, John J. "Back to the Future: Instability in Europe after the Cold War," *International Security* 15 (summer 1990) 5–56.

Mearsheimer, John J. "The False Promise of International Institutions," *International Security* 19 (No. 3, 1994/95) 332–376.

Mearsheimer, John J. "Offensive Realism," Paper delivered at the annual meeting of the American Political Science Association, Atlanta, September 2–5, 1999.

Mearsheimer, John J. "A Realist Reply," *International Security* 20 (summer 1995) 82–93.

Meernik, James. "Presidential Decision Making and the Political Use of Military Force," *International Studies Quarterly* 38 (March 1994) 121–138.

Meernik, James and Peter Waterman. "The Myth of the Diversionary Use of Force by American Presidents," *Political Research Quarterly* 49 (September 1996) 573–590.

Merritt, Richard L. "Measuring Events for International Political Analysis," *International Interactions* 20 (Nos. 1/2, 1994) 3–33.

Meyer, John W., David J. Frank, Ann Hironaka, Evan Schoter, and Nancy Brandon Tuma. "The Structuring of a World Environmental Regime, 1870–1990," *International Organization* 51 (Autumn, 1997) 623–652.

Midlarsky, Manus I. "Environmental Influences on Democracy," *Journal of Conflict Resolution* 39 (June 1995) 224–262.

Midlarsky, Manus I. *The Onset of World War.* Boston: Unwin Hyman, 1988.

Midlarksy, Manus I. "Polarity and International Stability," *American Political Science Review* 87 (March 1993) 173–177.

Midlarsky, Manus I. "Power, Uncertainty, and the Onset of International Violence," *Journal of Conflict Resolution* 18 (September 1974) 395–431.

Midlarsky, Manus I. "Systemic Wars and Dyadic Wars," *International Interactions* 16 (No. 3, 1990) 171–182.

Miller, Judith. "U.S. Relations with UN Languish," *New York Times,* August 5, 1999, p. A6 [California edition].

Miller, Ross A. "Regime Type, Strategic Interaction, and the Diversonary Use of Force," *Journal of Conflict Resolution* 43 (June 1999) 388–402.

Mintz, Alex. "The Decision to Attack Iraq: A Noncompensatory Theory of Decision Making," *Journal of Conflict Resolution* 37 (December 1993) 595–618.

Modelski, George, ed. *Exploring Long Cycles.* Boulder: Lynne Rienner Publishers, 1987.

Modelski, George. "Is World Politics Evolutionary Learning?" *International Organization* 44 (winter 1990) 1–24.

Modelski, George. "The Long Cycle of Global Politics and the Nation-State," *Comparative Studies in Society and History* 20 (No. 2, 1978), 214–235.

Modelski, George and Sylvia Modelski, eds. *Documenting Global Leadership.* Seattle: University of Washington Press, 1988.

Modelski, George and William R. Thompson. *Leading Sectors and World Powers: The Coevolution of Global Politics and Economics.* Columbia, SC: University of South Carolina Press, 1996.

Moll, Kendall D. and and Gregory M. Luebbert. "Arms Race and Military Expenditure Models," *Journal of Conflict Resolution* 24 (March 1980) 153–186.

Moore, Will H. "Reciprocity and the Domestic-International Conflict Nexus during the 'Rhodesia Problem'," *Journal of Conflict Resolution* 39 (March 1995) 129–167.

Moran, Theodore H. "Grand Strategy: The Pursuit of Power and the Pursuit of Plenty," *International Organization* 50 (winter 1996) 175–205.

Moravcsik, Andrew. "A New Statecraft? Supranational Entrepreneurs and International Cooperation," *International Organization* 53 (spring 1999) 267–306.

Morgan, T. Clifton and Kenneth N. Bickers, "Domestic Discontent and the External Use of Force," *Journal of Conflict Resolution* 36 (March 1992) 25–52.

Morgan, T. Clifton and Sally H. Campbell. "Domestic Structure, Decisional Constraints, and War," *Journal of Conflict Resolution* 35 (June 1991) 187–211.

Morgan, T. Clifton and Valerie L. Schwebach. "Fools Suffer Gladly: The Use of Economic Sanctions in International Crises," *International Studies Quarterly* 41 (March 1997) 27–50.

Morgan, T. Clifton and Valerie L. Schwebach. "Take Two Democracies and Call Me in the Morning: A Prescription for Peace? *International Interactions* 17 (No. 4, 1992) 305–320.

Morgenthau, Hans. *Politics among Nations*. 3d. ed. New York: Knopf, 1965.

Morrow, James D., Randolph M. Siverson, and Tressa E. Taberes. "The Political Determinants of International Trade: The Major Powers, 1907–1990," *American Political Science Review* 92 (September 1998) 649–662.

Morrow, James D. Randolph M. Siverson and Tressa E. Taberes. "Correction to 'Political Determinants to International Trade,'" *American Political Science Review* 93 (December 1999) 931–933.

Mousseau, Michael. "Democracy and Compromise in Militarized Interstate Conflicts, 1816–1992," *Journal of Conflict Resolution* 42 (April 1998) 210–230.

Moynihan, Daniel P. *Pandaemonium: Ethnicity in International Politics*. Oxford: Oxford Univesity Press, 1993.

Mueller, John. *Retreat from Doomsday: The Obsolescence of Major War*. New York: Basic Books, 1989.

Muller, Harald. "The Internalization of Principles, Norms, and Rules by Governments: The Case of Security Regimes," in Volker Rittberger (ed.), *Regime Theory and International Relations*. Oxford: Clarendon Press, 1993. Pp. 361–390.

Murphy, Craig. "Review Essay," *Review of International Political Economy* 1 (spring 1994), 193–197.

Nasar, Sylvia. "The Top Draft Pick in Economics," *New York Times*, April 21, 1995, p. C1 [California edition].

Nau, Henry R. "From Integration to Interdependence: Gains, Losses, and Continuing Gaps," *International Organization* 33 (winter 1979) 119–147.

Nau, Henry R. *The Myth of America's Decline*. New York: Oxford University Press, 1990.

Nayar, Baldev Raj. "Regimes, Power and International Aviation," *International Organization* 49 (winter 1995) 139–170.

Newman, John. *JFK and Vietnam: Deception, Intrigue, and the Struggle for Power*. New York: Warner Books, 1992.

Nicholson, Michael. "The Conceptual Bases of *The War Trap*," *Journal of Conflict Resolution* 31 (June 1987) 346–369.

Nicolson, Harold. *Diplomacy*. New York: Oxford University Press, 1963.

Nincic, Miroslav. "Loss Aversion and the Domestic Context of Military Intervention," *Political Research Quarterly* 50 (March 1997) 97–120.

Norris, Floyd. "Last Big Wall Street Bear Changes His Mind," *New York Times*, December 5, 1995, p. C1.

Nye, Joseph S. "As China Rises, Must Others Bow?" *The Economist*, June 17, 1998. Pp. 23–25.

Nye, Joseph S. *Bound to Lead*. New York: Basic Books, 1990.

Nye, Joseph S. "Nuclear Learning," *International Organization* 41 (summer 1987) 371–402.

Nye, Joseph S. *Peace in Parts: Integration and Conflict in Regional Organization.* Boston: Little, Brown, 1971.

O'Loughlin, John and Luc Anselin. "Bringing Geography Back to the Study of International Relations," *International Interactions* 17 (No. 1, 1991) 29–61.

Onate, Andres. "The Conflict Interactions of the People's Republic of China, 1950–1970," *Journal of Conflict Resolution* 18 (December 1974) 578–594.

Oneal, John R. and James Lee Ray. "New Tests of the Democratic Peace Controlling for Economic Interdependence," *Political Research Quarterly* 50 (December 1997) 751–776.

Oneal, John R. and Bruce M. Russett. "The Classic Liberals Were Right: Democracy, Interdependence, and Conflict, 1950–1985," *International Studies Quarterly* 41 (June 1997) 267–294.

Onuf, Nicholas. "A Constructivist Manifesto," in Kurt Burch and Robert A. Denemark (eds.), *Constituting International Political Economy.* Boulder: Lynne Reinner Publishers, 1997. Pp. 7–17.

Oren, Ido. "The Subjectivity of the 'Democratic' Peace: Changing U.S. Perceptions of Imperial Germany," in Michael E. Brown, Sean M. Lynn-Jones, and Steven E. Miller (eds.), *Debating the Democratic Peace.* Cambridge, MA: MIT Press, 1996.

Organski, A.F.K. *World Politics.* 2d ed. New York: Knopf, 1968.

Organski, A.F.K. and Jacek Kugler. *The War Ledger.* Chicago: University of Chicago Press, 1980.

Osgood, Charles E. *An Alternative to War or Surrender.* Urbana: University of Illinois Press, 1962.

Ostrom, Charles W., Jr. "Evaluating Alternative Foreign Policy Decision-Making models," *Journal of Conflict Resolution* 21 (June 1977) 235–266.

Ostrom, Charles W. and John H. Aldrich. "The Relationship between Size and Stability in the Major Power International System," *American Journal of Political Science* 22 (1978) 743–771.

Ostrom, Charles W., J. and Brian Job. "The President and the Political Use of Force," *American Political Science Review* 80 (June 1986) 541–566.

Paige, Glenn. *The Korean Decision.* New York: Free Press, 1968.

Park, K. and M. Ward, "A Research Note on the Correlates of War National Capability Data," *International Interactions* 14 (No. 3, 1988) 191–199.

Partell, Peter J. "Executive Constraints and Success in International Crises," *Political Research Quarterly* 50 (September 1997) 503–528.

Partell, Peter J. and Glenn Palmer. "Audience Costs and Interstate Crises: An Empirical Assessment of Fearon's Model of Dispute Outcomes," *International Studies Quarterly* 43 (June 1999) 389–406.

Passell, Peter. "A Lot of Money Spent on Nuclear Arms Was Wasted," *New York Times* December 14, 1995, C2.

Passell, Peter. "Trade Pacts by Regions," *New York Times* February 4, 1997, C1 [California edition].

Patchen, Martin. "Conflict and Cooperation in American-Soviet Relations: What Have We Learned from Quantitative Research?" *International Interactions* 17 (No. 2, 1991) 127–144.

Patchen, Martin. "Models of Cooperation and Conflict: A Critical Review," *Journal of Conflict Resolution* 14 (September 1970) 389–408.

Patchen, Martin. "Strategies for Eliciting Cooperation from an Adversary: Laboratory and Internation Findings," *Journal of Conflict Resolution* 31 (March 1987) 164–185.

Pauly, Louis W. and Simon Reich. "National Structures and Multinational Corporate Behavior," *International Organization* 51 (winter 1997) 1–30.

Peceny, Mark. "Forcing Them to Be Free," *Political Research Quarterly* 52 (September 1999) 549–582.

Pentagon Papers, New York Times Edition. New York: Bantam Books, 1971.

Perez, Mathias J. "External Threat-Bloc Cohesion Revisited," University of Arizona, Department of Political Science, mimeo, spring, 1993.

Perlez, Jane. "Czechs Gear Up to Resume Weapons Exports," *New York Times* July 4, 1993, section F, P. 7.

Peters, Tom. *In Search of Excellence.* New York: Harper and Row, 1982.

Peters, Tom. "10 Years Later: 'Excellence' Lessons Need a Second Look," *Arizona Daily Star,* September 15, 1992.

Peterson, V. Spike, ed. *Gendered States: Feminist (Re)Visions of International Relations Theory.* Boulder, CO: Lynne Rienner Publishers, 1992.

Pevehouse, Jon C. and Joshua S. Goldstein. "Serbian Compliance or Defiance in Kosovo?" *Journal of Conflict Resolution* 43 (August 1999) 538–546.

Pfaff, William. "Social Justice Must Again Enter Economics Policy Debate," *Arizona Daily Star,* October 22, 1993, p. 15.

Phillips, Warren. "The Conflict Environment of Nations," in Jonathan Wilkenfeld, Ed., *Conflict Behavior and Linkage Politics.* N.Y.: David McKay, 1973. Pp. 124–147.

Polachek, Solomon William. "Conflict and Trade," *Journal of Conflict Resolution* 24 (March 1980) 55–78.

Pollins, Brian M. "Conflict, Cooperation, and Commerce: The Effects of International Political Interactions on Bilateral Trade Flows," *American Journal of Political Science* 33 (August 1989) 737–761.

Pollins, Brian M. "Global Political Order, Economic Change, and Armed Conflict: Coevolving Systems and the Use of Force," *American Political Science Review* 90 (March 1996) 103–117.

Post, Jerrold M. "Woodrow Wilson Re-examined," *Political Psychology* 4 (June 1983) 289–306.

Powell, Robert. "Guns, Butter, and Anarchy," *American Political Science Review* 87 (March 1993) 115–132.

Puchala, Donald J. "International Transactions and Regional Integration," *International Organization* 24 (autumn 1970) 732–763.

Puchala, Donald J. and Raymond F. Hopkins. "International Regimes: Lessons from Inductive Analysis," *International Organization* 36 (spring 1982) 245–276.

Rajmaira, Sheen. "Indo-Pakistani Relations: Reciprocity in Long-Term Perspective," *International Studies Quarterly* 41 (September 1997) 547–560.

Rapoport, Anatol, and Albert M. Chammah, *Prisoner's Dilemma.* Ann Arbor: University of Michigan Press, 1965.

Raphael, Theodore D. "Integrative Complexity Theory and Forecasting International Crises," *Journal of Conflict Resolution* 26 (September 1982) 423–450.

Rapkin, David, William R. Thompson, and Jon A Christopherson. "Bipolarity, Bipolarization, and the Cold War," *Journal of Conflict Resolution* 23 (June 1979) 261–295.

Rasler, Karen A. "Spending, Deficits, and Welfare-Investment Tradeoffs: Cause or Effect of Leadership Decline?" in David P. Rapkin (ed.), *World Leadership and Hegemony: Yearbook of International Political Economy.* Boulder, CO: Lynne Rienner Publishers, 1990. Pp. 169–190.

Rasler, Karen A. and William R. Thompson. *The Great Powers and Global Struggle, 1490–1990.* Lexington: University Press of Kentucky, 1994.

Rasler, Karen A. and William R. Thompson. "Technological Innovation, Capability Positional Shifts, and Systemic War," *Journal of Conflict Resolution* 35 (September 1991) 412–442.

Rattinger, Hans. "Armaments, Detente, and Bureaucracy: The Case of the Arms Race in Europe," *Journal of Conflict Resolution* 19 (December 1975) 571–595.

Ray, James Lee. *Democracy and International Conflict.* Columbia, SC: University of South Carolina Press, 1995a.

Ray, James Lee. "The End of Slavery and the Abolition of International War," *International Organization* 43 (summer 1989) 405–440.

Ray, James Lee. *Global Politics.* 7th ed. Boston: Houghton Mifflin, 1998.

Ray, James Lee. "Promise or Peril? Neorealism, Neoliberalism, and the Future of International Politics," in Charles W. Kegley (ed.), *Controversies in International Relations Theory: Realism and the Neoliberal Challenge.* New York: St. Martin's Press, 1995b. Pp. 335–355.

Ray, James Lee. "Wars between Democracies: Rare or Nonexistent?" *International Interactions* 18 (No. 3, 1993) 251–276.

Raymond, Gregory A. "Democracies, Disputes, and Third-Party Intermediaries," *Journal of Conflict Resolution* 38 (March 1994) 24–42.

Reiter, Dan and Allan C. Stam III. "Democracy and Battlefield Military Effectiveness," *Journal of Conflict Resolution* 42 (June 1998a) 259–278.

Reiter, Dan and Allan C. Stam III. "Democracy, War Initiation, and Victory," *American Politial Science Review* 92 (June 1998b) 377–389.

Remmer, Karen L. "Does Democracy Promote Interstate Cooperation? Lessons from the Mercosur Region," *International Studies Quarterly* 42 (March 1998) 25–52.

Reus-Smit, Christian. "The Constitutional Structure of International Society and the Nature of Fundamental Institutions," *International Organization* 51 (autumn 1997) 555–589.

Rhodes, Edward. "Do Bureacratic Politics Matter? Some Disconfirming Findings from the Case of the U.S. Navy," *World Politics* 47 (October 1994) 1–41.

Richardson, Lewis F. *Statistics of Deadly Quarrels.* Pittsburgh: Boxwood Press, 1960.

Risse-Kappen, Thomas. "Ideas Do Not Float Freely: Transnational Coalitions, Domestic Structures, and the End of the Cold War," *International Organization* 48 (spring 1994) 185–214.

Rittberger, Volker, ed. *Regime Theory and International Relations.* Oxford: Clarendon Press, 1993.

Rochester, J. Martin. "The Rise and Fall of International Organization as a Field of Study," *International Organization* 40 (autumn 1986) 777–813.

Rosati, Jerel A. "Failures of Deterrence: Who Won the Cold War?" *Mershon International Studies Review* 39 (April 1995) 142–145.

Rosecrance, Richard. "Bipolarity, Multipolarity, and the Future," *Journal of Conflict Resolution* 10 (June 1966) 314–327.

Rosecrance, Richard. "International Theory Revisited," *International Organization* 35 (autumn 1981) 691–714.

Rosecrance, Richard. "Long Cycle Theory and International Relations," *International Organization* 41 (spring 1987) 283–302.

Rosecrance, Richard. "Reply to Waltz," *International Organization* 36 (summer 1982) 682–685.

Rosecrance, Richard. *The Rise of the Trading State.* New York: Basic Books, 1985.

Rosecrance, Richard and Chih-Cheng Lo. "Balancing, Stability, and War: The Mysterious Case of the Napoleonic International System," *International Studies Quarterly* 40 (December 1996) 479–500.

Rosenau, James N. "Games International Relations Scholars Play," *Journal of International Affairs* 21 (No. 2, 1967) 293–303.

Rosenau, James N. "Pre-theories and Theories of Foreign Policy," in R. Barry Farrel (ed.), *Approaches to Comparative and International Politics.* Evanston: Northwestern University Press, 1966.

Rosenau, James N. *Turbulence in World Politics.* Princeton: Princeton University Press, 1990.

Rosenau, James N. and Michael Fagen. "A New Dynamism in World Politics: Increasingly Skillful Individuals?" *International Studies Quarterly* 41 (December 1997) 655–686.

Rothstein, Robert L. "Regime-Creation by a Coalition of the Weak: Lessons from the NIEO and the Integrated Problem for Commodities," *International Studies Quarterly* 28 (September 1984) 307–328.

Rousseau, David L., Christopher Gelpi, Dan Reiter, and Paul K. Huth. "Assessing the Dyadic Nature of the Democratic Peace, 1918–1988," *American Political Science Review* 90 (September 1996) 512–533.

Ruggie, John G. "Changing Frameworks of International Collective Behavior," in Nazli Choucri and Thomas W. Robinson (eds.), *Forecasting in International Relations: Theory, Methods, Problems, Prospects.* San Francisco: W.H. Freeman and Co., 1978. Pp. 384–406.

Ruggie, John G. "Continuity and Transformation in the World Polity: Towards a Neorealist Synthesis," in Robert O. Keohane (ed.), *Neorealism and Its Critics.* New York: Columbia University Press, 1986.

Ruggie, John G. "Continuity and Transformation in the World Polity: Toward a Neorealist Synthesis," *World Politics* 35 (January 1983) 261–285.

Ruggie, John G. "International Responses to Technology: Concepts and Trends," *International Organization* 40 (summer 1975) 557–583.

Ruggie, John G. "International Structure and International Transformation: Space, Time, and Method," in Ernst-Otto Czempiel and James N. Rosenau (eds.), *Global Changes and Theoretical Challenges*. Lexington: D.C. Heath, 1989. Pp. 21–35.

Ruggie, John G. "Territoriality and Beyond: Problematizing Modernity in International Relations," *International Organization* 47 (winter 1993) 139–174.

Rummel, R.J. "Democracy, Power, Genocide, and Mass Murder," *Journal of Conflict Resolution* 39 (March 1995) 3–26.

Rummel, R.J. "Dimensions of Conflict Behavior within and between Nations," *General Systems: Yearbook of the Society for General Systems Research* 8 (1963).

Rummel, R.J. *Dimensions of Nations*. Beverly Hills: Sage, 1972.

Rummel, R.J. "Field Theories and Indicators of International Behavior," Research Report No. 29. Paper Delivered at the 65th annual meeting of the American Political Science Association, New York, September, 1969a.

Rummel, R.J. "Indicators of Cross-National and International Patterns," *American Political Science Review* 63 (March 1969b) 127–147.

Rummel, R.J. "Libertarianism and International Violence," *Journal of Conflict Resolution* 27 (March 1983) 27–71.

Rummel, R.J. "The Relationship between National Attributes and Foreign Conflict Behavior," in J. David Singer (ed.), *Quantitative International Politics: Insights and Evidence*. New York: Free Press, 1968.

Rummel, R. J. "Some Dimensions in the Foreign Behavior of Nations," in James N. Rosenau (ed.), *International Politics and Foreign Policy*. Rev. ed. New York: Free Press, 1969c.

Rummel, R. J. "U.S. Foreign Relations: Conflict, Cooperation, and Attribute Distances," in Bruce M. Russett (ed.), *Peace, War, and Numbers*. Beverly Hills: Sage, 1972.

Russett, Bruce M. "The Calculus of Deterrence," *Journal of Conflict Resolution* 7 (June 1963) 97–109.

Russett, Bruce M. "Economic Decline, Electoral Pressure, and the Initiation of International Conflict," in Charles Gochman and Alan Sabrosky (eds.), *Prisoners of War?* Lexington, KY: Lexington Books, 1990.

Russett, Bruce M. *Grasping the Democratic Peace*. Princeton: Princeton University Press, 1993.

Russett, Bruce M. *International Regions and the International System*. Chicago: Rand McNally, 1967.

Russett, Bruce M. "The Mysterious Case of Vanishing Hegemony," *International Organization* 39 (spring 1985) 207–231.

Russett, Bruce M. et al. *World Handbook of Political and Social Indicators*. New Haven: Yale University Press, 1964.

Russett, Bruce, John Oneal, and David R. Davis. "The Third Leg of the Kantian Tripod for Peace: International Organizations and Militarized Disputes, 1950–1985," *International Organization* 52 (summer 1998) 441–468.

Salmore, Steven A. and Charles F. Hermann. "The Effect of Size, Development and Accountability on Foreign Policy," *Peace Research Society Papers* 14 (1970).

Sample Susan G. "Military Buildups, War, and Realpolitik," *Journal of Conflict Resolution* 42 (April 1998) 156–175.

Sayrs, Lois W. "The Long Cycle in International Relations," *International Studies Quarterly* 37 (June 1993) 215–238.

Sayrs, Lois W. "Trade and Conflict Revisited," *International Interactions* 15 (No. 2, 1989) 155–176.

Schafer, Mark and Scott Crichlow. "Antecedents of Groupthink," *Journal of Conflict Resolution* 40 (September 1996) 415–435.

Schaller, Michael. *The American Occupation of Japan: The Origins of the Cold War in Asia*. New York: Oxford University Press, 1985.

Schampel, James H. "Change in Material Capabilities and the Onset of War: A Dyadic Approach," *International Studies Quarterly* 37 (December 1993) 395–408.

Schampel, James H. "Change in Material Capabilities and the Onset of War: A Dyadic Approch," *International Studies Quarterly* 37 (December 1993) 395–408.

Schampel, James H. "Parity or Preponderance," *International Studies Notes* 19 (No. 3, 1994) 1–6.

Schelling, Thomas. *Micromotives and Macrobehavior.* New York: W.W. Norton, 1978.

Schelling, Thomas. *The Strategy of Conflict.* New York: Oxford University Press, 1963.

Schmieglow, Henrik and Michele Schmieglow. "How Japan Affects the International System," *International Organization* 44 (autumn 1990) 553–588.

Schroeder, Paul W. "Correspondence; History vs. Neo-realism: A Second Look," *International Security* 20 (summer 1995) 193–195.

Schrodt, Philip A. "The Statistical Characteristics of Event Data," *International Interactions* 20 (No. 1/2, 1994) 35–53.

Schrodt, Philip A., Shannon G. Davis and Judith L. Weddle. "Political Science: KEDS—A Program for Machine Coding Events Data," *Social Science Computer Review* 12 (fall 1994) 561–588.

Schultz, Kenneth A. "Do Democratic Insitutions Constrain or Inform? Contrasting Two Institutional Perspectives on Democracy and War," *International Organization* 53 (spring 1999) 233–266.

Schweller, Randall L. "New Realist Research on Alliances: Refining, Not Refuting, Waltz's Balancing Proposition," *American Political Science Review* 91 (September 1997) 927–930.

Schweller, Randall L. "Tripolarity and the Second World War," *International Studies Quarterly* 37 (March 1993) 73–104.

Schweller, Randall L. and David Priess. "A Tale of Two Realisms: Expanding the Institutions Debate," *Mershon International Studies Review* 41 (May 1997) 1–32.

Sharp, Paul. "For Diplomacy: Representation and the Study of International Relations," *International Studies Review* 1 (spring 1999) 33–58.

Shepard, Graham H. "Personality Effects on American Foreign Policy, 1969–1984," *International Studies Quarterly* 32 (March 1988) 91–123.

Shimko, Keith L. *Images and Arms Control: Perceptions of the Soviet Union in the Reagan Administration.* Ann Arbor: University of Michigan Press, 1991.

Signorino, Curtis S. and Jeffrey M. Ritter. "Tau-B or Not Tau-B: Measuring the Similarity of Foreign Policy Positions, *International Studies Quarterly* 43 (March 1999) 115–144.

Simmel, Georg. *Conflict.* Glencoe, IL: Free Press, 1955.

Simon, Herbert. *Administrative Behavior.* New York: Free Press, 1947.

Singer, J. David. "Inter-nation Influence: A Formal Model," *American Political Science Review* 57 (June 1963) 420–430.

Singer, J. David. "Review: *The Two Faces of National Interest,*" *American Political Science Review* 89 (March 1995) 247–248.

Singer, J. David, Stuart Bremer, and John Stuckey. "Capability Distribution, Uncertainty, and Major Power War, 1820–1965," in Bruce Russett (ed.), *Peace, War, and Numbers.* Beverly Hills: Sage, 1972.

Singer, J. David and Melvin Small. "Alliance Aggregation and the Onset of War, 1815–1945," in J. David Singer (ed.), *Quantitative International Politics.* New York: Free Press, 1968. Pp. 247–286.

Singer, J. David and Melvin Small. *The Wages of War.* New York: John Wiley, 1972.

Singer, J. David and Michael D. Wallace. "Intergovernmental Organization and the Preservation of Peace, 1816–1964: Some Bivariate Relationships," *International Organization* 24 (summer 1970) 520–547.

Siverson, Randolph M. "Demcracies and War Participation: In Defense of the Institutional Constraints Argument," *European Journal of International Relations* 1 (No. 4, 1995) 481–489.

Siverson, Randolph M. "Role and Perception in International Crisis," *International Organization* 27 (summer 1973) 329–346.

Siverson, Randolph M. and Juliann Emmons. "Birds of a Feather," *Journal of Conflict Resolution* 35 (June 1991) 285–306.

Siverson, Randolph M. and Harvey Starr. *The Diffusion of War.* Ann Arbor: University of Michigan Press, 1991.

Siverson, Randoph M. and Michael P. Sullivan. "Alliances and War: A New Examination of an Old Problem," *Conflict Management and Peace Science* 8 (1984) 1–15.

Siverson, Randolph M. and Michael P. Sullivan. "The Distribution of Power and the Onset of War," *Journal of Conflict Resolution* 27 (September 1983) 473–494.

Smith, Dale L. and James Lee Ray. "European Integration: Gloomy Theory versus Rosy Reality," in Dale L. Smith and James Lee Ray. *The 1992 Project and the Future of Integration in Europe.* Armonk, NY: M.E. Sharpe, 1993.

Smith, Theresa Clair. "Arms Race Instability and War," *Journal of Conflict Resolution* 24 (June 1980) 253–284.

Smith, Theresa Clair. "Risky Races? Curvature Change and the War Risk in Arms Racing," *International Interactions* 14 (No. 3, 1988) 201–228.

Snyder, Glenn. *Deterrence and Defense: Toward A Theory of National Security.* Princeton: Princeton University Press, 1961.

Snyder, Glenn and Paul Diesing. *Conflict among Nations: Bargaining, Decision-Making, and System Structure in International Crises.* Princeton: Princeton University Press, 1977.

Snyder, Jack and Robert Jervis, eds. *Coping with Complexity in the International System.* Boulder: Westview Press, 1993.

Snyder, Richard. "A Decision-Making Approach to the Study of Political Phenomena," in Roland Young (ed.), *Approaches to the Study of Politics* (Evanston, IL.: Northwestern University Press, 1958).

Snidal, Duncan. "The Game *Theory* of International Politics," in Kenneth Oye (ed.), *Cooperation under Anarchy.* Princeton: Princeton University Press, 1986.

Somit, Albert. "Review Essay: Humans, Chimps, and Bonobos: The Biological Bases of Aggression, War, and Peacemaking," *Journal of Conflict Resolution* 34 (September 1990) 553–582.

Sorokin, Pitirim. *Society, Culture, and Personality: Their Structures and Dynamics.* New York: Harper and Row, 1947.

Spezio, K. Edward. "British Hegemony and Major Power War, 1815–1939: An Empirical Test of Gilpin's Model of Hegemonic Governance," *International Studies Quarterly* 34 (June 1990) 165–181.

Spiro, David E. "The Insignificance of the Liberal Peace," *International Security* 19 (fall 1994) 50–86.

Spruyt, Hendrik. "Institutional Selection in International Relations: State Anarchy as Order," *International Organization* 48 (autumn 1994) 527–558.

Starr, Harvey. "Diffusion Approaches to the Spread of Democracy," *Journal of Conflict Resolution* 35 (June 1991a) 356–381.

Starr, Harvey. *Henry Kissinger: Perceptions of International Politics.* Lexington, KY: University of Kentucky Press, 1984.

Starr, Harvey. "Joining Political and Geographic Perspectives," *International Interactions* 17 (No. 1, 1991b) 1–9.

Starr, Harvey and Benjamin A. Most. "The Substance and Study of Borders in International Relations Research," *International Studies Quarterly* 20 (December 1976) 581–620.

Starr, Harvey and Benjamin A. Most. "A Return Journey: Richardson, 'Frontiers,' and Wars in the 1946–1965 Era," *Journal of Conflict Resolution* 22 (September 1978) 441–468.

Stein, Arthur. "Coordination and Collaboration: Regimes in an Anarchic World," *International Organization* 36 (spring 1982) 299–324.

Stein, Janice Gross. "Deterrence and Compellence in the Gulf, 1990–1991: A Failed or Impossible Task?" *International Security* 17 (fall 1992) 147–179.

Stein, Janice Gross. "Deterrence and Reassurance," in Philip E. Tetlock, Jo L. Husbands, Robert Jervis, Paul C. Stern, and Charles Tilly (eds.), *Behavior, Society, and Nuclear War.* New York: Oxford University Press, 1991. Pp. 8–72.

Stein, Janice Gross. "Political Learning by Doing: Gorbachev as Uncommitted Thinker and Motivated Learner," *International Organization* 48 (spring 1994) 155–184.

Stein, Janice Gross. "The Wrong Strategy in the Right Place," *International Security* 14 (winter 1988/89) 142–167.

Steinberg, Blema S. *Shame and Humiliation: Presidential Decision-Making on Vietnam.* Montreal: McGill-Queens University Press, 1996.

Sterling, Richard W. *Macropolitics: International Politics in a Global Society.* New York: Knopf, 1974.

Stevens, William K. "U.S. and Japan Key to Outcome in Climate Talks," *New York Times,* August 12, 1997, p. B7.

Stokke, Olav Schram. "Regimes as Governance Systems," in Oran R. Young, (ed.), *Global Governance: Drawing Insights from Environmental Experience.* Cambridge, MA: MIT Press, 1997. Pp. 27–64.

Stoll, Richard and Michael Champion. "Capability Concentration, Alliance Bonding, and Conflict among the Major Powers," in A. Ned Sabrosky (ed.), *Polarity and War.* Boulder: Westview Press, 1985.

Strang, David. "Global Patterns of Decolonization, 1500–1987," *International Studies Quarterly* 35 (December 1991) 429–454.

Strange, Susan. *Casino Capitalism.* Oxford, UK: Basil Blackwell, 1986.

Strange, Susan. "*Cave! Hic Dragones:* A Critique of Regime Analysis," *International Organization* 36 (spring 1982) 479–496.

Strange, Susan. "The Persistent Myth of Lost Hegemony," *International Organization* 41 (autumn 1987) 551–574.

Strange, Susan. "Political Economy and International Relations," in Ken Booth and Steve Smith (eds.), *International Relations Theory Today.* Cambridge: Polity Press, 1995. Pp. 154–174.

Strange, Susan. "The Structure of Finance in the World System," in Yoshikazu Sakamoto (ed.), *Global Transformation: Challenges to the State System.* New York: United Nations University Press, 1994. Pp. 228–249.

Strange, Susan. "Toward a Theory of Transnational Empire," in Ernst-Otto Czempiel and James N. Rosenau (eds.), *Global Changes and Theoretical Challenges.* Lexington, MA: Lexington Books, 1989.

Strange, Susan. *The Retreat of the State.* Cambridge: Cambridge University Press, 1996.

Suedfeld, Peter. "Bilateral Relations between Countries and the Complexity of Newspaper Editorials," *Political Psychology* 13 (No. 4, 1992) 601–611.

Suedfeld, Peter and Philip Tetlock. "Integrative Complexity of Communications in International Crises," *Journal of Conflict Resolution* 21 (March 1977) 169–184.

Suedfeld, Peter, Michael D. Wallace, and Kimberly L. Thachuk. "Changes in Integrative Complexity among Middle East Leaders during the Persian Gulf Crisis," *Journal of Social Issues* 49 (No. 4, 1993) 183–199.

Sullivan, Michael P. "Commitment and the Escalation of International Conflicts," *Western Political Quarterly* 25 (March 1972) 23–38.

Sullivan, Michael P. "Competing Frameworks and the Study of Contemporary International Politics," *Millennium: Journal of International Studies* 7 (autumn 1978a) 93–110.

Sullivan, Michael P. "Escalatory and Non-Escalatory 'Systems'," *American Journal of Political Science* 18 (August 1974a) 549–558.

Sullivan, Michael P. "Foreign Policy Articulations and U.S. Conflict Behavior," in J. David Singer and Michael Wallace (eds.), *To Auger Well: Early Warning Indicators in World Politics.* Beverly Hills, CA.: Sage 1979.

Sullivan, Michael P. "International Organizations and World Order: A Reappraisal," *Journal of Conflict Resolution* 22 (March 1978b) 105–120.

Sullivan, Michael P. *International Relations: Theories and Evidence.* Englewood Cliffs, NJ: Prentice-Hall, 1976.

Sullivan, Michael P. *Power in Contemporary International Politics.* Columbia, SC: University of South Carolina Press, 1990.

Sullivan, Michael P. "The Question of Relevance in Foreign Policy Studies," *Western Political Quarterly* [*Political Research Quarterly*] 26 (June 1973) 314–324.

Sullivan, Michael P. "Review of 'Compliance and Public Authority,'" *American Political Science Review* 75 (March 1981) 282–283.

Sullivan, Michael P. "'That Dog Won't Hunt': The Cottage Industry of Realist Criticism, or 'Must You Play that Waltz Again?'." Mimeo. Department of Political Science, University of Arizona, September, 2000.

Sullivan, Michael P. "Transnationalism, Power Politics, and the Realities of the Present System," in Ray Maghroori and Bennett Ramberg (eds.), *International Relations' Third Debate: Globalism Versus Realism.* Boulder: Westview Press, 1982. Pp. 195–221.

Sullivan, Michael P. "Vietnam: Calculation or Quicksand? An Analysis of Competing Decision-Making Models," in Fred Sondermann, William Olson, and David McClellan (eds.), *The Theory and Practice of International Relations.* 4th ed. Englewood Cliffs, NJ: Prentice-Hall, 1974b.

Sullivan, Michael P. *The Vietnam War: A Study in the Making of American Policy.* Lexington: University of Kentucky Press, 1985.

Sullivan, Michael P. and Randolph M. Siverson. "Theories of War: Problems and Prospects," in P. Terrence Hopmann, Dina A. Zinnes, and J. David Singer (eds.), *Cumulation in International Relations Research.* Monograph Series in World Affairs Vol. 18, No. 3. Denver, CO: University of Denver, 1981. Pp.9–38.

Sylvan, David and Stephen Majeski. "A Methodology for the Study of Historical Counterfactuals, "*International Studies Quarterly* 42 (March 1998) 79–108.

Sylvester, Christine. *Feminist Theory and International Relations in a Postmodern Era.* Cambridge: Cambridge University Press, 1994.

Tanter, Raymond. "Dimensions of Conflict Behavior within and between Nations, 1958–1960," *Journal of Conflict Resolution* 10 (March 1966) 41–64.

Taubman, Philip. "Russia's Blood Feud: The Enmity That Shaped History," *New York Times,* June 24, 1996, p. A10.

Taylor, Charles Lewis et al., *World Handbook of Political and Social Indicators.* 2d ed. 1972. 3d ed. 1983. New Haven: Yale University Press.

Tetlock, Philip E. "Identifying Victims of Groupthink from Public Statements of Decision-Makers," *Journal of Personality and Social Psychology* 37 (1979) 1314–1324.

Tetlock, Philip E. "Monitoring the Integrative Complexity of American and Soviet Policy Rhetoric," *Journal of Social Issues* 44 (No. 2, 1988) 101–131.

Tetlock, Philip E. and Aaron Belkin, eds. *Counterfactual Thought Experiments in World Politics.* Princeton: Princeton Univeristy Press, 1996.

Tetlock, Philip E. and Richard Boettger, "Cognitive and Rhetorical Styles of Traditionalist and Reformist Soviet Politicians," *Political Psychology* 10 (June 1989) 209–232.

Tetlock, Philip E., Randall S. Peterson, Charles McGuire, Shi-jie Chang, and Peter Feld. "Assessing Political Group Dynamics: A Test of the Groupthink Model," *Journal of Personality and Social Psychology* 63 (No. 3, 1992) 403–425.

t'Hart, P. "Irving L. Janis's Victims of Groupthink," *Political Psychology* 12 (June 1991) 247–278.

Thompson, Kenneth W. *Schools of Thought in International Relations.* Baton Rouge: Louisiana State University Press, 1996.

Thompson, William R. "Democracy and Peace: Putting the Cart before the Horse?" *International Organization* 50 (winter 1996) 141–174.

Thompson, William R. *On Global War.* Columbia, SC: University of South Carolina Press, 1988.

Thompson, William R., Robert B. Duval, and Aahmed Dia. "Wars, Alliances, and Military Expenditures," *Journal of Conflict Resolution* 23 (December 1979) 629–654.

Thompson, William R. and David P. Rapkin. "Collaboration, Consensus, and Detente: The External Threat-Bloc Cohesion Hypothesis," *Journal of Conflict Resolution* 25 (December 1981) 615–638.

Thompson, William R. and Karen A. Rasler, "War and Systemic Capability Reconcentration," *Journal of Conflict Resolution* 32 (June 1988) 335–366.

Thompson, William R., Karen A. Rasler, and Richard P.Y. Li. "Systemic Interaction Opportunities and War Behavior," *International Interactions* 7 (No. 1, 1980) 57–85.

Thompson, William R. and Rafael Reuveny. "Tariffs and Trade Fluctuations," *International Organization* 52 (spring 1998) 421–440.

Thompson, William R. and Richard Tucker. "A Tale of Two Democratic Peace Critiques," *Journal of Conflict Resolution* 41 (June 1997a) 428–454.

Thompson, William R. and Richard Tucker. "Bewitched, Bothered, and Bewildered," *Journal of Conflict Resolution* 41 (June 1997b) 462–477.

Thompson, William R. and Lawrence Vescera. "Growth Waves, Systemic Openness, and Protectionism," *International Organization* 46 (spring 1992) 493–532.

Thomson, Janice E. *Mercenaries, Pirates, and Sovereigns: State-Building and Extraterritorial Violence in Early Modern Europe.* Princeton: Princeton University Press, 1994.

Thomson, Janice E. and Stephen D. Krasner. "Global Transactions and the Consolidation of Sovereignty," in Ernst-Otto Czempiel and James N. Rosenau (eds.), *Global Changes and Theoretical Challenges.* Lexington, MA: D.C. Heath, 1989. Pp. 195–220.

Tickner, J. Ann. "You Just Don't Understand: Troubled Engagements between Feminists and IR Theorists," *International Studies Quarterly* 41 (December 1997) 611–632.

Toynbee, Arnold J. *A Study of History.* Vol. 9. London: Oxford University Press, 1954.

Trudeau, G. B. *This War Had Such Promise.* New York: Holt, Rinehart, and Winston, 1973.

Tuchman, Barbara. *The March of Folly: From Troy to Vietnam.* New York: Ballantine Books, 1984.

Van Evera, Stephen. "Why Cooperation Failed in 1914," in Kenneth Oye (ed.), *Cooperation under Anarchy.* Princeton: Princeton University Press, 1986. Pp. 80–119.

Van Wyk, Koos and Sarah Radloff. "Symmetry and Reciprocity in South Africa's Foreign Policy," *Journal of Conflict Resolution* 37 (June 1993) 382–396.

Vasquez, John A. "Distinguishing Rivals That Go to War from Those That Do Not," *International Studies Quarterly* 40 (December 1996) 531–558.

Vasquez, John A. "The Realist Paradigm and Degenerative Versus Progressive Research Programs," *American Political Science Review* 91 (December 1997) 899–912.

Verdier, Daniel. "Democratic Convergence and Free Trade," *International Studies Quarterly* 42 (March 1998) 1–24.

Viotti, Paul R. and Mark V. Kauppi. *International Relations Theory: Realism, Pluralism, Globalism and Beyond.* 3d. ed. Boston: Allyn and Bacon, 1999.

Volgy, Thomas J. and Lawrence E. Imwalle. "Hegemonic and Bipolar Perspectives on the New World Order," *American Journal of Political Science* 39 (November 1995) 819–834.

Volgy, Thomas J. and Stacey Mayhall. "Status Inconsistency and International War," *International Studies Quarterly* 39 (March 1995) 67–84.

Volgy, Thomas J. and Jon E. Quistgard. "Learning about the Value of Global Cooperation: Role-Taking in the United Nations as a Predictor of World-Mindedness," *Journal of Conflict Resolution* 19 (June 1975) 349–376.

Walker, Stephen G. "The Interface between Beliefs and Behavior: Henry Kissinger's Operational Code and the Vietnam War," *Journal of Conflict Resolution* 21 (September 1977) 129–168.

Walker, Stephen G. "Power, Perception, and Personality in the Gulf War: A Review," *Mershon International Studies Review* 38 (April 1994) 166–170.

Walker, Stephen G. "Psychodynamic Processes and Framing Effects in Foreign Policy Decision-Making: Woodrow Wilson's Operational Code," *Political Psychology* 16 (No. 4, 1995) 697–717.

Walker, Stephen G., Mark Schafer, and Michael D. Young. "Presidential Operational Codes and Foreign Policy Conflicts in the Post–Cold War World," *Journal of Conflict Resolution* 43 (October 1999) 610–625.

Walker, Stephen G. and George L. Watson, "Integrative Complexity and British Decisions during the Munich and Polish Crises," *Journal of Conflict Resolution* 38 (March 1994) 3–23.

Wallace, Michael D. "Alliance Polarization, Cross-Cutting, and International War, 1815–1964," *Journal of Conflict Resolution* 17 (December 1973) 575–604

Wallace, Michael D. "Arms Races and Escalation," *Journal of Conflict Resolution* 23 (March 1979) 3–16.

Wallace, Michael D. "Some Persistent Findings: A Reply to Professor Weede," *Journal of Conflict Resolution* 24 (June 1980) 289–292.

Wallace, Michael D. "Status, Formal Organization, and Arms Levels as Factors Leading to the Onset of War, 1820–1964," in Bruce Russett (ed.), *Peace, War, and Numbers.* Beverly Hills: Sage, 1972.

Wallace, Michael D., Peter Suedfeld, and Kimberly Thachuk. "Political Rhetoric of Leaders under Stress in the Gulf Crisis," *Journal of Conflict Resolution* 37 (March 1993) 94–107.

Wallerstein, Immanuel. *The Modern World-System.* Vol. I. New York: Academic Press, 1974.

Wallerstein, Immanuel. "The Rise and Future Demise of the World Capitalist System," in Immanuel Wallerstein, *The Capitalist World-Economy.* Cambridge: Cambridge University Press, 1979.

Walt, Stephen M. "The Progressive Power of Realism," *American Political Science Review* 91 (December 1997) 931–935.

Walt, Stephen M. "The Renaissance of Security Studies," *International Studies Quarterly* 35 (June 1991) 211–239.

Walt, Stephen M. "Rigor or Rigor Mortis? Rational Choice and Security Studies," *International Security* 23 (spring 1999) 5–48.

Waltz, Kenneth. "The Emerging Structure of International Politics," in Michael E. Brown, Sean M. Lynn-Jones, and Steven F. Miller (eds.), *The Perils of Anarchy: Contemporary Realism and International Security.* Cambridge, MA: MIT Press, 1995.

Waltz, Kenneth. "Evaluating Theories," *American Political Science Review* 91 (December 1997) 913–917.

Waltz, Kenneth. "Letter to the Editor," *International Organization* 36 (summer 1982) 679–681.

Waltz, Kenneth. *Man, the State, and War.* New York: Columbia University Press, 1959.

Waltz, Kenneth. "The Origins of War in Neorealist Theory," in Rotberg, Robert I. and Theodore K. Rabb (eds.), *The Origin and Prevention of Major Wars.* New York: Cambridge University Press, 1989. Pp. 39–52.

Waltz, Kenneth. "Review of *Macropolitics: International Relations in a Global Society*," *American Political Science Review* 70 (March 1976) 296–297.

Waltz, Kenneth. *Theory of International Politics.* Reading, MA: Addison Wesley, 1979.

Wang, Kevin H. "Presidential Responses to Foreign Policy Crises: Rational Choice and Domestic Politics," *Journal of Conflict Resolution* 40 (March 1996) 68–97.

Ward, Michael D. "Cooperation and Conflict in Foreign Policy Behavior," *International Studies Quarterly* 26 (March 1982) 87–126.

Ward, Michael D. "Differential Paths to Parity: A Study of the Contemporary Arms Race," *American Political Science Review* 78 (1984) 297–317.

Ward, Michael D. "Power in the International System," Richard J. Stoll and Michael D. Ward (eds.), *Power in World Politics.* Boulder: Lynne Rienner Publishers, 1989. Pp. 121–134.

Ward, Michael D. and Jordin S. Cohen. "Replication by Any Other Name Is . . . Research." Paper prepared for the 1995 annual meetings of the International Studies Association, Chicago, February 21–24, 1995.

Ward, Michael D. and Kristian S. Gleditsch. "Democratizing for Peace," *American Political Science Review* 92 (March 1998) 51–62.

Ward, Michael D. and Sheen Rajmaira. "Reciprocity and Norms in U.S.-Soviet Foreign Policy," *Journal of Conflict Resolution* 36 (June 1992) 342–368.

Wayman, Frank Whelon. "Bipolarity, Multipolarity and the Threat of War," in A. Ned Sabrosky (ed.), *Polarity and War.* Boulder: Westview Press, 1985.

Wayman, Frank Whelon and Paul F. Diehl. "Realism Reconsidered," in Frank W. Wayman and Paul F. Diehl (eds.), *Reconstructing Realpolitik.* Ann Arbor: University of Michigan Press, 1994. Pp. 3–16.

Webb, Michael C. "International Economic Structures, Government Interests, and International Coordination of Macroeconomic Adjustment Policies," *International Organization* 45 (summer 1991) 309–342.

Weber, Steven. "The End of the Business Cycle?" *Foreign Affairs* 76 (July/August, 1997) 65–83.

Weber, Steven. "Origins of the European Bank for Reconstruction and Development," *International Organization* 48 (winter 1994) 1–38.

Weede, Erich. "Arms Races and Escalation," *Journal of Conflict Resolution* 24 (June 1980) 285–288.

Weede, Erich. "Democracy and War Involvement," *Journal of Conflict Resolution* 28 (December 1984) 649–664.

Weede, Erich. "Overwhelming Preponderance as a Pacifying Condition among Contiguous Asian Dyads, 1950–1969," *Journal of Conflict Resolution* 20 (September 1976) 395–412.

Welch, David A. "Crisis Decision Making Reconsidered," *Journal of Conflict Resolution* 33 (September 1989) 430–445.

Wendt, Alexander. "The Agent-Structure Problem in International Relations Theory," *International Organization* 41 (summer 1987) 335–370.

Wendt, Alexander. "Anarchy Is What States Make of It: The Social Construction of Power Politics," *International Organization* 46 (spring 1992) 391–426.

Wendt, Alexander. "Collective Identity Formation and the International State," *American Political Science Review* 88 (June 1994a) 384–396.

Wendt, Alexander. "Constructing International Politics," *International Security* 20 (summer 1995) 71–81.

Wendt, Alexander. "Review of *Ideas and Foreign Policy,*" *American Political Science Review* 88 (December 1994b) 1040–1041.

Werner, Susanne and Douglas Lemke. "Opposites Do Not Attract: The Impact of Domestic Institutions, Power, and Prior Commitments on Alignment Choices," *International Studies Quarterly* 41 (September 1997) 529–546.

White, Ralph K. "Empathizing with Saddam Hussein," *Political Psychology* 12 (June 1991) 291–308.

White, Ralph K. "Images in the Context of International Conflict: Soviet Perceptions of the U.S. and the USSR." in Herbert C. Kelman (ed.), *International Behavior: A Social-Psychological Analysis.* New York: Holt, Rinehart and Winston. 1965.

White, Ralph K. *Nobody Wanted War.* New York: Doubleday, 1968.

Whitworth, Sandra. *Feminism and International Relations.* London: MacMillan Press, 1994.

Wicker, Tom. *JFK and LBJ: The Influence of Personality upon Politics.* New York: Morrow, 1968.

Wilkenfeld, Jonathan. "Models for the Analysis of Foreign Conflict Behavior of States," in Bruce M. Russett (ed.), *Peace, War, and Numbers.* Beverly Hills: Sage Publications, 1972.

Williams, John T. and Michael D. McGinnis. "The Dimensions of Superpower Rivalry," *Journal of Conflict Resolution* 36 (March 1992) 86–118.

Winter, David G. "Personality and Foreign Policy," in Eric Singer and Valerie Hudson (eds.), *Political Psychology and Foreign Policy.* Boulder: Westview Press, 1992. Pp. 79–102.

Winter, David G., Margaret G. Hermann, Walter Weintraub, and Stephen G. Walker. "Theory and Predictions in Political Psychology: The Personalities of Bush and Gorbachev Measured at a Distance," *Political Psychology* 12 (June 1991a) 215–246.

Winter, David G., Margaret G. Hermann, Walter Weintraub, and Stephen G. Walker. "The Personalities of Bush and Gorbachev at a Distance: Follow-up on Predictions," *Political Psychology* 12 (September 1991b) 457–464.

Wish, Naomi. "Foreign Policy Makers and Their National Role Conceptions," *International Studies Quarterly* 24 (December 1980) 532–554.

Woodall, Pam. "A Survey of the World Economy," The *Economist*, October 7, 1995. (Special Survey: pp. 1–38.)

Woodward, Bob. *The Commanders*. New York: Simon and Schuster, 1991.

Wright, Quincy. "The Escalation of International Conflicts," *Journal of Conflict Resolution* 9 (December 1965) 434–449.

Wright, Quincy. "The Form of a Discipline of International Relations," in James Rosenau, ed. *International Politics and Foreign Policy*. Rev. ed. New York: Free Press, 1969.

Wright, Quincy. *A Study of War*. 2 Vols. Chicago: University of Chicago, 1942.

Wright, Quincy. *A Study of War*. Abridged. Chicago: University of Chicago Press, 1964.

Wright, Quincy. "Toward a Universal Law for Mankind," in Richard A. Falk and Saul H. Mondlovitz (eds.), *Toward a Theory of War Prevention*. New York: World Law Fund, 1966.

Wu, Samuel S. G. "To Attack or Not to Attack: A Theory and Empirical Assessment of Extended Immediate Deterrence," *Journal of Conflict Resolution* 34 (September 1990) 531–552.

Young, Michael D. and Mark Shafer. "Is There Method in Our Madness? Ways of Assessing Cognition in International Relations," *Mershon International Studies Review* 42 (May 1998) 63–96.

Young, Oran. "Anarchy and Social Choice," *World Politics* 30 (January 1978) 241–263.

Young, Oran. "Comment on Andrew Moravcsik, 'A New Statecraft?'" *International Organization* 53 (autumn 1999) 805–810.

Young, Oran. *Compliance and Public Authority*. Baltimore: Johns Hopkins University Press, 1979.

Young, Oran. *International Cooperation: Building Regimes for Natural Resources and the Environment*. Ithaca: Cornell University Press, 1989.

Young, Oran. *The Politics of Force: Bargaining during International Crises*. Princeton: Princeton University Press, 1968.

Young, Oran R. and Gail Osherenko, "Testing Theories of Regime Formation," in Volker Rittberger (ed.), *Regime Theory and International Relations*. Oxford: Clarendon Press, 1993. Pp. 223–251.

Zacher, Mark W. and Richard A. Matthew. "Liberal International Theory: Common Threads, Divergent Strands," in Charles W. Kegley, Jr., (ed.), *Controversies in International Relations Theory: Realism and the Neoliberal Challenge*. New York: St. Martin's Press, 1995. Pp. 107–150.

Zakaria, Fareed. "The Rise of Illiberal Democracy," *Foreign Affairs* 76 (Nov/Dec., 1997) 22–44.

Zinnes, Dina A. "An Analytical Study of the Balance of Power Theories," *Journal of Peace Research* 4 (No. 3, 1967) 270–288.

Zinnes, Dina A. "Prerequisites for the Study of System Transformation," in Ole R. Holsti, Randolph M. Siverson, and Alexander M. George (eds.), *Change in the International System* Boulder, CO: Westview Press, 1980.

Zinnes, Dina A. and Jonathan Wilkenfeld. "An Analysis of Foreign Conflict Behavior of Nations," in Wolfram Hanreider (ed.), *Comparative Foreign Policy*. New York: David McKay, 1971. Pp. 167–213.

Zurn, Michael. "Bringing the Second Image (Back) In: About the Domestic Sources of Regime Formation," in Volker Rittberger (ed.), *Regime Theory and International Relations*. Oxford: Clarendon Press, 1993. Pp. 282–313.

Name Index

Subject Index